Chemistry 2
FOR OCR

David Acaster
Lawrie Ryan

Brian Ratcliff

Helen Eccles

Anne McCarthy

CAMBRIDGE
UNIVERSITY PRESS

CAMBRIDGE UNIVERSITY PRESS
Cambridge, New York, Melbourne, Madrid, Cape Town, Singapore, São Paulo, Delhi

Cambridge University Press
The Edinburgh Building, Cambridge CB2 8RU, UK

www.cambridge.org
Information on this title: www.cambridge.org/9780521746045

© Cambridge University Press 2009

First published 2009

Printed in the United Kingdom at the University Press, Cambridge

A catalogue record for this publication is available from the British Library

ISBN 978-0-521-74604-5 paperback and CD-ROM

ACKNOWLEDGEMENTS
Project management: Sue Kearsey
Front cover photograph: Fireworks/Magrath Photography/Science Photo Library
Page layout, illustration and preparation of interactive PDFs: HL Studios, Long Hanborough

Contents

Advice

Contents

Introduction

Cambridge OCR Advanced Sciences

The new *Cambridge OCR Advanced Sciences* course provides complete coverage of the revised OCR AS and A2 Level science specifications (Biology, Chemistry A and Physics A) for teaching from September 2008. There are two books for each subject – one covering AS and one covering A2. Some material has been drawn from the existing *Cambridge Advanced Sciences* books; however the majority is new.

The course has been developed in an innovative format, featuring Cambridge's new interactive PDFs on CD-ROM in the back of the books, and free access to a dedicated website. The CD-ROM provides additional material, including detailed objectives, hints on answering questions, and extension material. It also provides access to web-based e-learning activities to help students visualise abstract concepts, understand calculations and simulate scientific processes.

The books contain all the material required for teaching the specifications, and can be used either on their own or in conjunction with the interactive PDFs and the website.

In addition, *Teacher Resource CD-ROMs* with book PDFs plus extra material such as worksheets, practical activities and tests, are available for each book. These CD-ROMs also provide access to the new *Cambridge OCR Advanced Sciences* Planner website with a week-by-week adaptable teaching schedule.

Introduction to Chemistry 2 for OCR – the chemistry A2 text

This book covers the entire OCR A2 Chemistry A specification for first examination in 2010. Chapter 1 revisits AS Level organic chemistry. Chapters 2 to 10 correspond to Unit F324, Rings, Polymers and Analysis. Chapters 11 to 17 correspond to Unit F325, Equilibria, Energetics and Elements. Each chapter covers one of the numbered sections within the three Modules in Unit F324, and within the three Modules in Unit F325. The content of the chapters is generally arranged in the same sequence as in the specification.

The book builds on the material covered in *Chemistry 1 for OCR*. The language is kept simple, to improve accessibility for all students, while still maintaining scientific rigour throughout. Care is taken to introduce and use all the specialist terms that students need to gain a complete understanding of the chemical concepts introduced. In the text, key terms are highlighted in bold.

The depth and breadth of treatment of each topic is pitched at the appropriate level for OCR A2 students. The accompanying CD-ROM also contains some extension material that goes a little beyond the requirements of the specification, which should interest and stretch more able students.

Some of the text and illustrations are based on material from the endorsed text *Chemistry 2*, which covered the earlier OCR specification, while some is completely new. All of it has been reviewed and revised, ensuring that the new specification is fully covered. In addition to the main content in each chapter, there are also How Science Works boxes, describing issues, applications or events, which put the chemical content introduced into a social context.

Self-assessment questions (SAQs) in each chapter provide opportunities to check understanding. They often address misunderstandings that commonly appear in examination answers, and will help students to avoid such errors. Some SAQs are marked, with a vertical red bar, as 'stretch and challenge' questions. These ask students to draw together their ideas about a topic, and to organise and discuss these in a well-structured and broad-ranging answer. These questions give students the opportunity to demonstrate their potential, and may help them to recognise areas of weakness in which further work is needed. Past examination questions at the end of each chapter allow students to practise answering exam-style questions. The answers to these, along with exam-style mark schemes and hints on answering questions, are found on the accompanying CD-ROM.

Acknowledgements

We would like to thank the following for permission to reproduce images:

Cover Magrath Photography/Science Photo Library; pp. 9*t*, 9*c*, 16, 17*t*, 21, 23, 24, 30, 31*l*, 40, 41, 42, 43, 53, 130, 142, 174, 175, 182, 184, 196*r*, 198, 199, 203, 205, 206, 210 Andrew Lambert Photography/ Science Photo Library; p. 9*b* Tick Ahearn; p. 11 © The Print Collector/Alamy; p. 13 © Imagestate; p. 15*l* © B. Kuiter/flpa-images.co.uk; p. 15*r* Dan Sams/A-Z Botanical Ltd; pp. 17*b*, 20*t*, 27, 31*r*, 63 © Michael Brooke; p. 34 © Powered by Light/ Alan Spencer/Alamy; p. 35*l* Garden Matters/ Wildlife Matters; p. 35*r* Martin Bond/Science Photo Library; p. 47 Damien Lovegrove/Science Photo Library; p. 50 Courtesy of Aventis Pasteur; pp. 54, extension ch. *7 polythene film* © Imperial Chemical Industries Limited; p. 56 courtesy of James Evans; p. 57 Cordelia Molloy/Science Photo Library; p. 58 Britstock-IFA/Amadeus; p. 75 © Reuters/Corbis; p. 77*l* © speedpix/Alamy; p. 77*r* Hank Morgan/ Science Photo Library; p. 82 Colin Cuthbert/Science Photo Library; p. 89*l* Paul Shambroom/Science Photo Library; p. 89*r* Mehau Kulyk/Science Photo Library; p. 96 Jack Finch/Science Photo Library; p. 97 George Porter; p. 107 Elenac/BASF; p. 125 David Frazier/Science Photo Library; p. 147 Barry Slaven, Peter Arnold inc./Science Photo Library; p. 148 Gary Parker/Science Photo Library; p. 158 © Robert Harding World Imagery; p. 189 Reuters/ Corbis; p. 191 Alfred Pasieka/Science Photo Library; p. 192 BP Photographic Services; p. 196*l* Peter Ryan/ Science Photo Library; p. 207 © Corbis; extension ch. 5 *springbok* Rafi Ben-Shahar/OSF; extension ch. 5 *Watson and Crick* A. Barringon Brown/SPL; extension ch. 10 *mobile mass spectrometer* © Bruker Daltonik GmbH, Leipzig, Germany; extension ch. 10 *infrared spectrometer* Geoff Lane/CSIRO/Science Photo Library; extension ch. 12 *crocodile* Mark Deeble & Victoria Stone/OSF; extension ch. 12 *purifying haemoglobin* Baxter Haemoglobin Therapeutics, USA; extension ch. 13 *baby* La Belle Aurore.

We would like to thank OCR for permission to reproduce exam questions from past examination papers.

Chapter 1

AS level organic chemistry revisited

e-Learning

Objectives

Some revision

Unit F324, *Rings, Polymers and Analysis* continues the study of organic chemistry that you began in AS Unit F322 *Chains, Energy and Resources* (covered in Chapters 10–14 of *Chemistry 1*). You should have a sound knowledge and understanding of the organic chemistry from *Chemistry 1* before you study the new A2 material introduced in this unit. This chapter provides an opportunity for you to review and extend appropriate material from *Chemistry 1*.

We can study organic chemistry in a particularly structured and systematic manner. That is because each different atom or group of atoms attached to a carbon atom in an organic compound has its own characteristic set of reactions. Chemists call these different groups of atoms **functional groups**. In *Chemistry 1*, you studied the reactions of the alkene functional group ($>C=C<$).

The functional groups that you will study in this unit are shown in Table 1.1.

Table 1.1 provides you with the classes and structures of these functional groups. An example is also provided of a simple molecule containing each functional group. Each functional group gives rise to a **homologous series**. For example, the alcohol functional group gives rise to the homologous series of alcohols. The first four of these are methanol (CH_3OH), ethanol (CH_3CH_2OH), propan-1-ol ($CH_3CH_2CH_2OH$) and butan-1-ol ($CH_3CH_2CH_2CH_2OH$). The members of a homologous series all have similar chemical properties.

Organic compounds are also classified as either aliphatic or aromatic. **Aromatic compounds** contain one or more arene rings; all other organic compounds are **aliphatic compounds**.

Chemists use different types of formulae to represent organic molecules.

- A **general formula** may be written for each homologous series. For example, the general formula of the aliphatic alcohols is $C_nH_{2n+1}OH$ (where n is the number of carbon atoms present).
- **Empirical formulae** (simplest formulae) are determined by experiments. They give the simplest whole-number ratio of elements present in a compound. However, they give no indication of structure. For example, the empirical formula of ethene, whose molecules contain two carbon atoms and four hydrogen atoms, is CH_2.
- The **molecular formula** of a compound tells us the actual numbers of atoms of each element in one molecule of a compound. So the molecular formula of ethene is C_2H_4. The molecular formula is used when you need to calculate the molecular mass of a compound.
- **Structural formulae** are particularly useful when writing equations involving aliphatic compounds. For example, the structural formula of 3-methylpentane is $CH_3CH_2CH(CH_3)CH_2CH_3$.
- **Skeletal formulae** are the clearest and easiest way to represent cyclic compounds in equations. For example, cyclohexane is represented by a simple hexagon.
- **Displayed formulae** (sometimes called full structural formulae) show all the atoms and bonds in a molecule in a 2D drawing. They are useful in checking that you have included the correct number of atoms and bonds. Examination questions often ask you to provide displayed formulae. However, remember that they do not give a true indication of the shape of a molecule. Shapes are best represented using **three-dimensional formulae** which attempt to show the actual arrangement of atoms in space by using some bonds that appear to stick out from or retreat into the plane of the page.

Class of functional group	Structure of functional group	Name of example	Structural formula of example
alkenes	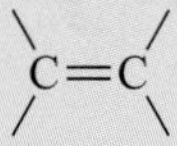 $\begin{array}{c}\diagdown\\C=C\\\diagup\end{array}$	ethene	$CH_2=CH_2$
arenes	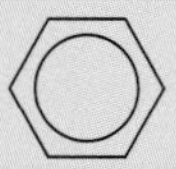 (benzene ring)	benzene	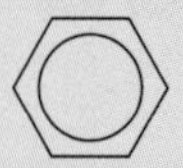 (benzene ring)
halogenoalkanes	$-X$, where $X = F, Cl, Br, I$	chloromethane	CH_3Cl
alcohols and phenols	$-OH$	methanol, phenol	CH_3OH, 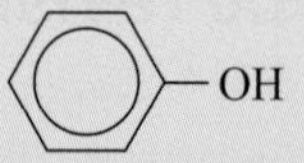 (phenol)—OH
aldehydes	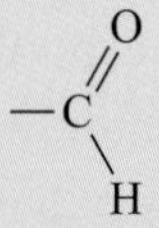 $-C\overset{O}{\underset{H}{\diagup}}$	ethanal	CH_3CHO
ketones	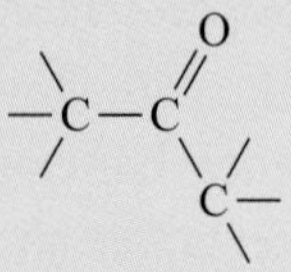 $-C-C\overset{O}{\diagup}$	propanone	CH_3COCH_3
carboxylic acids	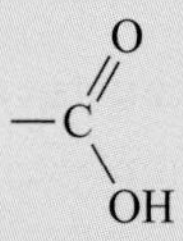 $-C\overset{O}{\underset{OH}{\diagup}}$	ethanoic acid	CH_3COOH
esters	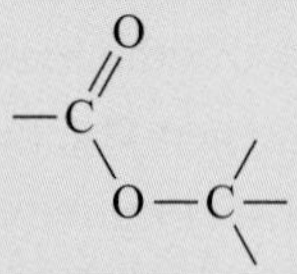 $-C\overset{O}{\underset{O-C}{\diagup}}$	ethyl ethanoate	$CH_3COOC_2H_5$
amines	$-NH_2$	methylamine	CH_3NH_2
amides	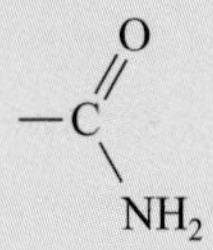 $-C\overset{O}{\underset{NH_2}{\diagup}}$	ethanamide	CH_3CONH_2
nitriles	$-C\equiv N$	ethanenitrile	CH_3CN

Table 1.1 The functional groups you will meet in this unit.

SAQ

1 Draw the following types of formulae for 2-methylbutan-2-ol:

  a displayed

  b structural

  c skeletal.

Answer

2 What is the molecular formula of 2-bromobutane?

Answer

You will see various computer-generated images of molecules where appropriate throughout this book. The colours used in these images are shown in Table 1.2.

Another type of image that will be used in this book is a space-filling model. In space-filling models, atoms are shown as including the space occupied by their electron orbitals. As their orbitals overlap significantly, a very different image from the ball-and-stick model results. Figure 1.1 shows these two types of model for lactic acid.

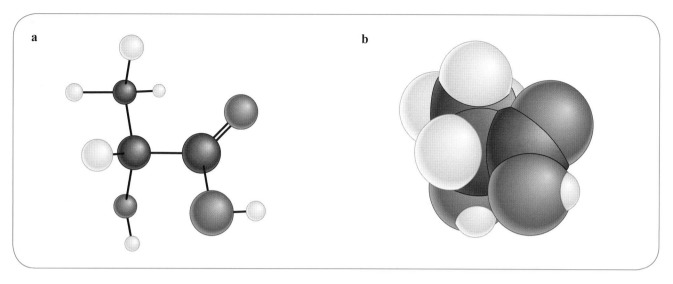

Figure 1.1 Different model types for lactic acid (2-hydroxypropanoic acid): **a** ball-and-stick model; **b** space-filling model.

Colour	Element
white	hydrogen
dark grey	carbon
red	oxygen
blue	nitrogen
yellow-green	fluorine
green	chlorine
orange-brown	bromine
brown	iodine
violet	phosphorus
pale yellow	sulfur

Table 1.2 The colours used for elements in molecular models.

Naming organic compounds

The names used in this section are known as **systematic** names. Such names precisely describe the structure of a molecule and enable chemists to communicate clearly. International rules of **nomenclature** have been agreed for the systematic naming of organic compounds.

The basic rules for naming hydrocarbons are as follows.

1 The number of carbon atoms in the longest chain provides the stem of the name. Simple **alkanes** consist entirely of unbranched chains of carbon atoms. They are named by adding -ane to this stem, as shown in Table 1.3.

2 Branched-chain alkanes are named in the same way. The name given to the longest continuous carbon chain is then prefixed by the names of the shorter side chains. The same stems are used for the side chains, but with the suffix -yl. Hence CH_3- is methyl (often called a methyl group). In general, such groups are called alkyl groups. The position of an alkyl group is indicated by a number. The carbon atoms in the longest carbon chain are numbered from one end of the chain. Numbering starts from the end which produces the lowest possible numbers for the side chains. For example, the molecule below is 2-methylpentane, *not* 4-methylpentane.

$$CH_3 - CH - CH_2 - CH_2 - CH_3$$
$$|$$
$$CH_3$$

3 Each side chain must be included in the name. If there are several identical side chains, the name is prefixed by di-, tri-, etc. For example, 2,2,3-trimethyl- indicates that there are three methyl groups: two on the second carbon atom and one on the third carbon atom of the longest chain. Note that two numbers are separated by a comma, whilst a number and a letter are separated by a hyphen.

4 Where different alkyl groups are present, they are placed in alphabetical order, as in 3-ethyl-2-methylpentane.

Molecular formula	Number of carbon atoms in longest chain	Stem	Name
CH_4	1	meth-	methane
C_2H_6	2	eth-	ethane
C_3H_8	3	prop-	propane
C_4H_{10}	4	but-	butane
C_5H_{12}	5	pent-	pentane
C_6H_{14}	6	hex-	hexane
C_7H_{16}	7	hept-	heptane
C_8H_{18}	8	oct-	octane
C_9H_{20}	9	non-	nonane
$C_{10}H_{22}$	10	dec-	decane
$C_{20}H_{42}$	20	eicos-	eicosane

Table 1.3 Naming simple alkanes

5 Compounds containing a ring of carbon atoms are prefixed by cyclo-. Cyclohexane is represented by:

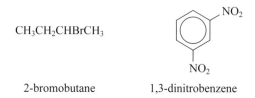

displayed formula   skeletal formula

6 Hydrocarbons containing one double bond are called **alkenes**. The same stems are used (eth-, prop-, etc.), but they are followed by -ene. The position of an alkene double bond is indicated by the lower number of the two carbon atoms involved. This number is placed between the stem and -ene. Hence $CH_3CH=CHCH_3$ is but-2-ene.

7 The simplest **arene** is benzene. When one alkyl group is attached to a benzene ring, a number is not needed because all the carbon atoms are equivalent. When two or more groups are attached, they will require numbers. For example:

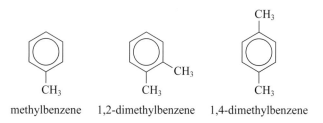

methylbenzene   1,2-dimethylbenzene   1,4-dimethylbenzene

8 Halogeno or nitro compounds are named in the same way as alkyl-substituted alkanes or arenes:

$CH_3CH_2CHBrCH_3$

2-bromobutane   1,3-dinitrobenzene

9 Aliphatic alcohols and ketones are named in a similar way to alkenes:

$CH_3CH_2CH_2OH$ $CH_3CH_2COCH_2CH_3$

propan-1-ol   pentan-3-one

10 Aliphatic aldehyde and carboxylic acid groups can only be found at the end of a carbon chain, so they do not need a number. There is only one possible butanoic acid, $CH_3CH_2CH_2COOH$, or butanal, $CH_3CH_2CH_2CHO$. Note that the names of aldehydes, carboxylic acids and nitriles include the carbon atom of the functional group in the stem of the name. Hence CH_3COOH is ethanoic acid and CH_3CN is ethanenitrile.

11 Amines are named using the alkyl- or aryl- prefix followed by -amine. Hence $CH_3CH_2NH_2$ is ethylamine.

SAQ

3 Give the systematic names of these compounds:

a   b   c

$BrCH_2CO_2H$

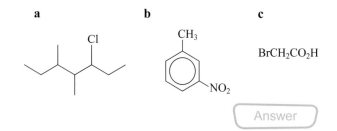

Answer

4 Draw structural formulae for these compounds:
   a aminoethanoic acid
   b 2-hydroxybenzoic acid
   c 2,4,6-tribromophenol.

   [Hint] [Answer]

Isomerism

Structural isomers have the same molecular formula but different structural formulae. For example, 1-bromopropane and 2-bromopropane are structural isomers. They both have the molecular formula C_3H_7Br. Their skeletal formulae are as follows:

1-bromopropane   2-bromopropane

SAQ

5 Draw six structural isomers containing a carboxyl group,

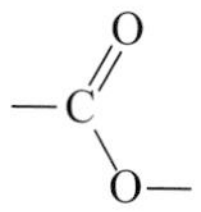

   [Hint]

   and with the molecular formula $C_4H_8O_2$.

   [Answer]

E/Z (cis–trans) **isomerism** arises in alkenes because rotation about a double bond cannot occur unless a π (pi) bond is broken. The molecule must have two different groups attached to each carbon atom of the C=C bond to exhibit *E/Z* isomerism. If two of the attached groups on adjacent carbon atoms are the same, the molecule can exhibit the special form of *E/Z* isomerism known as *cis–trans* isomerism.

SAQ

6 Draw and label the *cis–trans* (*E/Z*) isomers of butenedioic acid, HOOCCH=CHCOOH.

   [Hint] [Answer]

Isomers which contain the same atoms with the same order of bonds but with different spatial arrangements of atoms are called **stereoisomers**. *E/Z (cis–trans)* isomerism is one type of stereoisomerism. Another type is optical isomerism. You will find out more about optical isomerism and stereoisomerism in Chapter 6.

Summaries of reactions from AS Chemistry

Alkanes

Apart from combustion and substitution by halogens, alkanes are relatively unreactive. This is due to their strong covalent bonds and a lack of polarity.

In general, hydrocarbons burn. Many are important sources of energy.

$$CO_2 + H_2O \xleftarrow[+ O_2]{combustion} \quad \underset{ethane}{C_2H_6} \quad \xrightarrow[\substack{UV\ light \\ + Cl_2}]{substitution} C_2H_5Cl + HCl$$

Substitution by a halogen on an alkane involves a (free) radical mechanism. Three stages are involved, as follows:

- **Initiation** to form Cl• radicals. Ultraviolet light provides sufficient energy to break the covalent bonds in chlorine, $Cl_2(g)$. Homolytic fission occurs and two chlorine radicals are formed.

   $Cl–Cl(g) \rightarrow Cl•(g) + Cl•(g)$

- **Propagation** involving a chain reaction to form C_2H_5Cl:

   $Cl•(g) + H–CH_2CH_3(g) \rightarrow Cl–H(g) + •CH_2CH_3(g)$
   $Cl–Cl(g) + •CH_2CH_3(g) \rightarrow Cl•(g) + Cl–CH_2CH_3(g)$

- **Termination** involves radical combination reactions. These reactions will predominate when the reactants are running out. Examples of possible termination steps include the following:

   $Cl•(g) + Cl•(g) \rightarrow Cl–Cl(g)$
   $•CH_2CH_3(g) + •CH_2CH_3(g) \rightarrow CH_3CH_2CH_2CH_3(g)$

SAQ

7 a Explain what we mean by *homolytic fission*.

<Hint>

b With reference to the mechanism for the reaction between ethane and chlorine, explain what is meant by the term *chain reaction*.

<Answer>

Alkenes

The C=C double bond undergoes a variety of addition reactions. These are summarised in Figure 1.2 for ethene.

SAQ

8 Limonene occurs naturally in oranges and lemons. Look at the structure of limonene.

<Hint>

limonene

How many moles of bromine, Br_2, will add to one mole of limonene?

<Answer>

The mechanism for the **electrophilic addition** of bromine is as follows. Notice how the bromine molecule becomes polarised and then can act as an electrophile:

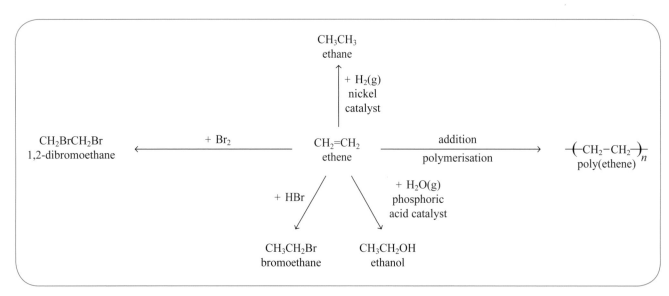

SAQ

9 a Explain what we mean by the term *electrophile*.

<Hint>

b The decolorisation of bromine water is frequently used as a test for an alkene functional group. When ethene is bubbled through bromine water, 2-bromoethanol is formed as well as 1,2-dibromoethane. Suggest a reason why 2-bromoethanol is also formed.

<Answer>

Figure 1.2 A summary of the addition reactions of ethene.

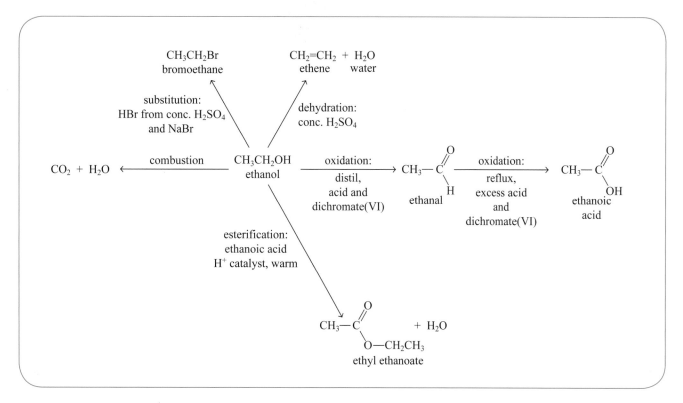

Figure 1.3 A summary of the reactions of ethanol.

Alcohols

Alcohols undergo a wide variety of reactions. These are summarised in Figure 1.3 for ethanol.

Halogenoalkanes

The hydrolysis of halogenoalkanes involves a **nucleophilic substitution**. The mechanism of this reaction is shown in Figure 1.4 for bromomethane, CH_3Br.

SAQ

10 Explain what we mean by the term *nucleophile*.

Answer

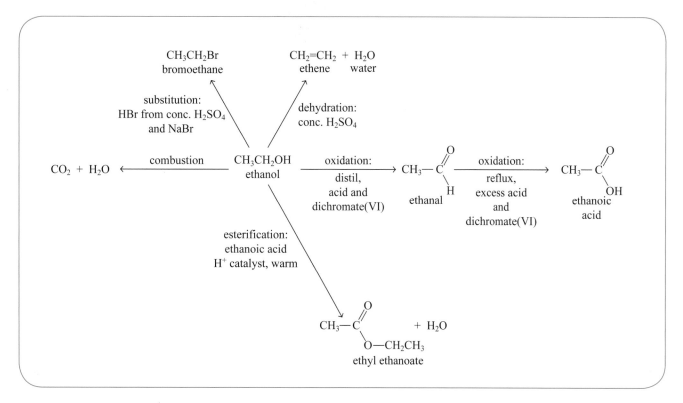

Figure 1.4 Nucleophilic substitution of CH_3Br.

Summary

Glossary

- All organic compounds contain carbon and most contain hydrogen. Most organic compounds also contain other elements, such as oxygen, nitrogen and chlorine.

- Functional groups, which have their own characteristic reactions, are attached to the hydrocarbon framework of an organic molecule. Alkenes, arenes, halogen atoms, alcohols, aldehydes and ketones, carboxylic acids, esters, amines, amides and nitriles are examples of functional groups.

- Chemists use a wide variety of formulae to represent organic molecules. These include general, empirical, molecular, structural, skeletal, displayed and three-dimensional formulae.

- Various types of molecular models (ball-and-stick, space-filling) are used to visualise organic molecules.

- Organic molecules are named in a systematic way, related to their structures.

- Organic molecules with the same molecular formula but with different structural formulae are called isomers. Three common types of isomerism are structural, *E/Z* (*cis–trans*) and optical isomerism. Structural isomers have different structural formulae, *E/Z* (*cis–trans*) isomers have different displayed formulae (and optical isomers have different three-dimensional formulae – see Chapter 6).

- The study of organic reactions is traditionally organised by functional group. Each functional group has its own characteristic reactions.

- Alkanes are relatively unreactive due to strong covalent bonds and low polarity. They burn in air to produce carbon dioxide and water. In ultraviolet light, they undergo radical substitution reactions with halogens, forming halogenoalkanes.

- Alkenes typically undergo addition reactions with hydrogen, bromine, hydrogen bromide and steam. They also undergo addition polymerisation. The reaction of bromine with ethene involves an electrophilic addition mechanism.

- Alcohols burn in air producing carbon dioxide and water. They may be dehydrated to alkenes by concentrated sulfuric acid. Substitution by HBr produces a bromoalkane. Esters are formed on refluxing with a carboxylic acid and a strong acid catalyst. Primary alcohols are oxidised to aldehydes and then to carboxylic acids with acidified dichromate(VI).

- Halogenoalkanes undergo nucleophilic substitution reactions with aqueous alkali to form alcohols.

- Reaction mechanisms may involve electrophiles, nucleophiles or (free) radicals. Each of these reagents is capable of forming a new covalent bond to the atom attacked. Electrophiles attack atoms with a high electron density, nucleophiles attack atoms with a low electron density. Radicals are highly reactive, attacking any atom with which they are capable of forming a bond.

- Covalent bonds may be broken homolytically to form two radicals, each with an unpaired electron. Polar bonds will frequently break heterolytically to form one cation and one anion.

- Curly arrows show the movement of pairs of electrons in a reaction mechanism.

- Electrophiles must be capable of accepting a pair of electrons; nucleophiles must have a lone-pair of electrons available for bond formation.

Chapter 2

Arenes

Objectives

Benzene

The simplest arene is the liquid called benzene, C_6H_6. It is added to unleaded petrol and is used to make many other chemicals, such as alkylbenzenes. Benzene is the feedstock for the manufacture of compounds as varied as medicines, detergents, dyes and explosives (see Figure 2.1). You will not use benzene in a school laboratory as it is believed to cause leukaemia.

Benzene is a planar, hexagonal-shaped molecule. This structure has considerable chemical stability.

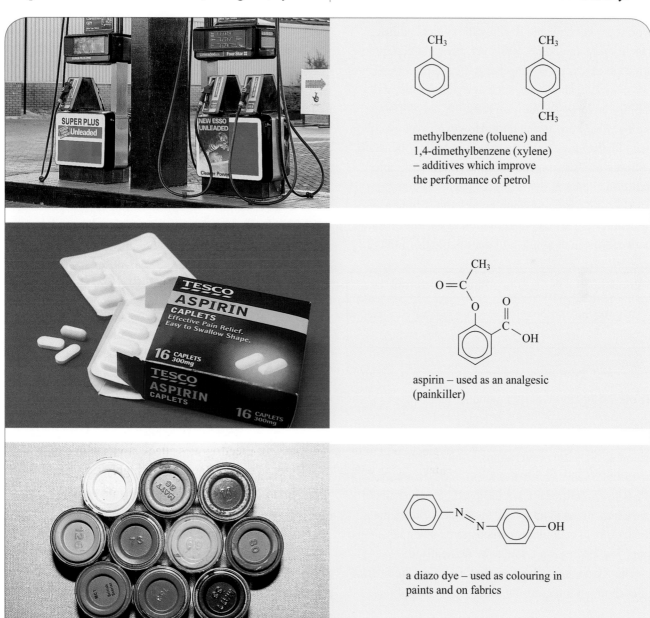

methylbenzene (toluene) and 1,4-dimethylbenzene (xylene) – additives which improve the performance of petrol

aspirin – used as an analgesic (painkiller)

a diazo dye – used as colouring in paints and on fabrics

Figure 2.1 Some compounds manufactured from benzene.

Friedrich Kekulé was the first to suggest that benzene was a cyclic molecule, but he also thought benzene had alternating single and double carbon–carbon bonds. Such a structure would have two different lengths for the carbon–carbon bonds and you would be able to put the single and double bonds in two alternative positions:

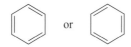

These are known as the Kekulé structures of benzene.

If Kekulé's structure for benzene was correct, you would expect benzene to show the typical addition reactions of an alkene. However, benzene undergoes addition reactions far less easily than a typical alkene. For example, an alkene, such as cyclohexene, will rapidly undergo an addition reaction, decolorising aqueous bromine in the dark. However, you would need the bromine to be dissolved in boiling benzene, with the mixture exposed to ultraviolet light, before addition occurs in benzene (see page 14).

Also, the carbon–carbon bond lengths in benzene molecules are all identical, with lengths intermediate between those of single and double bonds (Table 2.1).

Bond	Bond length/nm
C–C	0.154
C=C	0.134
benzene C–C	0.139

Table 2.1 Carbon–carbon bond lengths.

Our current model of the bonding in benzene accounts for these observations. Each carbon atom contributes one electron to a π (pi) bond. However, the π bonds formed are not localised between pairs of carbon atoms as in an alkene molecule: instead, the π bonds spread over all six carbon atoms in the hexagonal ring. The electrons are said to be **delocalised**.

The π bonding in benzene is formed by the overlap of carbon p atomic orbitals, one from each of the

six carbon atoms. To achieve maximum overlap, the benzene molecule must be planar. The lobes of the p orbitals merge to form a ring of delocalised electrons above and below the plane of the carbon atoms in the benzene molecule:

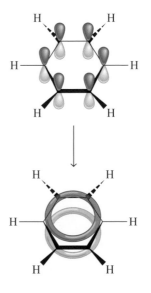

overlap of p orbitals produces a ring of delocalised electrons above and below the plane of benzene's carbon atoms.

This model produces six C–C bonds of the same length, as seen in Table 2.1. We can see the planar shape clearly in a space-filling molecular model of benzene:

SAQ

1 a How many electrons are found in the π bonding system above and below the plane of the atoms in the benzene molecule? 〔Hint〕

b From which atomic orbitals do the π bonding electrons originate in the benzene molecule?

c Why are the π bonding electrons described as 'delocalised' electrons? 〔Answer〕

Kekulé – the chemical dreamer

In the middle of the 19th century, new dyes could be made based on benzene. Chemists had known that the chemical formula of benzene was C_6H_6 since 1834, but they could not work out how the atoms were arranged in its molecules. It was the chemical dreamer, Friedrich August Kekulé (Figure 2.2), who solved the problem. In 1853, when Kekulé was in his twenties, he had his first 'chemical' dream.

Figure 2.2 Friedrich August Kekulé (1829–1896).

On his way home from a friend's house in London, Kekulé took a horse-drawn bus through the streets, which were quiet at that time of night. He had been discussing chemistry with his friends, so that probably explains why, as he slipped into a light sleep, his dream was about carbon atoms. He saw them moving around, joining to form pairs.

Then pairs would join to form chains that increased in length as each pair joined the end. This was his first insight into organic chemistry: the fact that carbon atoms can form chains.

About 12 years later, when working in Belgium, Kekulé was dozing in front of his fire when he dreamt of chains of carbon atoms making snake-like movements. Suddenly one snake bit its own tail and whirled around before his eyes. Kekulé woke up immediately and started sketching his visions.

Kekulé came to conclusion that the mysterious benzene molecule, C_6H_6, was a closed hexagonal ring.

Kekulé was also one of the first chemists to suggest that carbon atoms can form four bonds to other atoms. He therefore proposed this structure for benzene (Figure 2.3):

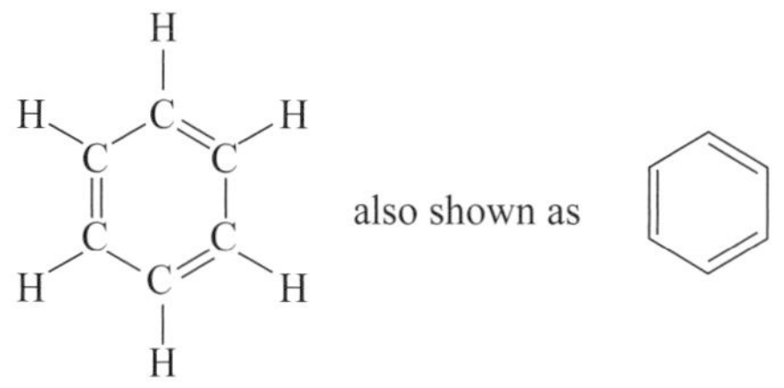

Figure 2.3 Kekulé's model for the bonding in benzene.

This was a great breakthrough for chemistry. Now chemists could start to understand the reactions they were discovering in their research, even though we now have convincing evidence that Kekulé's model did not accurately represent the carbon–carbon bonding in benzene.

Energetic stability of benzene

The reluctance of benzene to undergo addition reactions is due to the increased energetic stability that the delocalised system gives it. We can show this by considering the reactions of both benzene and the theoretical Kekulé structure with hydrogen. We know the actual value of the heat of hydrogenation of benzene using data from experiments:

benzene + $3H_2$ ⟶ cyclohexane $\Delta H = -208$ kJ mol^{-1}

We can measure the enthalpy of hydrogenation of cyclohexene, which contains one double bond:

cyclohexene + H_2 ⟶ cyclohexane $\Delta H = -121$ kJ mol^{-1}

If we think of benzene as having its Kekulé structure with three double bonds, it seems reasonable to multiply the value for cyclohexene by 3 to get the enthalpy of hydrogenation of benzene. This gives us an enthalpy of hydrogenation for the Kekulé structure, of $(-121 \times 3) = -363$ kJ mol^{-1}.

We can show the values for benzene and for its theoretical Kekulé structure on an enthalpy level diagram (Figure 2.4).

You can see from Figure 2.4 that the actual benzene molecule is about 155 kJ mol^{-1} more stable than its theoretical Kekulé structure. This stability comes from its delocalised π bonding electrons. Therefore, when benzene reacts it tends to keep its benzene ring intact, unless extreme conditions are used.

The high electron density associated with π bonding means that both arenes and alkenes attract electrophiles (acceptors of an electron pair). However, benzene undergoes electrophilic *substitution* reactions around the delocalised benzene ring whereas alkenes undergo electrophilic *addition* reactions which take place across the localised π bonding in the C=C double bond.

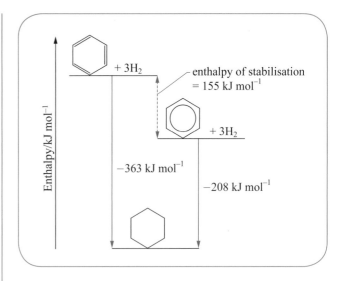

Figure 2.4 Enthalpies of hydrogenation used to calculate benzene's enthalpy of stabilisation.

SAQ

2   List three pieces of evidence that you could use to argue against Kekulé's model as representing the correct bonding between carbon atoms in benzene.

Answer

Substitution reactions

Breaking the delocalised π bonding electron system on benzene requires a considerable input of energy. Arenes such as benzene undergo many reactions in which the delocalised system is retained. The majority of these are substitution reactions. In these reactions one or more hydrogen atoms on the benzene ring are directly replaced by atoms or groups such as halogen atoms, nitro ($-NO_2$) groups and alkyl groups.

The formation of nitroarenes

The explosive trinitrotoluene (TNT) is made by substituting nitro groups, $-NO_2$, for hydrogen atoms on the benzene ring of methylbenzene. It is explosive because the nitro groups bring six oxygen atoms near to the carbon atoms of the benzene ring. When detonated (Figure 2.5), the compression pushes these atoms closer together, causing the rapid formation of carbon dioxide and water vapour, and leaving the nitrogen atoms to join together as nitrogen molecules. The explosion is caused by the very large and rapid increase in volume as the solid TNT is converted to gases.

Figure 2.5 The use of trinitrotoluene (TNT) as an explosive in quarrying.

As well as its use in explosives, the nitro group is also used in the preparation of drugs and dyestuffs.

To substitute a nitro group into an arene requires the use of **nitrating mixture**. This is a mixture of concentrated nitric acid and concentrated sulfuric acid. To make nitrobenzene from benzene, the reaction mixture is heated gently under reflux at a temperature of about 50–55 °C. Careful temperature control is needed to minimise the formation of dinitrobenzene. The reaction equation is:

$$\text{benzene} + HNO_3 \longrightarrow \text{nitrobenzene (NO}_2\text{)} + H_2O$$

This is a substitution in which a hydrogen atom is replaced by the nitro group, $-NO_2$.

The mechanism of nitration involves an **electrophilic substitution**. The function of the sulfuric acid in the nitrating mixture is to generate the electrophile from the nitric acid. The benzene ring has a high electron charge density associated with the delocalised π electrons. Hence an electrophile, which is electron deficient, is attracted by this negative charge. An electrophile must be capable of forming a new covalent bond to carbon if it is to react successfully. The electrophile produced in the nitrating mixture is the nitronium ion, NO_2^+ (sometimes called the nitryl cation):

$$HNO_3 + H_2SO_4 \longrightarrow H_2NO_3^+ + HSO_4^-$$
$$H_2NO_3^+ \longrightarrow NO_2^+ + H_2O$$

There are two stages in the mechanism of electrophilic substitution by the NO_2^+ ion. Figure 2.6 shows this mechanism using curly arrows.

● *Stage 1* Electrophilic attack by the nitronium ion takes place as the positively charged ion is attracted by the delocalised π electrons on benzene. A new covalent bond forms to one of the carbon atoms in the benzene ring. This carbon atom is now saturated, so the delocalised π electrons, together with the positive charge from the NO_2^+, are shared by the other five carbon atoms.

● *Stage 2* Loss of a proton (H^+) produces nitrobenzene and restores the full delocalised π electron system. Thus in electrophilic substitution, the chemical stability of the benzene ring is retained.

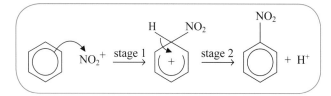

Figure 2.6 Electrophilic substitution on benzene.

● *Stage 1* Notice that the curly arrow starts at the delocalised π electrons and finishes on the nitrogen atom in NO_2^+. Two electrons are lost from the delocalised π electrons to produce a new covalent bond to the nitrogen atom in NO_2^+.

   The intermediate is a cation with a single positive charge and a 'horseshoe' representing delocalisation of four electrons over five carbon atoms.

● *Stage 2* The second curly arrow moves two electrons from the C–H bond to restore the full delocalised system of six π electrons. Nitrobenzene and H^+ are formed. The circle in the benzene ring of the product shows that the full delocalised π electron system has been restored.

SAQ

3 a Draw and name three isomers which might be produced following electrophilic substitution of NO_2^+ for one hydrogen atom in methylbenzene. **Hint**

  b TNT has the systematic name 1-methyl-2,4,6-trinitrobenzene. Draw the structural formula of TNT. **Answer**

The formation of halogenoarenes

Benzene also undergoes an electrophilic substitution reaction with chlorine or bromine. For example, if chlorine is bubbled through benzene at room temperature, in the presence of a halogen carrier, chlorobenzene is formed:

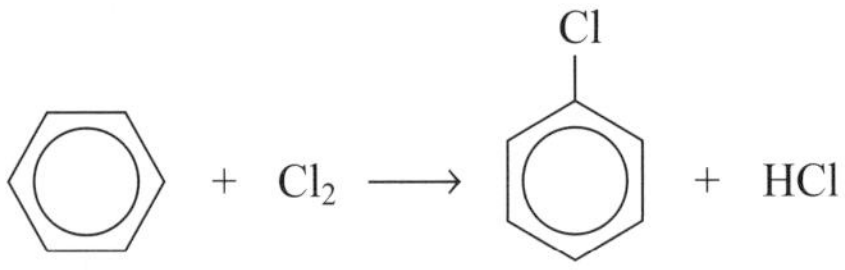

The halogen carrier is usually introduced as metallic iron. This reacts with the chlorine to produce anhydrous iron(III) chloride. Iron(III) chloride is a covalent chloride and is soluble in the benzene. The effect of the iron(III) chloride is to polarise the chlorine molecule so that it behaves as an electrophile:

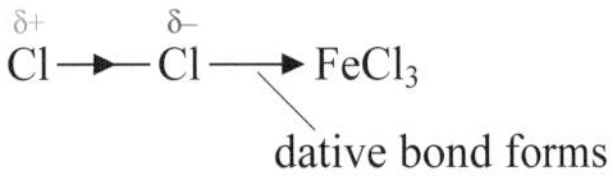

The arrow represents a dative bond between a chlorine atom and the iron(III) chloride. This has the effect of drawing the electrons from the Cl–Cl bond, leaving one Cl atom with a partial positive charge. We can think of the Cl–Cl bond as breaking heterolytically to form the electrophile Cl^+ and $[FeCl_4]^-$:

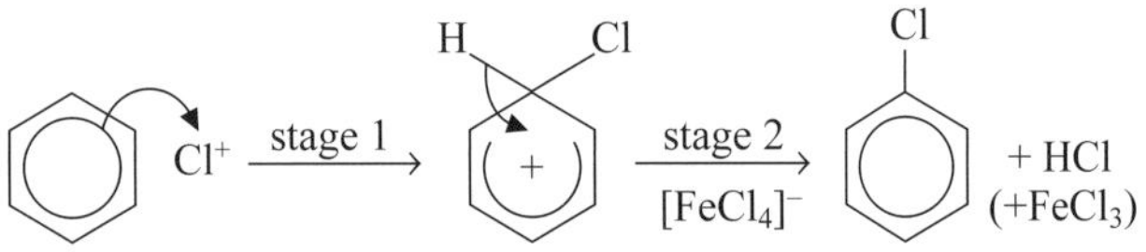

Anhydrous aluminium chloride may also be used as a halogen carrier. We can also represent the creation of the electrophile, Cl^+, by the equation:

$$Cl–Cl + AlCl_3 \longrightarrow Cl^+ + [AlCl_4]^-$$

SAQ

4 Suggest a mechanism for the electrophilic substitution reaction between benzene and chlorine in the presence of aluminium chloride.

Answer

Addition of halogens to benzene

The Kekulé structure of benzene with three alternating C=C double bonds would suggest that benzene might readily undergo an addition reaction with a halogen such as chlorine or bromine. We have already seen that chlorine and bromine, in the presence of a halogen carrier, produce substituted products. For example, bromine in the presence of anhydrous iron(III) bromide produces bromobenzene:

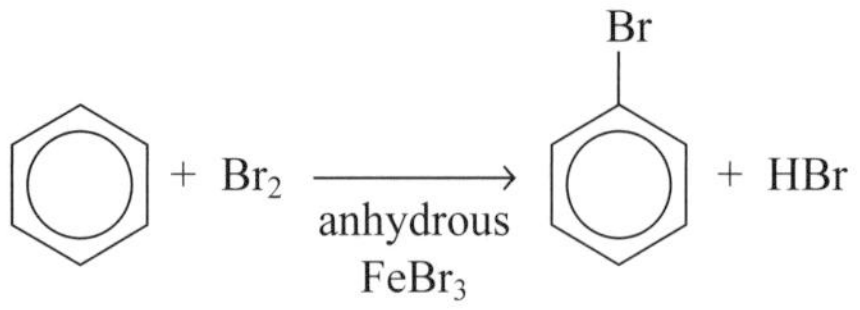

The *addition* of bromine to benzene is much more difficult to achieve. This is somewhat surprising if we represent benzene by the Kekulé structure.

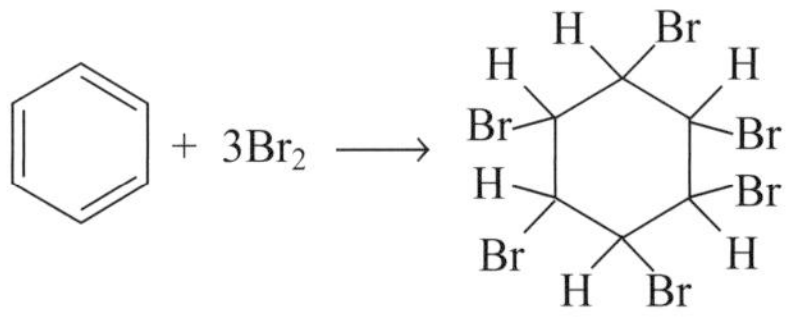

Our knowledge of the addition of bromine to an alkene such as cyclohexene would suggest that this reaction would require mild reaction conditions. Cyclohexene produces 1,2-dibromocyclohexane on shaking with bromine water. Indeed, this reaction is used as a quick test to show the presence of an alkene:

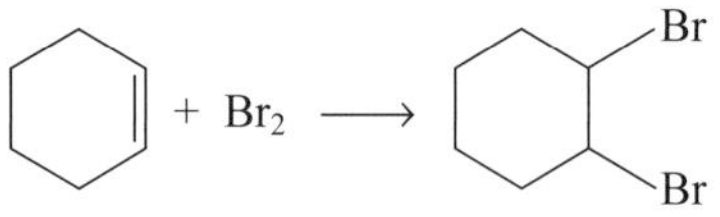

The relative resistance of benzene to bromination as compared to cyclohexene may be explained in terms of delocalisation of the π electrons in the benzene ring.

Benzene requires more vigorous reaction conditions for the addition of a halogen such as chlorine or bromine because of the chemical stability of the delocalised π electron system.

Extra energy is required to overcome this stability (see page 12). For example, the chlorination of benzene needs sunlight for the reaction to take place:

$$\text{benzene} + 3Cl_2 \longrightarrow \text{hexachlorocyclohexane}$$

(see page 12)

SAQ

5 **a** What does the use of ultraviolet light suggest about the nature of the attacking species in the addition of chlorine to benzene? [Hint]

b How does your suggestion compare to the attacking species in the addition of chlorine to an alkene? [Answer]

Benzene has been used to manufacture the chlorinated insecticide Lindane. However, the use of chlorinated hydrocarbon insecticides has now virtually ceased. This follows the discovery of a link between their use and a decline in the population of predator species, for example peregrine falcons (Figure 2.7).

[Extension]

Figure 2.7 Peregrine falcon populations have increased significantly since chlorinated hydrocarbon insecticides have been replaced by new, safer alternatives.

Phenols and their properties

Phenols, like alcohols, occur widely in nature. Phenol itself is a white crystalline solid at 25 °C, and has the formula C_6H_5OH. Its structural formula is:

In all phenols, the –OH group is joined to a benzene ring. For example, vanillin is found in the seed pods of the vanilla orchid (Figure 2.8). Vanillin is widely used as a flavouring in foods such as chocolate and ice cream.

The structure of vanillin is:

SAQ

6 **a** Copy the structure of vanillin and label the phenolic –OH group.

b Identify and label any other functional groups present. [Hint] [Answer]

Figure 2.8 Vanilla orchids.

Solubility in water

Phenol is sparingly soluble in water. The –OH group forms hydrogen bonds to water, whilst the benzene ring reduces the solubility because it has only weak van der Waals' interactions with other molecules. Two liquid layers are formed if sufficient phenol crystals are added to water (Figure 2.9). The excess phenol absorbs water (again, by forming hydrogen bonds) and produces a lower liquid layer. This lower layer is a solution of water in phenol and the upper layer is a solution of phenol in water.

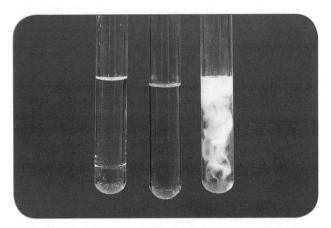

Figure 2.9 The left-hand tube shows phenol in water: the phenol does not mix, and settles out at the bottom of the tube. The central tube contains phenol dissolved in alkali. The right-hand tube shows the formation of a milky emulsion when the alkaline phenol is acidified.

Reactions in which the O–H bond is broken

Reaction with bases

As phenol is a weak acid, it neutralises strong bases. For example, with sodium hydroxide the products are the salt called sodium phenoxide and water:

$$\text{C}_6\text{H}_5\text{—OH} + \text{NaOH} \longrightarrow \text{C}_6\text{H}_5\text{—O}^-\text{Na}^+ + \text{H}_2\text{O}$$

Sodium phenoxide is an ionic compound. Phenol dissolves completely in aqueous sodium hydroxide, but it is only sparingly soluble in water.

Reaction with sodium

Phenol reacts vigorously with sodium:

$$2\,\text{C}_6\text{H}_5\text{—OH} + 2\text{Na} \longrightarrow 2\,\text{C}_6\text{H}_5\text{—O}^-\text{Na}^+ + \text{H}_2$$

Sodium phenoxide is formed and hydrogen gas is given off.

SAQ

7 **a** Name the products formed when phenol reacts with potassium hydroxide.

b Write an equation to show the reaction in part **a**.

Answer

Reactions involving the benzene ring

Phenol undergoes electrophilic substitution reactions far more readily than benzene. The hydroxyl group, –OH, raises the electron charge density of the benzene π bonding system, considerably enhancing the reactivity of phenol towards electrophiles. The carbon–oxygen bond in phenol has about 16% double-bond character. This is caused by a partial delocalisation into the benzene ring of lone-pair electrons on the oxygen. The increased electron charge density is greatest at the 2, 4 and 6 positions on the benzene ring.

Substitution with bromine

Aqueous phenol decolorises bromine water to form a white precipitate of 2,4,6-tribromophenol (Figure 2.10)

Similar reactions occur with chlorine and iodine. Contrast these very mild conditions with the need to use pure bromine and pure benzene, together with an iron(III) bromide catalyst, to produce the mono-substituted bromobenzene.

The presence in phenol of the –OH group increases the susceptibility of the benzene ring to electrophilic attack. The oxygen in the –OH group has two lone-pairs of electrons in p orbitals. These can overlap with the delocalised π electrons in the benzene ring, partially extending delocalisation to the oxygen atom. Overall, the π electron charge density is increased (especially at the 2, 4 and 6 positions). Chemists say the –OH group activates the benzene ring.

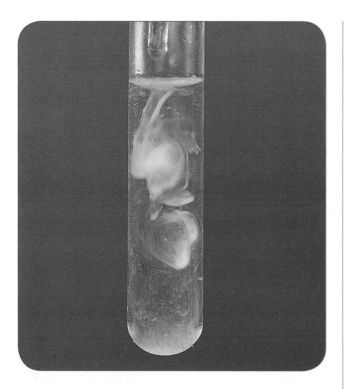

Figure 2.10 The reaction that occurs when bromine water is added to aqueous phenol.

SAQ

8 How does bromine in aqueous solution become sufficiently polar to achieve electrophilic substitution on phenol?

Hint

Answer

Uses of phenols

Phenol is used to manufacture a wide range of useful chemical products (Figure 2.11). A dilute aqueous solution of phenol was first used in 1865 as an antiseptic by Joseph Lister. Phenol was soon widely used in hospitals and greatly reduced the number of infections, particularly during surgery. Phenol as the solid or in concentrated form is harmful by skin absorption and can cause burns. Safer compounds such chlorophenols have now largely replaced phenol in antiseptics and disinfectants. Phenols are also used in the production of plastics and resins for paints.

Figure 2.11 Compact discs, Araldite and TCP are all manufactured using phenol as a raw material.

Summary

Glossary

- Arenes have considerable energetic stability because of the delocalised π bonding electrons. Arenes require much more vigorous reaction conditions than alkenes to undergo addition reactions because of this extra stability.

- Arene chemistry is dominated by electrophilic substitution reactions that enable arenes to retain the delocalised π electrons. Hydrogen atoms on the benzene ring may be replaced by a variety of other atoms or groups including halogen atoms and nitro ($-NO_2$) groups.

- The variety of substitution reactions on benzene provides access to many useful compounds including medicines, dyes, explosives and polymers.

- When the $-OH$ group is joined directly to a benzene ring, the resulting alcohol is called a phenol.

- Phenols are weakly acidic and form salts, called phenoxides, plus water on reaction with sodium hydroxide.

- The reaction of sodium with phenol produces sodium phenoxide and hydrogen gas.

- The $-OH$ group enhances the reactivity of the benzene ring towards electrophiles. Bromine water is decolorised by phenol, producing a white precipitate of 2,4,6-tribromophenol.

Questions

1 Phenol reacts readily with dilute nitric acid at room temperature in a nitration reaction to produce a mixture of products as shown below.

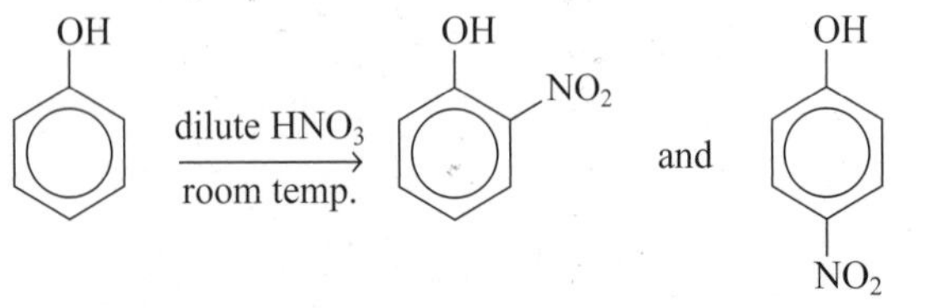

  a Suggest the structure of another organic product that is likely to be formed in the nitration of phenol. [1]

  b Assuming a yield by mass of 27% for 4-nitrophenol, calculate the mass of 4-nitrophenol that would be produced from 100 g of phenol. Show your working. Give your answer to an appropriate number of significant figures. [4]

Hint

OCR Chemistry A2 (2814) January 2006   [Total 5]

Answer

continued

2 *In this question, one mark is available for the quality of spelling, punctuation and grammar.*
Describe, with the aid of suitable diagrams, the bonding and structure of a benzene molecule. [6]
Quality of written communication [1]
OCR Chemistry A2 (2814) January 2007 [Total 7]

Hint

Answer

3 The diagram below shows some reactions of phenol.

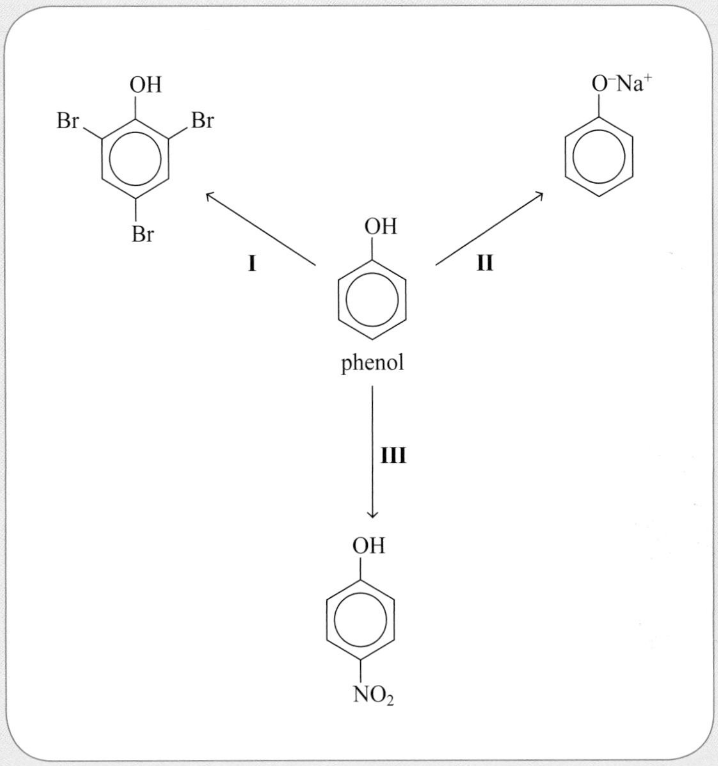

a On the diagram above, identify suitable reagents that could be used to carry out reactions **I**, **II** and **III**. [3]

b Phenol reacts much more readily with bromine than benzene does. Explain why electrophiles, such as bromine, react much more readily with phenol than with benzene. [3]

OCR Chemistry A2 (2814) June 2007 [Total 6]

Hint

Answer

Chapter 3

Carbonyl compounds

Objectives

Aldehydes and ketones

You first met carbonyl compounds in AS Unit F322, *Chains, Energy and Resources*, when you studied aldehydes and ketones (Figure 3.1). Aldehydes are formed in the first stage of oxidation of primary alcohols, whilst ketones are the only product formed on oxidation of secondary alcohols (see *Chemistry 1*, Chapter 13).

Figure 3.1 The ketone, heptan-2-one, is responsible for the odour of blue cheese, and benzaldehyde contributes to the flavours of many fruits.

Both aldehydes and ketones contain the carbonyl group, C=O.

- In aldehydes, the carbon atom of this group is joined to at least one hydrogen atom. The aldehyde group is often written as –CHO. (This must not be confused with the hydroxyl functional group in alcohols, which is written as COH.) For example:

$$H-\overset{\overset{\displaystyle H}{|}}{\underset{\underset{\displaystyle H}{|}}{C}}-C\overset{\displaystyle O}{\underset{\displaystyle H}{\diagdown}} \quad \text{ethanal} \\ (CH_3CHO)$$

- In ketones, the carbonyl group is joined to two other carbon atoms, so the simplest ketone, propanone, must contain three carbon atoms.

$$H-\overset{\overset{\displaystyle H}{|}}{\underset{\underset{\displaystyle H}{|}}{C}}-\overset{\overset{\displaystyle O}{\|}}{C}-\overset{\overset{\displaystyle H}{|}}{\underset{\underset{\displaystyle H}{|}}{C}}-H \quad \text{propanone} \\ (CH_3COCH_3)$$

Note that aldehydes are named by taking the alkane stem and replacing the '-e' with '-al'; with ketones the '-e' is replaced by '-one'. Ketones which are larger than butanone have numbers in their names to show the position of the C=O group. For example:

$$H-\overset{\overset{\displaystyle H}{|}}{\underset{\underset{\displaystyle H}{|}}{C}}-\overset{\overset{\displaystyle O}{\|}}{C}-\overset{\overset{\displaystyle H}{|}}{\underset{\underset{\displaystyle H}{|}}{C}}-\overset{\overset{\displaystyle H}{|}}{\underset{\underset{\displaystyle H}{|}}{C}}-\overset{\overset{\displaystyle H}{|}}{\underset{\underset{\displaystyle H}{|}}{C}}-H \quad \text{pentan-2-one} \\ (CH_3COCH_2CH_2CH_3)$$

$$H-\overset{\overset{\displaystyle H}{|}}{\underset{\underset{\displaystyle H}{|}}{C}}-\overset{\overset{\displaystyle H}{|}}{\underset{\underset{\displaystyle H}{|}}{C}}-\overset{\overset{\displaystyle O}{\|}}{C}-\overset{\overset{\displaystyle H}{|}}{\underset{\underset{\displaystyle H}{|}}{C}}-\overset{\overset{\displaystyle H}{|}}{\underset{\underset{\displaystyle H}{|}}{C}}-H \quad \text{pentan-3-one} \\ (CH_3CH_2COCH_2CH_3)$$

Table 3.1 shows the first few members of the homologous series of aldehydes and ketones.

Aldehydes		Ketones	
Name	**Structural formula**	**Name**	**Structural formula**
methanal	HCHO		
ethanal	CH_3CHO		
propanal	CH_3CH_2CHO	propanone	CH_3COCH_3
butanal	$CH_3CH_2CH_2CHO$	butanone	$CH_3COCH_2CH_3$

Table 3.1 The homologous series of aldehydes and ketones.

Extension

Physical properties of the carbonyl group

The carbonyl group is significantly polar:

$$\underset{/}{\overset{\backslash \delta+}{C}} = \overset{\delta-}{O}$$

The polarity is sufficient to enable the lower members of the homologous series of aldehydes and ketones to be completely miscible with water. Water will form hydrogen bonds to the carbonyl group:

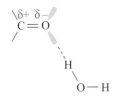

SAQ

1 Explain the following in terms of intermolecular forces:
'Aldehydes and ketones containing more than four carbon atoms become increasingly immiscible with water.'

Hint

Answer

Preparation: oxidation of alcohols

Primary and secondary aliphatic alcohols are oxidised on heating with acidified aqueous potassium dichromate(VI); tertiary alcohols do not react with this reagent (Figure 3.2).

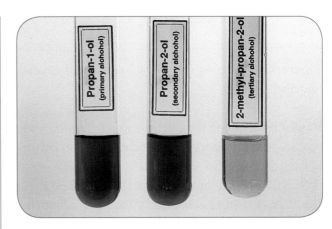

Figure 3.2 The colour changes that take place when primary, secondary and tertiary alcohols are heated with potassium dichromate(VI) acidified with dilute sulfuric acid.

- Primary alcohols produce aldehydes on gentle heating with aqueous potassium dichromate(VI) acidified with dilute sulfuric acid. As aldehydes are more volatile than their corresponding alcohols, they are usually separated by distillation as they are formed. On stronger heating under reflux with an excess of acidified potassium dichromate(VI), the aldehydes are further oxidised to form carboxylic acids.
- Secondary alcohols produce ketones on heating with acidified potassium dichromate(VI).
- Tertiary alcohols do not react with acidified dichromate(VI).

During the oxidation reactions that occur with primary and secondary alcohols, the orange colour of the dichromate(VI) ion, $Cr_2O_7^{2-}$(aq), changes to the green colour of the chromium(III) ion, Cr^{3+}(aq).

Ethanol, a primary alcohol, produces ethanal (an aldehyde) on gentle heating with acidified dichromate(VI). You can prepare a sample of aqueous

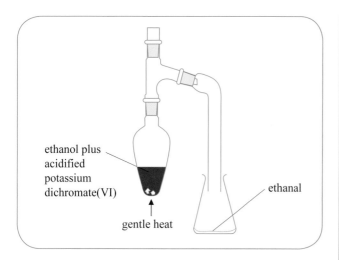

Figure 3.3 Preparing ethanal by oxidation of ethanol and distillation.

ethanal by distilling the aldehyde as it is formed when acidified dichromate(VI) is added dropwise to hot ethanol (Figure 3.3).

Simplified equations are frequently used for the oxidation of organic compounds. The oxygen from the oxidising agent, in this case the acidified potassium or sodium dichromate(VI), is shown as [O]:

$$CH_3CH_2OH + [O] \longrightarrow CH_3CHO + H_2O$$

Further oxidation, by refluxing ethanol with an excess of acidified dichromate(VI), produces a carboxylic acid, ethanoic acid (Figure 3.4):

$$CH_3CHO + [O] \longrightarrow CH_3COOH$$

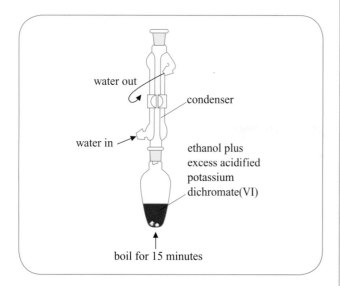

Figure 3.4 Preparing ethanoic acid by oxidation of ethanol and reflux.

You can separate aqueous ethanoic acid from the reaction mixture by distillation after it has been refluxing for about 15 minutes. You can detect the ethanoic acid by its characteristic odour of vinegar and by its effect on litmus paper, which turns red.

SAQ
2   We can oxidise butan-1-ol to form butanal ($CH_3CH_2CH_2CHO$) and to butanoic acid ($CH_3CH_2CH_2COOH$).
    a   What reagents and conditions should be used to oxidise butan-1-ol to butanal?
    b   Write a balanced chemical equation for this oxidation. Oxygen from the oxidising agent should be shown as [O].
    c   What reagents and conditions should be used to oxidise butan-1-ol to butanoic acid?
    d   Write a balanced chemical equation for this oxidation. Again, show oxygen from the oxidising agent as [O].   *Answer*

The secondary alcohol propan-2-ol, on heating with acidified dichromate(VI), produces propanone (a ketone). No further oxidation products can be obtained even with prolonged refluxing with an excess of acidified potassium dichromate(VI).

$$CH_3CH(OH)CH_3 + [O] \longrightarrow CH_3COCH_3 + H_2O$$

Reduction

As we have just seen, aldehydes are obtained by mild oxidation of primary alcohols, and ketones are formed when secondary alcohols are oxidised. Conversely, aldehydes or ketones may be reduced to their respective alcohols.

Sodium tetrahydridoborate (also known as sodium borohydride), $NaBH_4$, is a suitable reducing agent. The aldehyde or ketone is warmed with the reducing agent using water or ethanol as a solvent. It is usual to represent $NaBH_4$ by [H] in the equation for the reduction. (Compare this to the use of [O] in the equations for the oxidation of alcohols with acidified dichromate(VI).)

Here are two examples:

Ethanal is reduced to ethanol:

$$CH_3CHO + 2[H] \longrightarrow CH_3CH_2OH$$

Propanone is reduced to propan-2-ol:

$$CH_3COCH_3 + 2[H] \longrightarrow CH_3CH(OH)CH_3$$

SAQ

3 Draw the structural formulae for the products obtained when the following are treated with aqueous $NaBH_4$:

   a butanone

   b butanal.

   Answer

The reduction reactions may also be considered to be the addition of hydrogen to the carbonyl (C=O) double bond. The mechanism of attack is called **nucleophilic addition**, as the attacking species can be thought of as the H^- (hydride) ion from $NaBH_4$. Remember that nucleophiles can donate a pair of electrons. The mechanism can be represented in two steps:

● *Step 1* Nucleophilic attack by the hydride ion:

a negatively charged intermediate

● *Step 2* Protonation of the intermediate by water:

an alcohol

SAQ

4 Propanal is reduced by $NaBH_4$ in water.

   a What do we call the mechanism of attack in this reaction?

   b Give the name and formula of the nucleophile.

   c Show the mechanism for the reaction and name the organic product.

   Hint

   Answer

Characteristic tests

A test for the presence of the carbonyl group, C=O

When a solution of 2,4-dinitrophenylhydrazine is added to an aldehyde or a ketone, a deep yellow or orange precipitate is formed (Figure 3.5).

Here is the structure of 2,4-dinitrophenylhydrazine:

2,4-dinitrophenylhydrazine

This test is used specifically to identify the presence of an aldehyde or ketone carbonyl bond (C=O). No precipitate is produced with carboxylic acids or with esters, although both of these classes of compounds also contain carbonyl groups. The yellow/orange precipitate is a 2,4-dinitrophenylhydrazone.

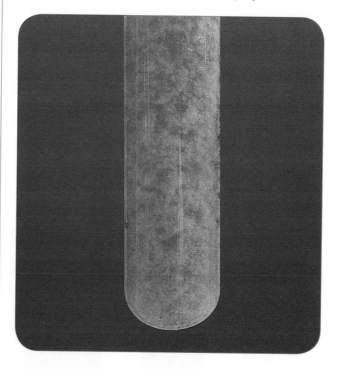

Figure 3.5 Propanone reacts with 2,4-dinitrophenylhydrazine to form a 2,4-dinitrophenylhydrazone.

Oxidising agent	Conditions	Observation on oxidation of an aldehyde	Explanation of observation
acidified potassium dichromate(VI)	boil gently (reflux)	the orange solution turns green	the orange dichromate(VI) ion, $Cr_2O_7^{2-}$, is reduced to green chromium(III), Cr^{3+}
Tollens' reagent (an aqueous solution of silver nitrate in excess ammonia)	warm	a silver mirror forms on the sides of the test tube from the colourless solution	the silver(I) ion is reduced to silver metal

Table 3.2 The effects of oxidising agents on aldehydes. With ketones, there is no reaction.

We use 2,4-dinitrophenylhydrazine rather than phenylhydrazine because it gives better precipitates. These precipitates are easily recrystallised to obtain pure samples with very sharp melting points. Recrystallisation, followed by the determination of the melting point of the 2,4-dinitrophenylhydrazone product can help to identify an unknown carbonyl compound.

(Note: you do not need to know the structure of these hydrazone derivatives or the equation for their formation for your examination.)

Distinguishing between aldehydes and ketones

Aldehydes are oxidised to form carboxylic acids when treated with mild oxidising agents. However, ketones are not oxidised by these reagents so no change is observed.

Suitable mild oxidising agents, together with the observations seen when they are used to oxidise an aldehyde, are shown in Table 3.2.

The observations are shown in Figure 3.6.

With Tollens' reagent, the silver ion (oxidation state = +1) is reduced to silver metal (oxidation state = 0) as it oxidises an aldehyde to a carboxylic acid. For example, with propanal:

$$CH_3CH_2CHO + [O] \longrightarrow CH_3CH_2COOH$$

SAQ

5 Describe and explain the difference observed when pentanal is warmed with Tollens' reagent in a test tube and then the same test is performed on pentan-3-one.

Hint

Answer

Figure 3.6 'Before' and 'after' situations for the oxidation of ethanal by **a** acidified potassium dichromate(VI) and **b** Tollens' reagent.

Summary

Glossary

- Aldehydes and ketones contain the carbonyl group, C=O. In aldehydes the carbonyl group is joined to just one other carbon atom (and a hydrogen atom); in ketones the carbonyl group is joined to two other carbon atoms.

- The systematic names of aldehydes are derived from the name of the alkane, with the '-e' replaced by '-al'. Similarly, ketones are named with the '-e' replaced by '-one'.

- As the carbonyl group is very polar, aldehydes and ketones are soluble in water.

- Carbonyl compounds are readily reduced by $NaBH_4$. Reduction of an aldehyde produces a primary alcohol; reduction of a ketone produces a secondary alcohol.

- The polar nature of the carbonyl group in aldehydes and ketones enables them to undergo nucleophilic addition by reacting with the hydride ions (H^-) from $NaBH_4$.

- Aldehydes are readily oxidised under mild conditions to carboxylic acids. Ketones are not oxidised under mild conditions.

- The reagent 2,4-dinitrophenylhydrazine produces a yellow/orange precipitate with aldehydes and ketones. The melting point of the product is used to identify particular aldehydes and ketones.

- As aldehydes are readily oxidised, they may be distinguished from ketones on warming with suitable oxidising reagents. With aldehydes, acidified potassium dichromate(VI) turns from orange to green, and Tollens' reagent produces a silver mirror.

Questions

1 But-2-enal, $CH_3CH=CHCHO$, is a pale yellow, flammable liquid with an irritating odour.
  a But-2-enal exists as two stereoisomers.
    Draw skeletal formulae to show the structure of the two stereoisomers of
    but-2-enal. [2]
  b i Describe a simple chemical test that would show that but-2-enal is an aldehyde. [2]   Hint
    ii Explain why this test gives a different result with aldehydes than it does
      with ketones. [1]
  c But-2-enal also reacts with sodium borohydride, $NaBH_4$.
    i Identify the organic compound formed in this reaction. [1]
    ii State the type of chemical reaction occurring. [1]
  d Precautions must be taken to prevent but-2-enal catching fire.
    Construct a balanced equation for the complete combustion of but-2-enal, C_4H_6O. [1]
OCR Chemistry A2 (2814) June 2007   [Total 8]

Answer

continued

2 a The reaction of trichloroethanal with water is a nucleophilic addition reaction. It can be catalysed by small amounts of hydroxide ions, OH^-.

Copy and complete the diagram below to suggest a mechanism for this reaction.

Show all the relevant dipoles and curly arrows.

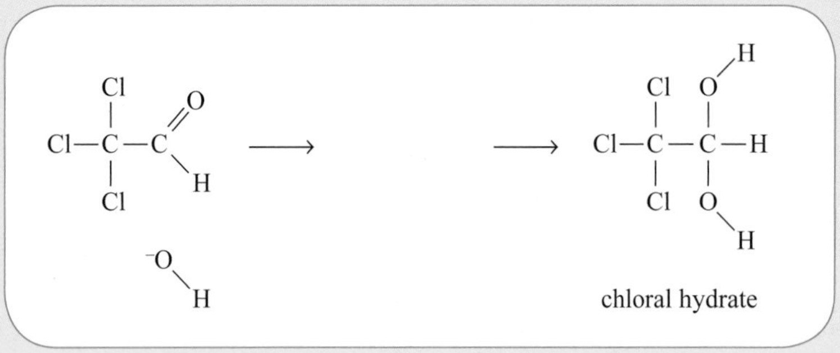

chloral hydrate

[5]

b The recommended adult dose of chloral hydrate as a sedative is 250 mg, three times a day.

Calculate the mass of trichloroethanal you would need to react with water to make one week's supply of chloral hydrate for an adult, assuming a 60% yield.

(M_r: chloral hydrate, 165.5; trichloroethanal, 147.5) [3]

c Chloral hydrate is broken down in the body after several hours. One reaction is oxidation to trichloroethanoic acid.

Copy and complete the equation for this reaction.

$Cl_3CCH(OH)_2 + [O] \longrightarrow$ [1]

OCR Chemistry A2 (2814) June 2007 [Total 9]

Chapter 4

Carboxylic acids and esters

e-Learning

Objectives

The carboxylic acid functional group is shown as –COOH in structural formulae. This consists of a hydroxyl group joined to a carbonyl group. Its structure is:

$$-C\overset{\displaystyle O}{\underset{\displaystyle O-H}{\big\|}}$$

We find simple carboxylic acids in many foods. The sharp acidic taste of vinegar is caused by ethanoic acid. Ethanoic acid has the formula CH_3COOH. The simplest aromatic carboxylic acid, benzoic acid, is used as a flavouring and a preservative in sparkling drinks such as lemonade. The acidity of lemons is caused by citric acid (Figure 4.1).

The structures of benzoic acid and citric acid are:

benzoic acid

citric acid

$$HOOC-CH_2-\overset{\displaystyle OH}{\underset{\displaystyle COOH}{C}}-CH_2-COOH$$

Esters are derivatives of carboxylic acids and are present in many foods. In esters, the hydrogen in the carboxylic acid group is replaced by an alkyl or an aryl group. Aliphatic esters have distinctive, fruity flavours. They are one of the main flavour components in most fruits (Figure 4.2). For example, ethyl 2-methylbutanoate is one component of the

Figure 4.1 Lemonade often contains benzoic acid as a preservative. Citric acid is present naturally in lemons.

Figure 4.2 Esters are the principal flavour components in ripe fruits.

flavour of ripe apples, while 3-methylbutyl ethanoate contributes to the flavour of ripe pears:

$$CH_3—CH_2—CH—C\underset{O—CH_2—CH_3}{\overset{O}{\Big\backslash}}$$
$$|$$
$$CH_3$$

ethyl 2-methylbutanoate

$$CH_3—C\overset{O}{\Big\backslash}$$
$$O—CH_2—CH_2—CH—CH_3$$
$$|$$

3-methylbutyl ethanoate CH_3

SAQ

1 Classify the following compounds as carboxylic acids or esters:

  a $CH_3CH_2CH_2COOCH_3$

  b $CH_2ClCOOH$

  c $HCOOCH_2CH_2CH_3$

[Answer]

Carboxylic acids

Carboxylic acids are named by taking the name of the alkane and replacing the final '-e' with '-oic acid'. The first four members of the homologous series of aliphatic carboxylic acids are shown in Table 4.1.

Structural formula	Systematic name
HCOOH	methanoic acid
CH_3COOH	ethanoic acid
CH_3CH_2COOH	propanoic acid
$CH_3CH_2CH_2COOH$	butanoic acid

Table 4.1 The first four members of the homologous series of carboxylic acids.

Note that the carbon atom of the carboxylic acid is counted as a carbon atom from the parent alkane. The general formula for the aliphatic carboxylic acids is $C_nH_{2n+1}COOH$.

Solubility of carboxylic acids

As with alcohols, we find that carboxylic acids contain hydrogen bonding – due to the presence in their molecules of hydrogen atoms bonded to strongly electronegative oxygen atoms.

In water, soluble carboxylic acids will ionise (dissociate) by losing an $H^+(aq)$ ion as the O–H bond breaks in some of their molecules:

$$CH_3C\underset{OH}{\overset{O}{\Big\backslash}} (aq) \rightleftharpoons CH_3C\underset{O^-}{\overset{O}{\Big\backslash}} (aq) + H^+(aq)$$

ethanoate ion

This only happens in a relatively small percentage of molecules as they are weak acids. This means that there are many undissociated molecules present in a solution of a carboxylic acid. These molecules will tend to form hydrogen bonds with water molecules via the O–H group. There will also be dipole–dipole interactions because of the C=O group in the acid.

The carboxylate anions will have strong dipole–dipole interactions with water molecules. This is because the negatively charged end of the COO^- ions will be attracted by the partial positive charges on the hydrogen atoms in the polar water molecules, which helps them to dissolve.

However, the longer the hydrocarbon chain, the less soluble a carboxylic acid gets. This is because the van der Waals' forces between the large non-polar parts of the molecule start to dominate its properties.

The acidic COOH group

Behaviour as acids

It is the proximity of the polar carbonyl group that enables the hydroxyl group to ionise partly in water. Hence carboxylic acids are weak acids – unlike alcohols, which do not ionise to any significant degree in water.

The ionisation of the carboxyl group is due to delocalisation of the negative charge over the carbon and two oxygen atoms. This delocalisation spreads out the negative charge and increases the energetic stability of the anion, producing an equilibrium in aqueous solution:

$$R—C\underset{O—H}{\overset{O}{\Big\backslash}} (aq) \rightleftharpoons R—C\underset{O}{\overset{O}{\Big\backslash}}{}^{\ominus} (aq) + H^+(aq)$$

Carboxylic acids form salts when they react with metals (such as magnesium or zinc), alkalis, carbonates and basic metal oxides.

Here are more details of these reactions:

- With metals they produce a salt (a carboxylate) plus hydrogen gas:

$$2CH_3COOH + Mg \longrightarrow (CH_3COO)_2Mg + H_2$$
magnesium ethanoate

- With alkalis and basic metal oxides they produce a salt (a carboxylate) plus water – for example, if you neutralise ethanoic acid with potassium hydroxide, you get potassium ethanoate and water:

$$CH_3COOH + KOH \longrightarrow CH_3COOK + H_2O$$
potassium ethanoate

- With carbonates they produce a salt (a carboxylate) plus water and carbon dioxide gas:

$$2CH_3COOH + CaCO_3$$
$$\longrightarrow (CH_3COO)_2Ca + H_2O + CO_2$$
calcium ethanoate

SAQ

2 Write balanced equations for the reactions of:

Hint

   a zinc with propanoic acid
   b sodium carbonate with methanoic acid
   c magnesium oxide with ethanoic acid
   d benzoic acid with sodium hydroxide.

Answer

Esters

The ester functional group is:

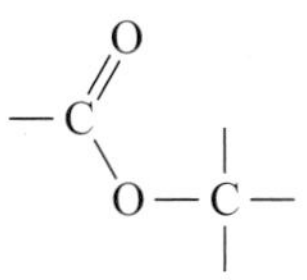

Esters are formed by the reaction of an alcohol with a carboxylic acid, using a strong acid catalyst. Water is also produced in the reaction.

The name of an ester comes partly from the parent alcohol and partly from the parent acid. The 'alcohol' part of the name is placed first and is separated by a

space from the 'acid' part of the name. An example is ethyl propanoate:

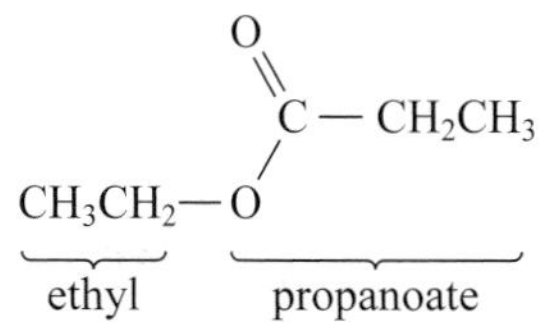

A range of isomers is possible by moving alkyl groups from one side of the ester group to the other. For example, methyl butanoate is an isomer of ethyl propanoate.

SAQ

3 a Draw skeletal formulae for the structural isomers of ethyl propanoate that are esters and do not have branched carbon chains, and name them.
   b Further isomers with the same molecular formula as ethyl propanoate are possible. Draw the skeletal formulae of as many of these as you can, and name them.

Answer

Formation of esters

The formation of an ester from a carboxylic acid and an alcohol is known as **esterification**. The general equation is:

$$carboxylic\ acid + alcohol \rightleftharpoons ester + water$$

You can prepare ethyl ethanoate by warming a mixture of ethanol and glacial ethanoic acid in the presence of concentrated sulfuric acid, which acts as a catalyst. (Glacial ethanoic acid is pure ethanoic acid, free of water. It is called *glacial* because it freezes in the bottle at $16.7\,°C$ (Figure 4.3).)

The equation for the formation of ethyl ethanoate is:

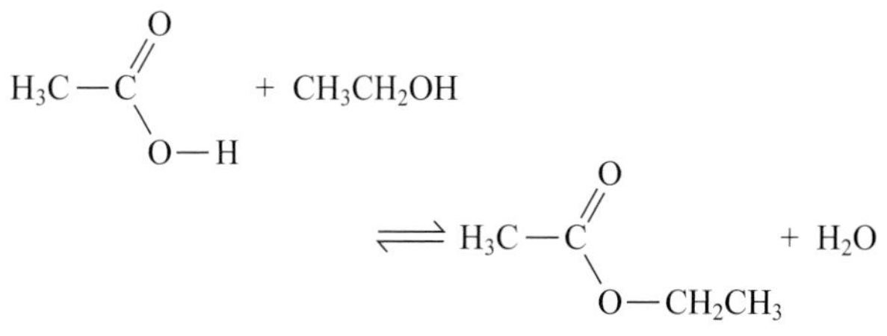

ethyl ethanoate

29

Figure 4.3 Glacial ethanoic acid freezes at 16.7 °C.

SAQ

4 a Draw the structural formula of
1-methylethyl propanoate. *(Hint)*

b Name the carboxylic acid and the alcohol
which would form 1-methylethyl propanoate.

c Write a balanced equation for the formation of
1-methylethyl propanoate
using structural formulae. *(Answer)*

5 a Name the ester formed on reaction of
methanoic acid with butan-1-ol.

b Write a balanced equation for the reaction of
methanoic acid with butan-1-ol
using structural formulae. *(Answer)*

Another way we can make esters of aliphatic alcohols
is by using an acid anhydride instead of a carboxylic
acid. Acid anhydrides are reactive compounds which
can be made from carboxylic acids or their salts. Here
is the structure of an acid anhydride:

$$CH_3 - C \underset{\diagdown O}{\overset{\diagup O}{=}}$$
$$CH_3 - C \underset{\diagdown O}{=}$$

ethanoic anhydride

The advantages of using an acid anhydride to prepare
an ester are that the reaction is not reversible (unlike
the reaction between a carboxylic acid and an
alcohol), and that no catalyst is needed.

The general equation is:

acid anhydride + alcohol
$$\longrightarrow ester + carboxylic\ acid$$

For example:

$$CH_3 - C \overset{O}{\underset{O}{\lessgtr}} + C_2H_5OH \longrightarrow CH_3 - C \overset{O}{\underset{C_2H_5}{\lessgtr}} + CH_3 - C \overset{O}{\underset{OH}{\lessgtr}}$$
$$CH_3 - C \underset{O}{=}$$

ethyl ethanoate

SAQ

6 Aspirin is an ester. It is made in the pharmaceutical
industry by reacting 2-hydroxybenzoic acid with
ethanoic anhydride. Complete the equation for
this reaction:

$$\underset{}{\overset{COOH}{\underset{OH}{\bigcirc}}} + \quad \begin{matrix} CH_3 - C \overset{O}{\underset{O}{\lessgtr}} \\ CH_3 - C \underset{O}{=} \end{matrix} \longrightarrow \ \dots + \dots$$

(Answer)

The hydrolysis of esters

Esters can be hydrolysed by heating under reflux with
either an acid or an alkali.

Refluxing with an acid simply reverses the
preparation of the ester from an alcohol and a
carboxylic acid. The acid catalyses the breakdown
of the ester by water. The reaction is reversible and
forms an equilibrium mixture; hence, there are always
molecules of both reactants and products present after
the reaction. The equation for the acid hydrolysis of
ethyl ethanoate is:

$$H_3C - C \overset{O}{\underset{O-CH_2CH_3}{\lessgtr}} + H_2O \underset{}{\overset{H^+(aq)}{\rightleftharpoons}} H_3C - C \overset{O}{\underset{O-H}{\lessgtr}} + CH_3CH_2OH$$

When an ester is refluxed with an alkali, such as
aqueous sodium hydroxide, it is fully hydrolysed
to the alcohol and the sodium salt of the acid. The
equation for the base hydrolysis of ethyl ethanoate is:

$$H_3C - C \overset{O}{\underset{O-CH_2CH_3}{\lessgtr}} + OH^- \longrightarrow H_3C - C \overset{O}{\underset{O^-}{\lessgtr}} + CH_3CH_2OH$$

When the ester is a benzoate, base hydrolysis with aqueous sodium hydroxide produces an aqueous solution of sodium benzoate. Subsequent addition of acid produces a white precipitate of benzoic acid. The benzoic acid is only sparingly soluble in water because of its non-polar benzene ring (Figure 4.4).

Figure 4.4 Benzoic acid precipitates out when sodium benzoate is acidified.

SAQ

7 **a** Write a balanced equation for the base hydrolysis of methyl benzoate by aqueous sodium hydroxide. Name the products.   Hint

  b Write a balanced equation for the acid hydrolysis of methyl propanoate. Name the products.   Answer

Fats as natural esters

Vegetable oils (Figure 4.5) and animal fats provide an important store of energy for plants and animals.

Oils and fats are esters of propane-1,2,3-triol (also known as glycerol). This alcohol has three hydroxyl (–OH) groups, each of which can form an ester link when reacted with a carboxylic acid.

Figure 4.5 Oleic acid can be obtained from olive oil, which contains an ester of oleic acid.

When only *one* of the alcohol groups in propane-1,2,3-triol has been esterified, the product is called a **monoglyceride**. In **diglycerides**, any *two* of the alcohol groups have been esterified. **Triglycerides** have had all *three* alcohol groups esterified. Figure 4.6 shows a molecular model of a triglyceride.

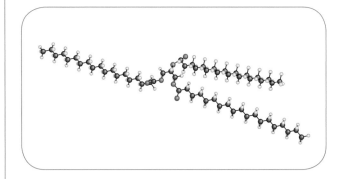

Figure 4.6 We can think of a triglyceride as a 'tri-ester' of propane-1,2,3-triol and fatty (long-chain) carboxylic acids.

We shall look more closely at the structure of one triglyceride containing the fatty acid octadecanoic acid (stearic acid). The structures of propane-1,2,3-triol and octadecanoic acid are:

propane-1,2,3-triol
(glycerol)

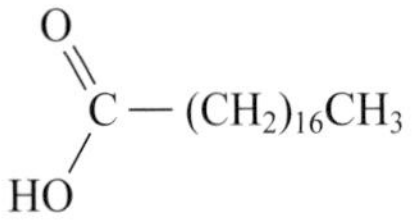

octadecanoic acid
(stearic acid)

The triglyceride formed from three moles of octadecanoic acid and one mole of propane-1,2,3-triol is:

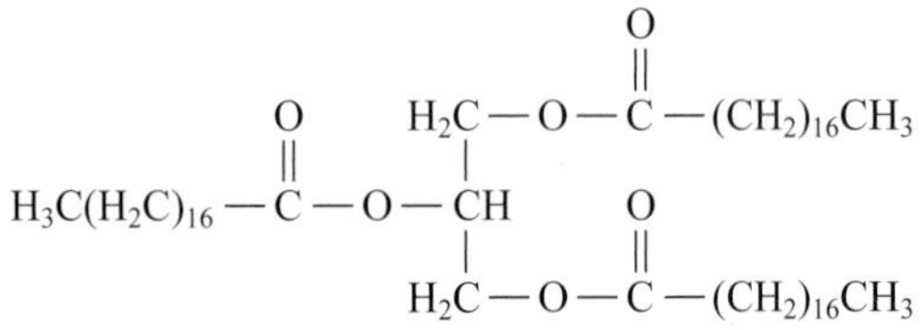

SAQ

8 a What is the other product when octadecanoic acid and propane-1,2,3-triol form a triglyceride?

[Hint]

b What type of reaction has taken place?

c How many moles of this second product are formed per mole of propane-1,2,3-triol?

d Write a balanced equation for the reaction using structural formulae.

[Answer]

Comparing saturated fats, unsaturated fats and fatty acids

Hydrolysis of these oils or fats provides an important source of carboxylic acids with longer chains of carbon atoms. Some examples are shown in Table 4.2.

In general, carboxylic acids that are obtained from oils or fats are called **fatty acids**. They usually contain an even number of carbon atoms and form unbranched chains. For example, octadecanoic acid contains 18 carbon atoms. Its structural formula is $CH_3(CH_2)_{16}COOH$. Its skeletal formula is shown as:

shorthand formula C18,0

This is abbreviated by scientists who work with fatty acids to C18,0. This means there are 18 carbon atoms and no C=C double bonds in the hydrocarbon chain. (You may also see this represented as C18:0.)

Fatty acids with one C=C double bond are said to be **monounsaturated**. Fatty acids are described as **polyunsaturated** if they contain more than one C=C double bond. Each double bond will give rise to *cis–trans* isomers (also referred to as *E/Z* or *Z/E* isomers).

To illustrate this, let's look at a common monounsaturated fatty acid we get from plant seeds. Its systematic name is octadec-9-enoic acid. Its shorthand formulae is C18,1(9) – this shows that it has 18 carbon atoms and one C=C double bond, which starts on the ninth carbon atom down the chain, beginning your counting from the carboxylic acid end (the C atom in –COOH is numbered 1).

Common name	Systematic name	Skeletal formula	Principal source
lauric acid	dodecanoic acid	 COOH	coconut oil
myristic acid	tetradecanoic acid	 COOH	nutmeg seed oil
stearic acid	octadecanoic acid	 COOH	animal fats
oleic acid	(9Z)-octadec-9-enoic acid or *cis*-octadec-9-enoic acid	 COOH	olive oil

Table 4.2 Some natural carboxylic acids.

Here are the skeletal formulae of its *cis* (Z) and *trans* (E) isomers:

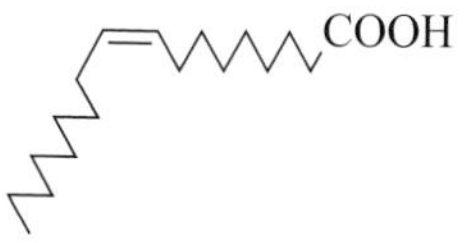

cis (Z) isomer
shorthand formula C18,1(*cis*-9)

trans (E) isomer
shorthand formula C18,1(*trans*-9)

Notice that the chains in the *trans* (E) isomer are in line whereas the *cis* (Z) isomer is bent. This means that the molecules of *trans* fatty acids can pack together better and so have the higher melting points.

Here is a polyunsaturated fatty acid with two C=C double bonds:

systematic name: (9E, 12E)-octadec-9,12-dienoic acid
shorthand formula: C18,2 (*trans*-9, *trans*-12)

SAQ

9 a Draw the skeletal formula of hexadecanoic acid (palmitic acid) – see Table 4.3.
  b Draw the skeletal formula of the *trans* isomer of oleic acid.
  c Name the following fatty acid:

Answer

10 Almond oil contains both saturated and unsaturated fatty acids, as shown by their shorthand formulae in the headings of Table 4.3. The table shows the percentages by weight for five fatty acids out of the total fatty acids in almond oil.

What percentage of the fatty acids shown in almond oil are:

  a saturated?
  b unsaturated?
  c monounsaturated?
  d polyunsaturated?
  e Why are there no numbers in brackets in the shorthand formula of stearic acid?

Answer

11 Coconut oil contains nearly 50% lauric acid. Use information from Table 4.3 to draw its skeletal formula.

Answer

12 Another edible fatty acid has the structural formula shown below:

Hint

$$CH_3CH_2CH=CHCH_2CH=CHCH_2CH=CH(CH_2)_7COOH$$

What is its shorthand formula?

Answer

	Lauric acid C12,0	Palmitic acid C16,0	Stearic acid C18,0	Oleic acid C18,1(9)	Linoleic acid C18,2(9,12)
Percentage in almond oil	0	7	2	69	17

Table 4.3 Percentages by weight for five fatty acids out of the total fatty acids in almond oil.

'Not-so-good-for-you' unsaturated fatty acids

Trans fatty acids have been making the news due to health scares about their use in foodstuffs. Plant oils are turned into 'spreadable' margarines by treating the oils with hydrogen to saturate some of the double bonds in their triglyceride molecules, straightening out their chains. This process also converts *cis* isomers into *trans* isomers, thus increasing their melting points (see page 33). *Trans* fatty acids are particularly associated with fast foods which are prepared by frying in partially hydrogenated oils (Figure 4.7).

Researchers claim to have found links between the amount of *trans* fats consumed and an increased risk of heart disease and strokes. The *trans* fats appear to increase the amount of low density lipoprotein (LDL) cholesterol (known as 'bad' cholesterol) and to lower the amount of high density lipoprotein (HDL) (known as 'good' cholesterol and which can have health benefits). Disturbing the balance in your blood between LDLs and HDLs can result in arteries furring up and narrowing, causing circulatory problems. This can result in high blood pressure, strokes and coronary heart disease. Some researchers claim that unsaturated *trans* fatty acids can do you even more harm than the saturated fatty acids we eat from animal sources. Most doctors recommend reducing our intake of *trans* fatty acids to avoid the problems associated with 'bad' cholesterol, as well as reducing our intake of saturated animal fats to fight obesity.

Figure 4.7 *Trans* fatty acids are one of the problems associated with eating fast food.

Flavour	Esters	Molecular model
apple	ethyl 2-methylbutanoate	
pear	3-methylbutyl ethanoate	
banana	1-methylbutyl ethanoate	
pineapple	butyl butanoate	

Table 4.4 Some esters and their associated flavours.

Uses of esters

The *flavours* and *fragrances* of different esters are widely used to produce food flavourings and perfumes. The natural flavours of fruits are the result of subtle blends of hundreds of organic compounds. Many of these compounds are esters of aliphatic alcohols and simple carboxylic acids. In this context, we have already mentioned ethyl 2-methylbutanoate and 3-methylbutyl ethanoate. Table 4.4 shows a number of esters with their approximate associated flavours and their molecular models.

The fragrance of a flower or plant is produced by volatile organic compounds. These may be extracted as the 'essential oil' of the flower or plant. These essential oils are the basis of the perfume industry. They contain a variety of compounds which include esters, aldehydes and phenols. Oil of jasmine (Figure 4.8), traditionally obtained from the plant jasmine, is now produced by chemical synthesis and is thus cheaply and readily available.

Figure 4.8 Oil of jasmine is a natural oil used in perfumes. It used to be obtained from the jasmine plant, but now is manufactured using phenylmethanol and ethanoic acid.

Oil of jasmine is phenylmethyl ethanoate:

The perfume industry now relies heavily on chemical synthesis to provide the basic fragrances for many expensive perfumes.

Biodiesel is another increasingly important use of esters of fatty acids. The triglyceride esters are extracted from plants, such as oilseed rape, corn and sunflowers. These are a rich, renewable energy source that might one day replace diesel obtained from crude oil (Figure 4.9).

The plant oils (you can even use discarded vegetable oils from cooking) are processed by heating them with a strong alkali which hydrolyses the natural triglyceride esters into propane-1,2,3-triol and its fatty acids. Methanol is then added and reacts with the carboxylic acids to make the methyl esters we use as biodiesel.

Figure 4.9 Biodiesel can be an alternative to traditional diesel from crude oil.

Biodiesel has been hailed as a 'carbon neutral' fuel as any carbon dioxide (a greenhouse gas) given off when it burns in engines was once absorbed from the air by the plants as they grew. However, this does not take into account conventional oil-based fuels used at present in nurturing, harvesting and processing the plants. Nonetheless, it is a genuine renewable fuel so it can definitely help conserve our diminishing supplies of crude oil.

An unforeseen disadvantage of producing biodiesel is the switch of land-use from food crops to plants for fuels. This can result in further deforestation to make fields for more crops to be grown, negating some of the benefits in terms of tackling global warming. Another knock-on effect is the increasing cost of staple foods such as corn, affecting many food prices. This can cause great hardship in developing countries where families have to live on very little money.

SAQ

13 Discuss the future of biofuels, such as ethanol and biodiesel. Include your own views in a conclusion to your report.

Answer

Summary

Glossary

- The carboxylic acid functional group is –COOH. Carboxylic acids are found naturally in many foods. The systematic name for a carboxylic acid derives from the name of the alkane, with the '-e' replaced by '-oic acid'.

- Carboxylic acids may be made by oxidation of primary alcohols.

- The close proximity of the carbonyl group to the hydroxyl group is responsible for the acidic behaviour of carboxylic acids. They readily form salts with many metals, alkalis, bases and carbonates.

- Esters are formed when carboxylic acids (or acid anhydrides) react with alcohols. A water molecule is also formed in the reaction. The ester functional group is:

- Esters of aliphatic alcohols have fruity odours and are principal components of the flavours of many fruits. Fats and oils are esters of propane-1,2,3-triol (glycerol) and long-chain carboxylic acids. *Trans* fatty acids in foods have been associated with 'bad' cholesterol which causes coronary heart disease and strokes.

- Esters are hydrolysed to form alcohols and carboxylic acids by warming the ester with an acid catalyst to form an equilibrium mixture. Warming an ester with an alkali breaks it down to form an alcohol and a carboxylic acid salt. Alkaline hydrolysis of fats or oils produces propane-1,2,3-triol and the salts of fatty acids.

- Esters are used as flavours and fragrances, as well as in the renewable fuel known as biodiesel.

Questions

1 An ester **D** with the formula, $CH_3CH_2COOCH_2CH(CH_3)_2$, is used in rum flavouring.
   a Draw a displayed formula of ester **D**. [2]
   b Outline how you could obtain a sample of ester **D**, starting with a named carboxylic acid and a named alcohol.

   Hint

   Include any essential reaction conditions and write an equation for the reaction.
   You do not need to include any details of the separation or purification of the ester. [6]

OCR Chemistry A2 (2814) June 2007 [Total 8]

Answer

2 This compound is tristearin, a triglyceride, which can be hydrolysed by heating with aqueous sodium hydroxide to make soap.

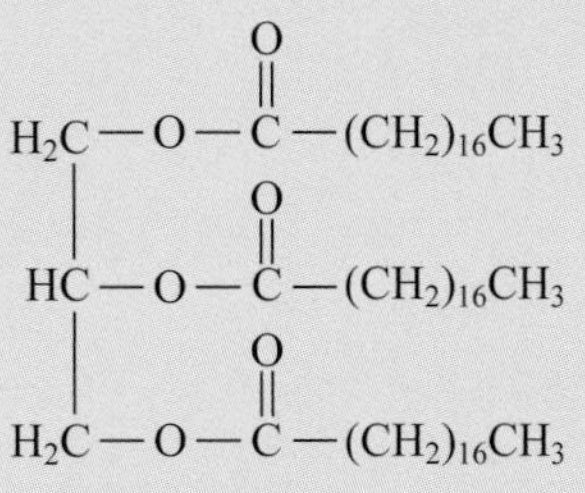

$$H_2C-O-\overset{\overset{\displaystyle O}{\|}}{C}-(CH_2)_{16}CH_3$$
$$HC-O-\overset{\overset{\displaystyle O}{\|}}{C}-(CH_2)_{16}CH_3$$
$$H_2C-O-\overset{\overset{\displaystyle O}{\|}}{C}-(CH_2)_{16}CH_3$$

tristearin

   a i Copy and complete and balance this equation for the soap-making reaction.

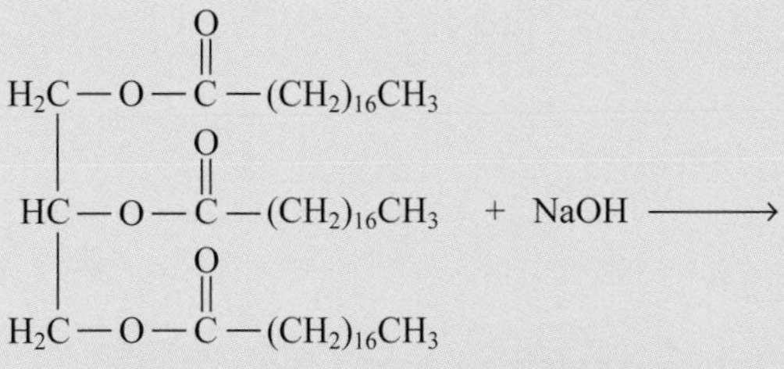

$$H_2C-O-\overset{\overset{\displaystyle O}{\|}}{C}-(CH_2)_{16}CH_3$$
$$HC-O-\overset{\overset{\displaystyle O}{\|}}{C}-(CH_2)_{16}CH_3 \quad + \quad NaOH \longrightarrow$$
$$H_2C-O-\overset{\overset{\displaystyle O}{\|}}{C}-(CH_2)_{16}CH_3$$

[3]

   ii Work out the mass of soap that could be produced from 1000 g of tristearin.
       M_r(tristearin) 890 g mol^{-1} [3]
   b Explain why compounds such as tristearin are soluble in non-polar solvents such as hexane. [3]
   c Triglycerides containing erucic acid, $C_{21}H_{41}COOH$, from rapeseed oil are now being used as high temperature lubricants.
       i Explain how you can tell from the formula that erucic acid is likely to be unsaturated. [1]
       ii Suggest <u>one</u> advantage of using high temperature lubricants derived from vegetable oils. [1]

OCR Chemistry A2 (2815/02) June 2003 [Total 11]

Answer

continued

3 Salicylic acid is used in the manufacture of aspirin tablets. In the UK around 3500 tonnes of salicylic acid are manufactured per year.

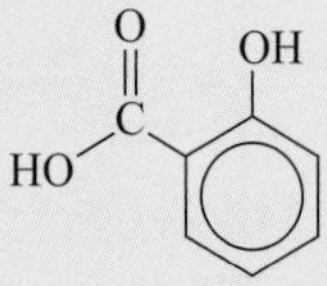

salicylic acid

Salicylic acid is manufactured from phenol in three stages.

a Phenol is first converted to sodium phenoxide, $C_6H_5O^- Na^+$.

   i State a reagent that could be used for this reaction. [1]

   ii Write a balanced equation for this reaction. [1]

b The phenoxide ion is then combined with carbon dioxide under high pressure to form the salicylate ion.

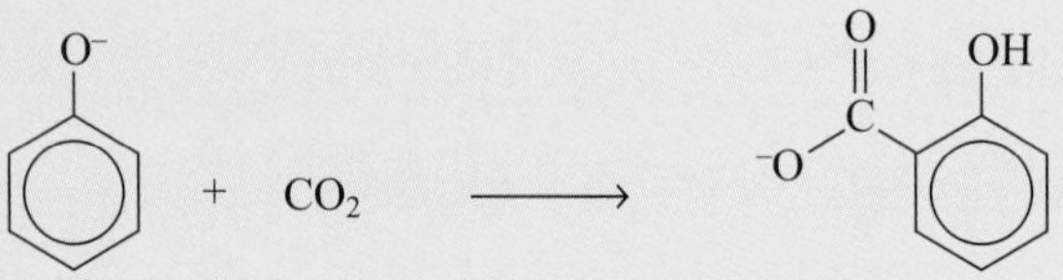

This reaction is an electrophilic substitution reaction, which occurs by the incomplete mechanism shown below. Carbon dioxide acts as the electrophile.

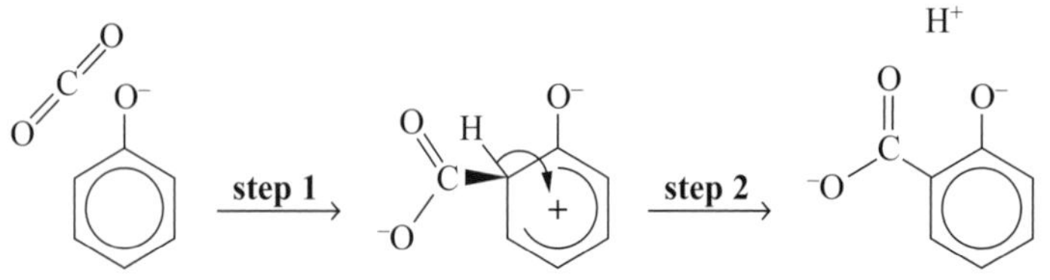

intermediate

   i Add partial charges δ+ and δ− to show the polarisation of the C=O bonds in the carbon dioxide molecule. [1]

   ii Copy and complete the mechanism by adding curly arrows to show the movement of electron pairs in step 1 to give the intermediate shown. [2]

   iii Carbon dioxide is normally a very poor electrophile. However, this reaction does occur because the benzene ring in the phenoxide ion is activated. Explain how the benzene ring in the phenoxide ion is activated. [3]

c In the final stage of this process, the salicylate ion is acidified to give salicylic acid. Assuming an overall yield by mass of 45% for this three stage process, calculate the mass of phenol (in tonnes) that is needed to produce the annual UK output of 3500 tonnes of salicylic acid.

   (M_r of phenol = 94.0; 1 tonne = 10^6 g) [4]

OCR Chemistry A2 (2814) June 2006 [Total 12]

Hint

Answer

Amines

Objectives

The amine functional group, –NH$_2$, occurs in a wide variety of compounds. These range from simple amines (Figure 5.1) to medicines, dyes and giant biological macromolecules.

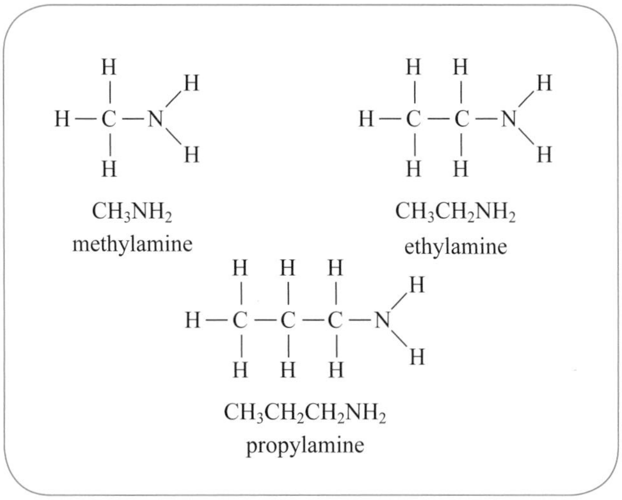

H—C—N (with H atoms shown)
CH$_3$NH$_2$
methylamine

H—C—C—N (with H atoms shown)
CH$_3$CH$_2$NH$_2$
ethylamine

H—C—C—C—N (with H atoms shown)
CH$_3$CH$_2$CH$_2$NH$_2$
propylamine

Figure 5.1 The displayed and structural formulae of some primary amines.

Figure 5.1 shows three examples of **primary amines** – the nitrogen atom is bonded to *one* alkyl group and two hydrogen atoms. The nitrogen atom in a **secondary amine** is bonded to *two* alkyl groups and one hydrogen atom and in a **tertiary amine** is bonded to *three* alkyl groups (Figure 5.2).

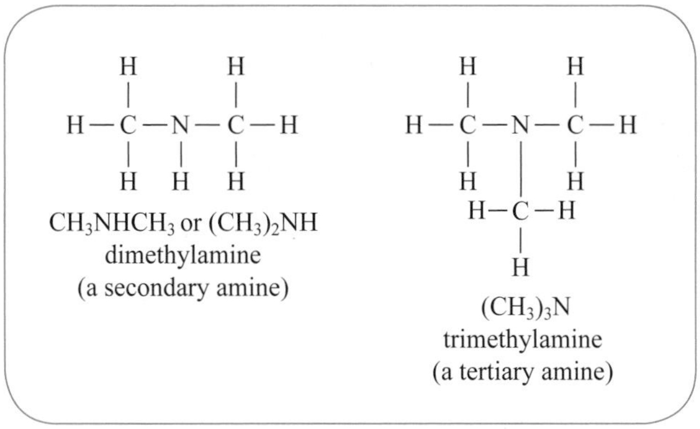

H—C—N—C—H (with H atoms shown)
CH$_3$NHCH$_3$ or (CH$_3$)$_2$NH
dimethylamine
(a secondary amine)

H—C—N—C—H with H—C—H below
(CH$_3$)$_3$N
trimethylamine
(a tertiary amine)

Figure 5.2 The displayed and structural formulae of a secondary amine and a tertiary amine.

SAQ

1 **a** What is the name of the amine with the structural formula CH$_3$CH$_2$CH$_2$CH$_2$NH$_2$?

   b Which of the following amines is a secondary amine?

Hint

   A NH$_2$(CH$_2$)$_2$NH$_2$
   B (C$_3$H$_7$)$_3$N
   C C$_2$H$_5$NHCH$_3$
   D C$_2$H$_5$NH$_2$

Answer

Primary amines

The primary amines which we shall study in detail are ethylamine (C$_2$H$_5$NH$_2$) and phenylamine (the simplest aromatic amine, C$_6$H$_5$NH$_2$). Space-filling models of their structures are shown in Figure 5.3.

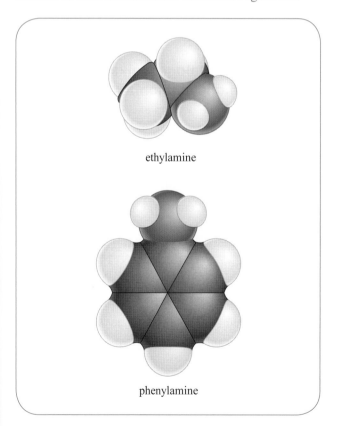

ethylamine

phenylamine

Figure 5.3 Space-filling models of ethylamine and phenylamine.

Primary aliphatic amines are generally water soluble. The hydrogen atoms in the amine group, $-NH_2$, form hydrogen bonds to the oxygen atoms in the water molecules. A hydrogen atom from a water molecule may also hydrogen-bond to the nitrogen of the amino group via its lone-pair of electrons (Figure 5.4). The solubility of the primary aliphatic amines in water reduces as the number of carbon atoms in the alkyl group increases.

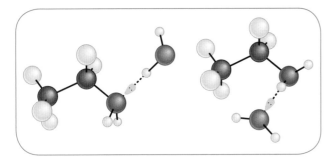

Figure 5.4 The formation of hydrogen bonds between water and ethylamine.

Extension ————————————————

The preparation of amines

Substitution of halogenoalkanes with excess ethanolic ammonia

Heating bromoethane with an excess of a hot, ethanolic solution of ammonia produces ethylamine:

$$CH_3CH_2Br + NH_3 \longrightarrow CH_3CH_2NH_2 + HBr$$

The ammonia acts as a nucleophile, donating the lone-pair on the nitrogen atom to the carbon atom bonded to the Br atom as the C–Br bond beaks.

The excess ammonia reacts with the HBr, forming ammonium bromide, NH_4Br:

$$NH_3 + HBr \longrightarrow NH_4Br$$

The primary amine formed is also a nucleophile, and so will react with bromoethane to form a secondary amine. This in turn could also react with bromoethane to form a tertiary amine; as a result, a mixture of amines can be produced. However, using excess ammonia decreases the chances of attack on bromoethane by the amine product. The conditions chosen are important in order to get a good yield of primary amine.

Reduction of nitroarenes using tin and concentrated hydrochloric acid

Phenylamine is prepared by reducing nitrobenzene:

$$\bigcirc - NO_2 + 6[H] \longrightarrow \bigcirc - NH_2 + 2H_2O$$

The reduction is carried out using tin and concentrated hydrochloric acid. The product is separated from the reaction mixture by steam distillation. This involves distilling by passing steam through the reaction mixture (Figure 5.5). Arenes are readily nitrated, so the reduction of nitroarenes provides a standard route to aromatic amines.

SAQ ————————————————————————

2 Give the name and structural formula of the organic product from the reactions of:
 a bromopropane with an excess of hot, ethanolic ammonia
 b 4-nitrophenol with tin and hydrochloric acid.

Hint

Answer

Figure 5.5 This student is reducing nitrobenzene during the preparation of phenylamine by steam distillation. After the reduction, he will heat the round-bottomed flask and the steam generated will pass into the reaction flask, separating the product from the reaction mxture.

Amines as bases

Amines are related to ammonia, which is a weak base. Weak bases will accept a proton from water to form an alkaline solution. The equation for the reaction of ammonia with water is:

$$H-\overset{\cdot\cdot}{\underset{H}{N}}-H \; + \; H_2O \; \rightleftharpoons \; \left[H-\overset{H}{\underset{H}{\overset{\uparrow\cdot\cdot}{N}}}-H \right]^+ + \; OH^-$$

Ammonia has a lone-pair of electrons on the nitrogen atom. This lone-pair accepts a proton from a water molecule to form the ammonium ion. A mixture of ammonia and ammonium ions is present in an aqueous solution of ammonia. If we represent a general amine by the formula RNH_2, the general equation for the reaction with water is:

$$RNH_2(aq) + H_2O(l) \rightleftharpoons RNH_3^+(aq) + OH^-(aq)$$

For example, ethylamine accepts a proton to form the ethylammonium ion:

$$H_3C-CH_2-\overset{\cdot\cdot}{\underset{H}{N}}-H \; + \; H_2O$$

$$\rightleftharpoons \; \left[H_3C-CH_2-\overset{H}{\underset{H}{\overset{\uparrow\cdot\cdot}{N}}}-H \right]^+ + \; OH^-$$

Making salts with amines

Bases are neutralised by acids to form salts. For example, reacting ammonia with hydrochloric acid produces ammonium chloride:

$$NH_3(aq) + HCl(aq) \longrightarrow NH_4^+(aq) + Cl^-(aq)$$

Amines also produce salts. Reacting ethylamine with hydrochloric acid forms ethylammonium chloride:

$$C_2H_5NH_2(aq) + HCl(aq)$$
$$\longrightarrow C_2H_5NH_3^+(aq) + Cl^-(aq)$$

Phenylamine forms phenylammonium chloride:

Phenylamine is only sparingly soluble in water, but it dissolves readily in hydrochloric acid because a soluble salt is formed. Addition of alkali to this salt solution causes phenylamine to be released. Initially, a milky emulsion forms, which usually breaks down into oily drops (Figure 5.6). (Compare this to the behaviour of a solution of phenol in aqueous alkali on treatment with hydrochloric acid (page 16).)

behaviour of a solution of phenol in aqueous alkali on treatment with hydrochloric acid (page 16).

SAQ

3 Write balanced equations for the reactions of:

> Hint

a dilute nitric acid with butylamine;
b dilute hydrochloric acid with 4-aminophenol;
c sodium hydroxide solution with 4-aminophenol.

> Answer

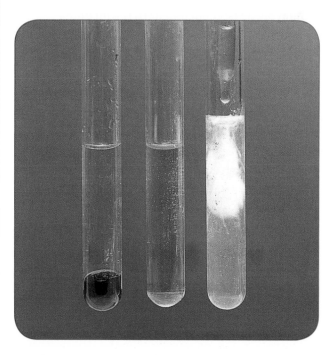

Figure 5.6 The left-hand tube contains brown phenylamine, which does not mix with water. The central tube contains a solution of phenylamine in acid. A white emulsion forms when alkali is added to this solution (the right-hand tube).

Reactions specific to phenylamine

Diazonium salt formation and coupling reactions

When a reaction mixture of phenylamine and nitrous acid is kept below 10 °C, a diazonium salt is formed (the diazonium ion is $-N_2^+$). This reaction is known as a **diazotisation** reaction:

phenyldiazonium
chloride

The nitrous acid (nitric(III) acid) needed for these reactions is unstable and is produced by reacting sodium nitrite (sodium nitrate(III)) with dilute hydrochloric acid:

$$NaNO_2 + HCl \longrightarrow HNO_2 + NaCl$$

The **diazonium ion**, $-N_2^+$, is rather unstable and decomposes readily, giving off nitrogen gas. However, delocalisation of the diazonium ion π-bonding electrons over the benzene ring stabilises phenyldiazonium sufficiently for it to form at low temperatures (below 10 °C).

The phenyldiazonium ion behaves as an electrophile, and will attack another arene molecule such as phenol. Electrophilic substitution takes place at the 4 position, producing 4-hydroxyphenylazobenzene (Figure 5.7).

The reaction is known as a **coupling reaction**:

The compound formed is an energetically stable, orange–yellow azo dye (the azo group is $-N=N-$). The stability is due to extensive delocalisation of the π-bonding electrons through the two benzene rings and across the $-N=N-$ azo link.

Figure 5.7 A diazonium dye is formed when phenyldiazonium chloride is added to an alkaline solution of phenol.

Figure 5.8 Methyl orange is used as an indicator.

The dye 4-hydroxyphenylazobenzene is just one of the wide range of dyes that can be made from reacting aromatic amines with other arenes. These are known as diazonium dyes. They are very stable, so they do not fade. Another example is the indicator methyl orange (Figure 5.8) which has the structure:

$$Na^+ \ {}^-O_3S \text{—} \bigcirc \text{—} N \!=\! N \text{—} \bigcirc \text{—} N \overset{CH_3}{\underset{CH_3}{<}}$$

SAQ

4 a Draw the displayed formula for the azo dye produced on reacting 4-aminophenol with nitrous acid (in dilute hydrochloric acid) below 10 °C and then coupling the resulting diazonium salt with phenol.

   b Write balanced equations for the reactions involved.

Hint

Answer

Summary

Glossary

- Primary amines contain the $-NH_2$ group.

- Ethylamine is prepared by treating bromoethane with an excess of hot, ethanolic ammonia.

- Phenylamine is prepared by reducing nitrobenzene using tin and concentrated hydrochloric acid.

- Like ammonia, amines behave as bases. Because of the lone-pair of electrons on their nitrogen atom, they can readily accept protons (H^+ ions), reacting to form salts.

- Phenylamine reacts with nitrous acid (nitric(III) acid) below 10 °C, to form phenyldiazonium chloride and water; this reaction is called diazotisation.

- Diazonium salts react with other aromatic compounds (such as phenol) to form dyes; this is known as a coupling reaction. Diazonium dyes are commercially useful.

- The stability of diazonium dyes arises from the extensively delocalised π-electron system.

Questions

1   A dye can be made from 4-methylphenylamine and 2,6-dimethylphenol, shown below.

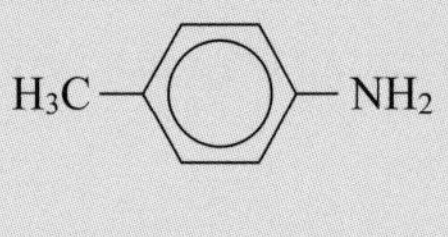

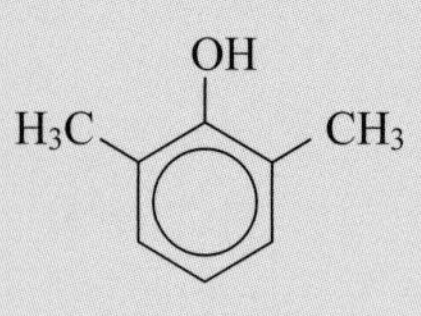

4-methylphenylamine   2,6-dimethylphenol

4-methylphenylamine is dissolved in ice-cold hydrochloric acid and sodium nitrite is added. This mixture is then slowly added to an alkaline solution of the phenol to form the dye.

a   Identify the inorganic nitrogen-containing compound formed by the mixture of hydrochloric acid and sodium nitrite.   [1]

b   Draw the structure of the organic compound formed in the ice-cold acidic mixture, showing a displayed formula of the nitrogen-containing group.   [1]

c   State the name of the type of organic compound drawn in **b**.   [1]

d   Suggest why the mixture must be kept at a low temperature.   [1]   Hint

e   Suggest the structure of the dye.   [2]   Hint

OCR Chemistry A2 (2814) June 2006   [Total 6]

Answer

2   Copy and complete the equation:

$$C_6H_5NO_2 \xrightarrow[\text{heat}]{\text{Sn and conc. HCl}} \dots$$

OCR Chemistry A2 (2814) June 2002   [Total 1]

Answer

3   2-methylphenylamine is used in the large-scale production of a variety of dyes, pesticides and pharmaceuticals.
It can be manufactured from benzene in three stages, as shown below.

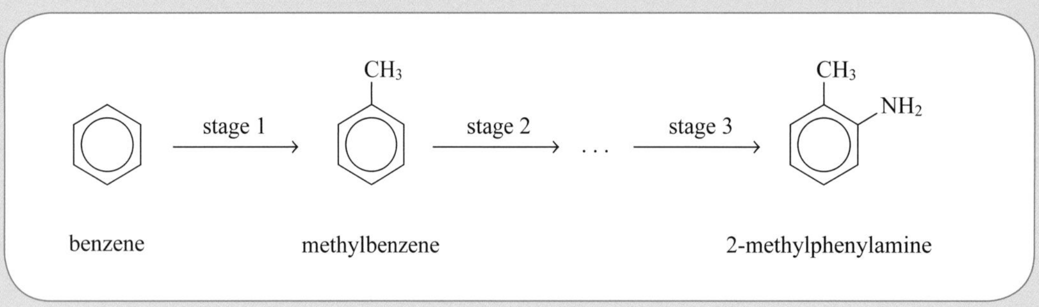

benzene   methylbenzene   2-methylphenylamine

Draw the structure of the compound formed in stage 2.

OCR Chemistry A2 (2814) January 2004   [Total 1]

Answer

continued

4 1,4-diaminobenzene is used in the manufacture of a variety of materials including dyes and polymers.

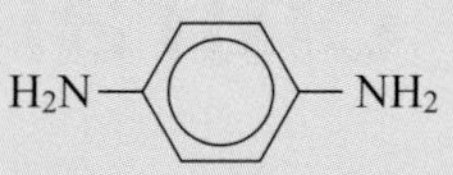

$$H_2N - \bigcirc - NH_2$$

1,4-diaminobenzene

a Explain what is meant by the term *1,4-diamino* in the name of this compound. [2]

b 1,4-diaminobenzene can be manufactured from 1,4-dinitrobenzene.

$$O_2N - \bigcirc - NO_2 \longrightarrow H_2N - \bigcirc - NH_2$$

1,4-dinitrobenzene   1,4-diaminobenzene

    i What type of reaction is this? [1]
   ii State reagents and conditions that could be used to carry out this reaction. [2]
  iii Copy, complete and balance the equation below for this reaction.

$$O_2N - \bigcirc - NO_2 \ + \ \ldots [H] \longrightarrow H_2N - \bigcirc - NH_2 \ + \ \ldots$$

[2]

c 1,4-diaminobenzene is used to make permanent black dye for hair.
1,4-diaminobenzene can irritate the skin because it is basic. Therefore, it is
sometimes neutralised with <u>excess</u> hydrochloric acid to give the salt.
    i Explain how the amino groups in a primary amine such as 1,4-diaminobenzene
allow the molecule to act as a base. [2]
   ii Draw the structure of the salt formed in this reaction. [2]

OCR Chemistry A2 (2814) June 2005   [Total 11]

Answer

Chapter 6

Amino acids and chirality

e-Learning

Objectives

Amino acids

There are about 20 naturally occurring **amino acids**, with the general formula $RCH(NH_2)COOH$. Their general structure is:

$$
\begin{array}{c}
NH_2 \\
| \\
R-C-H \\
| \\
COOH
\end{array}
$$

They are all α-amino acids, which means they have the amino group ($-NH_2$) and the carboxylic acid group ($-COOH$) attached to the same carbon atom. In the simplest amino acid, glycine, the 'R' is a hydrogen atom. In the next simplest amino acid, alanine, the 'R' is a methyl group, CH_3.

Amino acids are **bifunctional**, that is they have two functional groups present in the molecule: the carboxylic acid group, $-COOH$, and the amino group, $-NH_2$. As one of these groups is acidic and the other group is basic, they can interact with one another. The $-COOH$ group donates a proton to the $-NH_2$ group. This forms an 'internal' salt known as a **zwitterion**:

$$
\begin{array}{c}
NH_2 \\
| \\
R-C-H \\
| \\
COOH
\end{array}
\longrightarrow
\begin{array}{c}
\overset{+}{N}H_3 \\
| \\
R-C-H \\
| \\
COO^-
\end{array}
$$

a zwitterion

The zwitterion has a significant effect on the properties of amino acids. It is the predominant form of the amino acid in the solid phase or in aqueous solution. The ionic charges increase the attractive forces between the amino acids in the solid, and so raise the melting point significantly above that of related compounds with similar numbers of atoms and electrons. For example, the amino acid glycine, NH_2CH_2COOH, decomposes at 262 °C without melting, whereas propanoic acid, CH_3CH_2COOH, melts at −21 °C.

Amino acids form salts when reacted with acids or bases. On addition of a dilute solution of a strong acid (for example, aqueous hydrochloric acid), the zwitterion will accept a proton. The product now carries a net positive charge and may be crystallised as the chloride salt:

$$
\begin{array}{c}
\overset{+}{N}H_3 \\
| \\
R-C-H + H^+ \\
| \\
COO^-
\end{array}
\longrightarrow
\begin{array}{c}
\overset{+}{N}H_3 \\
| \\
R-C-H \\
| \\
COOH
\end{array}
$$

Addition of dilute aqueous sodium hydroxide removes the proton from the $-NH_3^+$ group in the zwitterion. This leaves a negatively charged ion:

$$
\begin{array}{c}
\overset{+}{N}H_3 \\
| \\
R-C-H + OH^- \\
| \\
COO^-
\end{array}
\longrightarrow
\begin{array}{c}
NH_2 \\
| \\
R-C-H + H_2O \\
| \\
COO^-
\end{array}
$$

Hence at high pH, amino acids tend to be negatively charged in aqueous solution. At low pH, they tend to be positively charged.

At a certain pH value, a solution of an amino acid will be present at its maximum concentration of zwitterion. This is called the **isoelectric point** of that amino acid. If positive and negative electrodes are placed in the solution at this pH value, the amino acid will not be attracted to either electrode. The isoelectric point of glycine, NH_2CH_2COOH, is at a pH value of about 6. The value of the isoelectric point can vary depending on the nature of the R group in $RCH(NH_2)COOH$. If the R group is basic (e.g. if it contains another $-NH_2$), the amino acid will reach its isoelectric point at a higher pH. Similarly, acidic side chains (R groups) on the amino acid will produce lower isoelectric points.

SAQ

1 Give the structural formulae for the ions present when glycine, NH_2CH_2COOH, is dissolved in
   a aqueous hydrochloric acid
   b aqueous sodium hydroxide.

Answer

2 Write balanced equations for the reaction of aqueous glycine with:
   a aqueous hydrochloric acid
   b aqueous sodium hydroxide.

[Answer]

3 Lysine has its isoelectric point at a pH of about 9.5. What does this mean? What can you deduce about the structure of lysine from this information?

[Answer]

Proteins and polypeptides

Proteins and polypeptides are important molecules in living organisms. Muscle and hair are composed of fibres containing long protein molecules (Figure 6.1). Enzymes are soluble proteins that catalyse many biochemical reactions. Proteins, as well as nylon, are also examples of polyamides.

Polypeptides are formed when amino acids undergo **condensation polymerisation**. Two amino acids join together via a **peptide link** to form a dipeptide and a water molecule – 'peptide link' is another name for the amide link in polypeptides and proteins:

Figure 6.1 Muscle tissue is largely protein, built up from amino acids in your food.

The sequence of amino acids in a protein is known as the **primary structure** of that protein. We show the sequence by abbreviating the amino acids to three letters, e.g. glycine is shown as Gly. Part of the primary structure of a protein could be shown as:
   Gly – Ser – His – Leu – Val – Glu – Ala –, etc.

SAQ

4 The R groups in the amino acids valine and serine are $(CH_3)_2CH–$ and $HO–CH_2–$ respectively.
   a Draw the displayed formula of the dipeptide formed by these two amino acids.
   b What else is formed in this reaction?   [Hint]
   c What do we call this type of reaction?   [Answer]

We can represent the peptide link in structural formulae as –CONH– or –NHCO–.

Three amino acids produce a tripeptide and two water molecules in a condensation reaction.

If these condensation reactions are repeated many times, we get polypeptides and proteins, which contain large numbers of amino acid units. (Proteins generally have much larger relative molecular masses than polypeptides.) In nature, proteins often consist of two or more polypeptides held together by intermolecular forces (such as hydrogen bonds).

Hydrolysis of a protein involves breaking the peptide links by reaction with water. So hydrolysis is the reverse of the condensation polymerisation of amino acids to form a polypeptide. The hydrolysis of the peptide link can be shown as:

In living organisms, condensation polymerisation of amino acids and hydrolysis of proteins are both catalysed by enzymes.

In the laboratory, acids or alkalis are used to catalyse the hydrolysis of proteins. Since each peptide link is broken, polyamides can also be hydrolysed to their monomers by refluxing with an acid catalyst.

With a strong acid, the products are α-amino acids. With a strong alkali, the α-amino acids react with excess alkali to form their carboxylate salts. For example:

$$\text{H} \quad \text{H} \quad \text{O}$$
$$\text{N}-\text{C}-\text{C}$$
$$\text{H} \quad \quad \text{O}^- \text{Na}^+$$
$$\text{R}$$

SAQ

5 Aspartame is the methyl ester of the dipeptide formed between aspartic acid and phenylalanine (Figure 6.2).

Its skeletal formula is:

It is used as a sweetener in many 'diet' soft drinks. Aspartame has two links that may be hydrolysed.

a Copy the skeletal formula of aspartame. Mark the bonds that | Hint | may be broken by hydrolysis, and label them with the names of the types of linkages present.

b Write a balanced equation for the acid hydrolysis of aspartame and name all the products. | Answer |

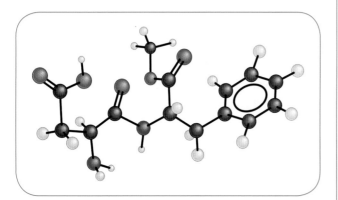

Figure 6.2 Aspartame.

Stereoisomerism

Stereoisomers contain the same atoms with the same order of bonds but with different spatial arrangements of atoms. Optical isomers and E/Z (or *cis–trans*) isomers are examples of stereoisomers.

E/Z (or *cis–trans*) isomerism

You studied E/Z (*cis–trans*) isomerism in Unit F322, *Chains, Energy and Resources* in *Chemistry 1* (Chapter 10). This type of isomerism occurs in alkenes where the carbon–carbon double bond, C=C, prevents rotation. Two identical atoms or groups on opposite sides of the double bond can then give rise to a Z or *cis* isomer and an E or *trans* isomer. For example, 1,2-dichloroethene has the following isomers:

cis-1,2-dichloroethene   *trans*-1,2-dichloroethene
(Z isomer)   (E isomer)

SAQ

6 Which of the following compounds show *cis–trans* (E/Z) isomerism? Draw and label the *cis* (Z) and *trans* (E) isomers where they exist.

A ... CHO   **B** ... CHO

| Answer |

Optical isomerism

Optical isomers are molecules that are non-superimposable mirror images of each other. Like other isomers, they have the same molecular formula. As stereoisomers, they have the same atoms and the same bonds between atoms. However, the bonds are arranged differently in space. The molecule CHBrClF provides a simple example of optical isomerism. Its displayed formula is:

$$\text{H}$$
$$\text{F}-\text{C}-\text{Br}$$
$$\text{Cl}$$

This displayed formula gives no indication of the spatial arrangement of the atoms in this molecule.

To display the optical isomers, we need to use three-dimensional formulae:

In these diagrams the solid wedge is coming towards you, the dashed wedge is going away from you.

Rotation of the right-hand structure about the C–H bond produces:

Notice that in the two structures the F, C and H atoms are in the same spatial position but the Br and Cl are interchanged. If the two optical isomers are placed on top of each other, as follows, they do not match. We say they are *non-superimposable*.

We call the two optical isomers **enantiomers**.

Place your hands together with the palms in contact. Hands are mirror images of each other. Put one hand on top of the other with both palms uppermost. Your thumbs are now on opposite sides. In effect, the enantiomers are rather like your right and left hands. They are non-superimposable images of each other.

Chemists use the term **chiral centre**, derived from the Greek for hand, to describe an atom that exhibits optical isomerism. A key feature of a chiral centre in an organic molecule is the presence of *four* different groups bonded to a carbon atom. The chiral centre in CHBrClF is labelled with an asterisk in this diagram:

SAQ

7 Copy these formulae and mark the chiral centres with an asterisk:

Hint

a $CH_3CH_2CHBrCH_3$

b

c

Answer

When drawing three-dimensional formulae by hand, it saves time to use a dashed line instead of the dashed wedge. In this book we use the dashed wedge to provide a more three-dimensional effect. You will find it easier to visualise these structures if you use a molecular model kit (or modelling software on a computer) to make these two isomers. (Use the colours shown in Table 1.2 on page 3 for the different atoms.) Molecular models of the optical isomers of CHBrClF are shown in Figure 6.3.

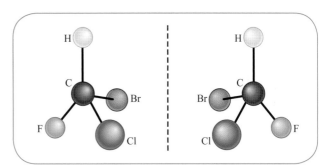

Figure 6.3 Ball-and-stick models of the optical isomers of CHBrClF.

Optical isomerism in amino acids

With the exception of glycine, the α-amino acids all have a chiral centre at the α-carbon atom (the α-carbon atom is the one next to the carboxylic acid group). For example, alanine has the structure:

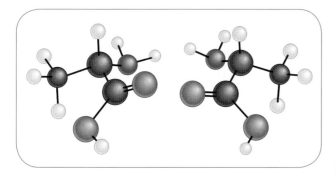

Figure 6.4 Ball-and-stick models of the two optical isomers of alanine.

The molecular models shown in Figure 6.4 illustrate the two optical isomers of alanine.

When you need to represent a pair of optical isomers, draw one isomer using the three-dimensional representation. Next, imagine reflecting this isomer in a mirror plane, and draw the other isomer opposite it.

SAQ

8 Draw three-dimensional formulae to show the two optical isomers of alanine.

  [Answer]

9 a Leucine has the structure:
   Draw three-dimensional formulae to show the

$$H_2N - \overset{\overset{\displaystyle H}{|}}{\underset{\underset{\displaystyle CH_2}{|}}{C}} - COOH$$
$$CH(CH_3)_2$$

   optical isomers of leucine.

 b Isoleucine has more than one chiral centre. It has the structure:
   Copy this structure and mark

$$H_2N - \overset{\overset{\displaystyle H}{|}}{\underset{\underset{\displaystyle CH_3}{|}}{C}} - COOH$$
$$CHCH_2CH_3$$

   the chiral centres with asterisks.

  [Answer]

Optical isomers in nature

Many of the molecules found in living organisms contain chiral centres. Usually only one of the isomers is biochemically active. This is not surprising when you consider the shape selectivity of, for example, enzymes. Medicines that have chiral molecules may need to be administered as a pure isomer. Synthetic organic reactions usually result in a mixture containing equal amounts of both isomers (a racemic mixture).

Purification of such mixtures can be done by crystallisation with a chiral acid or base. However, new separation techniques such as chiral high-performance liquid chromatography are enabling much better separations (Figure 6.5).

To avoid expensive separation techniques, a few 'leading technology companies' are now using synthetic routes which produce only the required isomer. You can read more about this in Chapter 8.

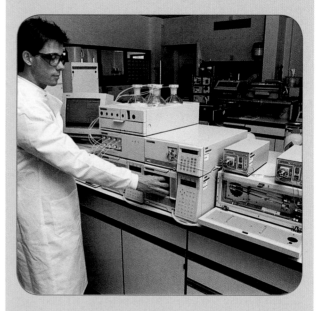

Figure 6.5 High-performance liquid chromatography equipment.

[Extension]

Summary

Glossary

- There are about twenty naturally occurring amino acids with the general formula $RCH(NH_2)COOH$. 'R' may be H, CH_3 or another organic group.

- The amino group interacts with the acid group to form an internal salt or zwitterion.

- Amino acids react with both acids and bases to form salts.

- Two amino acids react together in a condensation reaction, bonding together by a peptide (or amide) link to form a dipeptide and water. Repetition of this condensation reaction many times leads to the formation of polypeptides and proteins.

- Proteins or polypeptides are hydrolysed by refluxing in a strong acid, such as $HCl(aq)$, or a strong alkali, such as $NaOH(aq)$, to form α-amino acids. In acid hydrolysis, carboxylic acids are formed as the peptide links break, whereas in hydrolysis using alkali, carboxylate salts are formed.

- With the exception of glycine, amino acids possess a chiral carbon atom (a chiral centre has four different groups bonded to it) and so optical isomers (enantiomers) are possible.

Questions

1 Leucine (2-amino-4-methylpentanoic acid) is a naturally occurring α-amino acid that is often used in protein supplements.
   Leucine has a structural formula of $(CH_3)_2CHCH_2CH(NH_2)COOH$.
   a i State the general formula of an α-amino acid. [1]
      ii Draw a displayed formula of leucine. [1]
   b Leucine can exist as a zwitterion.
      i State what is meant by the term *zwitterion*. [1]
      ii Explain, with the aid of a diagram, how the zwitterion is formed from the functional groups in leucine. [2]
   c Leucine can be obtained from a source of protein such as meat.
      i State suitable reagents and conditions to break down a protein into amino acids. [2]
      ii State the type of reaction occurring. [1]
   d Leucine can also be synthesised in the laboratory from simpler compounds.
      i One reaction in this synthesis converts 2-chloro-4-methylpentanoic acid, $(CH_3)_2CHCH_2CHClCOOH$, into leucine.
        State the reagents and conditions needed for this reaction. [1]
      ii Explain how a purified sample of leucine synthesised in the laboratory would differ from a sample of leucine purified from meat. [3]

   Hint

OCR Chemistry A2 (2814) June 2006 [Total 12]

   Answer

continued

2 One of the final stages in winemaking involves the fermentation of malic acid to lactic acid. An equation for the reaction is shown below.

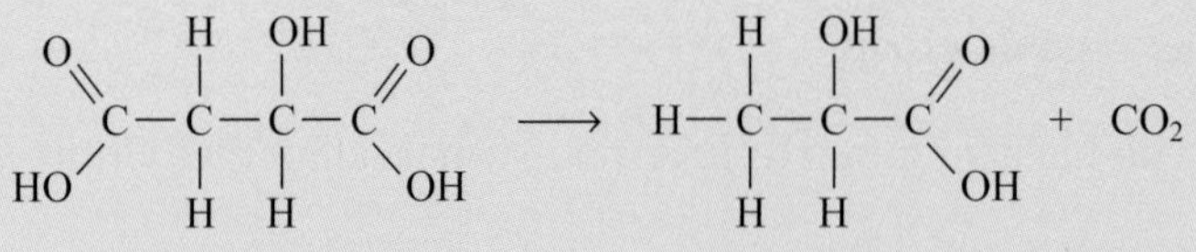

malic acid   lactic acid

Both acids contain a chiral centre.

a Copy the structure of malic acid and identify the chiral centre on the structure of malic acid using an asterisk *. [1]

b Draw a diagram to show the 3D arrangement of groups around the chiral centre in malic acid. [1]

OCR Chemistry A2 (2814) June 2006   [Total 2]

Hint

Hint

Answer

3 Alanine, $CH_3CH(NH_2)COOH$, is an α-amino acid that is found in human sweat. Its structure is shown below.

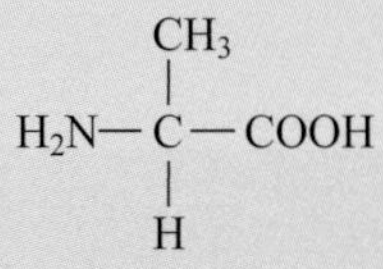

alanine

a Alanine reacts with an aqueous alkali such as sodium hydroxide to give a salt and another product.

   i Name the functional group in alanine which reacts with aqueous alkali. [1]

   ii Give the structural formula of the salt formed in the reaction of alanine with aqueous sodium hydroxide. [2]

   iii What is the other product of this reaction? [1]

b In sweat, alanine exists as a zwitterion. The structure of this zwitterion is shown below.

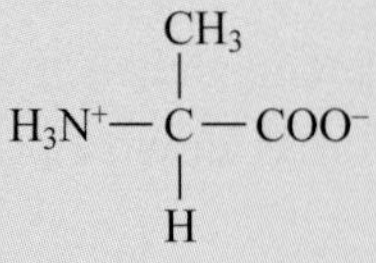

Show the structure that results when this zwitterion comes into contact with an alkali. [2]

c Human sweat also contains dipeptides in which alanine is combined with one other α-amino acid such as valine. The structure of valine is shown below.

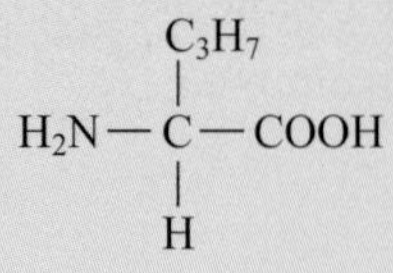

valine

Explain how α-amino acids combine to give peptides.

Include in your answer the displayed formulae of <u>two</u> different dipeptides that can be made from alanine and valine. [5]

OCR Chemistry A2 (2814) June 2004   [Total 11]

Answer

Chapter 7

Polyesters and polyamides

e-Learning

Objectives

Polymers are macromolecules that are built up from very large numbers of small molecules known as monomers.

Bakelite®

In 1872, Adolf von Baeyer made a resin by heating phenol with an aldehyde. He threw this resin away because he could not see a use for the material. The resin was re-investigated by Leo Hendrik Baekeland who, in 1910, set up a company to manufacture the material (which he called Bakelite®). It was used for a great variety of objects, including making electrical sockets and plugs.

Since Baekeland's day, the material used in sockets and plugs has changed several times. Polyester, polycarbonate and acrylonitrilebutadiene styrene copolymer (ABS) are used for these nowadays (Figure 7.1). Once Bakelite® has been formed it cannot be melted, so it is a **thermosetting** polymer. The newer materials can be melted and moulded many times (they are **thermoplastic** polymers), making recycling much easier.

Figure 7.1 Electrical sockets and plugs are made from thermoplastic polymers.

The formation of polymers

Addition polymerisation

Alkenes polymerise by addition reactions. The alkene undergoes an addition to itself. As further molecules are added, a long molecular chain is built up. The reactions are initiated in various ways and an initiating chemical (initiator) may become incorporated at the start of the polymer chain.

Ignoring the initiator, an addition polymer has the same empirical formula as the alkene it is made from. This type of reaction is called **addition polymerisation**. Many useful polymers are obtained by addition polymerisation of different alkenes.

Poly(ethene) was first produced accidentally by Eric Fawcett and Reginald Gibson in 1933. The reaction involves ethene adding to itself in a chain reaction. It is a very rapid reaction, with chains of up to 10 000 ethene units being formed in one second.

The product is a high molecular mass, straight-chain alkane. It is a polymer and a member of a large group of materials generally known as **plastics**. The alkene from which it is made is called the **monomer**. The section of polymer that the monomer forms is called the **repeat unit** (often shown within brackets in structural formulae):

Skeletal formulae for two other important addition polymers, poly(chloroethene) and poly(phenylethene), are:

poly(chloroethene)   poly(phenylethene)

They are more commonly known as PVC and polystyrene, respectively. Note how the systematic name is derived by putting the systematic name of the monomer in brackets and prefixing this with 'poly'. The skeletal formulae of the monomers, chloroethene (old name vinyl chloride) and phenylethene (old name styrene), are as follows:

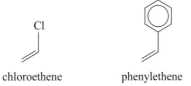

chloroethene   phenylethene

There are several ways of bringing about the addition polymerisation of alkenes. These different conditions produce polymers with different properties, which provide the wide variety of poly(alkene)s for the many applications of these versatile materials.

SAQ

1 a Acrylic fibre is often used as a furnishing fabric or as a wool substitute in sweaters. It is an addition polymer of propenenitrile, CH_2=CHCN (also called acrylonitrile). Write a balanced equation for the polymerisation of propenenitrile. Use a displayed formula in your equation to indicate the repeat unit of this polymer.

   b A polymer which is often used to make plastic boxes for food storage has the structure:

   $$CH_3 \quad CH_3 \quad CH_3 \quad CH_3$$

   Draw displayed formulae to show the repeat unit of this polymer and the monomer from which it is made. Label your diagrams with the appropriate systematic names.

   Answer

Extension

Condensation polymerisation

Polyester formation

A significant proportion of clothing is made using polyester fibre. Polyester is also used to make plastic bottles for drinks (Figure 7.2).

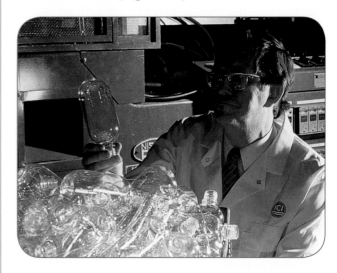

Figure 7.2 Poly(ethylene terephthalate), a polyester, is widely used for drinks bottles as a replacement for glass.

One polyester, Terylene®, is made by polymerising ethane-1,2-diol with benzene-1,4-dicarboxylic acid (terephthalic acid). As each ester link is made, a water molecule is lost – a condensation reaction occurs. So the formation of a polyester is an example of **condensation polymerisation**.

The reaction requires a catalyst such as antimony(III) oxide at about 280 °C. An equation for the reaction is:

The resulting polymer is fairly rigid because of the 1,4 links across the benzene ring. The 1,4 links produce a more linear polymer, which enables the polymer chains to pack more closely. Close packing produces strong intermolecular forces, which enable the polymer to be spun into strong threads for the clothing industry.

SAQ

2 The external mirror housings of some vehicles have been made from PBT, or poly(butylene terephthalate). This material provides excellent protection to the mirror glass whilst driving off-road. The structure of PBT is:

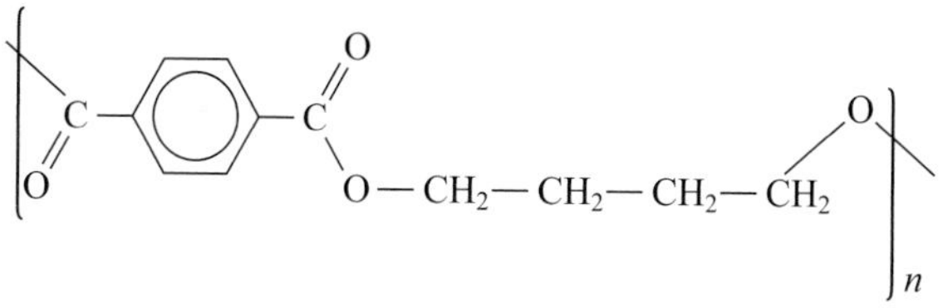

a Draw displayed formulae to show the two monomers used to make PBT.

b Write an equation for the reaction.

Answer

Poly(lactic acid), PLA

Another polyester is poly(lactic acid), known as PLA. This polymer has been getting a lot of attention lately because the starting material used to produce it comes from plant starch, not from chemicals made from our dwindling supplies of crude oil. Crops such as corn, wheat, beet and potatoes can all be used. PLA also has other advantages, such as its biodegradability (see page 59). It has also been shown that the lifecycle of PLA, starting from the crop and ending at scrapping, reduces greenhouse gas emissions by between 30 and 50% compared with traditional oil-based plastics.

We can summarise the process used to make PLA in Figure 7.3.

We can think of this as the polymerisation of lactic acid (systematic name, 2-hydroxypropanoic acid), even though in industry the more reactive lactide derivative is used to make the PLA. The lactic acid molecules can undergo esterification (a condensation reaction, forming water as well as the polymer).

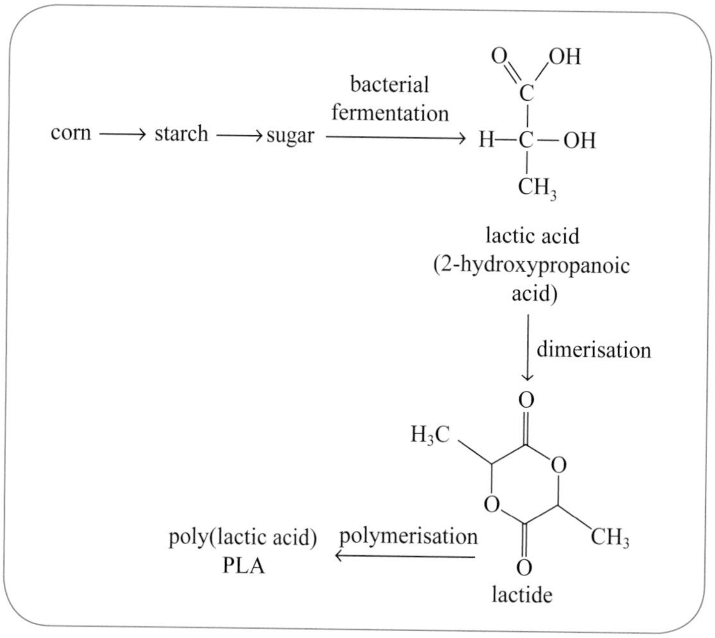

Figure 7.3 The production of poly(lactic acid), PLA.

Notice that the lactic acid (2-hydroxypropanoic acid) molecule has an alcohol and a carboxylic acid group within each molecule. Therefore the molecules can react to form ester links between one another:

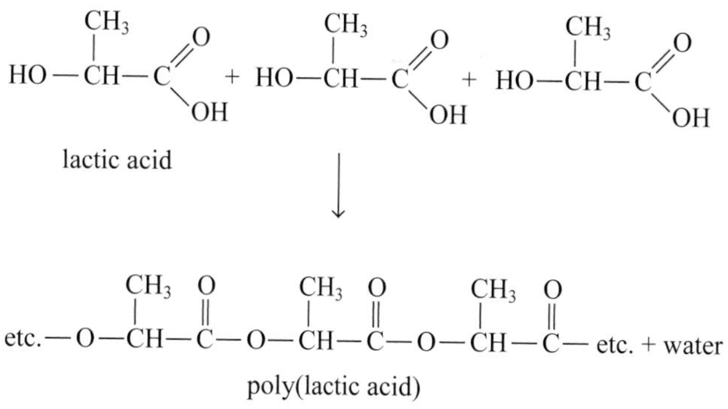

We can show the repeat unit in the PLA polymer as:

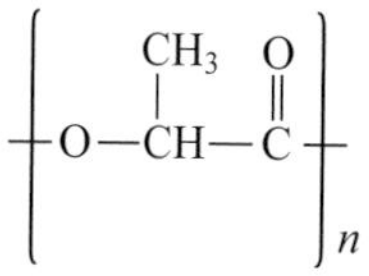

SAQ

3 a Draw the skeletal formula of 2-hydroxypropanoic acid (lactic acid).

b Draw the repeat unit of PLA in skeletal form.

Answer

Polyamide formation

Wallace Carothers carried out research for Du Pont (a chemical company based in the USA) in 1928 in order to find new polymers that might be used for making fabric. At that time, it was known that wool and silk were proteins and that they contained the peptide linkage, –NHCO– (see Chapter 6). Because of this, Carothers set out to make polymers systematically, using condensation reactions involving amines and carboxylic acids.

In order to make a polymer, he realised that he needed monomers which had two functional groups present. The monomer could have an amino group (–NH_2) at one end and a carboxylic acid group (–COOH) at the other. Alternatively, two monomer units could be used, one with amino groups at both ends, and the other with carboxylic acid groups at both ends. Both approaches led to the discovery of new polymers, which are now widely used to make fibres.

Use of the diamine, 1,6-diaminohexane, together with the dicarboxylic acid, hexanedioic acid, produces a nylon called nylon-6,6. An amino group undergoes a condensation reaction with a carboxylic acid group (see Chapter 6). A water molecule is released and a C–N bond is formed.

This reaction can occur at both ends of the two monomer molecules, so a condensation polymerisation is possible:

The product is a long chain of alternating monomer units linked by amide groups, –NHCO–. Such polymers are called **polyamides**.

Notice that each of the two monomer units contains six carbon atoms. This is why it is called nylon-6,6. Nylons are given names that indicate the number of carbon atoms in each monomer unit.

Nylon is formed into a very strong fibre by melt spinning, during which the molecules become oriented along the axis of the fibre. This increases the opportunities for hydrogen bonds to form between the molecules. The hydrogen bonds also provide nylon with greater elasticity than is present in fibres without hydrogen bonds (such as poly(propene)). The hydrogen bonds tend to pull the molecules back to their original positions after the fibre has been stretched. This is why nylon is the most popular fibre for making tights. Tights made from many other fibres would tend to sag and lose their shape. The combination of strength and elasticity are also important properties in a climbing rope (Figure 7.4).

Figure 7.4 Nylon has a very high tensile strength, coupled with considerable elasticity. Climbers rely on these properties to minimise the effects of a fall.

The discovery of Kevlar

In 1965 a new fibre was discovered by Stephanie Kwolek that had properties that even she found hard to believe. Stephanie had worked as a research chemist for DuPont for almost 30 years. She worked with a team of chemists in DuPont's Pioneering Research Laboratory, looking for new polymers.

In the 1960s people had already started to worry about a shortage of crude oil and DuPont wanted to make a new material for lightweight, but durable, car tyres. Their theory was that the new lighter tyres would help save fuel. Kwolek and her team worked on the problem and one day the chemicals she mixed formed a milky plastic, unlike the clear one she was expecting. Instead of throwing it away and starting again, her experience and intuition told her to test the product. This would involve 'spinning' it into fibres by forcing it through narrow jets in a machine called a spinneret.

She sent her discovery to the test lab, but they were reluctant to 'spin' it into a fibre, arguing that it would probably block up their spinneret. Eventually, they relented and sent the results of their tests on the fibre back to Stephanie. The results surprised everyone involved.

The fibre turned out to be nine times stronger than a similar mass of steel, but was only half the density of fibreglass. Kwolek insisted on re-testing the material until she was absolutely sure no mistake had been made.

She and her team then had to work out how to scale up the reaction she had performed in her laboratory into a process that could manufacture tonnes of the new fibre. This included the necessary safety and environmental checks on their process and on the new fibre. Finally in 1971, the new fibre was launched under the name of Kevlar. It is used to reinforce tyres but research continued and it is now used in hundreds of different applications. Some of these are called composites, in which Kevlar fibres are mixed with other materials to give new products with improved properties. For example, it is used extensively in sports equipment and commuter aircraft to reduce weight but maintain strength. But perhaps its most famous application is in bullet-proof vests and body armour (Figure 7.5).

Figure 7.5 Kevlar is used to make bullet-proof vests.

SAQ

4 Kevlar is a polyamide made by Du Pont. It has some remarkable properties, including fire resistance and a much higher tensile strength than steel. Kevlar is used to make protective clothing for fire-fighters, bullet-proof vests, crash helmets for motor cyclists and tail fins for jumbo jets, and it is used instead of steel in radial tyres. The structure of this remarkable polymer is:

a Draw a displayed formula to show the repeat unit in Kevlar and label the amide link clearly.
b Draw displayed formulae of the two monomers required to make Kevlar.
c Write a balanced equation for the reaction.
d Compare the polymerisation reaction to make Kevlar with the reaction to make poly(ethene). What are the similarities and differences in terms of the reaction, reactants and products?

[Hint]

[Answer]

Degradable plastics

It has been estimated that around 25% of the space in our landfill sites for dumping rubbish is taken up by waste plastics. One advantage of the poly(alkene) plastics is their resistance to water and chemical attack; this is an advantage *until* we try to get rid of them, when it becomes a disadvantage (Figure 7.6)!

We saw at AS level some of the methods chemists have developed to deal with this waste, such as recycling and reprocessing. Alternatively, poly(alkene) waste may be incinerated as a 'clean' fuel, although gas scrubbers are required to remove polluting gases such as hydrogen chloride from poly(chloroethene) incineration. (See Chapters 12 and 18 in *Chemistry 1*.)

Figure 7.6 Polymer waste is not easy to dispose of – it is usually not biodegradable.

However, chemists are designing new polymers to make plastics that will degrade in nature. Having polymerised monomers to make polymers, their task is to reverse this process somehow once the plastic is discarded.

As you have seen in Chapter 4 and Chapter 6, both esters and peptides will undergo hydrolysis. In esters the –COO– link is broken and in peptides the –NHCO– link is broken (in the presence of a strong acid or base).

With esters we get a carboxylic acid (or carboxylate salt with a base) and an alcohol formed. With peptides we get a carboxylic acid (or carboxylate salt with a base) and an amine formed. So if water and the natural acids found in soil can break down polyesters at their ester links and polyamides at their amide (peptide) links, they will decompose in landfill sites. The plastics will be biodegradable.

Poly(lactic acid), PLA, is a good example of a degradable condensation plastic. Its polymer chains can be hydrolysed at its ester links. This has led to its use in bags for storing rubbish, packaging for foods and disposable kitchenware. An interesting application of PLA is in degradable stitches used by surgeons inside patients during an operation.

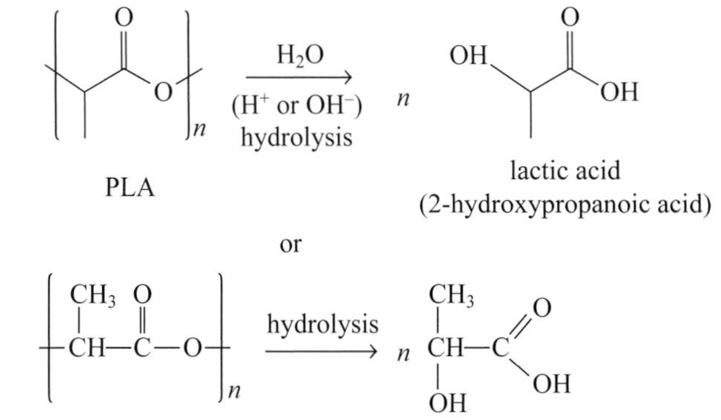

PLA

lactic acid
(2-hydroxypropanoic acid)

or

SAQ

5 Research a list of the advantages of PLA over poly(chloroethene) as a plastic for food packaging.

   Research some of the general disadvantages of PLA. Argue whether or not you think that PLA should replace poly(chloroethene) in the food packaging industry.

Hint

Answer

Some plastics have also been developed that are **photodegradable**, i.e. can be broken down using light energy. These use the fact that the C=O bond in some condensation polymers can absorb radiation from the Sun and can split the chain at this point. Some of the plastic webbing used to hold beer cans in place in their packaging is photodegradable.

The carbonyl (C=O) group can also be introduced into non-degradable plastics by adding a 'co-monomer' containing the photosensitive group to monomers such as ethene and phenylethene. The polymer chains will then break at the C=O groups, so this is a good idea for use in plastics that might end up as litter (which is exposed to sunlight).

Photodegradable plastics are usually designed to decompose over a period of between six weeks and two years. However, if they are buried in a landfill site, sunlight will not reach them and they will not decompose as quickly. Critics claim that false promises of degradability will merely encourage people to use more plastics and to be more careless when they discard them because of the belief that the plastics are 'harmless'. Some are also worried about the possible toxic effects of the products formed when photodegradable plastics, which can contain polymers with benzene rings, are broken down.

Summary

- Polymers are macromolecules that are built up from a very large number of small molecules known as monomers.

- Addition polymerisation occurs when a monomer joins to itself by an addition reaction. Alkenes polymerise in this way. Poly(ethene), poly(chloroethene) and poly(phenylethene) are important alkene-based polymers.

- Condensation polymerisation involves the loss of a small molecule (often water) in the reaction between two monomer molecules. Both polyesters and polyamides are formed by condensation polymerisation.

- A common polyester is formed by the condensation polymerisation of benzene-1,4-dicarboxylic acid with ethane-1,2-diol.

- Polyamides are formed by condensation polymerisation between an amine group and a carboxylic acid group. These groups may be at either end of the same monomer or on different monomers. Nylon-6,6 is formed in a condensation polymerisation between 1,6-diaminohexane and hexanedioic acid. The numbers in the names for nylons refer to the numbers of carbon atoms present in the monomers.

- Condensation polymerisation between the amino and carboxylic acid groups in amino acids produces a polypeptide or protein. The amide links in these polymers are also known as peptide links.

- Poly(alkene)s are non-biodegradable and are also very resistant to chemical decomposition. Disposal of poly(alkene) waste has become a problem.

- Condensation polymers can be designed that are degradable, e.g. photodegradable polymers which are broken down by the absorption of radiation at the C=O bonds in a polymer chain, or biodegradable polymers which are broken down by hydrolysis of amide or ester links.

Glossary

Questions

1 The 'Nylon Rope Trick' is a well-known laboratory demonstration for the formation of a condensation polymer from its monomers.

Two solutions, one containing each monomer, are placed in a beaker as shown. In this reaction, the more reactive hexanedioyl dichloride is used instead of hexanedioic acid. The nylon forms where the two immiscible liquids join, and can be pulled out from between the layers in a continuous strand.

nylon strand

hexanedioyl dichloride
dissolved in hexane

nylon forms where
the liquids meet

1,6-diaminohexane
dissolved in water

a Copy and complete the equation below to show the formation of the nylon polymer from its monomers. Show a repeat unit for the polymer and the other product formed.

Hint

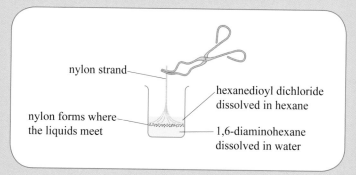

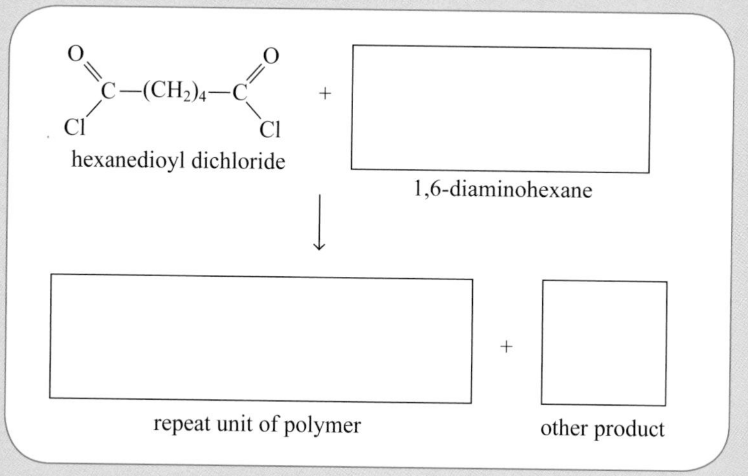

hexanedioyl dichloride

1,6-diaminohexane

repeat unit of polymer

other product

[4]

b Nylon is sometimes used for electrical insulation. However, if there is a risk of high temperatures then a polymer such as Nomex®, with a higher melting point, is used. The repeat unit of Nomex® is shown below.

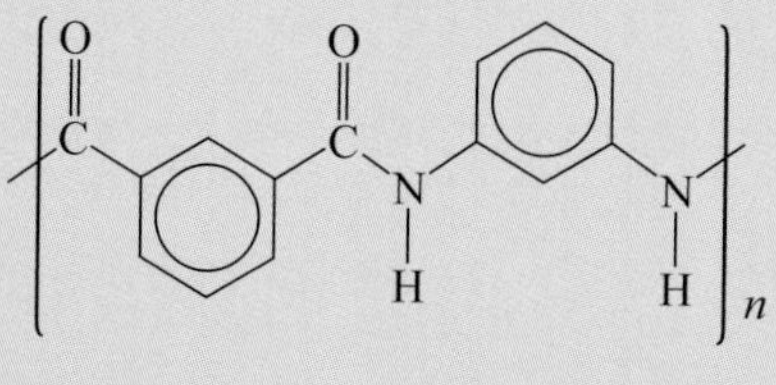

i Draw the structures of two monomers that could be used to form Nomex®. [2]

ii Suggest a reason why the melting point of Nomex® is higher than that of nylon. [1]

OCR Chemistry A2 (2814) June 2007

[Total 7]

Hint

Answer

continued

2 There are two major types of polymerisation: addition polymerisation and condensation polymerisation.

  a **i** Propene undergoes addition polymerisation.

        Give a balanced equation for this polymerisation, using structural formulae.   [2]

    ii Explain the differences between *addition* polymerisation and *condensation* polymerisation.   [2]

  b Polymer **G** is also formed by addition polymerisation.

a section of polymer G

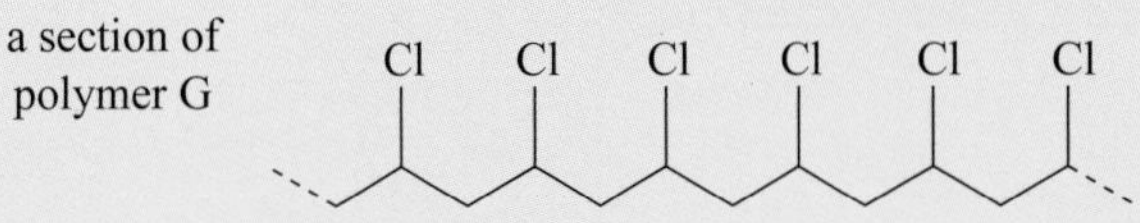

     Deduce the structure of a monomer from which **G** could be made.   [1]

  c The monomer shown below can form a condensation polymer, **H**.

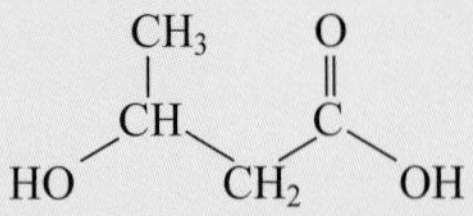

    i Suggest a structure for the polymer, showing <u>two</u> repeat units.   [2]   Hint

    ii Concentrated aqueous NaOH solution can be transported in containers made of poly(propene) but not in containers made of polymer **H**. Suggest reasons for this difference.   [3]

OCR Chemistry A2 (2814) June 2003   [Total 10]

Answer

3 Polymers can be made either from a single monomer or from more than one monomer. Two polymers, **L** and **M**, are shown below.

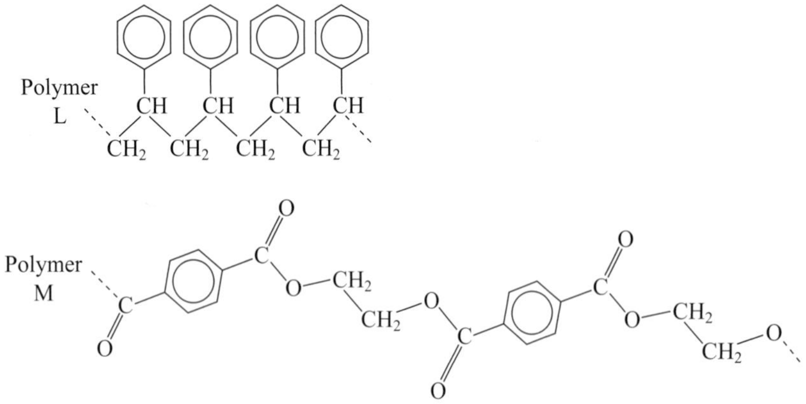

Deduce the structures of the monomers from which **L** and **M** could be obtained.

OCR Chemistry A2 (2814) January 2003   [Total 3]

Answer

Chapter 8

Synthesis

e-Learning

Objectives

How do we design molecules?

If we wish to design a molecule for a particular purpose, for example as a medicine, one approach is to identify the structural features that will achieve the desired result. The structural features of interest may be associated with:

- the shape of the molecule, or
- the functional groups present.

There is often a relationship between these structural features and the behaviour of the molecule in the body (**pharmacological activity**).

Some of the milder painkillers such as aspirin are derived from 2-hydroxybenzoic acid (salicylic acid). (These compounds are also used to reduce the effects of fevers.) Many modern medicines are related to naturally occurring compounds used in 'folk' medicine. For example, a derivative of salicylic acid, called salicin, is present in willow bark and willow leaves (Figure 8.1).

An infusion of willow leaves was recommended by Hippocrates (in 400 BC) for relieving pain whilst giving birth. A brew made from willow bark was used in the eighteenth century to reduce fever.

Figure 8.1 The leaves and bark of willow trees were used as a 'folk' medicine to reduce a fever and to relieve pain.

SAQ

1 The structures of aspirin, 2-hydroxybenzoic acid and salicin are:

aspirin   2-hydroxybenzoic acid   salicin
(salicylic acid)

Copy these diagrams and circle the common structural feature.

Answer

The part of the molecules that you have circled in SAQ 1 is the part which gives rise to their similar pharmacological activity. Investigation of other potential painkillers might focus on making similar molecules with this common structural feature.

SAQ

2 Which of these compounds might have potential as mild painkillers?

A   B   C

Answer

Medicines act by binding to **receptor molecules** present in the body. In order to bind to a receptor molecule and produce the desired pharmacological effect, the medicine molecule must have:

● a shape which fits the receptor molecule
● groups which are capable of forming intermolecular bonds to complementary groups on the receptor molecules – these intermolecular bonds may involve hydrogen bonding, ionic attraction, dipole–dipole forces or instantaneous dipole–induced dipole forces (van der Waals' forces).

Molecular modelling

Computers are now used to examine the relationship between a molecule and a receptor site. Such *molecular modelling* has greatly speeded up the process of designing new medicines. The interactions and fit of a potential medicine with a biological receptor molecule can be studied before the medicine is synthesised (Figure 8.2).

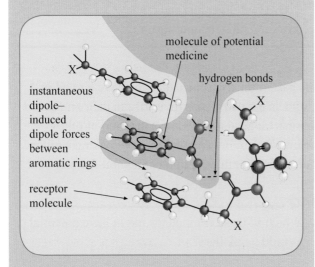

Figure 8.2 The interaction between a receptor molecule and a potential medicine.

Before molecular modelling became available, the synthesis of a new medicine involved far more trial and error, with many more compounds being prepared for testing. With molecular modelling, only those molecules that show potential after computer testing are made in the laboratory.

Molecular modelling on a computer thus provides a powerful tool for the design of medicines and many other compounds (such as pesticides and polymers).

3 Which of these compounds would you choose to investigate for pharmacological activity at the receptor site shown in Figure 8.2?

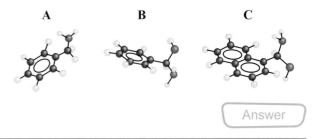

Answer

Routes to new molecules

Even simple molecules such as aspirin may have several functional groups present. There may be a suitable, readily available molecule with a structure very close to the one desired. If such a starting material exists, it may be possible to achieve the desired product in a *one-step synthesis*.

In a one-step synthesis, the starting material is converted to the product by means of a single reaction. For example, a natural penicillin can be modified to produce a new penicillin with enhanced antibacterial activity.

However, it is much more likely that several separate reactions will be needed to convert a suitable starting compound to the desired product. In other words, a *multi-step synthesis* is required.

Planning a multi-step synthesis requires a sound knowledge of many different reactions. The reactions that you have met in your study of advanced chemistry provide you with the basis for planning the syntheses of a wide range of organic compounds. We shall now review these reactions.

This review should enable you to use reactions effectively in planning multi-step syntheses of your own, as well as helping you to learn the reactions more thoroughly. The reactions can be divided into two groups:

● aliphatic reactions
● aromatic reactions.

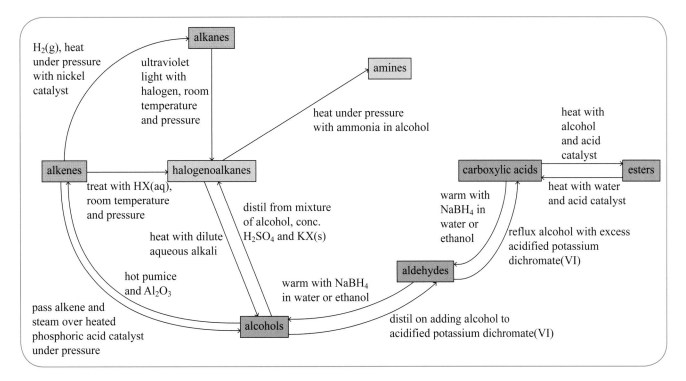

Figure 8.3 A summary of reactions of the functional groups.

Aliphatic reactions

You may have already seen a connection between the reactions of a number of functional groups. These are summarised in Figure 8.3, which shows the names of the functional groups, together with arrows to indicate the interconversions possible. Note the importance of halogenoalkanes in these synthetic routes.

Aromatic reactions

Figure 8.4 provides you with a summary of reactions involving aromatic compounds.

You could copy the reaction summaries (from Figure 8.3 and Figure 8.4) and display them where you will look at them regularly – this will help you to learn the reactions and their conditions.

You can use the reaction summaries to plan multistep syntheses.

Suppose we wish to convert ethene to ethanoic acid. A possible route is to convert ethene to ethanol, which is then oxidised to ethanoic acid. Alternatively, ethene could be converted to bromoethane, which is then hydrolysed to ethanol, and this is oxidised to ethanoic acid. This second alternative involves an extra reaction step – you should usually try to complete a synthesis in as few steps as possible. Remember that material is lost at each stage when preparing organic compounds: reaction yields seldom approach 100%.

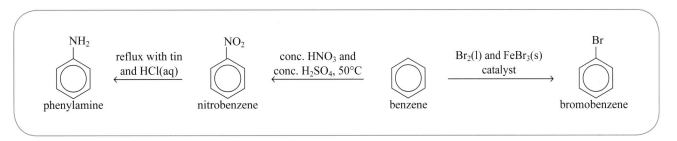

Figure 8.4 A summary of reactions involving aromatic compounds.

SAQ

4 Outline how you might carry out the following conversions [Hint]
involving two- or three-step syntheses. Include the conditions required for the reactions.
a Ethene to ethylamine.
b Benzaldehyde to ethyl benzoate.
c 1-bromobutane to butanoic acid.
d Butan-2-one to 2-aminobutane. [Answer]

[Extension]

Chirality in pharmaceutical synthesis

The pharmaceutical industry is constantly searching for new drugs. Their research chemists have discovered that most of these drugs contain at least one **chiral centre**. Remember that a molecule containing a carbon atom bonded to four different atoms or groups of atoms can exist as two non-superimposable mirror images called **enantiomers**. The two isomers will be optically active. They differ only in their ability to rotate the plane of polarised light to the left or to the right.

Using conventional organic reactions to make the desired product will yield a 50:50 mixture of the two enantiomers. We call this a racemic mixture. Although the physical properties of the enantiomers will be identical, each differs in its 'pharmacological activity', i.e. the effect the drug has on the body. For example, naproxen is a drug used to treat the pain caused by arthritis (see Figure 8.5). One enantiomer will ease the pain but the other can cause liver damage. In the treatment of tuberculosis, one enantiomer of the drug ethambutol is effective whereas the other can cause blindness. Therefore, chemists ideally need a single pure enantiomer to put in their drug product. (About 80% of new drugs patented are single enantiomers.)

Using pure enantiomers will be beneficial as it:
- reduces the patient's dosage by half as the pure enantiomer is more potent, cutting costs and minimising the risk of side-effects
- protects drugs companies from possible litigation as people sue for damages when serious side-effects do occur.

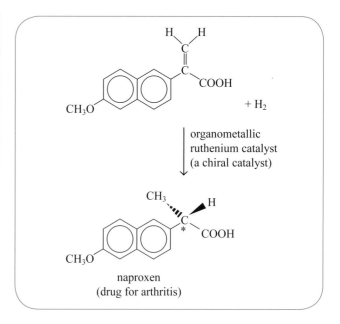

Figure 8.5 Using the chiral Ru catalyst ensures that only one of the enantiomers is formed. The catalyst can be immobilised on a solid support.

SAQ

5 Why are pure enantiomers rather than racemic mixtures the better option for use as pharmaceutical drugs from the point of view of:
a a patient
b a pharmaceutical company? [Answer]

6 Find out why the drug thalidomide resulted in litigation against its manufacturer. [Answer]

There are three ways to prepare pure enantiomers:
1 separate the products of the reaction
2 use optically active starting materials
3 use enzymes (optically active catalysts).

1 Optical resolution

In this method, you follow a traditional synthetic route to make the compound, resulting in a racemic mixture. Then you *separate* the two enantiomers in a process called **optical resolution**. This involves using a pure enantiomer of another optically active compound that will react with the compounds to be separated. The two different products formed will now have different physical properties and so can be separated by physical means. For example, their solubility in a given solvent may differ so they can be separated by fractional crystallisation.

The crystallisation is repeated many times to ensure purity. This method is difficult, time-consuming, uses extra reagents and involves the disposal of half the original racemic mixture.

Large volumes of organic solvents (often harmful to the environment) are used in the process. However, chemists are now using supercritical carbon dioxide as a solvent which is much safer. Supercritical fluids have properties between those of a liquid and a gas. At 31 °C and 73 atmospheres pressure, carbon dioxide is a suitable non-polar solvent for many drug derivatives in the process of optical resolution. The solubility of the derivatives changes by simply varying the density of the supercritical carbon dioxide while the solvent (which is non-toxic) is easily removed by reducing the pressure.

The reaction used to form the derivatives is then reversed to form the original compound again, which will now be in an optically pure form.

We can also use high-pressure liquid chromatography (see Chapter 9) to separate a racemic mixture, as long as the stationary medium (e.g. the solid that packs the column) is itself optically active.

2 Optically active starting materials

We can also use starting materials that are themselves optically active, in the same orientation as the desired product. These are often naturally occurring compounds, such as carbohydrates or L-amino acids. (Most amino acids exist as two optical isomers – the D- and L-forms – with the vast majority of amino acids found naturally in proteins having the L-structure.) The synthetic route is designed to keep any intermediates and the final product in the same enantiomeric form. There is therefore no need to carry out the costly separation process needed when a racemic mixture is produced.

Chemists are also developing new chiral catalysts that ensure only one specific enantiomer is formed in a reaction. The benefits of these catalysts are that only small quantities are needed and they can be used over and over again, although the catalyst itself can be expensive. For example, a ruthenium (Ru) organometallic catalyst is used in the production of naproxen (Figure 8.5).

Often a combination of optical resolution and chiral synthesis is needed in the production of a pharmacologically active, pure enantiomer.

3 Using enzymes

The pharmaceutical industry can also use enzymes to promote stereo-selectivity and produce single-enantiomer products. The specific shape and the nature of the molecular interactions at the active site of an enzyme ensure that only one enantiomer will be formed (as in living things). The enzymes are often immobilised (fixed in place) on inert supports so that reactants can be passed over them without the need to separate the product from the enzymes after the reaction. However, isolating enzymes from living things can be expensive. Using whole organisms, such as bacteria, can reduce this cost.

Nowadays, synthetic enzymes can also be made, designed for a particular synthesis. Therefore a search for a suitable enzyme from the limited pool available from natural sources is not always necessary.

Overall, using an enzyme process might take longer to develop than a conventional synthetic route but in the long run the benefits generally outweigh the disadvantages as there are fewer steps needed, resulting in a 'greener' process.

SAQ

7 Why are modern enzyme-based processes for manufacturing pure enantiomers more sustainable than traditional synthetic routes used by the pharmaceutical industry?

Answer

Summary

Glossary

- Many multi-step syntheses can be planned using the reactions of the functional groups discussed in this book.

- Molecular design of a new medicine is made possible with a sound understanding of the structural features that produce medical effects. The computerised study of the interactions between molecules and biological receptors has become a powerful tool in the search for new medicines.

- The preparation of a new compound will involve safety considerations, making decisions on quantities of reagents to use, establishing what conditions provide the best yield, and purification and characterisation of the product, taking into account any issues of sustainability.

- Optical isomers are molecules that are non-superimposable mirror images of each other. Such molecules contain a carbon atom which is a chiral centre. This chiral centre has four different atoms or groups attached to it.

- Both natural biochemicals and modern medicines contain chiral molecules. Generally, only one of the enantiomers is beneficial to living organisms. The other isomer may have undesirable effects. The beneficial isomer has the appropriate shape and pattern of intermolecular forces to interact with a receptor molecule in a living organism.

- Chemists are now producing medicines containing single enantiomers rather than a racemic mixture of isomers. This enables the dose to be halved, improves pharmacological activity (i.e. behaviour of the molecule in an organism), reduces side-effects and minimises litigation against manufacturers.

Questions

1 A commercial synthesis of the ester **A** is shown below.

$$C_6H_5CH_2Cl \xrightarrow[\text{stage I}]{} C_6H_5CH_2OH \xrightarrow[\text{stage II}]{\text{CH}_3\text{COOH, conc. H}_2\text{SO}_4} C_6H_5CH_2OOCCH_3$$

B   **A**

a Stage I:

    i Suggest a suitable reagent.   [1]

Hint

    ii State the type of reaction occurring.   [2]

    iii Write the equation for this reaction.   [1]

b Stage II:

    i Draw the displayed formula for the ester **A**.   [1]

    ii Write the equation.   [1]

    iii Suggest a general use for esters such as **A**.   [1]

    iv **A** can also be made directly from **B** by reaction with $CH_3COO^-Na^+$.

        Suggest a possible mechanism for this reaction.   [3]

Hint

OCR Chemistry A2 (2814) June 2002   [Total 10]

Answer

continued

2 Compound **C** is currently being tested as a possible anti-allergic drug.

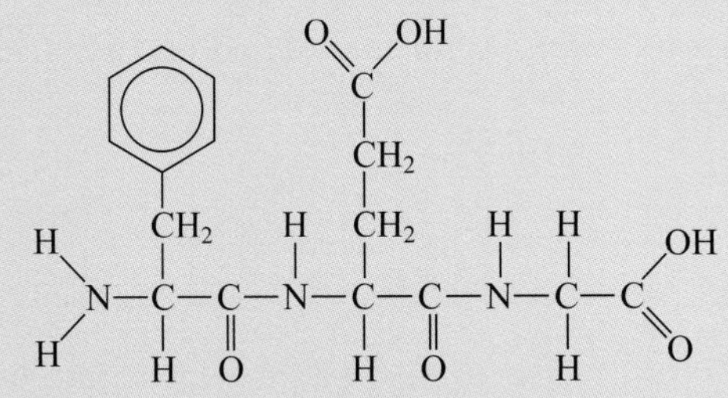

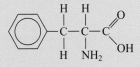

compound C

a Compound **C** can be hydrolysed to form three organic products.
  i Name a suitable reagent and conditions for the hydrolysis of compound **C**. [2]
  ii The three organic products all belong to the same class of compound. State
  the general name for this class of organic compound. [1]
  iii Draw the structure of <u>one</u> of the organic products from the hydrolysis of **C**
  using the reagent you have given in part **a i** above. [2]
  iv Explain what is meant by the term *hydrolysis*. Use this reaction to illustrate
  your answer. [2]

b Compound **C** can exist as a number of stereoisomers, but only one of them is
pharmacologically active as the anti-allergic drug.
  i Explain what causes stereoisomerism in compounds such as **C**. [3]
  ii Explain why there are <u>four</u> different stereoisomers of compound **C**. [2]
  iii Suggest how a drug company could synthesise compound **C** so that the drug
  contains only the one pharmacologically active stereoisomer. [1]
  iv Sometimes it is difficult to manufacture a drug containing only the one
  pharmacologically active stereoisomer.
  Describe <u>two</u> possible disadvantages of producing a drug containing a mixture
  of several stereoisomers. [2]

OCR Chemistry A2 (2814) June 2005 [Total 15]

Answer

3 Phenylalanine is a naturally occurring α-amino acid. Its structure is shown below.

phenylalanine

a State the general formula of an α-amino acid. [1]
b Phenylalanine exists at pH 7 in the body as a zwitterion.
Copy and complete the displayed formula of phenylalanine below to show
the zwitterion of phenylalanine.

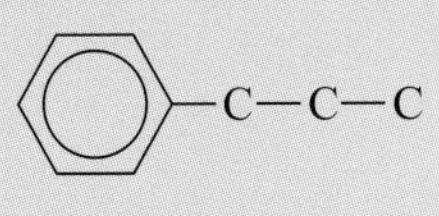

[2]

continued

c Phenylalanine has two stereoisomers.

i What is the name of the type of stereoisomerism shown by phenylalanine? [1]

ii Copy and complete the structures below to show the three-dimensional arrangement of the two stereoisomers of phenylalanine.

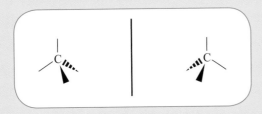

[2]

d Compound **D** is used to make a drug that inhibits the action of the HIV virus.

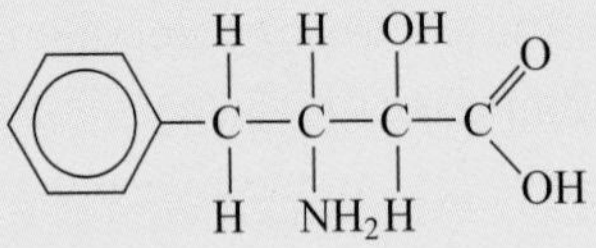

compound **D**

Compound **D** is a β-amino acid, whereas most naturally occurring amino acids are α-amino acids.

State <u>three</u> differences between the structures of compound **D** and phenylalanine. [3]

e Compound **D** contains two chiral centres and its stereochemistry has been found to be significant in the action of the drug. The drug works because it has the right shape to inhibit an enzyme that is needed by the HIV virus.

i Identify the <u>two</u> chiral centres in compound **D** by placing an asterisk * by the appropriate atoms on a drawing of the structure of **D**. [2]

ii State whether the compound **D** made by a three-step chemical process will contain a single stereoisomer or a mixture containing more than one stereoisomer. Explain your answer. [1]

f To finally make the drug, compound **D** is made into a dipeptide by combining it with an α-amino acid such as glycine, H_2NCH_2COOH.

Copy and complete the diagram to show the displayed formula of the peptide bond between compound **D** and glycine.

[2]

[Total 14]

OCR Chemistry A2 (2814) January 2004

Answer

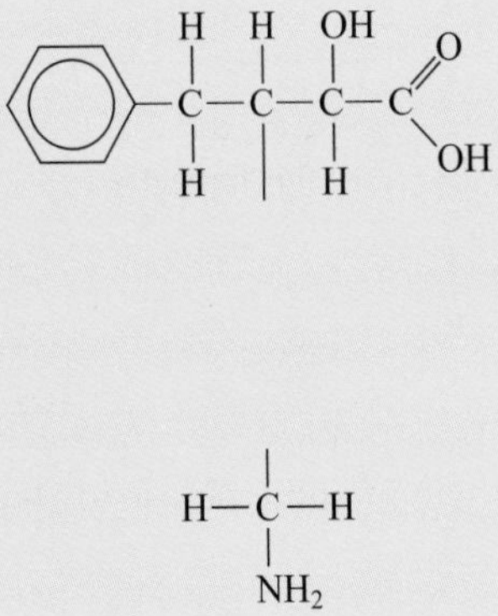

Chapter 9

Chromatography

e-Learning

Objectives

You probably remember doing experiments to split up the components of ink from felt-tip pens or separating the colours of Smarties® on filter paper (Figure 9.1).

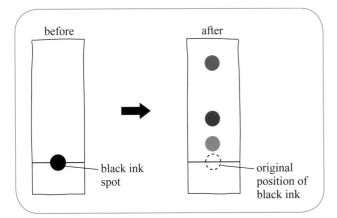

Figure 9.1 Separating the components of black ink from a felt-tip pen. Chromatography shows that the black ink is a mixture of three different colours.

This type of simple experiment has been developed, so that we can now separate many different kinds of substances. The separation of substances by their slow movement through or over a separating material is called **chromatography**.

The word 'chromatography' means 'colour writing'. It was first used in 1903 to describe the separation of plant pigments by pouring a solution of plant pigments through a column of calcium carbonate packed into a glass tube (Figure 9.2). Different pigments moved at different rates and formed different coloured areas in the column, and so could be separated. Although many of the substances that we now separate by more modern methods are colourless, we still use the term 'chromatography'.

You can see in Figure 9.2 how the solution of pigments is placed on top of the column and is washed down the column with a solvent. This simple process, and the more advanced methods of chromatography, all have the following principles in common.

There are two phases in the chromatography process – the **stationary phase** and the **mobile phase**.

The stationary phase stays in place inside the column or in the fibres of the paper. If the stationary phase is packed into a column it usually consists of solid particles or a viscous liquid coated onto a solid surface. In a technique called thin-layer chromatography (TLC) the stationary phase is a solid coated onto the surface of plastic or glass, for example, onto a microscope slide (see page 74).

The mobile phase, which is the **solvent**, moves through the solid in the column or on the microscope slide, or over the paper, and is either a liquid or a gas.

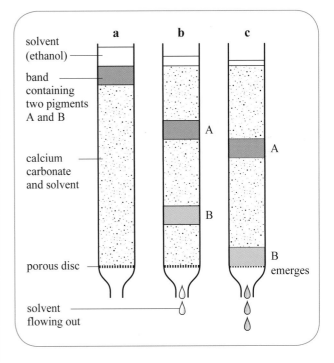

Figure 9.2 The separation of plant pigments – the first example of chromatography.

a The mixed pigments are added to the top of a column of calcium carbonate.

b The pigments flow downwards with the solvent, but at different rates.

c The pigments reach the bottom of the column at different times and can be collected separately.

SAQ

1 Plant pigment was dissolved in ethanol and passed through the column shown in Figure 9.2.

   a Name the stationary phase.

   b Name the mobile phase.

Answer

Mechanisms of chromatographic separation

The separation of the mixture we want to study occurs because the components of the mixture interact with the stationary phase to differing extents. The dissolved components are called **solutes**.

There are two mechanisms for the separation process:

- partition (also referred to as 'relative solubility')
- adsorption.

Partition and relative solubility

To understand the term **partition**, it is helpful to look at what happens to a solute when it is added to two liquids that do not mix but which are in contact with one another. For example, when bromine is added to a mixture of water and tribromomethane ($CHBr_3$), two liquid layers form and the bromine molecules pass upwards and downwards across the interface between the liquids (Figure 9.3).

When the rates of movement of the solute molecules up and down between the two liquids become equal, we say that *equilibrium* has been reached. At equilibrium, the solute molecules are distributed between the two liquids in a definite ratio which depends on their relative solubilities in the two liquids; the solute has been partitioned between the two liquids. (For more information about equilibria, see *Chemistry 1*, Chapter 17.)

During the separation process in partition chromatography, the solutes move between the stationary phase and the mobile phase (Figure 9.4a) and are partitioned between them. Solutes in the mobile phase move forward with it.

When the stationary and mobile phases are both liquids, the rate of movement of each solute depends on its *relative solubility* in the two phases. Solutes that are more soluble in the mobile phase will move faster than the others and will either move further or leave the column earlier. When the mobile phase is a gas, the rate of movement of the solutes depends on their *volatility* and their *relative solubility*.

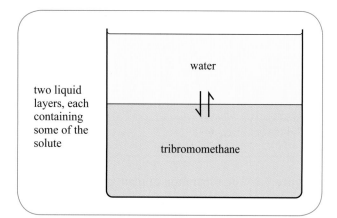

Figure 9.3 Bromine partitioned between water and tribromomethane.

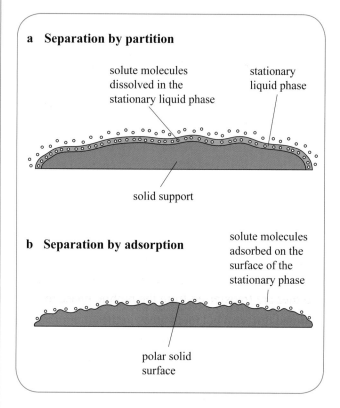

Figure 9.4 The two mechanisms of separation: **a** partition chromatography; **b** adsorption chromatography.

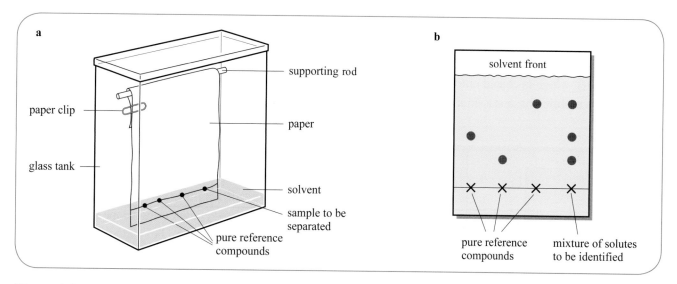

Figure 9.5 **a** Paper chromatography. **b** Components of the unknown mixture can be identified by comparison with pure reference compounds.

Adsorption

In **adsorption chromatography**, the solute molecules are held on the surface of the stationary phase (Figure 9.4b). The stationary phase is a polar solid and the solutes are polar molecules. Strongly polar stationary phases attract and retain the polar solutes. The separation of the solutes depends on the *difference in their polarity*; the more polar solutes are more readily adsorbed than the less polar solutes. (For more information about polarity see *Chemistry 1*, Chapter 6.)

Paper chromatography

In paper chromatography we use filter paper because the cellulose fibres from which the paper is made contain water. This trapped water is the stationary phase and the filter paper is called the **support**. The mobile phase is the liquid solvent that moves over the paper.

Figure 9.5a shows how the method works. The solutes are transferred from the mobile phase to the stationary phase by partition between the two liquids because of their different solubilities in the two liquids. The solutes that are more soluble in the mobile phase move further forward with the solvent.

When the solvent comes towards the top of the paper, we remove the paper from the chromatography tank and the solvent is allowed to evaporate. We can see the coloured components of a mixture directly. When colourless components are involved, we can spray the paper with chemicals so that the colourless components form coloured compounds.

For example, when sprayed with ninhydrin, amino acids show up as lilac-blue spots.

Figure 9.5b shows how the components of the mixture are identified by comparing their positions on the filter paper with those of known pure compounds.

Another way to identify the components of a mixture is to calculate their **retardation factors** (**R_f values**). The movement of any solute relative to the solvent is a characteristic property of the solute. The R_f value is defined as:

$$R_f = \frac{\text{distance moved by centre of solute spot}}{\text{distance moved by front of mobile phase}}$$

The method for calculating an R_f value is shown in Figure 9.6.

Extension

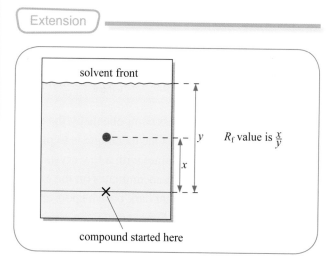

Figure 9.6 Calculation of R_f values.

Thin-layer chromatography

In thin-layer chromatography (TLC), the stationary phase is a thin layer of silica (SiO_2) or aluminium oxide (Al_2O_3), which is coated onto a glass or plastic surface. The mobile phase is a liquid (Figure 9.7).

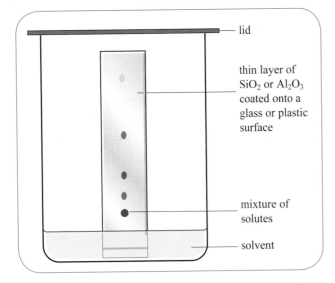

Figure 9.7 Thin-layer chromatography.

The silica or aluminium oxide is first heated to a high temperature so that all water is removed from it. In this state these compounds act as polar solids and the solutes are transferred to them from the mobile phase by adsorption onto their surfaces. However, both these stationary phases readily attract water molecules, so that the thin layers become $SiO_2.xH_2O$ (silica gel) or $Al_2O_3.xH_2O$ (alumina). The water, incorporated in the solid, then becomes the stationary phase and the solutes are separated by partition. On partially dried thin layers, both adsorption and partition may occur.

A thin layer of cellulose powder can also be used as the stationary phase, but, as the cellulose retains water, the separation in this case is by partition rather than adsorption.

We can detect colourless components by the use of appropriate chemicals. One technique is to place the plate in a closed container with a few crystals of iodine. The iodine vapour accumulates on the spots of separated solutes, so that dark brown spots appear on a yellow background. For example, the products resulting from the nitration of phenol (2-nitrophenol and 4-nitrophenol) can be separated and located in this way.

A second technique involves shining ultraviolet light onto a plate that contains a fluorescent material. The glow is reduced by the solutes, which will then appear as dark spots on a bright plate.

The solutes are identified in the same way as for paper chromatography, using R_f values and a database of pure reference compounds.

Thin-layer chromatography is about three times as fast as paper chromatography and it will work with very small samples. You may be able to try it yourself using a coated microscope slide. Also, because the thin layer can be made from different solids, a wide range of mixtures can be separated and the components of the mixtures identified by careful choice of both the stationary and mobile phases. For example, a thin layer of silica will separate chlorinated insecticides, steroids, or alkaloids such as morphine and opium.

Thin-layer chromatography can also be used to select the conditions for larger-scale separations. Different combinations of stationary and mobile phases can be tested quickly to find the most effective method for a particular separation.

Thin-layer chromatography is mainly used for the separation of organic compounds and has applications in clinical diagnosis, forensic testing and quality control.

SAQ

2   State *two* advantages of thin-layer chromatography over paper chromatography.

Answer

3   The results of a thin-layer chromatography separation on silica gel are shown in the table.

Hint

Compound	Distance travelled /cm
compound 1	1.5
compound 2	9.1
solvent	12.5

Calculate the R_f values of the compounds and comment on their values.

Answer

TLC and forensics

Examples of the use of thin-layer chromatography in forensic science are the well-publicised cases of the 'Maguire Seven' and the 'Birmingham Six'. These cases involved men and women suspected of terrorist activities involving explosives.

The Maguire family were arrested on the basis of the results of the thin-layer chromatography analysis of ether extracts of cotton-wool swabs taken from their hands and nail scrapings. The suspects were convicted. The case was re-opened years later. It became known that the TLC tests had been carried out by an 18-year-old scientific officer who had only a few weeks' experience of using TLC, but who was said to have been working under supervision.

The Court of Appeal was concerned that accidental contamination of the samples from the suspects could have occurred from other materials, for example from some pharmaceutical product. There was also concern that the inexperienced analyst might have confused samples with standards.

The evidence from the TLC tests was discredited and the convictions were quashed. Because of similar uncertainties in the forensic evidence in the 'Birmingham Six' case, this was also referred to the Court of Appeal, and again the convictions were quashed (Figure 9.8).

Although more sensitive chromatographic methods have been developed, TLC is still widely used for the identification of cannabis. The stationary phase used is a thin layer of silica that has been sprayed with silver nitrate solution and then dried. Methylbenzene (toluene) is used as the mobile phase.

TLC has retained its usefulness primarily because of its simplicity, low cost and reliability when used with control samples and selected locating agents.

Figure 9.8 The validity of TLC evidence has been questioned and convictions quashed in the Court of Appeal.

Gas chromatography (GC)

Gas chromatography (also known as gas–liquid chromatography) is used to separate and identify very small samples of gases, liquids and volatile solids.

In this technique, a vaporised sample is carried by an inert gas (the mobile phase) over the surface of a solid or a liquid (the stationary phase) on a solid support. A diagram of the apparatus and how it works is shown in Figure 9.9.

The mobile phase, which is called the carrier gas, flows through the column of stationary phase at a constant rate. Nitrogen, which is a relatively unreactive gas, is frequently used as the carrier gas.

The stationary phase is often a non-volatile liquid on a solid support, for example, a long-chain alkane of high boiling point coated onto the surface of SiO_2. In this case the components of the mixture are partitioned between the mobile and stationary phases to different extents, so that they move through the column at different rates depending on:

- their volatility and
- their solubility in the stationary phase.

When the stationary phase is non-polar, the rate of movement of each component through the column is determined principally by its volatility, which is related to boiling point. However, when the stationary phase is polar it will tend to attract and retain polar components. For example, if a mixture of non-polar octane (C_8H_{18}) and polar pentan-1-ol ($C_5H_{11}OH$) is separated using a polar stationary phase, the octane would leave the column before the pentan-1-ol.

Stationary phases, such as the non-volatile liquids coated onto a solid support, are selected for their suitability for the separation of different substances.

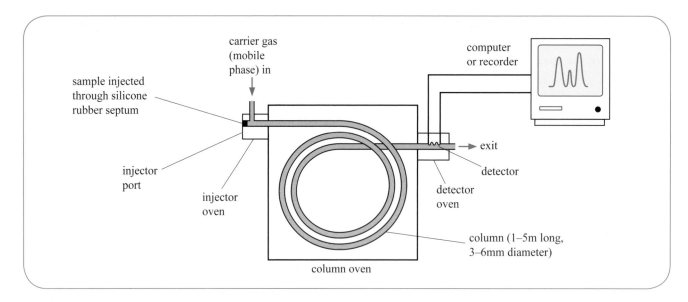

Figure 9.9 A gas chromatograph. The oven is needed to keep the temperature constant.

The components of a mixture leave the column after definite intervals of time, characteristic of each component. As they leave the column they are monitored by a detector designed to record changes in the composition of the carrier gas as the components are separated.

Figure 9.10 shows a diagram of a chromatogram for a mixture of liquids. The time taken for each of these components to pass through the column is found by measuring the distance on the chromatogram between the injection of the mixture (defined as 0 minutes) and the centre of the peak for that component. We call this value the **retention time**.

Since each solute has its own retention time, we can identify an unknown compound by comparing its retention time with the retention times of known compounds. However, remember that the conditions used in the experiments with unknown compounds and with known reference samples must be exactly the same:

● the same carrier gas
● the same flow rate
● the same stationary phase
● the same temperature.

The gas chromatogram also tells us how much of each component is present in the mixture. The *area* under a component peak in the chromatogram is related to the *amount* of that component in the mixture.

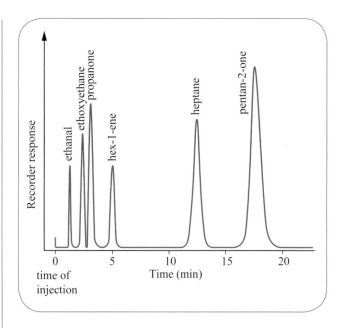

Figure 9.10 A gas chromatogram of a mixture of organic compounds.

However, analysis by gas chromatography does have some limitations. For example, similar compounds will have similar retention times and if a newly discovered compound is detected it will not have a match in the computer's database of retention times.

Determination of the percentage composition of a mixture by GC

For quantitative analysis, the component peaks are first identified and then the area of each is measured.

The peaks are roughly triangular in shape so their area is about:

$$\frac{1}{2} \times \text{base} \times \text{height}$$

(i.e. the area of a triangle).

The GC machine usually measures the area of the peak automatically and can print the results with the chromatogram. If the peaks are very narrow then *peak height* may be used instead of peak area to approximate the proportion of components in a mixture.

For this method:

- the chromatogram must show peaks for all the components in the mixture
- all the components of the mixture must be separated
- the detector must respond equally to the different components so that peak area is directly proportional to the component concentration.

The amount of each component in a mixture is found by expressing it as a percentage of the sum of the areas of all the peaks. For example, for a mixture of three ketones A, B and C:

(approximate) percentage of ketone A

$$= \frac{\text{peak area (or height) of A} \times 100}{\text{sum of the areas (or heights) of A, B and C}}$$

GC is used in testing for steroids in competing athletes and for testing the fuels used in Formula One motor racing (Figure 9.11). It is also used for medical purposes where it is possible to determine the percentages of dissolved oxygen, nitrogen, carbon dioxide and carbon monoxide in blood samples as small as $1\,cm^3$.

Figure 9.11 A Formula One car being refuelled. GC is used to test the fuel, checking that the amounts of various additives and performance-enhancing compounds are within allowed limits.

SAQ

4 For GC separations explain:
   a how retention time is measured;
   b how the areas under the component peaks are used.

   Answer

5 What can you use to approximate the proportion of a component in a mixture from a GC chromatogram which produces sharp peaks?

   Answer

High-performance liquid chromatography (HPLC)

When we want to separate small samples of *non-volatile* substances and find out how much of each component is present, we use high-performance liquid chromatography (HPLC), also referred to as high-pressure liquid chromatography. This is an improved form of the original chromatography method used to separate plant pigments.

It is similar to GC, except that the mobile phase is a liquid that moves under high pressure through a column containing the stationary phase. The chromatogram produced resembles a GC chromatogram in the information it gives us. UK Sport use the technique to detect the presence of the stimulant caffeine in competing athletes (Figure 9.12).

Figure 9.12 HPLC is used to test the urine of athletes for banned compounds such as steroids and stimulants such as caffeine.

SAQ

6   A gas chromatogram of the alcohols found in the space above the beer in a beer can showed the presence of ethanol, butan-1-ol, methanol and 2-methylbutan-1-ol (Figure 9.13 and Table 9.1).

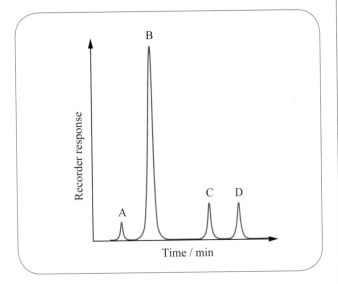

Figure 9.13 A gas chromatogram of the vapour found above the beer in a beer can.

Alcohol	Peak areas (arbitrary units)
A	50
B	500
C	100
D	100

Table 9.1

a   Suggest which peak on the chromatogram was formed by each alcohol.

  Hint

b   Determine the approximate percentage composition of each alcohol in the mixture of alcohols.

  Answer

Gas chromatography–mass spectrometry (GC-MS)

Another way of identifying the separated solutes as they emerge from the column is by linking the GC apparatus directly to a mass spectrometer. The mass spectrum of a substance is like a fingerprint – the heights and distribution of the peaks in the mass spectrum will identify a substance (see *Chemistry 1*, Chapter 15). Figure 9.14 shows a typical mass spectrum.

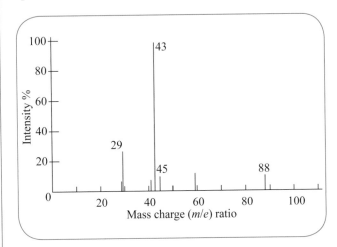

Figure 9.14 This is the mass spectrum of ethyl ethanoate. Its characteristic mass spectrum can be used to identify this compound. Its relative molecular mass is given by the molecular ion peak at 88.

GC-MS is very sensitive, and any two solutes that can be separated with a time gap of *one second* on a GC column can be identified almost instantly by the mass spectrometer without first being collected. Identification is by comparison with the mass spectra of known compounds, using a computer's spectral database. The data generated is complex, as there can be many components in a mixture, each with a peak at its particular retention time on the chromatogram, and each peak will generate its own characteristic series of lines in the mass spectrometer. We can combine the chromatogram and the mass spectra to display the data on a 3D graph (Figure 9.15).

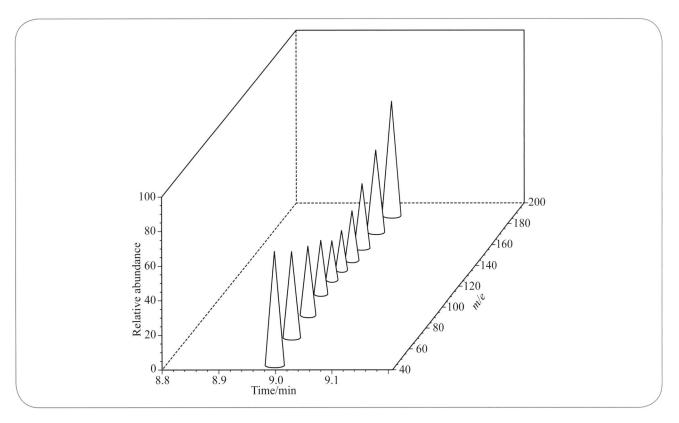

Figure 9.15 The *x*-axis shows retention time, the *y*-axis the amounts and the *z*-axis the charge/mass ratio of the mass spectra. This 3D representation shows the peaks on a mass spectrum for one component in the gas chromatogram.

SAQ

7 Look at Figure 9.15.

   a What is the retention time of the compound shown?

      [Hint]

   b What is the approximate relative molecular mass of the compound shown?

      [Hint]

   c How would the compound be identified?

      [Hint]

      [Answer]

GC-MS is used for analysing complex mixtures, for example for identifying the hydrocarbons in a sample of crude oil. Its fast, reliable results are also ideal for use in forensics, environmental analysis and airport security. It has even been used on space probes to analyse rocks on Mars.

An interesting example of the use of the combined technique of GC and mass spectrometry in forensic science is the case of a husband who killed his wife while she was a patient in hospital. He poisoned her with cyanide and then had her body cremated. However, the police found strands of the victim's hair on a hospital pillow and detected cyanide in the hair follicles. This led to a criminal conviction.

Summary

Glossary

- Chromatography separates mixtures of substances for identification.

- In chromatography, the mobile phase moves the components of a mixture through or over the stationary phase. Separation occurs by the transfer of the components to the stationary phase either by:
  - partition between two liquids (due to the different solubilities of solutes in the mobile phase and in the stationary phase),
  - partition between a gas and a liquid or
  - adsorption on to a solid surface.

- The stationary phase may be solid or liquid; the mobile phase may be liquid or gas.

- In paper and thin-layer chromatography (TLC) the components of a mixture are identified by their R_f values.

- In gas chromatography (GC) the components of a mixture are identified by their retention times; the amount of each component is found by measuring the area of each peak (estimates can be made from peak heights).

- Gas chromatography–mass spectrometry (GC-MS) provides a more powerful tool for identifying the components in a mixture than GC alone (compounds can have similar retention times but can be 'fingerprinted' by their unique mass spectra).

- GC-MS is used in airport security checks, the petroleum and food industries, and in forensic and medical testing.

Questions

1 a *In this question, one mark is available for the quality of written communication.*
      Describe how the components in a mixture of volatile liquids may be separated
      and analysed using gas–liquid chromatography. You may use a diagram to help
      with your description.   [5]
      Quality of written communication   [1]
   b State what is meant by the following terms used in chromatography.
      i R_f value   [1]
      ii retention time.   [1]

OCR Chemistry A2 (2815/04) January 2004   [Total 8]

Answer

2 a Thin-layer chromatography relies on a different physical process from paper chromatography.
      i   Identify this process.   [1]
      ii Give <u>two</u> advantages of thin-layer chromatography over paper chromatography.   [2]

continued

b The diagram shows the print-out from a gas–liquid chromatography analyser.

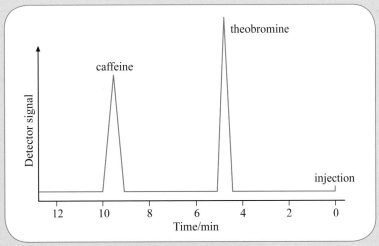

i Which component is held <u>least</u> strongly on the column? [1]

ii Calculate the percentage of this component in the mixture. [2]

iii Suggest why gas–liquid chromatography is <u>not</u> generally a suitable technique for analysing mixtures of dyes. [1]

OCR Chemistry A2 (2815/04) January 2002 [Total 7]

Hint

Answer

3 Chromatography is the name given to a range of techniques which may be used to separate mixtures. The techniques use the principles of partition and adsorption.

a Using gas–liquid chromatography as an example, state clearly what is meant by the following terms.

i mobile phase [1]

ii stationary phase [1]

b The diagram shows the output from a gas chromatograph. Determine the percentage of each component in the mixture.

Hint

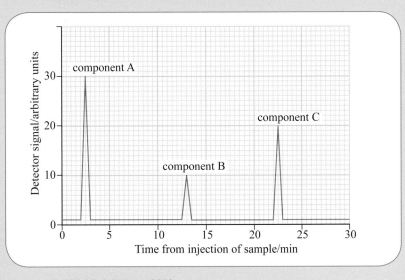

[3]

OCR Chemistry A2 (2815/04) January 2003 [Total 5]

Answer

Chapter 10

Spectroscopy

e-Learning

Objectives

Chemists now have a wide range of instrumental methods available for identifying the structure of a compound. In *Chemistry 1*, Chapter 15, you met two of these methods, mass spectrometry and infrared spectroscopy. You saw how we can use mass spectrometry to determine the structure of unknown organic compounds and how infrared spectroscopy is used to identify the functional groups –OH and >C=O in simple organic compounds such as alcohols or carboxylic acids. Another important method, known as NMR, is discussed in the following sections.

Nuclear magnetic resonance spectroscopy

Nuclear magnetic resonance spectroscopy (NMR spectroscopy) is a particularly powerful tool for finding out the structure of an organic compound.

NMR spectroscopy was developed from work by both chemists and nuclear physicists. The technique relies on the interaction between the magnetic properties of certain nuclei and their chemical environment. Some nuclei (those with odd mass numbers such as ^1H and ^{13}C) have a property called 'spin' (like electrons). This spin gives the nuclei magnetic properties so that they behave like very small bar magnets.

When a sample of a compound containing such nuclei is placed in a large magnetic field, and subjected to a pulse of radiofrequency radiation, some of the nuclei will absorb energy. NMR spectroscopy is the analysis of the spectra of energies absorbed by different nuclei. The energy involved is small, in the low-energy radiowave range of the electromagnetic spectrum.

In the following section we shall focus on the use of proton NMR spectroscopy. This technique enables the positions of protons (hydrogen nuclei, ^1H) in a compound to be determined.

Figure 10.1 Samples dissolved in a solvent, ready to place in the NMR spectrometer.

Choosing a solvent

The sample tested is often dissolved in a solvent to obtain its NMR spectrum (Figure 10.1).

The nuclei of any ^1H atoms (protons) in the molecules of a solvent will interact with the magnetic field applied in the NMR spectrometer and complicate the spectrum. For this reason CCl_4, which contains no H atoms and so doesn't produce an NMR spectrum of its own, or $CDCl_3$ can be chosen as the solvent. $CDCl_3$ is called a *deuterated solvent* as its hydrogen atoms have been replaced by deuterium atoms. Deuterium (D) is an isotope of hydrogen, ^2H. Remember that NMR only works with atoms whose mass number is an odd number, so using $CDCl_3$ as a solvent will not interfere with the NMR spectrum of the sample.

SAQ

1 Ethanol is commonly used as a solvent in chemistry. Why isn't it used to prepare a sample for an NMR spectrometer?

Hint

Answer

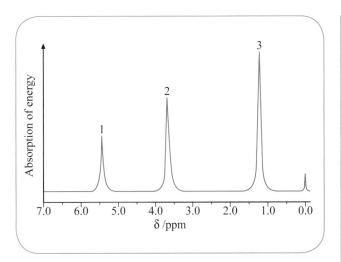

Figure 10.2 Low-resolution NMR spectrum of ethanol.

Low-resolution NMR

A low-resolution NMR spectrum of ethanol consists of three lines, as shown in Figure 10.2.

You will notice several features in this spectrum.

- Unusually, the horizontal scale increases from right to left.
- The scale is labelled in terms of chemical shift, δ/ppm.
- The small peak at 0 ppm is due to a compound, tetramethylsilane (TMS), whose formula is $(CH_3)_4Si$. This is used as a reference standard as it produces one sharp peak, given the δ value of 0 ppm, on an NMR spectrum.

- The spectrum consists of three sharp peaks. The numbers at the top of each peak show the relative areas of the peaks. The relative numbers of each type of proton are shown by relative peak areas. This can also be shown on a print-out of the spectrum by a stepped line called an **integration trace**. The height of each step corresponds to the relative numbers of each type of proton in the sample tested (Figure 10.3).

Ethanol has protons in three different chemical environments.

Look at the structural formula of ethanol, CH_3CH_2OH. There are:

- three protons on the first carbon
- two protons on the second carbon
- one proton on the oxygen atom.

Each atom has different neighbours and so has a different chemical environment.

Notice that the numbers 3 : 2 : 1 correspond to the relative peak areas in the NMR spectrum of ethanol (Figure 10.2 and Figure 10.3).

- The peak at a chemical shift of about 1.2 ppm is due to the $-CH_3$ protons.
- The peak at about 3.7 ppm is due to the $-CH_2-$ protons.
- The peak at about 5.4 ppm is due to the $-OH$ proton.

So for ethanol, a low-resolution NMR spectrum confirms the structure.

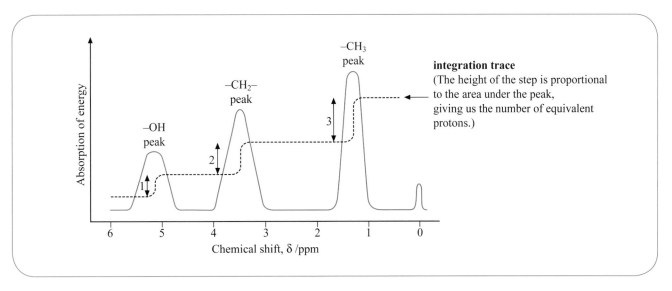

Figure 10.3 An integration trace tells us the relative areas under each peak and hence the number of equivalent hydrogen atoms (protons) in a sample.

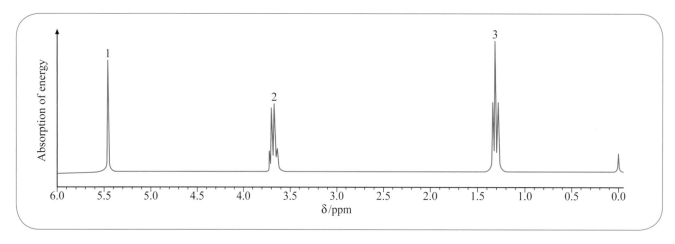

Figure 10.4 High-resolution NMR spectrum of ethanol.

High-resolution NMR

It is not always so easy to establish a structure from a low-resolution spectrum. Indeed, such spectra are not usually recorded. More information can be obtained from a high-resolution spectrum, as we shall see. The high-resolution spectrum of ethanol is shown in Figure 10.4.

Notice that there are still three main groups of peaks. Their areas are also in the same ratio as in a low-resolution spectrum. However, two of the peaks are split. The $-CH_3$ peak is split into three (a triplet), whilst the $-CH_2-$ peak is split into four (a quartet). This is called spin–spin splitting. It is caused by spins of protons on adjacent carbon atoms interacting with each other. Protons on the same carbon atom are equivalent and do not affect each other.

There is a general rule for predicting the number of signals in the *spin–spin splitting* pattern of protons on a carbon atom caused by protons on an adjacent carbon. It is known as the $n+1$ rule, where n is the number of protons on the adjacent carbon.

Hence for a $-CH-$ proton on an adjacent C atom, $n = 1$ so $n + 1 = 2$, and a doublet (two peaks) is produced. For $-CH_2-$ on an adjacent C atom, $n + 1 = 3$ so a triplet is formed, and for $-CH_3$, a quartet is produced.

SAQ

2 a How many peaks would you   ⟨ Hint ⟩
expect to see on a low-resolution NMR spectrum of propanal, CH_3CH_2CHO? Explain your answer.

b Use the $n+1$ rule to predict the   ⟨ Hint ⟩
spin–spin splitting of the $-CH_3$ peak in a high-resolution NMR spectrum of propanal.   ⟨ Answer ⟩

Interpreting high-resolution NMR

We will now look at the interpretation of an NMR spectrum. Table 10.1 provides information on the chemical shifts of different types of proton.

Let's consider an unknown molecule of molecular formula, C_2H_4O. Its NMR spectrum is shown in Figure 10.5.

The information contained in Figure 10.5 can be summarised as in Table 10.2.

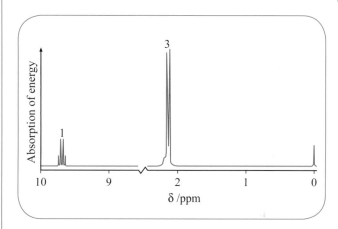

Figure 10.5 The NMR spectrum of an unknown molecule, C_2H_4O.

Type of proton			Chemical shift, δ/ppm
R–CH$_3$			0.7–1.6
N–H	R–OH		1.0–5.5*
R–CH$_2$–R			1.2–1.4
R$_3$CH			1.6–2.0
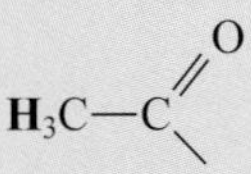 H$_3$C–C(=O)	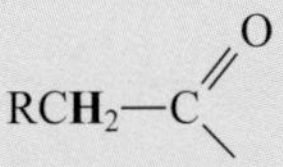 RCH$_2$–C(=O)	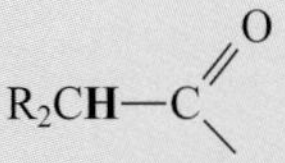 R$_2$CH–C(=O)	2.0–2.9
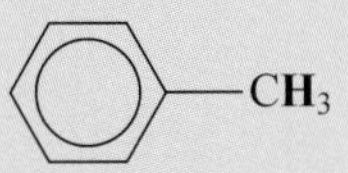 ⬡—CH$_3$	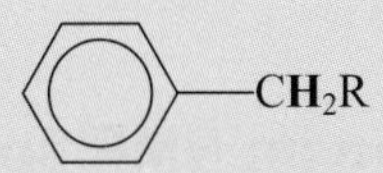 ⬡—CH$_2$R	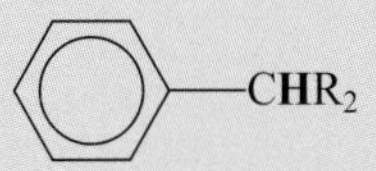 ⬡—CHR$_2$	2.3–2.7
N–CH$_3$	N–CH$_2$R	N–CHR$_2$	2.3–2.9
O–CH$_3$	O–CH$_2$R	O–CHR$_2$	3.3–4.3
Br or Cl–CH$_3$	Br or Cl–CH$_2$R	Br or Cl–CHR$_2$	3.0–4.2
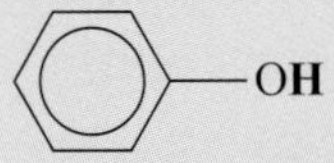 ⬡—OH			4.5–10.0*
–CH=CH–			4.5–6.0
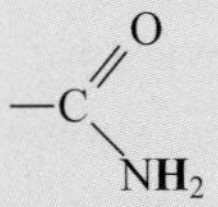 –C(=O)NH$_2$	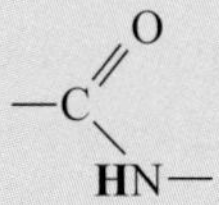 –C(=O)HN–		5.0–12.0*
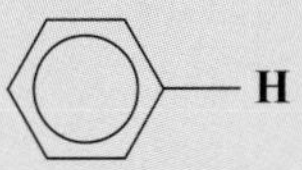 ⬡—H			6.5–8.0
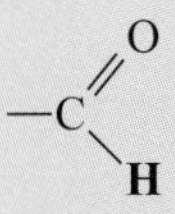 –C(=O)H			9.0–10
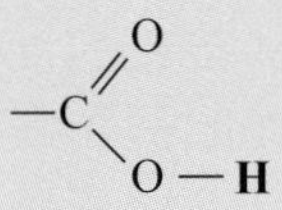 –C(=O)O—H			11.0–12.0*

Table 10.1 1H NMR chemical shifts relative to TMS.

Chemical shifts are typical values and can vary slightly depending on the solvent, concentration and substituents.

*OH and NH chemical shifts are very variable (sometimes outside these limits) and are often broad. Signals are not usually seen as split peaks.

Chemical shift, δ/ppm	Relative number of protons	Splitting pattern
2.2	3	doublet
9.8	1	quartet

Table 10.2 Summary of information from NMR spectrum shown in Figure 10.5.

From the splitting patterns given, the following can be deduced:

- to produce a quartet, the single proton at chemical shift 9.8 must be adjacent to a –CH$_3$ group.
- to produce a doublet, the three protons at chemical shift 2.2 must be adjacent to a –CH– proton.

The types of proton are shown in Table 10.3.

Chemical shift, δ/ppm	Type of proton
2.2	$\underset{}{\overset{\displaystyle O}{\overset{\displaystyle \|}{CH_3\!-\!C\!-\!R}}}$
9.8	$\underset{}{\overset{\displaystyle O}{\overset{\displaystyle \|}{R\!-\!C\!-\!H}}}$

Table 10.3 Types of proton present in C_2H_4O.

The structure of the compound is thus CH_3CHO (ethanal), which agrees with the molecular formula C_2H_4O.

SAQ

3 A compound has the molecular formula $C_4H_8O_2$. The NMR spectrum of this compound is shown in Figure 10.6. The compound shows a strong sharp absorption in its infrared spectrum at $1750\,cm^{-1}$, typical of a C=O bond.

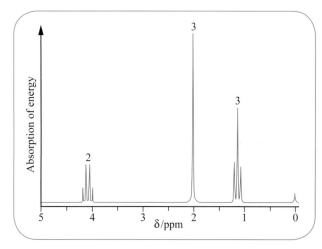

Figure 10.6 The NMR spectrum of the compound with molecular formula $C_4H_8O_2$.

a Summarise the information from the NMR spectrum in a table similar to Table 10.2. [Hint]

b From the splitting patterns, deduce which protons are on adjacent carbon atoms.

c Use Table 10.1, together with the infrared data given above, to identify the types of proton present.

d Deduce the structural formula for this compound. [Answer]

Predicting an NMR spectrum

When research chemists set out to synthesise a compound, they may predict the NMR spectrum of the desired compound. They can then compare the spectrum of the product with that of their desired compound. Computer programs are now available to make predictions of NMR spectra from chemical structures. (You will not be able to use such a program in an examination when you are asked to predict the spectrum of a simple compound. Fortunately, the process is quite straightforward for simple compounds, as the following example shows.)

Suggest the chemical shifts and splitting patterns that you might observe for butanone.

Butanone has the structure:

$$CH_3\!\!\diagdown\!\!\underset{CH_2}{}\overset{\overset{\displaystyle O}{\overset{\displaystyle \|}{C}}}{}\!\!\diagup\!\!CH_3$$

First we check Table 10.1 for the chemical shifts. Then we can create a table for our predictions (Table 10.4).

Type of proton	Chemical shift, δ/ppm	Relative number of protons	Splitting pattern
CH_3–R	0.7–1.6	3	triplet
$\overset{\displaystyle O}{\overset{\displaystyle \|}{-C-CH_3}}$	2.0–2.9	3	singlet
$\overset{\displaystyle O}{\overset{\displaystyle \|}{-C-CH_2\text{–}R}}$	2.0–2.9	2	quartet

Table 10.4 Predicting the NMR spectrum of butanone.

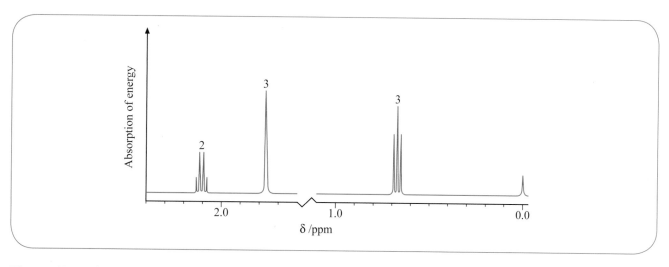

Figure 10.7 The NMR spectrum of butanone. Note that the chemical shift values differ from the predicted values. Such variation is not uncommon.

The NMR spectrum for butanone is shown in Figure 10.7.

Note that both –CH$_3$ peaks are outside the range given in Table 10.1. The ranges given in Table 10.1 may not always be appropriate. The chemical shift for a particular group of protons can be affected by factors outside the molecule, such as the solvent used to run the spectrum, the concentration or the temperature.

SAQ

4   Record in a table the chemical shifts (see Table 10.1) and splitting patterns for each type of proton you might observe in the high-resolution proton NMR of methyl propanoate, CH$_3$CH$_2$COOCH$_3$.

$\boxed{\text{Hint}}$

$\boxed{\text{Answer}}$

Identifying the –OH or –NH– signal

The –OH signal in the high-resolution NMR spectrum of ethanol appears as a single peak. You may have wondered why the signal is not split by the protons on the neighbouring –CH$_2$– group. The reason for this is that the –OH proton exchanges very rapidly with protons in any traces of water (or acid) present as follows:

$$CH_3CH_2OH + H_2O \rightleftharpoons CH_3CH_2OH + HOH$$

The hydrogen atoms involved in this reversible proton exchange have been coloured red and blue to help you to see what takes place.

This exchange is so rapid that the signal for the –OH protons becomes a single peak.

Table 10.1 shows that –OH signals range from a chemical shift of 1.0–5.5 (for R–**OH** protons) through 4.5–10.0 (for phenol protons) to 11.0–12.0 (for carboxylic acid protons). Some of these ranges overlap with the signals for other protons and can make an NMR spectrum less clear.

Fortunately, there is a simple remedy to this lack of clarity. The signal for the –OH group can be easily removed from the spectrum by adding a small amount of deuterium oxide, D$_2$O, to the NMR sample. The deuterium atoms in D$_2$O (known as 'heavy water') exchange reversibly with the protons in the –OH groups:

$$-OH + D_2O \rightleftharpoons -OD + HOD$$

Deuterium atoms (^{2}H) do not absorb in the same region of the electromagnetic spectrum as protons (^{1}H). So the –OH signal disappears from the NMR spectrum. This enables the –OH signal in the original NMR spectrum, before the D$_2$O was added, to be identified and any overlapping signals clarified.

In some organic compounds containing nitrogen, proton exchange also occurs with D$_2$O and so can be used to identify the peaks formed in NMR spectra by –NH– groups. This technique is often used when investigating peptides (which have –NH–CO– links):

$$\underset{\text{NH peak}}{-NH-CO-} + D_2O \rightleftharpoons \underset{\text{no NH peak}}{-ND-CO-} + HOD$$

The ^{1}H proton in the –OH or –NH– group is referred to as a 'labile' proton – these can be readily identified using D_2O in high-resolution NMR.

SAQ

5 Look back to Figure 10.4 on page 84. The high-resolution NMR spectrum was produced from a sample of ethanol containing traces of water. What difference would you see in the NMR spectrum using D_2O as a solvent?

Answer

Carbon-13 NMR spectroscopy

As well as proton NMR, carbon-13 NMR is another analytical tool frequently used by organic chemists. The vast majority of the carbon atoms in any organic compound will be carbon-12, which has an even mass number and as such is unsuitable for analysis by NMR. However, about 1% of the carbon atoms will be the carbon-13 isotope, which will interact with a magnetic field and can produce an NMR spectrum.

Carbon-13 NMR produces a spectrum with different chemical shifts for non-equivalent carbon atoms in a molecule. Typical ^{13}C NMR chemical shifts are shown in Table 10.5. As in proton NMR, the chemical shifts are measured with reference to the TMS peak at 0 ppm on any spectrum (see page 83).

The analysis of the ^{13}C NMR spectra is similar to proton NMR, looking to match peaks to characteristic chemical shifts. However, in carbon-13 NMR, spectra are often shown as single lines (without the complicated splitting patterns caused by protons from ^{1}H atoms in the molecules). The heights of the lines are *not* usually proportional to the number of equivalent ^{13}C atoms in the molecules.

Let's consider a few examples of ^{13}C NMR spectra. The solvent used is $CDCl_3$, so the small signal near 80 ppm can be ignored as it shows the carbon atom in the solvent. Figure 10.8 shows the spectrum for propanone, $(CH_3)_2CO$.

Notice that there are only two peaks: one for the C atom in the carbonyl group (C=O) and one for the C in –CH$_3$. Although there are two –CH$_3$ groups, they are both equivalent and so appear as only one peak (just as equivalent H atoms do in proton NMR).

Type of carbon	Chemical shift, δ/ppm
C–C (alkanes)	5–55
C–C with =O	20–30
C–Cl or **C–Br**	30–70
C–N (amines)	35–60
C–O	50–70
aromatic	110–165
C=C (alkenes)	115–140
carbonyl (ester, carboxylic acid, amide)	160–185
carbonyl (aldehyde, ketone)	190–220

Table 10.5 ^{13}C NMR chemical shifts relative to TMS. Notice that their values cover a much wider range than those for proton NMR.

Chemical shifts are typical values and can vary slightly depending on the solvent, concentration and substituents.

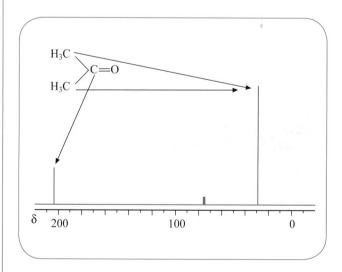

Figure 10.8 The carbon-13 NMR spectrum of propanone.

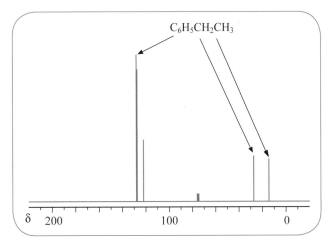

$C_6H_5CH_2CH_3$

δ 200   100   0

Figure 10.9 The carbon-13 NMR spectrum of ethylbenzene.

Figure 10.9 shows another example, that of ethylbenzene, $C_6H_5C_2H_5$.

The carbon atoms in the benzene ring are almost equivalent but will be affected to slightly different extents by the ethyl group. Hence the series of lines clustered at about 125 ppm.

SAQ

6 Look at the series of lines clustered at about 125 ppm in Figure 10.9. One line is separated slightly from the main grouping – which carbon atom do you think produced that signal?

[Hint]

[Answer]

Magnetic resonance imaging (MRI)

MRI scanners have been in use in hospitals since the 1980s. A patient is placed inside the scanner, within a large coil used to create a powerful magnetic field (Figure 10.10).

The scanner works using the same technology and principles as an NMR spectrometer, with the nuclei of ^1H atoms in water interacting with the magnetic field and radiowave pulses of energy.

This amazing medical breakthrough enables doctors to look at 2D images across any plane through the body (Figure 10.11). A computer can build these up to make incredibly detailed 3D internal images of the body.

MRI scanning has no known side-effects and so is a safer option than using harmful X-rays for imaging the body. However, it costs a hospital a lot more money to buy and maintain an MRI scanner than a traditional CT scanner that uses X-rays.

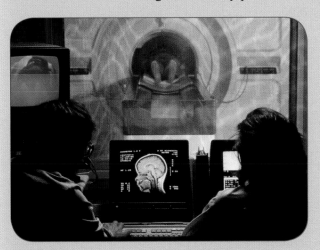

Figure 10.10 A patient has to stay perfectly still inside an MRI scanner for anything from 20 minutes to over 90 minutes.

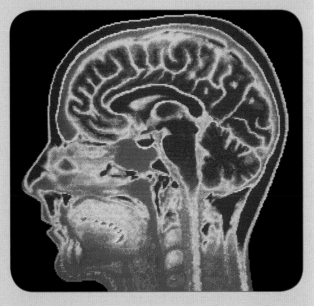

Figure 10.11 The image from an MRI scanner enables doctors to 'see' what is happening inside the body.

SAQ

7 Predict the carbon-13 NMR spectrum of benzene.

Hint

Answer

8 Explain the number of signal peaks you would expect to see in a carbon-13 NMR spectrum of:
a propan-1-ol
b propan-2-ol.

Answer

Combined techniques

You will have noticed by now that the interpretation of spectra from instrumental analysis involves using reference data that often overlap and can vary from molecule to molecule, with ranges quoted (as opposed to specific values). That is why chemists will often use more than one technique when investigating a compound. Combining techniques involves recognising the important features of each spectrum and fitting the information together like the pieces of a jigsaw puzzle.

The contribution that each type of spectrum can make to our knowledge of a compound can be summarised as follows.

Mass spectrometry
(see *Chemistry 1*, Chapter 15, and *Chemistry 2*, Chapter 9)
- Accurate molecular mass from the molecular ion peak.
- Possible structure from the fragmentation pattern.
- The identity of the compound by 'fingerprinting' using a computer database.

Extension

Infrared spectroscopy
(see Table 10.6, and *Chemistry 1*, Chapter 15)
- The presence of functional groups from the wavenumbers of the absorption bands found in the region between $1500 \, cm^{-1}$ and $3500 \, cm^{-1}$.
- The identity of the compound using the 'fingerprint' region ($700–1500 \, cm^{-1}$), by comparison with spectra of known compounds.

Extension

Nuclear magnetic resonance
(see Table 10.2 and Table 10.5)
- The identity of chemical groups containing protons from chemical shift in proton NMR spectra.
- The arrangement of proton-containing groups in the molecule from the spin–spin splitting pattern.
- The identity of non-equivalent carbon atoms from chemical shift in carbon-13 NMR spectra.

Suggesting a structure
It is not always necessary to record and interpret all three spectra to identify and to suggest a structure for an unknown compound.

In infrared spectra, the O–H stretching absorption bands are broad because of hydrogen bonding. They will only appear as sharp peaks if the sample is in dilute solution or in the vapour phase.

Example
The three spectra from an unknown compound, 'A', are shown in Figure 10.12.

Bond	Location	Wavenumber/cm^{-1}
C–O	alcohols, esters, carboxylic acids	1000–1300
C=O	aldehydes, ketones, carboxylic acids, esters, amides	1640–1750
O–H	hydrogen-bonded in carboxylic acids	2500–3300 (very broad)
C–H	alkanes, alkenes, arenes	2850–3100
N–H	amines, amides	3200–3500
O–H	hydrogen-bonded in alcohols, phenols	3200–3550 (broad)
O–H	free	3580–3670

Table 10.6 Characteristic ranges for infrared absorption due to stretching vibrations in organic molecules.

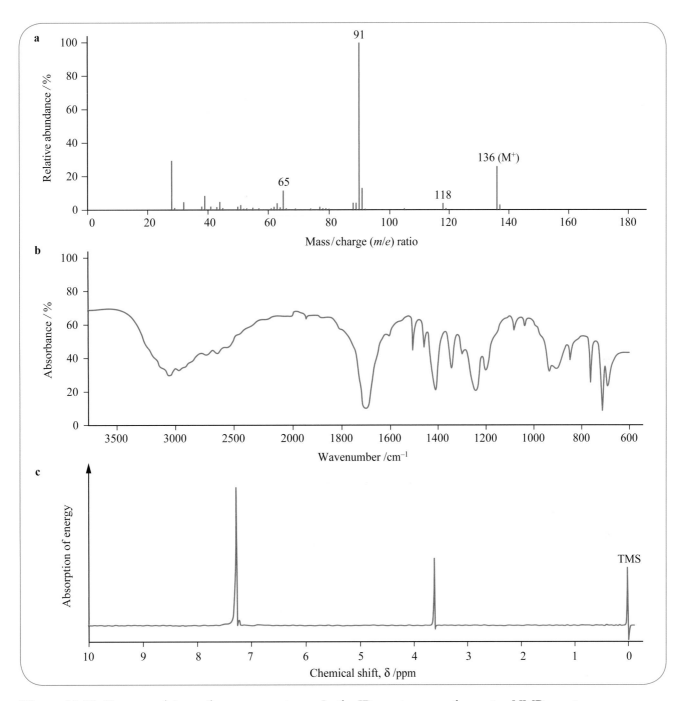

Figure 10.12 Compound A: **a** the mass spectrum; **b** the IR spectrum; **c** the proton NMR spectrum. Elemental analysis of A gave the following results: C, 70.7%; H, 6.0%; O, 23.3%.

	C	**H**	**O**
Percentage by mass	70.7	6.0	23.3
Amount/mol	$\dfrac{70.7}{12.0} = 5.89$	$\dfrac{6.0}{1.0} = 6.0$	$\dfrac{23.3}{16.0} = 1.46$
Divide by the smallest number (in this case 1.46) to give whole numbers of atoms per molecule	4	4	1

Table 10.7 Working out the empirical formula of A.

The IR spectrum shows an absorption band at $\sim 1700\,cm^{-1}$, which indicates the presence of a C=O bond. The broad band at 2500 to $3300\,cm^{-1}$ indicates the presence of an –OH group in a carboxylic acid.

The composition by mass of the elements is useful at this stage. You saw in *Chemistry 1*, Chapter 2, how the empirical formula of a compound is calculated from this information. The empirical formula is worked out in Table 10.7.

The empirical formula of A is therefore C_4H_4O, and the empirical formula mass is $M_r = 68.0$.

The mass spectrum shows that $M = 136$ (i.e. 2×68). Therefore, the molecular formula is $C_8H_8O_2$. This is a highly unsaturated molecule (the saturated hydrocarbon with eight carbon atoms is C_8H_{18}), which suggests the presence of a benzene ring.

Molecules that could fit this data are:

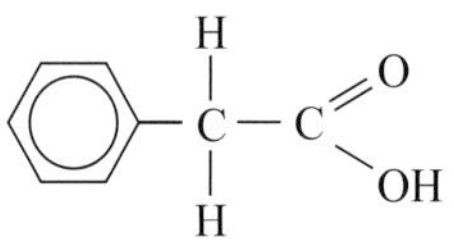

or one of the forms of:

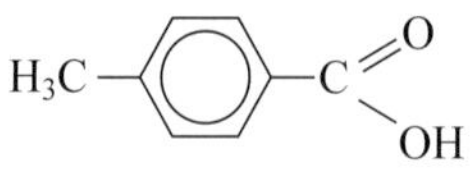

(i.e. 1,2-, 1,3- or 1,4-)

The mass spectrum shows a large peak at $m/e = 91$, but this could represent either of the the fragment ions $[C_6H_5CH_2]^+$ or

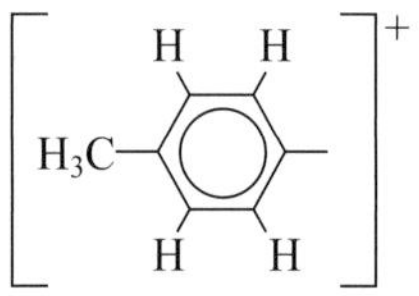

The proton NMR spectrum shows a single peak at $\delta = 7.3$, which indicates a phenyl group, and the single peak at $\delta = 3.7$ suggests the presence of a –CH_2– group. Neither of these peaks is split, so the proton groups are not adjacent.

If 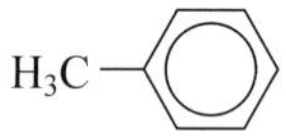 were present in the molecule, a peak would be expected at $\delta = \sim 2.3$. This peak is not found, so the compound is phenylethanoic acid:

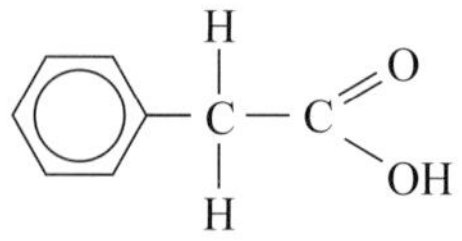

Further confirmation may be obtained by comparing one of the spectra with that obtained from a pure sample of phenylethanoic acid ('fingerprinting').

Confirmation of a structure

You can see from this example that, while all the spectra contribute in some way to the analysis of the compound, the evidence from one or two techniques can hold the key to solving the problem. With compound A, the final choice of structure was based on the evidence from the proton NMR spectrum.

In many cases, it is important to recognise what further evidence is required to confirm the structure of a compound. For example, in the analysis of a hydrocarbon that has two isomers, the infrared spectrum will only show absorptions due to C–H bonds. The mass spectrum will give the relative molecular mass and the fragmentation pattern may indicate the most likely structure. But to confirm a structure, a proton NMR spectrum would be required.

SAQ

9 Suggest, with reasons, which spectroscopic techniques would be essential to identify and find the structures of the following compounds.
   a $CH_3CH_2CH_2COOH$
   b CH_3COOCH_3
   c

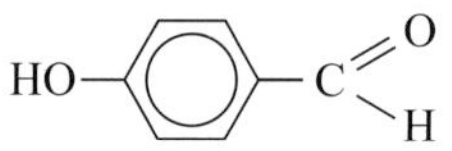

Answer

Summary

Glossary

- The proton NMR spectrum of a compound provides detailed information about the structure of the compound. In particular, the spectrum for the protons, ^1H, in a compound can provide a complete determination of the compound's structure.

- Protons in different chemical environments produce signals at different chemical shifts. The chemical shift provides information about the type of proton present.

- The area ratios of the signals (or heights of the steps in an integration trace) correspond to the numbers of protons in the different chemical environments.

- Protons on neighbouring carbon atoms cause signals to be split. The splitting pattern establishes which groups of protons are on adjacent carbon atoms. The $n+1$ rule predicts the splitting pattern.

- Protons on –OH and –NH– can be identified by the addition of D_2O to the NMR sample, which collapses the peak due to an –OH or an –NH– proton.

- A simple carbon-13 NMR spectrum can tell us the number of different types of (non-equivalent) carbon atoms in a compound. We can also match the signals against known chemical shifts for carbon atoms in different molecular environments.

- The infrared spectrum of a compound enables the presence of different functional groups to be established. Groups such as >C=O or –OH absorb radiation at different frequencies in the infrared range. In infrared spectroscopy, frequency is measured in units of cm^{-1} (called wavenumbers).

- The mass spectrum of a compound enables the relative molecular mass of the compound to be determined using the molecular ion peak. The molecular ion peak, M, is the peak produced by the loss of one electron from a molecule of the compound.

- Infrared, nuclear magnetic resonance and mass spectra are all used in the analysis of organic compounds. Frequently, it is not possible to establish an identity or structure from one technique alone.

- The compounds are most quickly and easily analysed by combining the three techniques. This is because the information provided by one spectrum may fill the gaps in information from another. The various spectra complement one another.

Questions

1 Here is the structure of lactic acid:

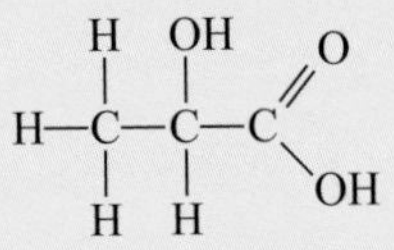

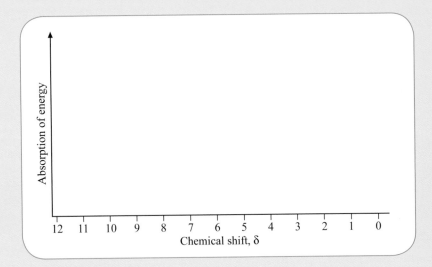

Lactic acid produces an NMR spectrum in D_2O with peaks at chemical shift values of 1.4 ppm and 4.3 ppm.

a Copy the axes below and sketch on the axes the high-resolution NMR spectrum of lactic acid in D_2O. Show any splitting patterns and state the relative areas of the two peaks. [4]

b How many peaks would you expect if the NMR spectrum of lactic acid was run in an inert solvent rather than in D_2O? Explain your answer. [2]

OCR Chemistry A2 (2814) June 2006 [Total 6]

Hint

Answer

2 a State a spectroscopic method that could be used to confirm that a sample of ester **D** has a molecular mass of 130. Explain how you would obtain the molecular mass of **D** from the spectrum. [2]

b *In this question, one mark is available for the quality of the use and organisation of scientific terms.*
Describe and explain the different ways that a high-resolution NMR spectrum can give information about a molecule. [7]
Quality of written communication [1]

OCR Chemistry A2 (2814) June 2007 [Total 10]

Hint

Answer

continued

Use Table 10.1 (page 85) to help you answer question **3**.

3 Unknown compounds are often identified by NMR spectroscopy.
Part of the NMR spectrum of <u>butanone</u> is shown on the axes below.

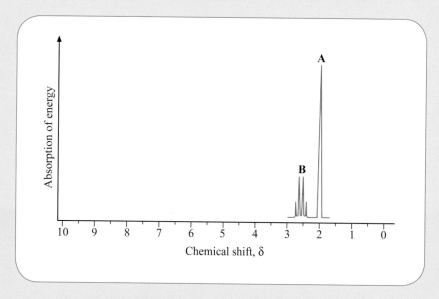

  a State which part of the butanone molecule is responsible for peak **A** at
    δ = 2.1. Explain your reasoning.   [2]
  b Explain why peak **B** is split into a quadruplet (quartet).   [1]
  c Predict the remainder of the NMR spectrum of butanone by copying the axes
    above and sketching it on the axes.   [2]
  d Write the relative peak area above each of the peaks on the completed
    spectrum of butanone.   [1]
OCR Chemistry A2 (2814) January 2007   [Total 6]

Answer

Chapter 11

How fast?

e-Learning

Objectives

In *Chemistry 1*, Chapter 17 you were introduced to the qualitative aspects of reaction rates. For example, you saw how we can use collision theory to explain the effect on reaction rate of changing concentration, pressure or temperature. Quantitative aspects were limited to making measurements during rate experiments and using the Boltzmann distribution and activation energy to explain the effect of temperature changes or catalysts on reaction rate.

A knowledge and understanding of the rate of a reaction for the production of a chemical is essential before work begins on the design of a manufacturing plant. In *Chemistry 1*, Chapter 17 you also saw how the work of Haber led to the industrial process for making ammonia.

Fast reactions

Over the past 25 years, the study of atmospheric chemistry has developed. There are many different chemical species present naturally in our atmosphere. Many more chemical species are present due to human activities. Studies of the atmosphere have shown that there is a great

Figure 11.1 The Northern Lights (*Aurora Borealis*) are the result of many complex reactions taking place in the upper atmosphere. A knowledge of reaction rates is needed to understand the natural reactions involved and how these might be disturbed by artificial emissions.

variety of reactions between these species. Many of these reactions require ultraviolet radiation. Some reactions are only possible in the upper atmosphere (Figure 11.1); others occur under the different conditions found close to the surface of the Earth.

Where the reaction rates are particularly fast, new techniques have been required to study them. Ronald Norrish and George Porter won the 1967 Nobel Prize for Chemistry, shared with Manfred Eigen. Norrish and Porter were working in Cambridge on the development of a technique to follow fast reactions.

Their technique, known as 'flash-photolysis' used a flashlight to 'freeze' reactions and observe intermediates with lifetimes of 10^{-6} to 10^{-3} s. Porter (Figure 11.2) subsequently refined the technique and developed the use of a laser to study reactions. The reaction is started by a very short, intense flash from the laser. This is very quickly followed by a second flash which allows the composition of the mixture to be studied spectroscopically.

The 1986 Nobel Prize for Chemistry went to Dudley Herschbach, Yuan Lee and John Polanyi. They used a crossed molecular beam technique to study even faster reactions, with lifetimes of intermediates in picoseconds (ps, 10^{-12} s).

continued

Figure 11.2 George Porter, who won a Nobel Prize with Ronald Norrish in 1967 for their work on measuring the rates of fast reactions.

Most recently, the Egyptian chemist Ahmed Zewail won the 1999 Nobel Prize for Chemistry for measurements of even faster reactions taking place in femtoseconds (fs, 10^{-15} s). Zewail's technique allows chemists to follow vibrations of individual bonds, which last 10–100 fs, for reactions which are complete in less than 200 fs.

SAQ

1 a Which region of the electromagnetic spectrum would enable the vibrations of individual bonds to be identified?   [Hint]

   b Write 200 fs in seconds using standard form.   [Hint] [Answer]

In this chapter you will find out about the quantitative aspects of reaction rates. In particular, you will meet the rate equation for a reaction and learn how to determine rate equations from measurements made whilst following a reaction.

You will also, like the Nobel Prize winners mentioned above, find out how a study of reaction rates leads to ideas for the intermediates present in reaction mechanisms. However, the reactions that you will study take place over several minutes rather than in split seconds!

The rate equation

The rate equation for the isomerisation of cyclopropane

A simple example of a rate equation is provided by the isomerisation of cyclopropane to propene:

$$\begin{array}{c} H_2C \\ | \quad \diagdown CH_2(g) \\ H_2C \diagup \end{array} \longrightarrow CH_3CH{=}CH_2(g)$$

cyclopropane   propene

Table 11.1 shows the changes in the concentrations of cyclopropane and propene at 500 °C. As temperature affects the rate of reaction, the measurements in Table 11.1 were all made at the same temperature.

Time/min	0	5	10	15	20	25	30	35	40
[cyclopropane]/mol dm^{-3}	1.50	1.23	1.00	0.82	0.67	0.55	0.45	0.37	0.33
[propene]/mol dm^{-3}	0.00	0.27	0.50	0.68	0.83	0.95	1.05	1.13	1.17

Table 11.1 Concentrations of reactant (cyclopropane) and product (propene) at 5 minute intervals (temperature = 500 °C (773 K)).

Notice the square brackets [ ] round 'cyclopropane' and 'propene'. These square brackets are the symbols that chemists use to indicate concentration, in this case the concentrations of cyclopropane and of propene. More usually, the brackets will be round the formula of the chemical species, but sometimes it is more helpful to write the name of the compound.

Figure 11.3 shows a plot of the cyclopropane concentration against time, using the data from Table 11.1.

The rate of a chemical reaction can be found by dividing the change in concentration by time. (Remember: speed is distance travelled divided by time taken.) For the cyclopropane reaction, writing Δ[cyclopropane] for a change in concentration over a time interval Δt, the rate of reaction is shown by the following expression:

rate of decrease of cyclopropane concentration

$$= \frac{\Delta[\text{cyclopropane}]}{\Delta t}$$

Figure 11.3 shows a method for measuring the reaction rate for the cyclopropane reaction. A tangent is drawn at a chosen point on the graph. This is drawn

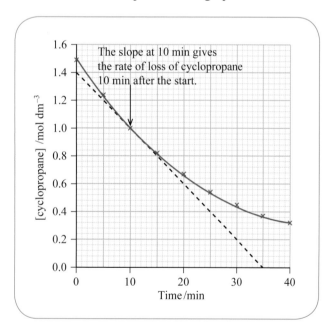

Figure 11.3 The rate of decrease of cyclopropane concentration over time as the reaction proceeds. The rate of reaction at a given time can be found by drawing a tangent and measuring its gradient.

so as to *just touch* the curve of the concentration against time plot. The two angles between the straight line and the curve should look very similar. Note that the tangent is then extended to meet the axes of the graph. By extending the tangent to the axes, we reduce the error in the measurements made from the graph.

The slope of the tangent is a measure of the rate of reaction at that time. Since the reactant concentration is decreasing, the gradient of the slope will be negative (and vice versa for increasing product concentration).

Ten minutes after the start of the reaction, the slope of the tangent is:

$$\text{slope} = \frac{0.00 - 1.40\,\text{mol dm}^{-3}}{35 \times 60\,\text{s}}$$

$$= -6.67 \times 10^{-4}\,\text{mol dm}^{-3}\,\text{s}^{-1}$$

$$= \text{rate of change of cyclopropane concentration}$$

Notice that the units for rate of reaction are (change in) concentration per second; compare them to the typical units for the speed of a runner, metres per second (m s^{-1}).

Take another look at Figure 11.3. Notice that, as time passes, the concentration of cyclopropane falls, as you would expect. The question to ask is: 'In what way does it fall?' Does it fall in a predictable way? Is there a mathematical way of describing it?

Figure 11.4 supplies some answers. We will use it to calculate the rate of reaction at different concentrations: $1.50\,\text{mol dm}^{-3}$, $1.00\,\text{mol dm}^{-3}$ and $0.50\,\text{mol dm}^{-3}$. (Again, we can measure the rate at any point on a graph by drawing the tangent to the curve and measuring its slope at that point.) The three measurements are shown in Table 11.2.

We can show the data from the table on a graph (Figure 11.5).

The data in Table 11.2 and Figure 11.5 show that the rate of the reaction depends directly upon the concentration of cyclopropane. We say that the rate is directly proportional to the concentration in this case. This means that if the concentration of cyclopropane drops to two-thirds, so does the reaction rate.

[cyclopropane]/mol dm^{-3}	1.50	1.00	0.50
Rate/mol dm^{-3} s^{-1}	1.00×10^{-3}	6.67×10^{-4}	3.30×10^{-4}
$\dfrac{\text{rate}}{\text{[cyclopropane]}}$ /s^{-1}	6.67×10^{-4}	6.67×10^{-4}	6.60×10^{-4}

Table 11.2 Rates of decrease for cyclopropane at different concentrations, calculated from Figure 11.4.

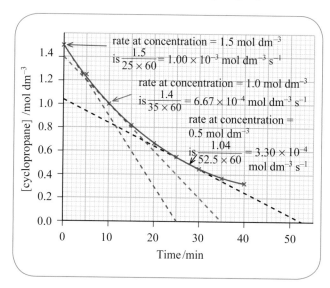

Figure 11.4 Calculation of the rate of decrease of cyclopropane concentration, made at regular intervals.

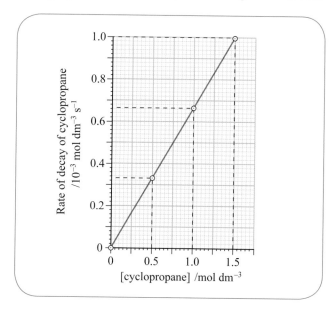

Figure 11.5 The rate of decrease of cyclopropane. Notice how the gradient (rate/concentration) is constant.

SAQ

2 Consider the cyclopropane reaction described above. What would happen to the reaction rate if the concentration of cyclopropane was halved? [Answer]

The third line in Table 11.2 shows that $\dfrac{\text{rate}}{\text{concentration}}$ is a number that is pretty well constant (between 6.60 and 6.67×10^{-4} s^{-1}). This can be expressed mathematically as:

rate of reaction $= k \times$ [cyclopropane]

The proportionality constant, k, is called the **rate constant**. For the reaction above, it has the units of rate divided by the units of concentration, which equal s^{-1}. For the data in Table 11.2, the value of the rate constant, k, is 6.6×10^{-4} s^{-1}.

SAQ

3 a Plot the data in Table 11.1 for yourself. Measure the rate after 10 minutes by drawing a tangent which is about 5 cm in length and not extended to the axes. Mark the horizontal and vertical measurements on your graph and calculate a value for the rate of reaction. Compare your value with the value given in Table 11.2. Which value do you consider to be more reliable? Explain your answer.

  b Draw two further tangents at the following cyclopropane concentrations: 1.25 and 0.75 mol dm^{-3}. Extend these tangents to meet both axes. Use the data from these measurements, together with the data in Figure 11.4 to plot your own version of Figure 11.5. Your points should also lie on, or close to, the straight line. [Answer]

More rate equations

We already have a rate equation for the isomerisation of cyclopropane:

rate = k [cyclopropane]

This rate equation was found by experiment – not by theoretical calculation.

The reaction between hydrogen gas and nitrogen monoxide, NO, at 800 °C produces water and nitrogen gas:

$$2H_2(g) + 2NO(g) \longrightarrow 2H_2O(g) + N_2(g)$$

Experiments show that doubling the concentration of hydrogen doubles the rate of reaction, tripling $[H_2]$ triples the rate, and so on. So:

rate $\propto [H_2]$ or   rate = $k_1 \times [H_2]$

Further experiments show that doubling the concentration of nitrogen monoxide quadruples the rate of reaction (2^2), tripling [NO] increases it by a factor of nine (3^2), and so on. Therefore:

rate $\propto [NO]^2$ or   rate = $k_2 \times [NO]^2$

The two equations can be combined as follows:

rate of reaction $\propto [H_2][NO]^2$

or

rate of reaction = $k_1 \times k_2 \times [H_2] \times [NO]^2$

$$= k \times [H_2] \times [NO]^2$$

which can be written as:

rate of reaction = $k[H_2][NO]^2$

More rate equations are shown in Table 11.3. They were all found by experiment. They cannot be predicted from the chemical equation.

The units for k can be different for each reaction; they must be worked out for each reaction. For example:

$k[H_2][NO]^2$ = rate of reaction in $mol\,dm^{-3}\,s^{-1}$

so k is in $\dfrac{(mol\,dm^{-3}\,s^{-1})}{(mol\,dm^{-3}) \times (mol\,dm^{-3})^2}$

i.e. k's units are $dm^6\,mol^{-2}\,s^{-1}$.

Order of reaction

The order of a reaction tells us how the concentration of a reagent affects the reaction rate. It is defined as follows: the **order of a reaction** with respect to a particular reactant is the power to which the concentration of that reactant is raised in the rate equation.

The easiest way to explain order is to use an example.

- Chemical equation:

$$2NO(g) + O_2(g) \longrightarrow 2NO_2(g)$$

- Experimental rate equation:

rate of reaction = $k[NO]^2[O_2]^1 = k[NO]^2[O_2]$

The order of the reaction as far as nitrogen monoxide (NO) is concerned is 2. It is the power of 2 in $[NO]^2$. We say the reaction is 'second order with respect to nitrogen monoxide'.

The order of reaction as far as oxygen is concerned is 1. We say the reaction is 'first order with respect to oxygen'.

The overall order of this reaction is $2 + 1 = 3$. Note how careful you should be when you talk about reaction orders. Always ask yourself the question: 'Order with respect to *what*?'

Equation for the reaction	Rate equation	Units for k
$2H_2(g) + 2NO(g) \longrightarrow 2H_2O(g) + N_2(g)$	rate = $k[H_2][NO]^2$	$dm^6\,mol^{-2}\,s^{-1}$
$H_2(g) + I_2(g) \longrightarrow 2HI(g)$	rate = $k[H_2][I_2]$	$dm^3\,mol^{-1}\,s^{-1}$
$NO(g) + CO(g) + O_2(g) \longrightarrow NO_2(g) + CO_2(g)$	rate = $k[NO]^2$	$dm^3\,mol^{-1}\,s^{-1}$

Table 11.3 Rate equations for some reactions.

SAQ

SAQ

4   What is the order of reaction for the isomerisation of cyclopropane to propene with respect to cyclopropane? What is the overall order of this reaction?

Hint

   The rate equation is
   rate of reaction = k[cyclopropane]

Answer

Zero-order reactions

Ammonia gas decomposes on a hot tungsten (W) wire:

$$2NH_3(g) \xrightarrow{W} N_2(g) + 3H_2(g)$$

By experiment, we find that the rate of decomposition does not depend upon the concentration of ammonia gas. The rate of reaction is fixed. Doubling or tripling the concentration of ammonia makes no difference to the rate at which the ammonia decomposes. Thus:

   rate of reaction = k

which can be written as:

   rate of reaction = $k[NH_3]^0$

(since any number raised to the power 0 equals 1). When a graph of rate of reaction against concentration is plotted for a zero-order reaction, a horizontal straight line is obtained, as shown in Figure 11.6.

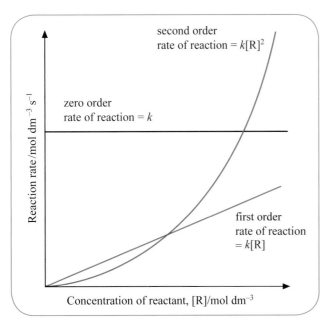

Figure 11.6 Zero-, first- and second-order reactions: how changes in the concentration of a reactant affect the reaction rate.

First-order reactions

The gas dinitrogen oxide, N_2O, decomposes on a heated gold (Au) surface:

$$2N_2O(g) \xrightarrow{Au} 2N_2(g) + O_2(g)$$

The rate of reaction depends directly upon the concentration of N_2O. If its concentration is doubled, its reaction rate also doubles. Thus:

   rate of reaction = $k[N_2O]$

which can be written as:

   rate of reaction = $k[N_2O]^1$

(since any number raised to the power 1 is unchanged). When a graph of rate of reaction against concentration is plotted for a first-order reaction, an inclined straight line is obtained, as shown in Figure 11.6.

Second-order reactions

Ethanal vapour (CH_3CHO) decomposes at 527 °C:

$$CH_3CHO(g) \longrightarrow CH_4(g) + CO(g)$$

The rate of reaction depends directly upon the square of the concentration of CH_3CHO. If its concentration is doubled, its rate of reaction quadruples. Thus:

   rate of reaction = $k[CH_3CHO]^2$

When a graph of rate of reaction against concentration is plotted for a second-order reaction, a curved line is obtained, as shown in Figure 11.6.

Concentration against time graphs

An alternative method of distinguishing between these three types is shown in Figure 11.7.

Figure 11.7 shows the differences between the concentration against time graphs for zero-, first- and second-order reactions. The zero-order graph is immediately recognisable as it is a straight line. Notice that the rate of reaction (as calculated by the slope of the line on this type of graph) does not change as the concentration of reactant changes.

Both the first- and second-order data produce a curve. In the next section you will see how we can distinguish between these curves, so we can identify a first-order reaction.

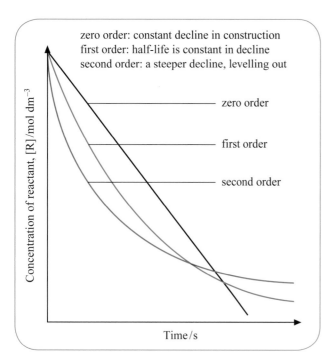

Figure within image, labelled:

zero order: constant decline in construction
first order: half-life is constant in decline
second order: a steeper decline, levelling out

zero order

first order

second order

Figure 11.7 Zero-, first- and second-order reactions: how changes in the concentration of a reactant affect the time taken for a reaction to proceed.

A generalised form of the rate equation for the reaction:

$$A + B \longrightarrow products$$

is:

rate of reaction = $k[A]^m[B]^n$

The powers m and n show the order of the reaction with respect to reactants A and B respectively, and can only be determined by experiment. The overall order of the reaction is $m + n$.

Half-life and reaction rates

In chemical reactions, the half-life ($t_{1/2}$) is the time taken for the concentration of a reactant to fall to half its original value.

A feature of a first-order reaction is that the half-life is independent of concentration. This is not true for zero- or second-order reactions. As you have just seen, a graph of *concentration against time* for a zero-order reaction produces a straight line, whereas such graphs for first- and second-order reactions are curves.

To distinguish between first-order and second-order reactions, measurements of two (or more) half-lives are made from the graph. Figure 11.8 and Table 11.4 show such measurements for the cyclopropane isomerisation reaction.

The three figures for the half-lives in Table 11.4 are quite close, producing a mean half-life for this reaction of 17.0 min. A second-order reaction shows significant increases when successive half-lives are measured in this way. A zero-order reaction shows significant decreases in half-lives.

As this book deals only with orders of 0, 1 or 2 with respect to an individual reagent, you may assume that a concentration–time curve with a half-life which increases with decreasing concentration is a second-order reaction. In general, this is not a satisfactory way of identifying a second-order reaction as orders of reaction other than 0, 1 or 2 do

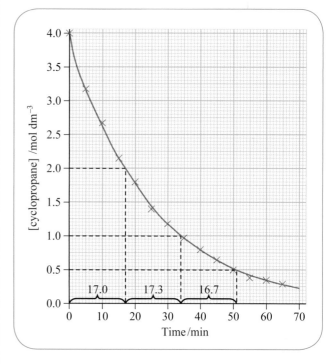

Figure 11.8 Measurement of half-life for cyclopropane isomerisation.

Δ[cyclopropane]/ mol dm^{-3}	Half-life/min
4.00 to 2.00	17.0
2.00 to 1.00	34.3 – 17.0 = 17.3
1.00 to 0.50	51.0 – 34.3 = 16.7

Table 11.4 A constant half-life indicates a first-order reaction.

exist. For example, orders of –1 and fractional orders are also known. Much less common are third-order reactions. Concentration against time graphs for these other orders may also be curves. However, you will only be expected to identify orders of 0, 1 or 2 from rate measurements.

Finding the order of reaction using raw data

We are now going to look at a more complex example. Keep clear in your mind the meanings of the terms 'rate of reaction', 'rate constant' and 'order of reaction'. You will also need to be able to work out the units you will use.

We can identify a sequence of steps in the processing of the experimental results:

- summarising the raw data in a table
- plotting a graph of raw data
- finding the rate at a particular concentration
- tabulating rate data
- plotting a graph of rate against concentration data.

Table 11.5 gives time and concentration data for the reaction of methanol with aqueous hydrochloric acid to give chloromethane and water at 298 K (25 °C):

$$CH_3OH(aq) + HCl(aq) \longrightarrow CH_3Cl(aq) + H_2O(l)$$

Figure 11.9 shows a graph of these data, and the beginnings of an exploration of the data.

Time/min	[HCl]/mol dm^{-3}	[CH$_3$OH]/mol dm^{-3}
0	1.84	1.84
200	1.45	1.45
400	1.22	1.22
600	1.04	1.04
800	0.91	0.91
1000	0.81	0.81
1200	0.72	0.72
1400	0.66	0.66
1600	0.60	0.60
1800	0.56	0.56
2000	0.54	0.54

Table 11.5 Data for the reaction between methanol and hydrochloric acid.

SAQ

5 The data in Table 11.5 could have been obtained by titrating small samples of the reaction mixture with a standard strong base. What can you find out by carrying out the titrations? How else might you monitor this reaction?

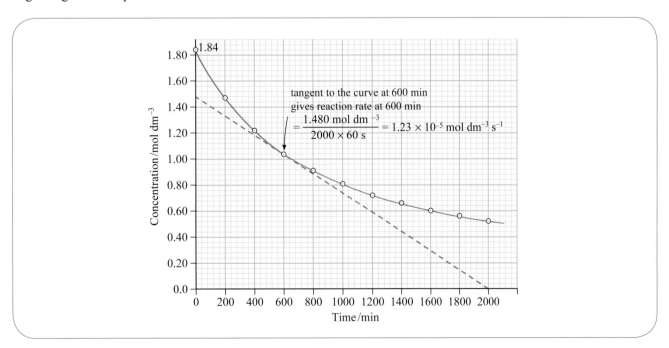

Figure 11.9 The concentration of hydrochloric acid and methanol fall at the same rate as time passes.

First look to see if there is a consistent half-life for this reaction. Half of the initial amount of each reagent is $\frac{1.84}{2}$ $mol\,dm^{-3} = 0.92\,mol\,dm^{-3}$. The first half-life from the graph is 780 min. However, this amount, $0.92\,mol\,dm^{-3}$, does not halve again in another 780 min. The second half-life (from 0.92 to $0.46\,mol\,dm^{-3}$) is off the end of the graph at around 1400–1500 min. The concentration–time graph has a long 'tail' at low concentration which is typical of a second-order reaction. The half-life increases – so the overall order of reaction is likely to be 2.

As with the previous reaction, we can draw tangents to the curve to derive approximate rates at different times. This is shown for $t = 600$ min in Figure 11.9. Other values have been calculated from these data and are shown in Table 11.6. Notice the different units used to quote the rates of reaction.

You can draw your own graph using the data in Table 11.5 to find out what results *you* obtain – they are likely to vary a bit due to the difficulty of drawing an accurate tangent by eye.

By examining the data in Table 11.6 you can see that the rate of reaction diminishes with time – unlike a zero-order reaction. A graph (Figure 11.10) shows that it most closely resembles a second-order plot (see Figure 11.6).

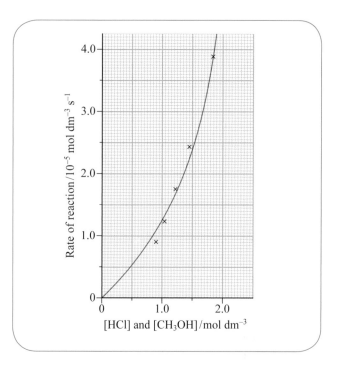

Figure 11.10 A graph showing how concentration changes of hydrochloric acid or methanol affect rate of reaction. The curve shows that the reaction is likely to be second order.

Time/min	Concentration/$mol\,dm^{-3}$	Rate from graph/ $mol\,dm^{-3}\,min^{-1}$	Rate from graph/ $mol\,dm^{-3}\,s^{-1}$
0	1.84	2.30×10^{-3}	3.83×10^{-5}
200	1.45	1.46×10^{-3}	2.43×10^{-5}
400	1.22	1.05×10^{-3}	1.75×10^{-5}
600	1.04	0.74×10^{-3}	1.23×10^{-5}
800	0.91	0.54×10^{-3}	0.90×10^{-5}

Table 11.6 Values calculated for the reaction between methanol and hydrochloric acid.

SAQ

6 Look again at the raw data in Table 11.5. Notice that the concentrations of both CH_3OH and HCl are changing.

   a Are both reactants affecting the rate or is only one reactant responsible for the data in Table 11.5?

   b Suggest how the experiment [Hint] might be re-designed to obtain data that would provide evidence for the effect of changing the HCl concentration whilst controlling the CH_3OH concentration. [Answer]

7 Further experiments have shown that the rate of this reaction is first order with respect to each of methanol, hydrogen ions and chloride ions. Suggest how these experiments could be carried out. [Answer]

The initial-rates method

We have seen that the rate of a reaction changes as the reactants are used up. For some reactions, measuring these changes over time may not be the best method for determining the rate equation. For instance, if the rate is quite slow, then obtaining a useful set of measurements would take an inconvenient amount of time.

However, we usually know the initial concentrations of the reactants that we mix together in the reaction flask, and we can measure the initial rate of reaction. (For example, look again at the graph in Figure 11.4: the rate we calculated at the concentration of 1.50 mol dm^{-3} is the initial rate.) We can carry out several experiments with different initial concentrations of reactants and measure the initial rates of these experiments. Then we can use these initial rates to determine the rate equation. The best way to illustrate this is with an example.

Dinitrogen pentoxide decomposes to nitrogen dioxide and oxygen:

$$2N_2O_5(g) \longrightarrow 4NO_2(g) + O_2(g)$$

Table 11.7 gives the values of the initial rate as it varies with the concentration of dinitrogen pentoxide.

Initial concentration, $[N_2O_5]$/mol dm^{-3}	Initial rate/ 10^{-5} mol dm^{-3} s^{-1}
3.00	3.15
1.50	1.55
0.75	0.80

Table 11.7 Data for the decomposition of dinitrogen pentoxide.

A graph of the data (Figure 11.11) shows that the initial rate of reaction is directly proportional to the initial concentration:

$$\text{rate of reaction} \propto [N_2O_5]$$
$$= k[N_2O_5]$$

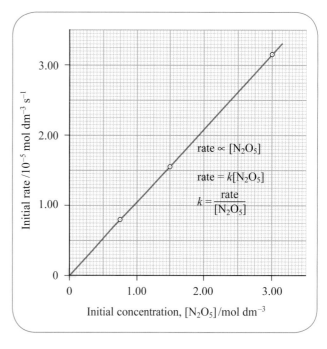

Figure 11.11 The initial rate of decomposition of dinitrogen pentoxide is directly proportional to the initial concentration.

SAQ

8 a What is the order of reaction for the decomposition of dinitrogen pentoxide?

   b Use the data for 3.00 mol dm^{-3} [Hint] N_2O_5 to calculate a value for the rate constant for this decomposition. [Answer]

Another example of the use of initial rates is provided by data from experiments to follow the acid-catalysed reaction of iodine with propanone:

$$CH_3COCH_3 + I_2 \xrightarrow{\ H^+\ } CH_3COCH_2I + HI$$
propanone

This reaction is readily followed using a colorimeter. The yellowish brown colour of the iodine fades as the reaction progresses.

Table 11.8 shows data obtained at 20 °C from four separate experiments to measure the initial rates of reaction.

The data are from real experiments, so we must bear in mind experimental errors. Note that in each experiment the initial concentration of just one reagent has been changed from the values used in experiment 1.

Compare experiments 1 and 2. You will see that the concentration of $H^+(aq)$ in experiment 2 is half the value of that in experiment 1. The initial rate has also been approximately halved. From this information we can deduce that the reaction is first order with respect to the acid (H^+) catalyst.

Now compare experiments 1 and 3. The propanone concentration in experiment 3 is half that in experiment 1. Again the initial rate has been approximately halved. We deduce that the reaction is first order with respect to propanone.

Finally, compare experiments 1 and 4. The iodine concentration has been halved but the initial rate stays approximately the same. We deduce that the reaction is zero order with respect to iodine.

SAQ

9 a Write the rate equation for the acid-catalysed reaction of iodine with propanone using the above deductions.

   b Calculate the rate constant for this reaction.

Rate constants and temperature changes

An increase in the temperature of a reaction mixture by 10 °C approximately doubles the rate of reaction. How can this increase in rate be explained by the rate equation?

A general form of the rate equation for the reaction of A and B to form products is:

$$\text{rate of reaction} = k\,[A]^m[B]^n$$

As temperature will not change the concentrations of A or B, the rate constant, k, must change if the reaction rate is to increase. The rate constant k remains constant if the temperature remains constant, but it varies if the temperature varies. So k is called a 'constant', but it's not!

We can predict that an increase in temperature will increase the value of k. An examination of the observed rate constants for a particular reaction over a range of temperatures confirms our prediction.

Table 11.9 shows the rate constants for the reaction of hydrogen and iodine at different temperatures. The equation for this reaction is:

$$H_2(g) + I_2(g) \longrightarrow 2HI(g)$$

Experiment	[HCl]/mol dm^{-3}	[propanone]/ 10^{-3} mol dm^{-3}	[iodine]/ 10^{-3} mol dm^{-3}	Initial rate/ 10^{-6} mol dm^{-3}
1	1.25	0.50	1.25	10.9
2	0.625	0.50	1.25	5.4
3	1.25	0.25	1.25	5.1
4	1.25	0.50	0.625	10.7

Table 11.8 Experimental results for the reaction of propanone with iodine at varying aqueous concentrations.

Temperature/K	Rate constant/dm^3 mol^{-1} s^{-1}
500	4.3×10^{-7}
600	4.4×10^{-4}
700	6.3×10^{-2}
800	2.6

Table 11.9 Rate constants for the reaction of hydrogen and iodine over a range of temperatures.

The rate equation is:

rate of reaction = k [H$_2$(g)][I$_2$(g)]

(However, remember that there is no correspondence between the balanced chemical equation for the reaction and its rate equation. We certainly cannot predict the rate equation from the balanced chemical equation. We can only work out the rate equation using data from experiments.)

Rate equations and mechanisms

Chemists are particularly interested in the mechanisms of chemical reactions. They want to find out which chemical bonds are broken, which are made and in what order. Such an understanding helps chemists to design the synthesis of new compounds.

Figure 11.12 A very thin film of polymer produced using a metallocene catalyst. The strength and puncture resistance are being tested using a ball-point pen.

For example, an understanding of the mechanism of polymerisation (see Chapter 7) has led to new catalysts for the polymerisation of ethene or propene. The polymers produced by the new catalysts (called metallocenes) are stronger and more tear-resistant than other polymers (see Figure 11.12). They can be used for food packaging as they are very impermeable to air and moisture.

By using the rate equation, sometimes along with other information, we can deduce something about the separate bond-making and bond-breaking processes that go to make up the overall reaction.

Some reactions may consist of a single step. For example, when aqueous sodium hydroxide is mixed with dilute hydrochloric acid, the reaction is simply one in which hydrogen ions react with hydroxide ions to form water. The other ions do not participate in the reaction – they are called spectator ions and just get left in solution:

$$Na^+(aq) + OH^-(aq) + H^+(aq) + Cl^-(aq)$$
$$\longrightarrow H_2O(l) + Na^+(aq) + Cl^-(aq)$$

Very frequently, a reaction is made up of a number of sequential steps. Each step will have a rate associated with it, but to find the overall rate of reaction, all we need to know is the rate of the *slowest* step (also called the **rate-determining step**). This is the case when all other steps are much faster. Fast steps, like selecting items off shelves in a supermarket, become insignificant when compared to the slow step, like queuing at the checkout.

We can use the rate equation to suggest a proposed reaction mechanism. If the concentration of a reactant appears in the rate equation, then that reactant, or something derived from it, takes part in the slow step (rate-determining step) of the reaction. If it does not appear in the rate equation, then neither the reactant nor anything derived from it participates in the slow step.

This is the key to using rate equations to propose mechanisms of reactions. We can now consider some of the reactions we have looked at above, in terms of what their rate equation, and other data, may tell us about their mechanism.

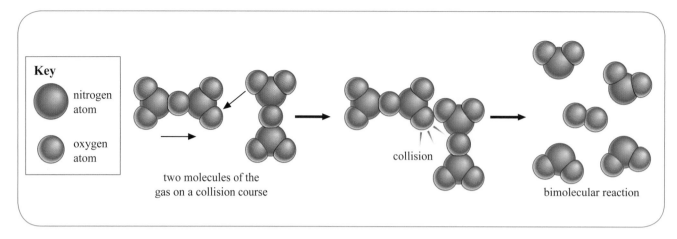

Figure 11.13 The equation for the decomposition of dinitrogen pentoxide (N_2O_5) suggests that a reaction between two molecules occurs (a bimolecular reaction). The rate equation tells us otherwise.

Reaction mechanisms

We can look again at the reaction for the decomposition of dinitrogen pentoxide:

$$2N_2O_5(g) \longrightarrow 4NO_2(g) + O_2(g)$$

You may have been surprised that this did not turn out to be a second-order reaction. The stoichiometry shows that two molecules of dinitrogen pentoxide are needed to balance the equation. So we can imagine that the reaction might start by two N_2O_5 molecules colliding and breaking up, as suggested in the mechanism shown in Figure 11.13.

But the rate equation tells us something different.

$$\text{rate of reaction} = k[N_2O_5]$$

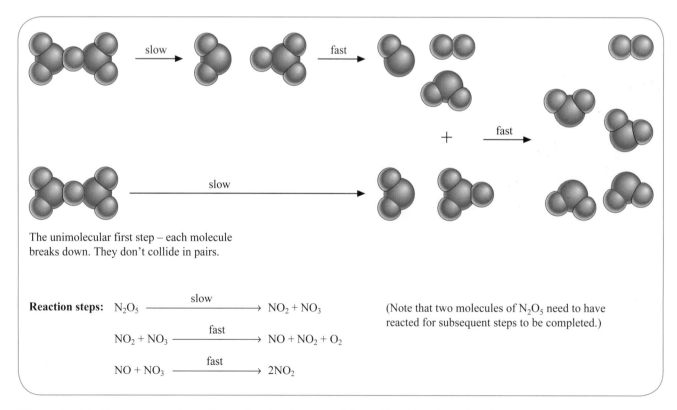

The unimolecular first step – each molecule breaks down. They don't collide in pairs.

Reaction steps:

$$N_2O_5 \xrightarrow{\text{slow}} NO_2 + NO_3$$

$$NO_2 + NO_3 \xrightarrow{\text{fast}} NO + NO_2 + O_2$$

$$NO + NO_3 \xrightarrow{\text{fast}} 2NO_2$$

(Note that two molecules of N_2O_5 need to have reacted for subsequent steps to be completed.)

Figure 11.14 The rate equation tells us that the decomposition of individual molecules of dinitrogen pentoxide is the rate-determining step. The subsequent reactions are very much faster by comparison, and do not influence the overall rate. Try to match the reaction steps with the illustrations to get a picture of what is happening.

The rate equation tells us that the slow step (the rate-determining step) of the reaction involves *one* molecule of dinitrogen pentoxide decomposing (to give nitrogen dioxide and nitrogen trioxide). This can be described as a unimolecular reaction – since only one chemical species is involved in the rate-determining step. In this case it is the first step. The subsequent steps are comparatively fast. The actual mechanism of this reaction is shown in Figure 11.14. The first step of the reaction is the slow step.

Now let's look at the acid-catalysed reaction of propanone with iodine:

$$CH_3COCH_3 + I_2 \xrightarrow{H^+} CH_3COCH_2I + HI$$

It appears that hydrogen ions from the acid are not directly involved. Either they are not used up or they are regenerated with the products, at the same rate as they are used up. In either case, the hydrogen ions behave as a catalyst.

The rate equation sheds some light on this (also see page 106). It is:

rate of reaction = $k[CH_3COCH_3]^1[H^+]^1[I_2]^0$

Therefore, the rate-determining step must involve propanone and hydrogen ions (but not iodine). The concentration of iodine does not need to be included in the rate equation as iodine does not participate in the rate-determining step – the reaction is zero order with respect to iodine.

The mechanism of the reaction is given in Figure 11.15. Notice that the slow step (rate-determining step) does not involve either propanone or hydrogen ions directly, but *something more rapidly derived from them both*, protonated propanone. Iodine comes in later in the sequence, in what must be a subsequent fast step.

We can picture the reaction sequence as follows. The propanone exists in equilibrium with its protonated form (we shall discuss something more of acid–base equilibria in Chapter 13). Every now and then one of these protonated molecules decomposes to lose H^+, not from the oxygen atom but from carbon, to yield the intermediate:

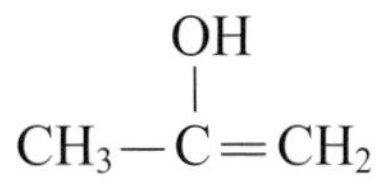

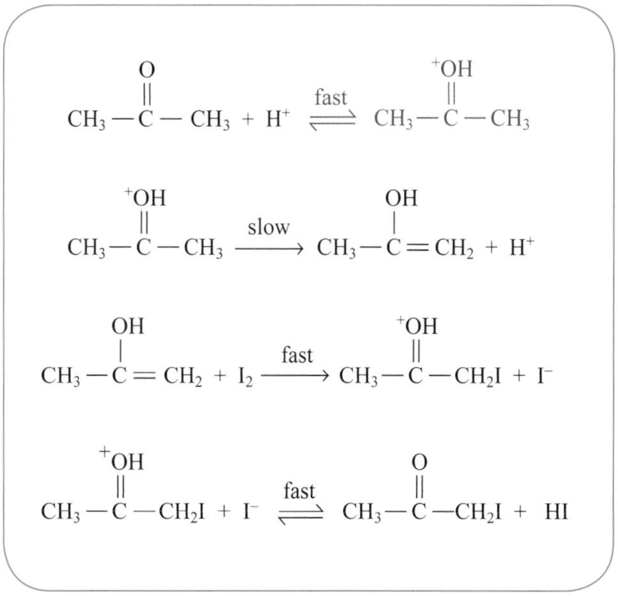

$$\underset{\displaystyle CH_3-C=CH_2}{\overset{\displaystyle OH}{}}$$

Figure 11.15 Propanone molecules rapidly accept hydrogen ions to form an intermediate that slowly forms propen-2-ol. This reacts rapidly with iodine to give the products.

We could not have deduced this reaction scheme precisely from the rate equation, but it does fit in with that equation. Confirmatory evidence is given by carrying out the reaction not with iodine, but with heavy water, D_2O. A deuterium atom, D (a hydrogen atom with a neutron as well as a proton in the nucleus) is taken up by the methyl group of the propanone at exactly the same rate as iodine is in the first reaction. The two reactions have the same rate-determining steps.

A reaction revisited

The rate equation for the reaction between methanol and hydrochloric acid:

$$CH_3OH(aq) + HCl(aq) \longrightarrow CH_3Cl(aq) + H_2O(l)$$

as established by experiment is (see pages 103–104):

rate of reaction = $k[CH_3OH][HCl]$

Extra information can help us to formulate a reaction mechanism. The rate equation suggests that a simple readjustment of bonds in a single-step reaction is involved (Figure 11.16).

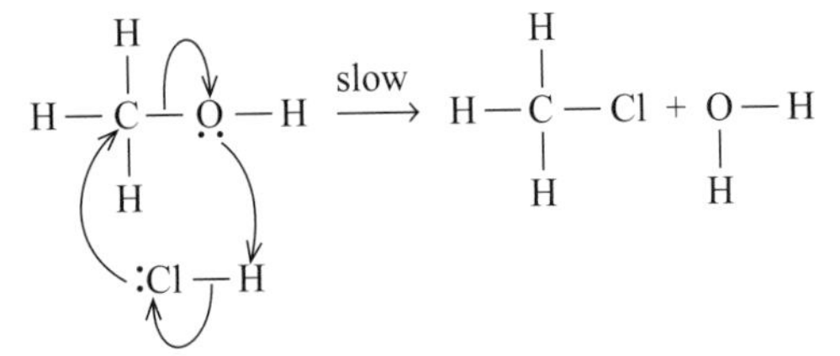

Bonds seem to break…and remake.

Figure 11.16 An apparent mechanism for the reaction between methanol and hydrochloric acid.

However, experiments show that the rate can be increased by adding a strong acid, H^+ ions, to the reaction mixture as well as by the addition of sodium chloride or a similar source of chloride ions, Cl^-. It is clear that the rate equation does not cater for the separate effects of varying concentrations of hydrogen ions and chloride ions. The new rate equation that is correct for hydrochloric acid, but also accounts for the separate effects of hydrogen ions and chloride ions, is:

$$rate = k\,[CH_3OH][H^+][Cl^-]$$

Now let us re-examine the proposed mechanism for this reaction in the light of the more general rate equation. The first stage consists of a protonation equilibrium:

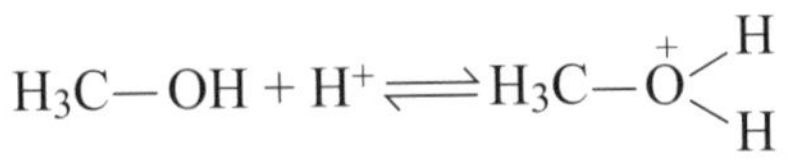

This is followed by an attack by the chloride ion.

SAQ

10 Suggest a possible second step in the reaction between methanol and hydrochloric acid, involving the attack by a chloride ion.

Answer

Summary

Glossary

- The rate of reaction is a measure of the rate at which reactants are used up or the rate at which products are formed. It is measured in units of concentration per unit time ($mol\,dm^{-3}\,s^{-1}$).

- The rate of reaction is related to the concentrations of the reactants by the rate equation, which (for two reactants A and B) is of the form:

  $$rate\ of\ reaction = k\,[A]^m[B]^n$$

  where k is the rate constant, [A] and [B] are the concentrations of the reactants, m is the order of reaction with respect to A and n is the order of reaction with respect to B.

- The rate equation cannot be predicted from the balanced chemical (stoichiometric) equation.

- The overall order of reaction is the sum of the orders with respect to the individual reactants. For the example above:

  $$overall\ order = m + n$$

- The order of reaction with respect to the different reactants may be determined by the initial-rates method, in which the initial rate is measured for several experiments using different concentrations of reactants. One concentration is changed whilst the others are fixed, so that we get a clear and systematic set of results to analyse.

continued

- The order of reaction with respect to a particular reactant may also be determined by monitoring a single experiment as it proceeds. The data gathered is used to produce a concentration–time graph. Tangents taken from several points on the graph give a measure of how the reaction rate changes with time. The rate of reaction at a particular point is the gradient of the graph at that point.

- The half-life of a reaction is the time taken for the concentration of a reactant to halve. For a first-order reaction the half-life is independent of the concentration(s) of reactant(s) – it remains constant throughout the reaction, as shown on a concentration–time graph.

- The increase in rate of a reaction with increasing temperature is accompanied by an increase in the value of the rate constant, k, for the reaction.

- The order of reaction with respect to a particular reactant indicates how many molecules of that reactant participate in the slowest step (rate-determining step) of a reaction mechanism. This slowest step determines the overall rate of reaction.

- Determination of the slowest step provides evidence for the mechanism of a reaction.

- The rate equation for a reaction may be deduced given its slowest step.

Questions

1 Benzenediazonium chloride, $C_6H_5N_2Cl$, decomposes above $10\,^{\circ}C$, releasing nitrogen gas.

$$C_6H_5N_2Cl(aq) + H_2O(l) \longrightarrow C_6H_5OH(aq) + N_2(g) + HCl(aq)$$

The graph below shows how the concentration of $C_6H_5N_2Cl$ changes with time at $50\,^{\circ}C$.

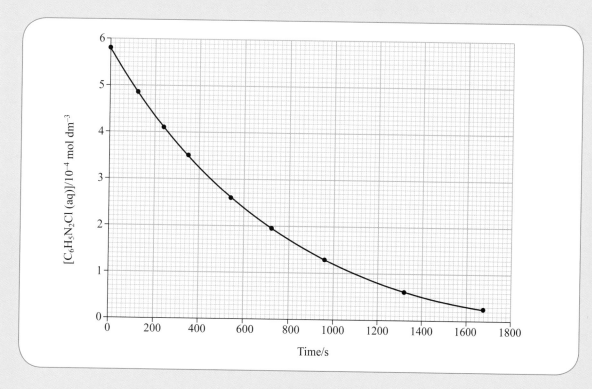

continued

a This reaction is first order with respect to $C_6H_5N_2Cl$. This can be confirmed from the graph using half-lives.

   i What is meant by the *half-life* of a reaction, $t_{1/2}$? [1]

   ii Use a copy of this graph to show that this reaction is first order with respect to $C_6H_5N_2Cl$. You should mark on the graph any working. [3]

   iii What would be the effect on the half-life of this reaction of doubling the initial concentration of $C_6H_5N_2Cl$? [1]

b For a first-order reaction, the rate constant, k, can be found using the following relationship.

$$k\,t_{1/2} = 0.693$$

Calculate the value for the rate constant, k, of this reaction. Include the units of k in your answer. [2]

c Write down the expression for the rate equation of this reaction. [1]

d The rate of this reaction can be calculated by using the graph and the rate equation together.

   i Read from the graph the concentration of $C_6H_5N_2Cl$ after 800 s. [1]

   ii Use the rate equation to calculate the rate of this reaction after 800 s. Include units in your answer. [2]

   iii How could you measure the reaction rate after 800 s directly from the graph alone? [1]

OCR Chemistry A2 (2816) January 2002   [Total 12]

Hint

Hint

Answer

2 Nitrogen dioxide is one of the major pollutants in air; it is formed by reaction of nitrogen monoxide with oxygen:

$$2NO(g) + O_2(g) \longrightarrow 2NO_2(g)$$

a What is meant by the *rate of reaction*? [1]

b A series of experiments was carried out to investigate the kinetics of this reaction. The results are shown in the table below.

Experiment	$[O_2]$/mol dm^{-3}	$[NO]$/mol dm^{-3}	Initial rate/ mol dm^{-3} s^{-1}
1	0.00100	0.00100	7.10
2	0.00400	0.00100	28.4
3	0.00400	0.00300	256

   i For each reactant, deduce the order of reaction. Show your reasoning. [4]

   ii Deduce the rate equation for this reaction. [1]

   iii Calculate the rate constant, k, for this reaction. State the units for k. [2]

continued

c Nitrogen dioxide reacts with carbon monoxide emitted from car exhausts in the following reaction.

$$NO_2 + CO \longrightarrow NO + CO_2$$

The rate equation for this reaction is rate = $k[NO_2]^2$.

This is a multi-step reaction. The first step is the rate-determining step.

i What is meant by the *rate-determining step*? [1]

ii Suggest a two-step reaction mechanism for this reaction that is consistent with the kinetic data and the overall reaction. [2]

OCR Chemistry A2 (2816) June 2006 [Total 11]

Hint

Answer

3 In an experiment, maltose, $C_{12}H_{22}O_{11}$, was hydrolysed to form glucose, $C_6H_{12}O_6$. The hydrochloric acid behaves as a catalyst for this reaction.

$$C_{12}H_{22}O_{11}(aq) + H_2O(l) \xrightarrow{H^+ \text{ catalyst}} 2C_6H_{12}O_6(aq)$$
maltose \qquad\qquad\qquad\qquad glucose

This reaction was carried out several times using different concentrations of maltose and of hydrochloric acid. The initial rate of each experimental run was calculated and the results are shown below. In each case, initial concentrations are shown.

Experiment	$[C_{12}H_{22}O_{11}(aq)]/$ mol dm^{-3}	$[HCl(aq)]/$ mol dm^{-3}	Initial rate/ mol dm^{-3} s^{-1}
1	0.10	0.10	0.024
2	0.20	0.10	0.048
3	0.10	0.15	0.036

a i Suggest what is meant by the *initial* rate of reaction. [1]

ii The initial rates measured in each experimental run are for the rate of <u>disappearance</u> of maltose.

For experiment 1, deduce the initial rate of <u>appearance</u> of glucose, in mol dm^{-3} s^{-1}. [1]

b i For each reactant, deduce the order of reaction. Show your reasoning. [4]

ii What is the overall order of this reaction? [1]

iii Deduce the rate equation for this reaction. [2]

c The experiment was repeated at a higher temperature.
State whether the rate constant would increase, decrease or stay the same. [1]

Hint

d Experiment 1 was repeated and the concentration of maltose was measured continuously until the reaction was complete.

The half-life of this reaction with respect to maltose was measured as 3 seconds.

Determine the concentrations of maltose and hydrochloric acid in experiment 1 after 3 seconds. In each case, explain how you have arrived at your answer. [3]

OCR Chemistry A2 (2816) June 2004 [Total 13]

Answer

continued

4   Bromine can be formed by the oxidation of bromide ions. This question compares the rates of two reactions that produce bromine.

   a   Bromine is formed by the oxidation of bromide ions with acidified bromate(V) ions.

$$5Br^-(aq) + 6H^+(aq) + BrO_3^-(aq) \longrightarrow 3Br_2(aq) + 3H_2O(l)$$

This reaction was carried out several times using different concentrations of the three reactants. The initial rate of each experimental run was calculated and the results are shown below. In each case, initial concentrations are shown.

Experiment	$[Br^-(aq)]/$ $mol\,dm^{-3}$	$[H^+(aq)]/$ $mol\,dm^{-3}$	$[BrO_3^-(aq)]/$ $mol\,dm^{-3}$	Initial rate/ $10^{-3}\,mol\,dm^{-3}\,s^{-1}$
1	0.10	0.10	0.10	1.2
2	0.10	0.10	0.20	2.4
3	0.30	0.10	0.10	3.6
4	0.10	0.20	0.20	9.6

     i   For each reactant, deduce the order of reaction. Show your reasoning.   [6]

     ii   Deduce the rate equation.   [1]

     iii   Calculate the rate constant, k, for this reaction. State the units for k.   [3]

   b   Bromine can <u>also</u> be formed by the oxidation of hydrogen bromide with oxygen. The following mechanism has been suggested for this multi-step reaction.

     step 1 $HBr \quad + \quad O_2 \longrightarrow HBrO_2$

     step 2 $HBrO_2 + HBr \longrightarrow 2HBrO$

     step 3 $HBrO \quad + HBr \longrightarrow Br_2 \quad + \quad H_2O$

     step 4 $HBrO \quad + HBr \longrightarrow Br_2 \quad + \quad H_2O$

               (a repeat of step 3)

     i   Explain the term *rate-determining step*.   [1]

     ii   The rate equation for this reaction is: rate $= k[HBr][O_2]$.

        Explain which of the four steps above is the <u>rate-determining step</u> for this reaction.   [2]

     iii   Determine the <u>overall</u> equation for this reaction.   [1]

OCR Chemistry A2 (2816) June 2003   [Total 14]

Hint

Answer

5   *In this question, one mark is available for the quality of use and organisation of scientific terms.*

Propanone reacts with iodine in the presence of dilute hydrochloric acid.

A student carried out an investigation into the kinetics of this reaction.

He measured how the concentration of propanone changes with time. He also investigated how different concentrations of iodine and hydrochloric acid affect the initial rate of the reaction.

continued

The graph and results are shown below.

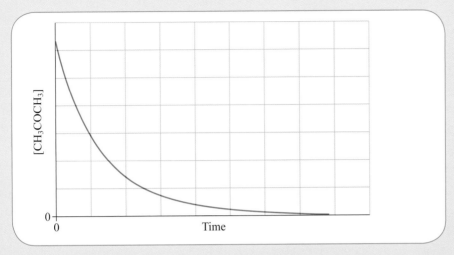

[CH$_3$COCH$_3$]/ mol dm^{-3}	[I$_2$]/mol dm^{-3}	[H$^+$]/mol dm^{-3}	Initial rate/ mol dm^{-3} s^{-1}
1.5×10^{-3}	0.0300	0.0200	2.1×10^{-9}
1.5×10^{-3}	0.0300	0.0400	4.2×10^{-9}
1.5×10^{-3}	0.0600	0.0400	4.2×10^{-9}

The overall equation for the reaction is given below.

$$CH_3COCH_3 + I_2 \longrightarrow CH_3COCH_2I + HI$$

This is a multi-step reaction.
- What conclusions can be drawn about the kinetics of this reaction from the student's investigation? Justify your reasoning.
- Calculate the rate constant for this reaction, including units.
- Suggest the equations for a possible two-step mechanism for this reaction. Label the rate-determining step and explain your reasoning. [13]

Quality of written communication [1]

OCR Chemistry A2 (2816) January 2006 [Total 14]

Hint

Answer

6 Nitrogen monoxide reacts with hydrogen at 500 °C as in the equation below.

$$2NO(g) + 2H_2(g) \longrightarrow N_2(g) + 2H_2O(g)$$

A series of experiments was carried out to investigate the kinetics of this reaction.

continued

The results are shown in the table below.

Experiment	[NO]/mol dm^{-3}	[H$_2$]/mol dm^{-3}	Initial rate/ mol dm^{-3} s^{-1}
1	0.10	0.20	2.6
2	0.10	0.50	6.5
3	0.30	0.50	58.5

a *In this question, one mark is available for the quality of spelling, punctuation and grammar.*

   i   For each reactant, deduce the order of reaction. Show your reasoning.   [4]
       Quality of written communication   [1]
   ii Deduce the rate equation for this reaction.   [1]
   iii Calculate the rate constant, k, for this reaction. State the units for k.   [3]

b Nitrogen monoxide, NO, is involved in the formation of ozone at low levels and the breakdown of ozone at high levels.

   i   In the lower atmosphere, NO is produced by combustion in car engines. Ozone is then formed following the series of reactions shown below.

   $$NO(g) + \tfrac{1}{2}O_2(g) \longrightarrow NO_2(g)$$

   $$NO_2(g) \longrightarrow NO(g) + O(g)$$

   $$O_2(g) + O(g) \longrightarrow O_3(g)$$

   - Write the overall equation for this reaction sequence.
   - Identify the catalyst and justify your answer.   [3]

   ii In the upper atmosphere, NO removes O$_3$ by the following reaction mechanism.

   $$NO(g) + O_3(g) \longrightarrow NO_2(g) + O_2(g) \quad \text{slow}$$

   $$O(g) + NO_2(g) \longrightarrow NO(g) + O_2(g) \quad \text{fast}$$

   Suggest the rate equation for this process. Explain your reasoning.   [2]

OCR Chemistry A2 (2816) January 2007   [Total 14]

Hint

Answer

7 This question looks at <u>two</u> different experiments that investigate rates of reaction.

a The decomposition of dinitrogen pentoxide, N$_2$O$_5$, at 45 °C was investigated. The reaction that takes place is shown below.

   $$2N_2O_5 \longrightarrow 4NO_2 + O_2$$

   In an experiment, N$_2$O$_5$ with a concentration of 0.60 mol dm^{-3} was decomposed at 45 °C.

continued

At this temperature, the reaction has a constant half-life of 1200 s.

i How can you tell that this reaction is first order with respect to N_2O_5? [1]

ii Write down an expression for the rate equation of this decomposition. [1]

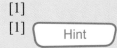

iii Copy the axes below onto a piece of graph paper. Complete the graph to show how the $[N_2O_5]$ changes over the first 3600 s. [2]

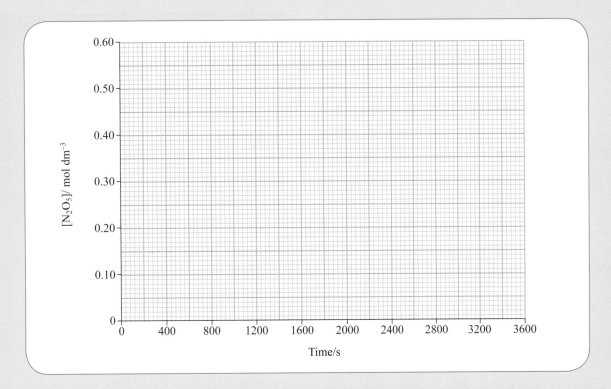

iv The rate of this reaction can be determined from this graph.
Show on the graph how the rate can be measured after 1200 s. [1]

v The rate can also be calculated from the rate equation. The rate constant for this reaction is $6.2 \times 10^{-4}\,s^{-1}$.
Calculate the initial rate of this reaction. State the units. [2]

b A student investigated the hydration of 2-methylpropene, $(CH_3)_2C{=}CH_2$, with dilute aqueous acid to form 2-methylpropan-2-ol, $(CH_3)_3COH$.
The following mechanism has been proposed for this hydration.

step 1 $(CH_3)_2C{=}CH_2 + H^+(aq) \longrightarrow (CH_3)_3C^+$ rate-determining step

step 2 $(CH_3)_3C^+ + H_2O \longrightarrow (CH_3)_3COH + H^+(aq)$

i Step 1 is the rate-determining step for this hydration.
What is meant by the term *rate-determining step*? [1]

ii Write a balanced equation for the overall hydration reaction. [1]

iii Suggest the role of $H^+(aq)$ in this mechanism. Explain your reason. [2]

iv Use the mechanism above to suggest the rate equation for this hydration. [1]

OCR Chemistry A2 (2816) June 2005 [Total 12]

Answer

Chapter 12

How far?

Objectives

This chapter develops the ideas that you met in *Chemistry 1*, Chapter 17, on chemical equilibria and introduces a more quantitative approach. You will find out how the concentrations of the reactants and products from the balanced chemical equation can be combined in the form of a constant known as the equilibrium constant.

We can use this constant to predict the effect of changing concentration, pressure or temperature on the position of equilibrium. In *Chemistry 1*, Chapter 17, **Le Chatelier's principle** was used for this purpose. However, by using the equilibrium constant, equilibrium concentrations may also be calculated.

From your previous work you might recall the characteristic features of a reacting mixture in which **dynamic equilibrium** has been established, as shown below:

- it is dynamic at the molecular or ionic level
- the position of equilibrium can be approached from either side of the chemical equation
- both forward and reverse processes occur at equal rates
- a closed system is required
- macroscopic properties remain constant.

Many reactions in living organisms involve chemical equilibria. A study of chemical equilibria leads us to a better understanding of such processes.

Extension

Dynamic equilibrium

When we view a system at equilibrium, we are not aware that constant change is taking place at the microscopic level of molecules and ions. Properties we can see or measure easily remain constant. We call these macroscopic properties. Once dynamic equilibrium is achieved, the macroscopic properties such as concentration, pressure, temperature, mass and volume remain constant.

Equilibria in organic reactions

Like many biochemical reactions, many of the organic reactions that you met in *Chemistry 1* and in the first ten chapters of this book also involve equilibria.

One example of an organic equilibrium reaction that you met earlier (Chapter 4 of this book) is the hydrolysis of the ester ethyl ethanoate, $CH_3COOCH_2CH_3$.

This ester hydrolyses slowly, forming ethanoic acid and ethanol when mixed with water and an acid catalyst such as sulfuric or hydrochloric acid. The equation for the reaction is as follows:

$$CH_3COOCH_2CH_3(l) + H_2O(l)$$
$$\rightleftharpoons CH_3COOH(l) + CH_3CH_2OH(l)$$

Table 12.1 shows the equilibrium concentrations for four experiments.

Experiment	Concentration/mol dm^{-3}				K_c
	$CH_3COOCH_2CH_3$	H_2O	CH_3COOH	CH_3CH_2OH	
1	7.22	2.07	2.03	2.03	
2	6.38	3.69	2.56	2.56	0.278
3	4.69	8.16	3.28	3.28	0.281
4	2.81	16.6	3.56	3.56	

Table 12.1 Data for the hydrolysis of ethyl ethanoate.

The mixtures were prepared by mixing together known masses of ester and water. The mixtures were placed in stoppered flasks and $1.00\,cm^3$ of concentrated sulfuric acid was added to each flask. The flasks were then left undisturbed for one week at room temperature. One week is necessary for the mixtures to reach equilibrium, even though a catalyst is used!

After one week, the flasks were opened and the contents analysed by titration with standardised sodium hydroxide. A separate titration was also carried out to determine the volume of sodium hydroxide required to neutralise the sulfuric acid catalyst.

The data in Table 12.1 were calculated from these titration results and the initial weighings. The last column of the table contains the symbol K_c, which is known as the equilibrium constant. The subscript 'c' refers to concentration. You will see that the values of K_c for the data in experiments 2 and 3 are in close agreement. So how is this constant calculated from the data? First of all we write the equation for the reaction:

$$CH_3COOCH_2CH_3(l) + H_2O(l)$$
$$\rightleftharpoons CH_3COOH(l) + CH_3CH_2OH(l)$$

Now we can write the equilibrium constant, K_c, as the ratio of the product concentrations (multiplied together) divided by the reactant concentrations (multiplied together), as follows:

$$K_c = \frac{[CH_3COOH][CH_3CH_2OH]}{[CH_3COOCH_2CH_3][H_2O]}$$

Note that this is an example of a homogeneous reaction as all the reactants and products are in the same state. You will only be asked to work out equilibrium constants for this type of reaction.

SAQ

1 Try substituting the data for experiment 2 in the above expression for K_c. Check your answer with the value in Table 12.1. Calculate the missing values of K_c. Remember the results are experimental, so not all values of K_c will be as close as those for experiments 2 and 3.

(Answer)

The amounts of substances present at equilibrium

Each line of data in Table 12.1 can be used to calculate a value for K_c. K_c can also be calculated if we start with less data than this, provided we use the chemical equation (see Worked example 1).

Worked example 1

0.100 moles of ethyl ethanoate are added to 0.100 moles of water. A little concentrated sulfuric acid is added as a catalyst and the volume of the mixture is made up to $1\,dm^3$ with an inert solvent. The mixture is left to reach equilibrium for five days at $30\,°C$. The equilibrium mixture is then analysed and found to contain exactly 0.0346 moles of ethanoic acid. Calculate the value of K_c.

The equation for the hydrolysis is:

$$CH_3COOCH_2CH_3 + H_2O$$
$$\rightleftharpoons CH_3COOH + CH_3CH_2OH$$

The equation says that the number of molecules of ethanoic acid produced is the same as the number of moles of ethanol produced. Therefore 0.0346 moles of ethanol must be present at equilibrium.

The equation says that the number of molecules of ethanoic acid produced is the same as the number of moles of ethyl ethanoate and water that are consumed. Therefore 0.0346 moles of ethyl ethanoate and water were consumed.

We started with 0.100 moles of ethyl ethanoate and water. Therefore there are $0.100 - 0.0346 = 0.0654$ moles of ethyl ethanoate and water present at equilibrium.

$$K_c = \frac{(0.0346) \times (0.0346)}{(0.0654 \times (0.0654)}$$

$$= 0.280 \text{ (no units)}$$

Note that the final answer is shown to 3 significant figures.

SAQ

2   0.500 moles of ethanol are added to 0.500 moles of ethanoic acid. Five drops of concentrated sulfuric acid are added as a catalyst and the volume of the mixture is made up to 1 dm^3 with an inert solvent. The mixture is left to equilibrate for one week at 30 °C. The equilibrium mixture is then analysed and found to contain exactly 0.1728 moles of ethanoic acid. The products of the reaction are ethyl ethanoate and water.

   a   Write a balanced chemical equation for the reaction.

   b   How many moles of ethanol are present at equilibrium?

   c   How many moles of ethyl ethanoate and water are present at equilibrium?   [Hint]

   d   Write an expression for K_c.

   e   Calculate the value of K_c to 3 significant figures.   [Answer]

3   Worked example 1 and SAQ 2 would both work even if you knew nothing about the volume of solvent added. Explain why this is.   [Answer]

Another equilibrium mixture

Iodine gas is purple. The more there is, the deeper the shade of purple. A colorimeter can be used to measure this intensity, and hence the concentration of iodine in a reaction vessel, over time.

   The equilibrium

$$H_2(g) + I_2(g) \rightleftharpoons 2HI(g)$$

can be approached from either side:

- by using a mixture of hydrogen gas and iodine gas (purple), which reacts to form colourless hydrogen iodide, or
- by using pure hydrogen iodide, which dissociates to form hydrogen and iodine.

Figure 12.1 illustrates what happens when 5.00 mol of hydrogen molecules and 5.00 mol of iodine molecules react at 500 K. As time passes, the purple colour of the iodine fades until a steady state is reached.

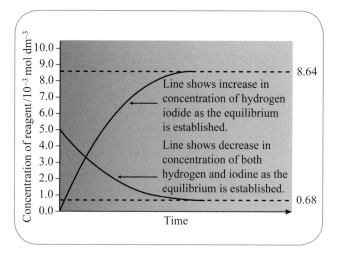

Figure 12.1 The changes in the concentrations of reagents as 5.00 mol of each of hydrogen and iodine react to form an equilibrium mixture with hydrogen iodide in a vessel of volume 1 m^3.

   Experimental analysis shows that the final amount of iodine is 0.68 mol. There must also be 0.68 mol of hydrogen left, as the chemical equation shows. Again using the balanced chemical equation, we can see that 4.32 mol of each gas have reacted and been converted to 8.64 mol of hydrogen iodide molecules.

SAQ

4   The same equilibrium can be achieved starting with 10.0 mol of hydrogen iodide molecules (Figure 12.2).

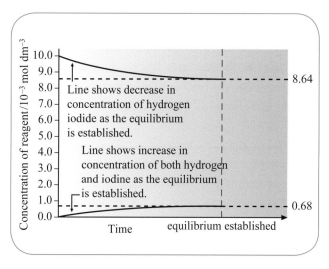

Figure 12.2 The changes in the concentrations of reagents as 10 mol of hydrogen iodide react to form an equilibrium mixture with hydrogen and iodine gases in a vessel of 1 m^3.

Describe what happens and satisfy yourself that, if 0.68 mol of iodine molecules are found to be in the equilibrium mixture, then there must be 8.64 mol of hydrogen iodide molecules present.

(Hint)

(Answer)

We can find the concentrations of H_2, I_2 and HI in any equilibrium mixture by analysing the amount of iodine present and by knowing the amount of H_2 and I_2 we had to start with. Table 12.2 shows some values obtained.

The fourth column shows the value of $\dfrac{[HI]^2}{[H_2][I_2]}$,

which, as you can see, is constant (allowing for experimental error). It is called the equilibrium constant, K_c, for the reaction. In this case K_c is given by the square of the equilibrium concentration of hydrogen iodide, divided by the equilibrium concentration of hydrogen multiplied by the equilibrium concentration of iodine.

$$K_c = \frac{[HI][HI]}{[H_2][I_2]}$$
$$= \frac{[HI]^2}{[H_2][I_2]}$$

Notice that the 2HI in the balanced chemical equation becomes $[HI]^2$ in the equilibrium constant expression. As a general rule, each concentration is raised to the power of the number of moles of the relevant substance in the balanced equation.

We can also work out the units of the equilibrium constant, K_c, for

$$H_2(g) + I_2(g) \rightleftharpoons 2HI(g)$$

by substituting in the units of concentration as they appear in the equilibrium expression for the reaction as written:

$$\frac{(\text{mol dm}^{-3})^2}{(\text{mol dm}^{-3}) \times (\text{mol dm}^{-3})}$$

As the units in this expression cancel each other out, this particular K_c has no units. However, each equilibrium constant must be considered individually.

(K_c will have no units whenever the equilibrium is homogeneous and the total number of molecules on both sides of the balanced equation is the same.)

Consider the equilibrium for the Contact process for the manufacture of sulfuric acid. In this process, a key stage involves the oxidation of sulfur dioxide to sulfur trioxide by oxygen. The chemical equation and expression for the equilibrium constant, K_c, for this reaction are:

$$2SO_2(g) + O_2(g) \rightleftharpoons 2SO_3(g)$$

$$K_c = \frac{[SO_3]^2}{[SO_2]^2 \times [O_2]}$$

$$\text{units of } K_c = \frac{(\text{mol dm}^{-3})^2}{(\text{mol dm}^{-3})^2 \times (\text{mol dm}^{-3})}$$

$$= \frac{1}{\text{mol dm}^{-3}}$$

$$= \text{dm}^3 \text{ mol}^{-1}$$

$[H_2]/\text{mol dm}^{-3}$	$[I_2]/\text{mol dm}^{-3}$	$[HI]/\text{mol dm}^{-3}$	$\dfrac{[HI]^2}{[H_2][I_2]}$
0.68×10^{-3}	0.68×10^{-3}	8.64×10^{-3}	161
0.50×10^{-3}	0.50×10^{-3}	6.30×10^{-3}	159
1.10×10^{-3}	1.10×10^{-3}	13.9×10^{-3}	160
1.10×10^{-3}	2.00×10^{-3}	18.8×10^{-3}	161
2.50×10^{-3}	0.65×10^{-3}	16.1×10^{-3}	160

Table 12.2 Equilibrium concentrations of hydrogen, $[H_2]$, iodine, $[I_2]$, and hydrogen iodide, $[HI]$, at 500 K.

SAQ

5 Write the expression for K_c for each of the following reactions, and work out the units for K_c assuming the concentrations of the gases are measured in $mol\,dm^{-3}$.

a $2NO_2(g) \rightleftharpoons N_2O_4(g)$

b $2NO(g) + O_2(g) \rightleftharpoons 2NO_2(g)$

c $N_2(g) + 3H_2(g) \rightleftharpoons 2NH_3(g)$

[Answer]

Use of the equilibrium constant expression has an additional advantage. If we can determine one equilibrium concentration and we know the initial concentrations of other compounds present, we can determine the equilibrium concentrations of the other chemical species present (see Worked example 2). As we have shown in Worked example 1, we can calculate a value for K_c from this information.

Worked example 2

Propanone reacts with hydrogen cyanide as follows:

A mixture initially containing $0.0500\,mol\,dm^{-3}$ propanone and $0.0500\,mol\,dm^{-3}$ hydrogen cyanide in ethanol is left to reach equilibrium at room temperature. At equilibrium, the concentration of the product is $0.0233\,mol\,dm^{-3}$. Calculate the equilibrium constant for this reaction under these conditions.

Step 1 Write out the balanced chemical equation, with the initial data underneath.

0.0500	0.0500	0

Initial concentrations /mol dm^{-3}

continued

Step 2 The equilibrium concentration of the only product is $0.0233\,mol\,dm^{-3}$. As 1 mol of each reactant produces 1 mol of product, the concentration of each of the reactants decreases by $0.0233\,mol\,dm^{-3}$.

Hence the equilibrium concentration of each reactant is now:

$$0.0500 - 0.0233\,mol\,dm^{-3} = 0.0267\,mol\,dm^{-3}$$

Write these equilibrium concentrations below the initial concentrations under the balanced chemical equation:

0.0500 – 0.0233 = 0.0267	0.0500 – 0.0233 = 0.0267	0.0233

Equilibrium concentrations /mol dm^{-3}

Step 3 Write the equilibrium constant for this reaction in terms of concentrations.

$$K_c = \frac{[product]}{[propanone][hydrogen\ cyanide]}\ dm^3\,mol^{-1}$$

The equilibrium concentrations can now be used to calculate K_c.

$$K_c = \frac{0.0233}{0.0267 \times 0.0267}\ dm^3\,mol^{-1}$$

$$= 32.7\,dm^3\,mol^{-1}$$

Note that the units are

$$\frac{\cancel{mol\,dm^{-3}}}{\cancel{mol\,dm^{-3}} \times mol\,dm^{-3}} = \frac{1}{mol\,dm^{-3}} = dm^3\,mol^{-1}$$

6 Calculate the equilibrium constant for the following reaction:

$$H_2(g) + CO_2(g) \rightleftharpoons CO(g) + H_2O(g)$$

The initial concentration of hydrogen is $10.00\,mol\,dm^{-3}$ and that of carbon dioxide is $90.00\,mol\,dm^{-3}$. At equilibrium, $9.47\,mol\,dm^{-3}$ of carbon monoxide are formed.

Hint

Answer

You should try to develop a 'feel' for values of K_c, so that when you look at equilibrium mixtures and the values for their equilibrium constants, you can begin to imagine the extent of the formation of product from reactant. High values of K_c indicate a high percentage of products compared to reactants. Conversely, low values of K_c indicate that the position of equilibrium lies in favour of the reactants (as written in the chemical equation).

K_c and Le Chatelier's principle

In *Chemistry 1*, Chapter 17, you saw how we can use Le Chatelier's principle to predict the effects of changes in concentration, pressure or temperature on the position of an equilibrium. For example, increasing the concentration of a reactant will lead to an increase in the concentrations of the products at a new position of equilibrium.

Le Chatelier's principle, expressed in modern language, states that

when any of the conditions affecting the position of a dynamic equilibrium are changed, then the position of that equilibrium will shift to minimise that change.

Predictions using Le Chatelier's principle of the effects of temperature changes are summarised, with examples, in Table 12.3.

K_c and temperature changes

A consequence of the effects shown in Table 12.3 of changing the temperature of a reaction is that the equilibrium constant, K_c, must also change. This is why we must carry out experiments to determine values of K_c at a constant temperature.

For example, the information in Table 12.3 states that an increase in temperature for an endothermic reaction, such as the decomposition of hydrogen iodide, causes more hydrogen and iodine to form (and vice versa). For this reaction:

$$K_c = \frac{[H_2][I_2]}{[HI]^2}$$

We can see that, if the concentrations of products increase, the concentration of HI must fall and so K_c must increase. Table 12.4 shows some values for the equilibrium constant for the decomposition of hydrogen iodide at different temperatures.

Example	Endothermic reaction, $2HI \rightleftharpoons H_2(g) + I_2(g)$	Exothermic reaction, $2SO_2(g) + O_2(g) \rightleftharpoons 2SO_3(g)$
temperature increase	equilibrium position shifts towards products: more hydrogen and iodine form	equilibrium position shifts towards reactants: more sulfur dioxide and oxygen form
temperature decrease	equilibrium position shifts towards reactant: more hydrogen iodide forms	equilibrium position shifts towards product: more sulfur trioxide forms

Table 12.3 The effects of temperature changes on equilibria.

Temperature/K	K_c
300	1.26×10^{-3}
500	6.25×10^{-3}
1000	18.5×10^{-3}

Table 12.4 Equilibrium constants at different temperatures for the decomposition of hydrogen iodide, $2HI \rightleftharpoons H_2 + I_2$.

SAQ

7 Deduce the effect of an increase in temperature on the value of K_c for the oxidation of NO, shown in the equation:

$$2NO(g) + O_2(g) \rightleftharpoons 2NO_2(g)$$
$$\Delta H = -115 \, kJ \, mol^{-1}$$

Answer

For the oxidation of SO_2 shown in Table 12.3, an increase in temperature produces less of the product, SO_3. The concentrations of the reactants will rise, so the value of K_c must decrease.

This reaction is the key stage in the manufacture of concentrated sulfuric acid, in which temperatures of 700 to 800 K are used. Despite these temperatures, a very high percentage conversion (over 99.5%) is achieved by passing the reactants through a total of four beds of the catalyst, vanadium(V) oxide (V_2O_5).

The effects of temperature changes on K_c are summarised in Table 12.5.

	Endothermic reaction, ΔH positive	Exothermic reaction, ΔH negative
temperature increase	equilibrium constant increases	equilibrium constant decreases
temperature decrease	equilibrium constant decreases	equilibrium constant increases

Table 12.5 The effects of temperature changes on equilibrium constants.

The equilibrium constant expression can also be used to predict the outcome of changes in concentration or pressure. However, unlike temperature changes, changes in concentration or pressure do not affect the value of K_c.

K_c and concentration changes

Consider again the decomposition of hydrogen iodide:

$$2HI(g) \rightleftharpoons H_2(g) + I_2(g)$$

The equilibrium constant, at 500 K, is:

$$K_c = \frac{[H_2][I_2]}{[HI]^2}$$
$$= 6.25 \times 10^{-3}$$

Suppose more hydrogen iodide is introduced into the equilibrium mixture, whilst maintaining a constant volume and a temperature of 500 K. [HI] will increase and the mixture will no longer be in a state of equilibrium. To restore equilibrium, both $[H_2]$ and $[I_2]$ must increase whilst [HI] decreases. Equilibrium will be restored when the values of these concentrations, when entered in the equilibrium constant expression, are such that the value of the expression once again equals the value of K_c at 500 K (6.25×10^{-3}).

K_c and pressure changes

A change in pressure may affect the position of equilibrium if gases are involved in the reaction. You can use Le Chatelier's principle to predict whether or not it does. An increase in pressure will shift the position of equilibrium in the direction which results in a lower number of gas molecules being formed. On the other hand, a decrease in pressure will shift the position of equilibrium in the direction which results in a greater number of gas molecules being formed. However, if a change in pressure does cause the position of equilibrium to shift, this happens without a change in the value of K_c.

K_c and catalysts

Adding a catalyst to a reaction mixture will cause equilibrium to be reached more rapidly but will not affect the composition of the equilibrium mixture. In other words a catalyst gives you the same yield, but you get it faster. Adding a catalyst therefore has no effect on the value of K_c.

SAQ

8 This question is about the Haber process:

$$N_2(g) + 3H_2(g) \rightleftharpoons 2NH_3(g)$$
$$\Delta H = -92 \, \text{kJ mol}^{-1}$$

Nitrogen and hydrogen are mixed in a reaction vessel at 400 °C and 200 atm pressure in the absence of a catalyst.

Predict what happens to the position of equilibrium, and to K_c, when the following changes are made. Explain your answers.

a The operating temperature is increased.
b The operating pressure is increased.
c An iron catalyst is added.

Answer

Pollution and the equilibrium $N_2(g) + O_2(g) \rightleftharpoons 2NO(g)$

At 1100 K, the value of K_c is very small, at 4×10^{-8}. However, calculations show that in 1 cm³ of air at this temperature there would be around 2×10^{15} molecules of nitrogen oxide in an equilibrium mixture – a small fraction of the total but enough to pose a pollution threat.

Vehicle engines are a significant source of nitrogen oxide molecules. They contribute to a complex series of reactions with other molecules such as carbon monoxide, sulfur dioxide and hydrocarbons.

Light energy plays its part, and the result can be a 'photochemical smog' of the form experienced in cities (Figure 12.3). The irritating chemicals produced include low-level ozone, O_3, and peroxyacetyl nitrates (PAN), which make your eyes water. Both of these are implicated in triggering asthma attacks.

Figure 12.3 Photochemical smog caused by light interacting with pollutant molecules.

In *Chemistry 1*, Chapter 18, you found out how the work of chemists contributed to the development of catalytic converters for use in cars. However, whilst these converters remove NO, CO and unburnt hydrocarbons, they are only really a stopgap solution. Vehicles that burn hydrocarbons contribute large quantities of CO_2 to the atmosphere. This CO_2 is now accepted as making a major contribution to global warming by the greenhouse effect.

Also, the metals in the catalytic converters, such as platinum, are gradually lost from catalytic converters. Measurable quantities of platinum have been found in road dust. This loss is a problem as these metals are very expensive and many people have an adverse reaction to platinum and its compounds.

The supplies of fossil fuels such as oil are limited and scientists are seeking alternatives. However, even these alternatives may have environmental consequences. A car burning hydrogen as a fuel will produce NO if the combustion temperature is high (since enough energy is available to break the covalent bonds in the nitrogen molecules in air).

In view of such problems we should be questioning our reliance on individual motorised transport and seeking major improvements in public transport in order to reduce the number of sources of pollutants.

Some photochemical smog occurs naturally. The haze of the Smoky Mountains in the USA seems to be caused by the reactions between oils from the pine forests and citrus groves with naturally occurring ozone. Atmospheric chemistry is both fascinating and complex; there will always be a need for research in this area.

Summary

Glossary

- An equilibrium constant, K_c (for concentrations) may be written using a balanced chemical equation for the reaction. For example, in the reaction:

$$N_2(g) + 3H_2(g) \rightleftharpoons 2NH_3(g)$$

$$K_c = \frac{[NH_3]^2}{[N_2][H_2]^3}$$

- The concentration (shown by square brackets) is raised to the power of the number of moles shown in the balanced chemical equation. Units must be worked out for each equilibrium constant. This is done by placing the units of concentration, i.e. $mol\,dm^{-3}$, in the equilibrium expression and cancelling out, as appropriate.

- In an equilibrium mixture, changes in pressure or concentration have no effect on the value of the equilibrium constant, K_c. However, an increase in temperature decreases the value of K_c for an exothermic reaction and increases the value of K_c for an endothermic reaction.

- Large values for equilibrium constants indicate high theoretical yields of product (and vice versa).

Questions

1 The formation of ethyl ethanoate and water from ethanoic acid and ethanol is a reversible reaction which can be allowed to reach equilibrium. The equilibrium is shown below.

$$CH_3COOH + C_2H_5OH \rightleftharpoons CH_3COOC_2H_5 + H_2O$$

   a Write the expression for K_c for this equilibrium system. [2]
   b A student mixed together 6.0 mol ethanoic acid and 12.5 mol ethanol. A small amount of hydrochloric acid was also added to catalyse the reaction. He left the mixture for two days to reach equilibrium in a water bath at constant temperature, after which time 1.0 mol ethanoic acid remained.

   i Copy and complete the table below to show the equilibrium composition of the equilibrium mixture.

Component	CH_3COOH	C_2H_5OH	$CH_3COOC_2H_5$	H_2O
Initial amount/mol	6.0	12.5	0.0	0.0
Equilibrium amount/mol				

[2]

   ii Calculate K_c to two significant figures. State the units, if any. The total volume of the equilibrium mixture is $1.0\,dm^3$. [2]

Hint

continued

c   The student was concerned that the mixture may <u>not</u> have reached equilibrium. What could he do to be sure that equilibrium had been reached? [2]

d   The student added more ethanol to the mixture.

   i   State, giving a reason, what would happen to the composition of the equilibrium mixture. [2]

   ii   What happens to the value of K_c? [1]

Hint

e   The student added more of the acid catalyst to the mixture. State, giving a reason, what would happen to the composition of the equilibrium mixture. [2]

f   The student repeated the experiment at a higher temperature and found that the value of K_c decreased.

   i   State, giving a reason, what would happen to the composition of the equilibrium mixture. [2]

   ii   What additional information does this information tell you about the reaction? [1]

OCR Chemistry A2 (2816) January 2004   [Total 16]

Answer

2   *Syngas* is a mixture of carbon monoxide and hydrogen gases, used as a feedstock for the manufacture of methanol.

A dynamic equilibrium was set up between carbon monoxide, CO, hydrogen, H_2, and methanol, CH_3OH. The equilibrium system is shown by Equilibrium 1 below.

   $CO(g) + 2H_2(g) \rightleftharpoons CH_3OH(g)$ *Equilibrium 1*

The equilibrium concentrations of the three components of this equilibrium are shown below.

Component	CO(g)	H_2(g)	CH_3OH(g)
Equilibrium concentration/ mol dm^{-3}	3.1×10^{-3}	2.4×10^{-2}	2.6×10^{-5}

a   State <u>two</u> features of a system that is in *dynamic equilibrium*. [2]

b   i   Write the expression for K_c for this equilibrium system. [2]

   ii   Calculate the numerical value of K_c for this equilibrium. [2]

Hint

c   The pressure was increased whilst keeping the temperature constant. The system was left to reach equilibrium. The equilibrium position of Equilibrium 1 shifted to the right.

   i   Explain why the equilibrium moved to the right. [2]

   ii   What is the effect, if any, on K_c? [1]

   iii   State and explain the effect on the rates of the forward and reverse reactions
      • when the pressure was first changed
      • when the system reached equilibrium. [4]

continued

d The temperature was increased whilst keeping the pressure constant. The system was left to reach equilibrium. The value of K_c for Equilibrium 1 decreased.

   i Explain what happens to the equilibrium position of Equilibrium 1. [2]

   ii Deduce the sign of the enthalpy change for the forward reaction shown in Equilibrium 1. Explain your reasoning. [1]

OCR Chemistry A2 (2816) January 2003 [Total 16]

Answer

3 Equilibrium 2, shown below, exists between $N_2(g)$, $O_2(g)$ and $NO(g)$.

$$N_2(g) + O_2(g) \rightleftharpoons 2NO(g) \qquad \textit{Equilibrium 2}$$

The equilibrium constant K_c for this reaction is 4.8×10^{-31} at 25 °C.

a i Write the expression for the equilibrium constant, K_c, for Equilibrium 2. [2]

   ii What does the value of K_c tell you about the equilibrium position in Equilibrium 2 at 25 °C? Explain your reasoning. [1]

Hint

   iii An equilibrium mixture of these three gases had the following equilibrium concentrations: $1.1 \, \text{mol dm}^{-3}$ $N_2(g)$ and $4.0 \times 10^{-16} \, \text{mol dm}^{-3}$ $NO(g)$. Calculate the equilibrium concentration of $O_2(g)$ in mol dm^{-3}. [3]

b In a car, nitrogen and oxygen gases in the air are drawn into the engine. The high temperature inside a working car engine increases the value of K_c for Equilibrium 2.

   i Deduce the sign of the enthalpy change for the forward reaction in Equilibrium 2. Explain your reasoning. [2]

   ii Compare the proportion of NO gas inside a working car engine to that at 25 °C. Explain your answer. [2]

   iii In the absence of a catalytic converter, the NO gas emerges from a car exhaust and then reacts with oxygen in the air. The oxidation number of the nitrogen increases to +4.
   Suggest an equation for this reaction. [2]

c *In this question, one mark is available for the quality of written communication.*
In industry, NO(g) is used in the manufacture of nitric acid. The production of NO(g) involves the oxidation of ammonia.

$$4NH_3(g) + 5O_2(g) \rightleftharpoons 4NO(g) + 6H_2O(g) \qquad \Delta H = -900 \, \text{kJ mol}^{-1}$$

The actual industrial conditions used are a temperature of about 1000 °C, a pressure of 10 atmospheres and a platinum–rhodium catalyst.
Giving reasons,

- predict the conditions required for an optimum equilibrium yield
- suggest reasons why the actual conditions used may be different from the optimum equilibrium conditions. [7]

Quality of written communication [1]

OCR Chemistry A2 (2816) June 2004 [Total 20]

Answer

continued

4 When heated, phosphorus pentachloride, PCl_5, dissociates.

$$PCl_5(g) \rightleftharpoons PCl_3(g) + Cl_2(g)$$

A chemist placed a mixture of the three gases into a container. The initial concentration of each gas was the same: $0.30 \, mol \, dm^{-3}$. The container was left until equilibrium had been reached.
Under these conditions, $K_c = 0.245 \, mol \, dm^{-3}$.

a Write an expression for K_c for this equilibrium. [1]

b **i** Use the value of K_c for this equilibrium to deduce whether the concentration of each gas increases, decreases or stays the same as the mixture approaches equilibrium. [1]

    ii Explain your deduction. [1]

c The chemist compressed the equilibrium mixture at constant temperature and allowed it to reach equilibrium under these new conditions.

    i Explain what happens to the value of K_c. [1]

    ii Explain what happened to the composition of the equilibrium mixture. [2]

d The chemist heated the equilibrium mixture and the equilibrium moved to the left.

    i Explain what happens to the value of K_c. [1]

    ii Explain what additional information this observation reveals about the reaction. [2]

e Phosphorus pentachloride reacts with magnesium oxide to form phosphorus(V) oxide, P_4O_{10}, and magnesium chloride.

    i Write a balanced equation for this reaction. [1]

    ii Calculate the mass of PCl_5 needed to form $100 \, g$ of P_4O_{10} in this reaction. [4]

OCR Chemistry A2 (2816) January 2007   [Total 14]

Hint

Answer

Acids, bases and buffers

Objectives

Definitions of acids and bases

In 1923, the Danish chemist J. N. Brønsted and the English chemist T. M. Lowry suggested that an acid may be defined as a 'proton donor', and a base as a 'proton acceptor'. A proton is a positive hydrogen ion, H^+. This is a long way from the first definitions you may have used for acids and bases.

Modern definitions are more precise than those which define an acid as something with a sour taste that turns blue litmus red, and a base as something that tastes bitter, feels soapy and turns red litmus blue (Figure 13.1). Such statements have some validity, but are limited and arbitrary. Health and safety legislation prevents us using taste to identify acids or bases in the laboratory. Nor do such statements help to explain what is going on when acids and bases take part in chemical reactions.

Figure 13.1 a The sour taste of lemons is due to citric acid and that of vinegar is due to ethanoic acid.
b Washing soda is a base used to soften water prior to washing clothes. A solution of washing soda feels soapy.

Acids and bases

Table 13.1 lists some definitions of acids and bases. (An alkali is a water-soluble base.)
Chemists tend to use the Brønsted–Lowry definition, as we will in this book.

Definition of acid	Definition of base	Advantage of definition
Tastes sharp or sour, like lemon	Tastes bitter, feels soapy or greasy	Is there any?
Turns purple cabbage juice red	Turns purple cabbage juice green or yellow	You can make your own indicator to test liquids
Turns blue litmus red	Turns red litmus blue	You can use test papers
Turns universal indicator red, orange or yellow	Turns universal indicator blue or purple	You can compare strengths of various acids and alkalis
Produces an excess of hydrogen ions, $H^+(aq)$, in aqueous solution (Arrhenius, 1884)	Produces an excess of hydroxide ions, $OH^-(aq)$, in aqueous solution (Arrhenius, 1884)	Enables acid–base reactions, e.g. neutralisation, to be explained as a reaction: $H^+(aq) + OH^-(aq) \longrightarrow H_2O(l)$
Donates protons during a chemical reaction (Brønsted and Lowry, 1923)	Accepts protons during a chemical reaction (Brønsted and Lowry, 1923)	Explains the role of water and why (for example) HCl(aq) is acidic but dry HCl(g) is not

Table 13.1 Acids and bases.

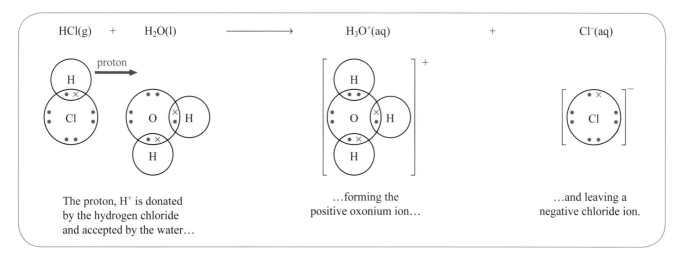

Figure 13.2 An acid is a proton donor. Hydrogen chloride is the acid in this reaction. A base is a proton acceptor. Water is the base in this reaction. Remember that a proton is a hydrogen ion, H^+.

The Brønsted–Lowry definition is particularly appropriate when considering the chemistry of aqueous solutions. We will start with the formation of one of the most familiar acids of all – hydrochloric acid. It is made when hydrogen chloride, a gas, dissolves and reacts in water.

In aqueous solution, hydrogen chloride donates a proton to water to form the oxonium ion, $H_3O^+(aq)$, (also known as a hydronium ion) as shown in Figure 13.2.

In contrast, a base will accept a proton to give the hydroxide ion, $OH^-(aq)$, as shown for ammonia in Figure 13.3.

Note that water behaves as a base in the hydrogen chloride solution, and as an acid in the ammonia solution. Substances which can act as an acid or a base are described as **amphoteric**. Aluminium oxide, Al_2O_3, is another example of an amphoteric compound.

In both cases we have omitted an important fact: the reactions should, strictly speaking, be written as equilibria. So for the first case we write:

$$HCl(g) + H_2O(l) \rightleftharpoons H_3O^+(aq) + Cl^-(aq)$$

When we think about the forward reaction, $HCl(g)$ is an acid because it donates a proton, H^+. Water is a base because it receives this proton.

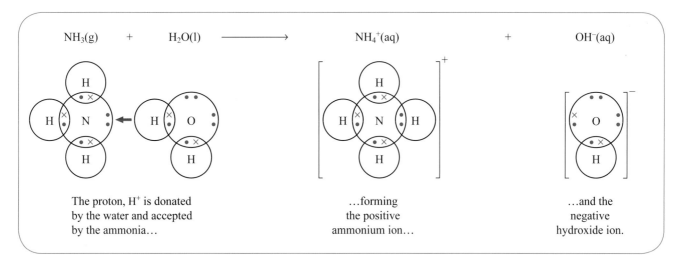

Figure 13.3 Water is the proton donor (it is the acid); ammonia is the proton acceptor (it is the base).

Hydrochloric acid is described as a *strong* acid. Strong acids are almost fully dissociated into ions in their solutions, so this equilibrium lies well to the right of the above reaction equation.

Now consider the reverse reaction:

$$H_3O^+(aq) + Cl^-(aq) \rightleftharpoons HCl(g) + H_2O(l)$$

The proton is donated to the chloride ion to form hydrogen chloride. (The oxonium ion, H_3O^+, a proton donor, is an acid.) Equally, we can say that the chloride ion, $Cl^-(aq)$, accepts a proton to become hydrogen chloride. The chloride ion, a proton acceptor, is therefore a base. This can be summarised as shown (B–L stands for Brønsted–Lowry):

conjugate pair

$$HCl(g) + H_2O(l) \rightleftharpoons H_3O^+(aq) + Cl^-(aq)$$

B–L acid   B–L base   B–L acid   B–L base

conjugate pair

Look at the relationship between the species. The chlorine-containing species, $HCl(g)$ and $Cl^-(aq)$, form a pair. They are acid and base respectively, with the acid the richer in protons. We call this couple a **conjugate pair**.

Now consider the equilibrium between ammonia and water. The conjugate pairs of acids and bases are shown in the following equation:

conjugate pair

$$NH_3(aq) + H_2O(l) \rightleftharpoons NH_4^+(aq) + OH^-(aq)$$

B–L base   B–L acid   B–L acid   B–L base

conjugate pair

An ammonia molecule accepts a proton from water. Ammonia is thus behaving as a Brønsted–Lowry base in forming an ammonium ion, which is its conjugate pair acid. Water is behaving as a Brønsted–Lowry acid (as it has donated a proton to an ammonia molecule) in forming a hydroxide ion. The hydroxide ion is water's conjugate pair base (as it accepts a proton to form water in the reverse reaction).

How to spot an acid or a base

You need to know these definitions:
- A Brønsted–Lowry acid is a proton (or H^+) donor.
- A Brønsted–Lowry base is a proton (or H^+) acceptor.

The Brønsted–Lowry definitions apply to chemical changes in which protons, H^+, are transferred. First of all examine the change, and find the donors and acceptors.

We shall now look at another example. Which are the conjugate pairs of acid and base in this reaction?

$$NH_4^+(aq) + CO_3^{2-}(aq) \rightleftharpoons HCO_3^-(aq) + NH_3(aq)$$

We can see that the ammonium ion (NH_4^+) donates a proton to the carbonate ion (CO_3^{2-}), and forms ammonia (NH_3). Thus the ammonium ion is an acid, and the ammonia is its conjugate base.

The carbonate ion accepts a proton, forming a hydrogencarbonate ion (HCO_3^-). Thus the carbonate ion is a base, and the hydrogencarbonate ion is its conjugate acid. In both cases the conjugate acids are richer in protons than their conjugate bases. The equation can therefore be annotated as shown below:

conjugate pair

$$NH_4^+(aq) + CO_3^{2-}(aq) \rightleftharpoons HCO_3^-(aq) + NH_3(aq)$$

B–L acid   B–L base   B–L acid   B–L base

conjugate pair

SAQ

1 Use the Brønsted–Lowry definition of acid and base to identify the acids and bases in these equilibria and their conjugate bases and acids. Note that one of the reactions is not occurring in aqueous solution, a situation that could not be covered by earlier definitions of acid and base.

  [Hint]

a $H_2SO_4(l) + H_2O(l) \rightleftharpoons H_3O^+(aq) + HSO_4^-(aq)$

b $CH_3COOH(aq) + H_2O(l)$
        $\rightleftharpoons CH_3COO^-(aq) + H_3O^+(aq)$

c $CH_3NH_2(aq) + H_2O(l)$
        $\rightleftharpoons CH_3NH_3^+(aq) + OH^-(aq)$

d $NH_3(g) + HCl(g) \rightleftharpoons NH_4^+Cl^-(s)$

  [Answer]

The role of water

Water seems a familiar, almost benign substance, not one to be involved when acids react with bases. For example, in the formation of sodium chloride from sodium hydroxide and hydrochloric acid, it seems to sit on the sidelines:

$$NaOH(aq) + HCl(aq) \rightleftharpoons NaCl(aq) + H_2O(l)$$

Don't be misled. Water is not an innocent bystander in acid–base reactions. Water plays a crucial part. It helps to understand this if you know more about pure water itself.

Water: facts and models

It is a fact that pure water conducts electricity, even if ever so slightly. It is quite unlike liquid helium, for example, or cyclohexane, which do not conduct electricity at all. Unlike these two substances, water contains ions that can carry charge. Indeed, pure water can be electrolysed by a direct current but its conductivity is very low.

SAQ

2   What does the low conductivity of water tell you about the number of ions available for carrying a direct current?

Answer

We can imagine a model for the formation of ions from water molecules, in terms of proton (H^+) transfer. Suppose every now and then one water molecule could react with another to form ions. It could be as shown in Figure 13.4. A proton leaves one molecule of water for another, ions are formed, and these ions can transfer electrons at the electrodes during electrolysis.

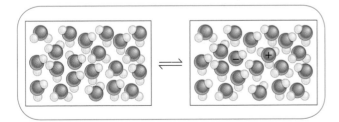

Figure 13.4 A proton is transferred from one water molecule to another, so that a positive ion, H_3O^+, is formed and a negative ion, OH^-, is left behind.

This reaction can be summarised as:

$$2H_2O(l) \rightleftharpoons H_3O^+(aq) + OH^-(aq)$$

or more simply as:

$$H_2O(l) \rightleftharpoons H^+(aq) + OH^-(aq)$$

SAQ

3   Experimental evidence tells us that the equilibrium constant for this reaction is very, very small. What does this tell you about the relative proportions of water molecules, protons and hydroxide ions? Does this fit in with your knowledge of the electrical conductivity of pure water?

Hint

Answer

Base behaviour and neutralisation

A base neutralises an acid because it reacts with the H^+ ions that the acid donates. This can be shown most clearly by writing an ionic equation. For example, when calcium oxide neutralises hydrochloric acid the balanced chemical equation is:

$$CaO(s) + 2HCl(aq) \longrightarrow CaCl_2(aq) + H_2O(l)$$

while the ionic equation is:

$$O^{2-}(s) + 2H^+(aq) \longrightarrow H_2O(l)$$

The calcium oxide neutralises the hydrochloric acid because the oxide ions react with the hydrogen ions to form water.

When magnesium carbonate neutralises hydrochloric acid the balanced chemical equation is:

$$MgCO_3(s) + 2HCl(aq) \longrightarrow MgCl_2(aq) + CO_2(g) + H_2O(l)$$

The ionic equation is:

$$CO_3^{2-}(s) + 2H^+(aq) \longrightarrow CO_2(g) + H_2O(l)$$

The magnesium carbonate neutralises the hydrochloric acid because the carbonate ions react with the hydrogen ions to form carbon dioxide and water.

When zinc metal neutralises hydrochloric acid the balanced chemical equation is:

$$Zn(s) + 2HCl(aq) \longrightarrow ZnCl_2(aq) + H_2(g)$$

The ionic equation is:

$$Zn(s) + 2H^+(aq) \longrightarrow Zn^{2+}(aq) + H_2(g)$$

The zinc metal neutralises the hydrochloric acid because the zinc atoms react with the hydrogen ions to form zinc ions and hydrogen gas.

When sodium hydroxide neutralises hydrochloric acid the balanced chemical equation is:

$$NaOH(aq) + HCl(aq) \longrightarrow NaCl(aq) + H_2O(l)$$

while the ionic equation is:

$$OH^-(aq) + H^+(aq) \longrightarrow H_2O(l)$$

The sodium hydroxide neutralises the hydrochloric acid because the hydroxide ions react with the hydrogen ions to form water.

SAQ

4 Write balanced chemical equations and ionic equations for the following neutralisation reactions:

   a sulfuric acid + copper(II) oxide
   b sulfuric acid + sodium carbonate
   c sulfuric acid + magnesium
   d sulfuric acid + potassium hydroxide.

> Answer

Enthalpy change of neutralisation

When an acid is neutralised by an alkali the reaction is exothermic. The enthalpy change of neutralisation is defined as 'the energy change when a sufficient amount of acid or alkali is neutralised to produce one mole of water'.

Since the ionic equation for such a neutralisation is always $OH^- + H^+ \longrightarrow H_2O$, the value of ΔH is almost unchanging for different strong acids and alkalis. It is always close to $-57\,kJ$ per mole of water produced. This can easily be investigated experimentally (Worked example 1).

Worked example 1

$50.0\,cm^3$ of $1.00\,mol\,dm^{-3}$ HCl, at a temperature of $18.0\,°C$, is neutralised by $50.0\,cm^3$ of $1.00\,mol\,dm^{-3}$ NaOH, also at a temperature of $18.0\,°C$. The temperature of the final mixture is $24.8\,°C$. No heat energy is lost. Assuming the specific heat capacity of the final mixture is $4.2\,J\,g^{-1}\,°C^{-1}$, and that $1.0\,cm^3$ of the final mixture has a mass of $1.0\,g$, calculate the enthalpy change of neutralisation.

Step 1 Calculate the heat energy released.

$$energy = mass \times specific\ heat\ capacity \\ \times temperature\ rise$$

Since $1.0\,cm^3$ of the final mixture has a mass of $1.0\,g$, the total mass is $(50.0 + 50.0)\,g = 100\,g$

$$energy = 100\,g \times 4.2\,J\,g^{-1}\,°C^{-1} \times 6.8\,°C \\ = 2856\,J$$

Step 2 Calculate the number of moles of water formed.

$50.0\,cm^3$ of $1.00\,mol\,dm^{-3}$ acid contain 0.05 moles of H^+ ions (i.e. $1 \times \left[\dfrac{50.0}{1000}\right]$).

$50.0\,cm^3$ of $1.00\,mol\,dm^{-3}$ alkali contain 0.05 moles of OH^- ions.

From the balanced chemical equation, we know this will produce 0.05 moles of water.

Step 3 Calculate the heat energy given out when 1 mole of water is formed.

$$enthalpy\ change\ of\ neutralisation = \frac{2856}{0.05} \\ = 57\,120\,J\,mol^{-1}$$

or $57\,kJ\,mol^{-1}$ to 2 significant figures.

As energy is released in this exothermic reaction we give it a negative sign, i.e. $-57\,kJ\,mol^{-1}$.

If you perform this experiment yourself, remember it is extremely unlikely that 'no heat energy is lost'!

SAQ

5 $100\,\text{cm}^3$ of $2.00\,\text{mol}\,\text{dm}^{-3}$ HCl, at a temperature of $19.5\,°C$, is neutralised by $100\,\text{cm}^3$ of $2.00\,\text{mol}\,\text{dm}^{-3}$ NaOH, also at a temperature of $19.5\,°C$. The temperature of the final mixture is $33.0\,°C$. No heat energy is lost. Assume the specific heat capacity of the final mixture is $4.2\,\text{J}\,\text{g}^{-1}\,\text{C}^{-1}$, and that $1.0\,\text{cm}^3$ of the final mixture has a mass of $1.0\,\text{g}$.

a Calculate the heat energy released in the reaction. [Hint]

b Calculate the number of moles of water formed in the reaction. [Hint]

c Calculate the enthalpy change of neutralisation. [Answer]

Acids and bases of varying strength

Strong acids and bases can be thought of as those which are totally ionised when dissolved in water. The strong acids include hydrogen halides and strong bases include the Group 1 metal hydroxides. Consider what happens when examples of these dissolve in water and then react.

For every mole of these solutes, a mole of each positive and negative ion is produced in solution:

$$LiOH(s) \xrightarrow{water} Li^+(aq) + OH^-(aq)$$

$$HCl(g) \xrightarrow{water} H^+(aq) + Cl^-(aq)$$

If a mole of protons reacts with a mole of hydroxide ions, they combine to form a mole of water molecules.

Weak acids and weak bases do not ionise totally when they dissolve in water; in fact, they may hardly ionise at all. When it comes to donating protons, weak acids are very limited. Ethanoic acid is a good example. Hardly any protons are produced when it reacts in water, so that the concentration of protons is low. In the reaction shown below, the equilibrium is very much to the left:

$$CH_3COOH(l) \xrightleftharpoons{water} H^+(aq) + CH_3COO^-(aq)$$

Organic acids such as ethanoic acid (the sharp-tasting liquid in vinegar) and citric acid (the mouth-watering stuff of lemons) are typical weak acids. As proton donors go, they are pretty feeble. Weak bases are similarly feeble when it comes to accepting protons. They include the conjugate bases of strong acids, such as chloride and sulfate ions.

Table 13.2 shows some examples of conjugate acid–base pairs, together with their relative strengths.

As you will see, the relative strengths of acids and bases need to be known in order to monitor reactions between them. You need to understand the arithmetic behind measuring their relative strengths.

Introducing K_w, the ionic product of water

As shown already, pure water dissociates according to this equation:

$$H_2O(l) \rightleftharpoons H^+(aq) + OH^-(aq); \Delta H^\ominus = +57\,\text{kJ}\,\text{mol}^{-1}$$

The equilibrium constant expression is:

$$K_c = \frac{[H^+][OH^-]}{[H_2O]}$$

	Acid				Base	
strongest acid	hydrochloric	HCl	$\rightleftharpoons$	$H^+ + Cl^-$	chloride	weakest base
	benzoic	C_6H_5COOH	$\rightleftharpoons$	$H^+ + C_6H_5COO^-$	benzoate	
	ethanoic	CH_3COOH	$\rightleftharpoons$	$H^+ + CH_3COO^-$	ethanoate	
	ammonium	NH_4^+	$\rightleftharpoons$	$H^+ + NH_3$	ammonia	
	phenol	C_6H_5OH	$\rightleftharpoons$	$H^+ + C_6H_5O^-$	phenoxide	
	hydrogencarbonate	HCO_3^-	$\rightleftharpoons$	$H^+ + CO_3^{2-}$	carbonate	
weakest acid	water	H_2O	$\rightleftharpoons$	$H^+ + OH^-$	hydroxide	strongest base

Table 13.2 Relative acid and base strengths of some conjugate acid–base pairs.

As $[H_2O]$ is effectively constant, we can write:

$$K_w = [H^+][OH^-]$$

The product, $[H^+] \times [OH^-]$, is called the **ionic product of water**, K_w.

At 298 K, $K_w = 1.00 \times 10^{-14} \, mol^2 \, dm^{-6}$. From the equation,

$$H_2O(l) \rightleftharpoons H^+(aq) + OH^-(aq),$$

we can see that the concentration of protons equals the concentration of hydroxide ions.

We have defined K_w:

$$K_w = [H^+][OH^-] = 1.00 \times 10^{-14} \, mol^2 \, dm^{-6} \text{ (at 298 K)}$$

This means that the concentration of each ion, $[H^+]$ and $[OH^-]$, is $1.00 \times 10^{-7} \, mol \, dm^{-3}$ in pure water (as $1.00 \times 10^{-7} \times 1.00 \times 10^{-7} = 1.00 \times 10^{-14}$).

Little numbers, large numbers and logs

Chemists deal with little and large. Minuscule molecules of water in enormous numbers are found in a sip of lemonade. To cope with this number range, we use powers of ten, as shown below:

Number of molecules of water in a sip of lemonade	300 000 000 000 000 000 000 000	3.00×10^{23}
Distance between the atoms in a molecule of water	0.000 000 0001 11 metres	$1.11 \times 10^{-10} \, m$

Other numbers that chemists might come across include the mass of the Earth ($5.97 \times 10^{24} \, kg$) and the mass of a hydrogen atom ($1.67 \times 10^{-27} \, kg$).

Ten to the power of 3 (10^3 or 1000) is ten times bigger than ten to the power of 2 (10^2 or 100). Powers of ten represent tenfold jumps in size and are called logarithms. Because we count in tens (unlike computers, which count in twos), we call these powers 'logarithms to the base ten', and write them as $\log_{10}$. In general, when we write 'number' $= 1 \times 10^x$, the value of x is $\log_{10}$('number'). Table 13.3 shows how $\log_{10}$ is used to represent the range of numbers we might use.

Example	Number	$\log_{10}$
Molecules of ozone in 1 cm^3 of air on a good day	100 000 000 000 000 = 10^{14}	14.0
Speed of light/m s^{-1}	300 000 000 $= 3 \times 10^8$	8.5
Solubility of Ca(OH)$_2$/mol dm^{-3}	0.0153 $= 1.53 \times 10^{-2}$	−1.8
Concentration of protons in pure water at 298 K/mol dm^{-3}	0.000 000 1 $= 1 \times 10^{-7}$	−7.0
Concentration of protons in 0.1 mol dm^{-3} NaOH/mol dm^{-3}	0.000 000 000 000 1 $= 1 \times 10^{-13}$	−13.0

Table 13.3 You will come across the term 'negative log' or '−$\log_{10}$'. This is not to complicate matters. It is simply a way of getting rid of the minus sign of the log.

Introducing pH

The concentration of protons and hydroxide ions in pure water is clearly very small. Because it is awkward to fiddle about with tiny numbers like 1.00×10^{-7} (0.0000001, a tenth of a millionth), chemists prefer to use logarithmic scales. They do the same for large numbers too.

Chemists define pH as $-\log_{10}[H^+]$, i.e. the negative logarithm to the base ten of the concentration of the hydrogen ion. (The negative part helps us to cope with very small numbers, actually negative powers of ten.)

$$pH = -\log_{10}[H^+]$$

Now you can show by calculation that pure water has a pH of 7:

$[H^+]$ is $1 \times 10^{-7}\,\text{mol}\,\text{dm}^{-3}$

$pH = -\log_{10}[H^+]$

$\quad = -\log_{10}[1 \times 10^{-7}]$

$\quad = 7$

You should ensure that you know how to carry out this calculation on your scientific calculator. Be careful to use the $\log_{10}$ (or $\lg_{10}$) button and *not* the ln button (which is $\log_e$). You can calculate the concentration of protons, $[H^+(aq)]$, by using the inverse log or 10^x button.

SAQ

6 Use this process to calculate the pH of these solutions:

a an aqueous solution with $[H^+] = 3.00 \times 10^{-4}\,\text{mol}\,\text{dm}^{-3}$ (e.g. a cola drink)
[Hint]

b an aqueous solution with $[H^+] = 1.00 \times 10^{-2}\,\text{mol}\,\text{dm}^{-3}$ (stomach contents!)

c an aqueous solution with $[H^+] = 4.00 \times 10^{-8}\,\text{mol}\,\text{dm}^{-3}$ (blood).
[Answer]

The pH values of some aqueous solutions with which you might be familiar are shown in Table 13.4.

Solution	pH
hydrochloric acid ($1.0\,\text{mol}\,\text{dm}^{-3}$)	0.0
hydrochloric acid ($0.1\,\text{mol}\,\text{dm}^{-3}$)	1.0
hydrochloric acid ($0.01\,\text{mol}\,\text{dm}^{-3}$)	2.0
stomach 'juices' (contains HCl(aq))	1.0–2.0
lemon juice	2.3
vinegar	3
coffee	around 5
rainwater (normal)	5.7
saliva	6.3–6.8
urine	6.0–7.4
fresh milk	around 6.5
pure water	7.0
blood	7.4
pancreatic juices	7.1–8.2
sea water	around 8.5
baking soda in water	around 9
milk of magnesia	10
soapy water (cheap soap!)	11
bench sodium hydroxide ($0.1\,\text{mol}\,\text{dm}^{-3}$)	13
bench sodium hydroxide ($1.0\,\text{mol}\,\text{dm}^{-3}$)	14

Table 13.4 pH values of some familiar aqueous solutions.

Calculating the pH of strong acids and strong bases

Strong acids dissociate completely. This means that we know, from the initial concentration of the strong acid, just how many protons are present in a solution. If one mole of a monobasic acid, such as HCl, which has one proton to lose, is present in a decimetre cube of solution, then the concentration of protons is $1.00\,\text{mol}\,\text{dm}^{-3}$. You can see this from the equation:

$$\underset{1\,\text{mol}}{HCl(g)} \xrightleftharpoons{\text{water}} \underset{1\,\text{mol}}{H^+(aq)} + \underset{1\,\text{mol}}{Cl^-(aq)}$$

The pH of a $1.00\,mol\,dm^{-3}$ solution of hydrochloric acid is therefore $-\log_{10}[H^+] = -\log_{10}(1.00)$, i.e. zero.

Strong bases also contain stoichiometric amounts of protons in solution, although it is much less obvious. We tend to think of strong bases as producers of hydroxide ions, but of course there are protons present too – only in very small quantities. Follow the calculation in Worked example 2, for the pH of a $0.0500\,mol\,dm^{-3}$ solution of sodium hydroxide.

Worked example 2

Sodium hydroxide ionises completely:

$$NaOH(s) \xrightarrow{\text{1 dm}^3 \text{ water}} Na^+(aq) + OH^-(aq)$$
$$0.0500\,mol \qquad\qquad 0.0500\,mol \quad 0.0500\,mol$$

The concentration of hydroxide ions in a $0.0500\,mol\,dm^{-3}$ NaOH solution is clearly $0.0500\,mol\,dm^{-3}$. Now the ionic product of water, K_w, is constant and (at 298 K) equals $1.00 \times 10^{-14}\,mol^2\,dm^{-6}$.

This means we can write:

$$K_w = [H^+][OH^-] = 1.00 \times 10^{-14}\,mol^2\,dm^{-6}$$

so

$$[H^+] = \frac{1.00 \times 10^{-14}\,mol^2\,dm^{-6}}{[OH^-]\,mol\,dm^{-3}}$$

$$= \frac{1.00 \times 10^{-14}}{0.0500}\,mol\,dm^{-3}$$

$$= 2.00 \times 10^{-13}\,mol\,dm^{-3}$$

so

$$pH = -\log_{10}[H^+] = -\log_{10}(2.00 \times 10^{-13}) = 12.7$$

There is a quicker way of getting the same answer: just find $-\log_{10}[OH^-]$ and subtract it from 14.0.

(This works because $-\log_{10}[H^+] - \log_{10}[OH^-] = 14$.)

SAQ

7   Find the pH of the following strong acids and strong bases, given that $K_w = 1.00 \times 10^{-14}\,mol^2\,dm^{-6}$ at 298 K:

   a $1.00\,mol\,dm^{-3}$ nitric acid, $HNO_3(aq)$ | Hint |

   b $0.500\,mol\,dm^{-3}$ nitric acid, $HNO_3(aq)$

   c   an aqueous solution containing 3.00 g of hydrogen chloride, HCl, per dm^3

   d   a $0.00100\,mol\,dm^{-3}$ potassium hydroxide solution, KOH(aq)

   e   an aqueous solution containing 0.200 g of sodium hydroxide, NaOH, per dm^3. | Answer |

Ionic equilibria: the definition of K_a and pK_a

The following ionic equation summarises all strong acid–strong base neutralisations:

$$H^+(aq) + OH^-(aq) \rightleftharpoons H_2O(l); \Delta H^\ominus = -57\,kJ\,mol^{-1}$$

In keeping with this, the same enthalpy change of reaction is observed whatever strong acid–strong base combination is involved (provided the solution is sufficiently dilute that the other ions do not interact).

Most acids are weak. They do not ionise completely in water. A good example is ethanoic acid, of which vinegar is a dilute solution. Here the ethanoic acid will donate a proton to water, so it is indeed an acid, but the reverse reaction, i.e. the acceptance of a proton by the ethanoate anion, must also be taken into account. When the two reactions are proceeding at the same rate, an equilibrium is set up:

$$CH_3COOH(aq) \rightleftharpoons H^+(aq) + CH_3COO^-(aq)$$

The expression for the equilibrium constant, K_a, can now be written:

$$K_a = \frac{[H^+][CH_3COO^-]}{[CH_3COOH]}$$

This constant, K_a, is called the **acid dissociation constant**. At 298 K for ethanoic acid, its value is $1.74 \times 10^{-5}\,mol\,dm^{-3}$. This value gives us a feel for the strength of the acid, and of course the extent to which it ionises in water.

Chemists often write the general formula for a monobasic acid as HA. Using this formula, the balanced equation for the ionisation of a weak acid becomes:

$$HA(aq) \rightleftharpoons H^+(aq) + A^-(aq)$$

so

$$K_a = \frac{[H^+][A^-]}{[HA]}$$

If the acid dissociates to a large extent, $[H^+]$ and $[A^-]$ are relatively large, and $[HA]$ is smaller. Both effects would make K_a comparatively big. You can see this in Table 13.5. Yet again we can be dealing with a large range of values, some of them very small. Just as pH was invented for hydrogen ion concentration, pK_a has been introduced to deal with the dissociation of acids:

$$pK_a = -\log_{10}K_a$$

SAQ

8 Look at Table 13.5. Work out which species are Brønsted–Lowry acids and which are their conjugate bases. Record your results in a table.

Answer

Calculating the pH of a weak acid

The pH of a weak acid may be calculated from the acid dissociation constant, K_a, the equilibrium constant expression and the concentration of the acid solution.

Unless we wish to determine pH to more than two decimal places, we make two assumptions to simplify the calculation:

- we assume that $[H^+] = [A^-]$, and that
- $[HA]$ is approximately equal to the concentration of the acid, making the assumption that only a very small number of the HA molecules have dissociated.

Acid or ion	Equilibrium in aqueous solution	K_a/mol dm^{-3}	pK_a
nitric	$HNO_3 \rightleftharpoons H^+ + NO_3^-$	about 40	−1.4
sulfuric(IV)	$H_2SO_3 \rightleftharpoons H^+ + HSO_3^-$	1.5×10^{-2}	1.8
hydrated Fe^{3+} ion	$[Fe(H_2O)_6]^{3+} \rightleftharpoons H^+ + [Fe(H_2O)_5(OH)]^{2+}$	6.0×10^{-3}	2.2
hydrofluoric	$HF \rightleftharpoons H^+ + F^-$	5.6×10^{-4}	3.3
nitric(III)	$HNO_2 \rightleftharpoons H^+ + NO_2^-$	4.7×10^{-4}	3.3
methanoic	$HCOOH \rightleftharpoons H^+ + HCOO^-$	1.6×10^{-4}	3.8
benzoic	$C_6H_5COOH \rightleftharpoons H^+ + C_6H_5COO^-$	6.3×10^{-5}	4.2
ethanoic	$CH_3COOH \rightleftharpoons H^+ + CH_3COO^-$	1.7×10^{-5}	4.8
propanoic	$CH_3CH_2COOH \rightleftharpoons H^+ + CH_3CH_2COO^-$	1.3×10^{-5}	4.9
hydrated Al^{3+} ion	$[Al(H_2O)_6]^{3+} \rightleftharpoons H^+ + [Al(H_2O)_5(OH)]^{2+}$	1.0×10^{-5}	5.0
carbonic	$CO_2 + H_2O \rightleftharpoons H^+ + HCO_3^-$	4.5×10^{-7}	6.35
silicic	$SiO_2 + H_2O \rightleftharpoons H^+ + HSiO_3^-$	1.3×10^{-10}	9.9
hydrogencarbonate ion	$HCO_3^- \rightleftharpoons H^+ + CO_3^{2-}$	4.8×10^{-11}	10.3
hydrogensilicate ion	$HSiO_3^- \rightleftharpoons H^+ + SiO_3^{2-}$	1.3×10^{-12}	11.9
water	$H_2O \rightleftharpoons H^+ + OH^-$	1.0×10^{-14}	14.0

Table 13.5 Acid dissociation constants, K_a, for a range of acids, for aqueous solutions in the region of 0.0–0.01 mol dm^{-3}.

The first of these assumptions may not seem to be an approximation until we remember that some water molecules will have dissociated to form hydrogen ions. As very few water molecules will have dissociated in this way, this approximation will not affect a pH calculated to two decimal places. Using this assumption, the expression for K_a simplifies to:

$$K_a = \frac{[H^+][A^-]}{[HA]} = \frac{[H^+]^2}{[HA]}$$

The second assumption relies on the fact that we are dealing with a weak acid. Clearly, some molecules will dissociate but the proportion is so small that the pH value calculated will not be significantly affected until we reach the third decimal place.

Having accepted that, for our purposes, these assumptions are sound, we can proceed to do a calculation (Worked example 3).

Worked example 3

What is the pH of $0.100\,\text{mol}\,\text{dm}^{-3}$ ethanoic acid? ($K_a = 1.74 \times 10^{-5}\,\text{mol}\,\text{dm}^{-3}$)

Step 1 Ethanoic acid dissociates as shown in the equation:

$$CH_3COOH(aq) \rightleftharpoons H^+(aq) + CH_3COO^-(aq)$$

Using our simplified expression for K_a:

[HA] = [CH₃COOH(aq)]
[H⁺] = [H⁺(aq)] and
[A⁻] = [CH₃COO⁻(aq)] = [H⁺(aq)]

$[HA] = [CH_3COOH(aq)]$
$[H^+] = [H^+(aq)]$ and
$[A^-] = [CH_3COO^-(aq)] = [H^+(aq)]$

So we can write:

$$K_a = \frac{[H^+]^2}{[CH_3COOH]}$$

Step 2 Putting numbers in we have:

$$1.74 \times 10^{-5} = \frac{[H^+]^2}{0.100}$$

Step 3 Rearrange this equation:

$$[H^+]^2 = 1.74 \times 10^{-5} \times 0.100 = 1.74 \times 10^{-6}$$

continued

Step 4 Take square roots:

$$[H^+] = 1.32 \times 10^{-3}\,\text{mol}\,\text{dm}^{-3}$$

Step 5 Now we can calculate pH:

$$pH = -\log_{10}(1.32 \times 10^{-3}) = 2.88$$

Check that you arrive at the same value by keying the data into your calculator. Use the 'square root' key to find the square root of 1.74×10^{-6}; remember to use $\log_{10}$ and to enter the powers of 10 using the 'exp' key (remembering the minus sign for this as well as a minus in front of the $\log_{10}$).

SAQ

9 Using the data from Table 13.5 work out:
   a the pH of a solution containing $0.020\,\text{mol}\,\text{dm}^{-3}$ of benzoic acid in water   Hint
   b the pH of an aqueous solution containing $0.010\,\text{mol}\,\text{dm}^{-3}$ of hydrated aluminium ions
   c the pH of a solution of $0.10\,\text{mol}\,\text{dm}^{-3}$ methanoic acid in water.   Answer

Calculating [H⁺] from a pH value

You have learned how to calculate the pH of a solution from the H^+ concentration, using the formula $pH = -\log_{10}[H^+]$. The calculation can also be performed in reverse, i.e. the H^+ concentration can be calculated from the pH (see Worked example 4). In this case the formula becomes:

$$[H^+] = 10^{-pH}$$

Worked example 4

What is the [H⁺] in a solution of pH 5.20?

Key into your calculator $10^{-5.20}$. Press '='.

The answer is 6.31×10^{-6}.   *continued*

A solution of pH 5.20 has an H^+ concentration of $6.31 \times 10^{-6} \, mol \, dm^{-3}$.

SAQ

10 Calculate the H^+ concentration of a solution whose pH is:

   a 2.90

   b 3.70

   c 11.2

Answer

Calculating the K_a of a weak acid

If you know the concentration of a solution of a weak acid, and the pH of the solution, it is possible to calculate the K_a of the acid.

   Consider the expression, $K_a = \dfrac{[H^+][A^-]}{[HA]}$.

If we know the pH of the solution we can calculate $[H^+]$. We know this is the same as $[A^-]$, so we

can change the expression to $K_a = \dfrac{[H^+]^2}{[HA]}$, using the

assumptions made previously. The method is demonstrated in Worked example 5.

Worked example 5

2-nitrophenol is a weak acid.
$0.100 \, mol \, dm^{-3}$ 2-nitrophenol has a pH of 4.10.

What is the K_a of 2-nitrophenol? *continued*

Since the pH is 4.10, the H^+ concentration is $10^{-4.1}$. This is $7.94 \times 10^{-5} \, mol \, dm^{-3}$.

$$K_a = \frac{[H^+]^2}{[HA]} = \frac{(7.94 \times 10^{-5})^2}{0.100}$$

$$= 6.31 \times 10^{-8} \, mol \, dm^{-3}$$

SAQ

11 Calculate the value of K_a for the following acids:

   a $0.0200 \, mol \, dm^{-3}$ 2-aminobenzoic acid, which has a pH of 4.30   Hint

   b $0.0500 \, mol \, dm^{-3}$ propanoic acid, which has a pH of 3.10

   c $0.0100 \, mol \, dm^{-3}$ methanoic acid, which has a pH of 2.90.

Answer

Measuring pH

Many dyes interact with acids and alkalis. Their molecular structure can be modified by changes in pH so that they change colour (Figure 13.5).

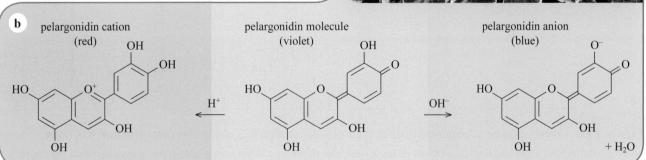

Figure 13.5 a The red petals of pelargoniums (geraniums) contain the dye pelargonidin. **b** Hydrogen or hydroxide ions can tweak its molecular structure to produce different colours.

Name of dye	Colour at lower pH	pH range	End-point	Colour at higher pH
methyl violet	yellow	0.0–1.6	0.8	blue
methyl yellow	red	2.9–4.0	3.5	yellow
methyl orange	red	3.2–4.4	3.7	yellow
bromophenol blue	yellow	2.8–4.6	4.0	blue
bromocresol green	yellow	3.8–5.4	4.7	blue
methyl red	red	4.2–6.3	5.1	yellow
bromothymol blue	yellow	6.0–7.6	7.0	blue
phenolphthalein	colourless	8.2–10.0	9.3	pink/violet
alizarin yellow	yellow	10.1–13.0	12.5	orange/red

Table 13.6 Some of the chemical indicators used to monitor pH, with their pH ranges of use and pH of end-point.

The pH affects the colour of some dyes in quite dramatic ways. The dyes are used in the laboratory, sometimes as mixtures, to monitor the pH of chemical changes; when used in this way, they are called **indicators**. They usually change colour over a pH range of between 1 and 2 pH units, with a recognised end-point somewhere in the middle. The end-point is the point where the indicator is most clearly seen to be between the two extremes of its colour.

For example, bromothymol blue is yellow in acidic solutions and blue in alkaline solutions. The colour change takes place from pH 6.0 to pH 7.6 and the end-point occurs when the pH is 7.0. The colours, ranges and end-points of indicators vary considerably, as can be seen in Table 13.6.

For example, phenolphthalein is colourless in solutions with a pH of less than 8.2 and does not reach its final pink colour until the pH is 10. Hydrogen or hydroxide ions have a considerable effect on the molecular structure, as shown in Figure 13.6.

Universal indicator is actually a mixture of dyes whose combined colours can create a range of

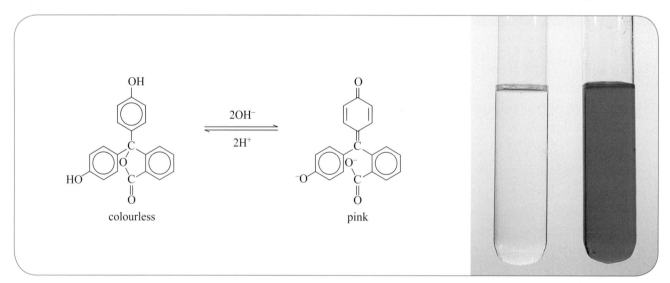

Figure 13.6 Colour change in phenolphthalein. At a pH of less than 8.2, the molecular structure has three isolated benzene rings, each with its own delocalised electrons in a different plane from the other two. In more alkaline solutions, the structure changes: a planar ion is formed (a flat ion!) and delocalised electrons extend over virtually the entire structure. This extended electron system absorbs most, but not all, of the light in the visible spectrum, so that the solution is pink.

colours, each corresponding to a pH unit – or even a fraction of a unit. Universal indicators can be designed to incorporate a wide pH range, e.g. 1–11, or for specific tasks over a smaller range, e.g. pH 4–6 in intervals of 0.2 of a pH unit.

Any measurement made using dyes must be subjective and will be far from accurate. There can also be problems with coloured solutions such as beer or wine (on which pH measurement is routine). For the accurate measurements required for research, particularly in biological and biochemical areas, pH measurement is done electrically. Great accuracy can be achieved with modern pH meters.

Acids with alkalis: monitoring change

Measuring the concentration of acid and alkaline solutions is a routine task. A traditional method involves titration, i.e. measuring just how much of a reagent of known concentration is needed to react completely with another reagent. Figure 13.7 shows a

familiar example, the titration of a strong acid against a strong base. Bear in mind that neutralisation means the reaction between equal amounts of hydrogen and hydroxide ions to form water (page 134).

Strong acids with strong bases

Figure 13.7 shows a strong acid being titrated 'against' a strong base. The acid is delivered slowly from the burette into the alkali in the flask, with constant stirring. The pH of the mixture is monitored using a pH meter, and values are recorded manually or by a data logger. The graph shows how the pH changes as drop after drop is added.

Note the sharp fall in the graph. In this region, tiny additional amounts of hydrogen ions from the acid have a dramatic effect on pH. The midpoint of this steep slope corresponds to a pH of 7. An indicator such as bromothymol blue, which changes from blue to yellow over the range 6.0–7.6, would register this change. Note, however, that the slope is steep over the range pH 3.5 to pH 10.5, so other

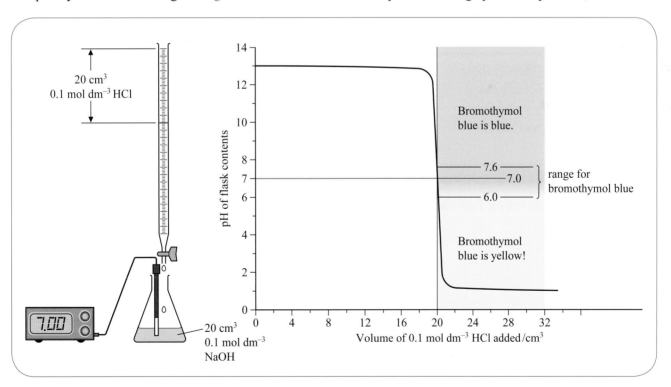

Figure 13.7 A strong acid–strong base titration produces a characteristic graph.

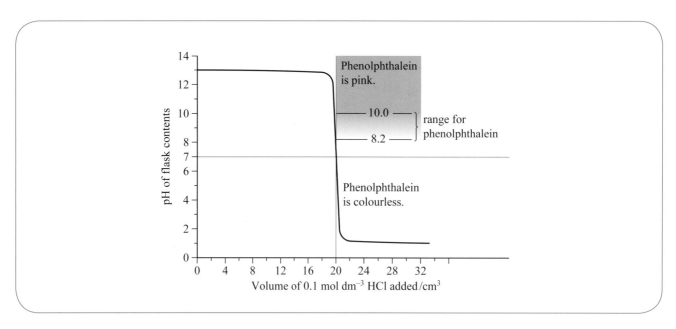

Figure 13.8 A strong acid–strong base titration with phenolphthalein as indicator.

indicators would also mark this sudden change. Phenolphthalein, effective in the pH range 8.2 to 10.0, could also be used (Figure 13.8), although it can be difficult to judge when a colour just disappears.

SAQ

12 Use Table 13.6 to identify those indicators which could be used for a strong acid–strong base titration like this, and those which could not.

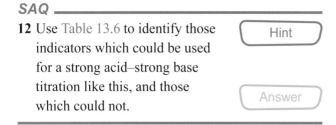

Strong acids with weak bases

A strong acid such as $0.10\,mol\,dm^{-3}$ nitric acid reacts with a weak base like ammonium hydroxide as shown in Figure 13.9. Which part of the graph corresponds to the graph in Figure 13.8? Methyl orange would be a suitable indicator, as the sudden decrease of pH occurs in the range in which methyl orange changes colour, i.e. 3.2–4.4.

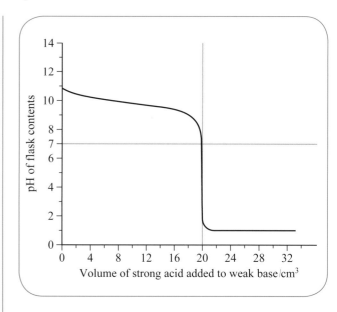

Figure 13.9 A typical strong acid–weak base titration.

SAQ

13 Use Table 13.6 to find those indicators which could be used for a strong acid–weak base titration, and those which could not.

Weak acids with strong bases

The change in pH for the reaction of a weak acid such as benzoic acid with a strong base such as potassium hydroxide is shown in Figure 13.10.

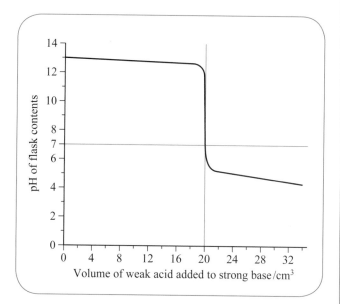

Figure 13.10 A typical weak acid–strong base titration.

14 Compare Figure 13.10 to Figure 13.8 and Figure 13.9, noticing similarities and differences. Phenolphthalein, with its colour change at 9.3, is a suitable indicator for the end-point in Figure 13.10. Why would methyl orange be unsuitable?

Answer

Weak acids with weak bases

As Figure 13.11 shows, there is no significant pH range in which the addition of a small amount of one reagent produces a sharp change. In circumstances like this, none of the indicators in Table 13.6 would be effective. In the example shown, bromothymol blue would start to change colour when $19.50\,cm^3$ of acid had been added, and would only finish changing after another $1.00\,cm^3$ had been added. Such a large range is unacceptable in situations when an accuracy of $0.05\,cm^3$ is desirable.

SAQ

15 Suggest a suitable indicator to find the end-points of the reactions between:

a $0.0500\,mol\,dm^{-3}$ nitric acid and $0.0500\,mol\,dm^{-3}$ aqueous ammonia

b $2.00\,mol\,dm^{-3}$ sodium hydroxide solution and $1.00\,mol\,dm^{-3}$ sulfuric acid

c $0.00500\,mol\,dm^{-3}$ potassium hydroxide and aspirin (2-ethanoyloxybenzoic acid), which has a K_a of $3.0 \times 10^{-4}\,mol\,dm^{-3}$.

Answer

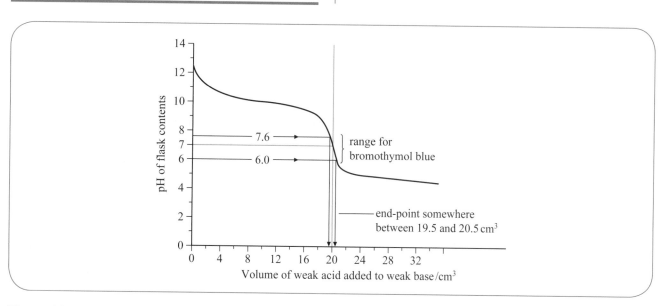

Figure 13.11 A typical weak acid–weak base titration.

Buffer solutions

In Table 13.4 the pH values of a number of commonly occurring solutions were given. Often it does not matter if these pH values vary slightly, but for biological solutions (stomach contents and saliva, for example), and for many industrial processes, it is important to maintain a steady pH value. It can be vital. If your blood pH increases or decreases by 0.5 pH units, you will lose consciousness and drift into a coma.

Your blood has to have some sort of control system to cope with increases in hydrogen or hydroxide ion concentration. It has to have a buffer – something to soak up any increase in the hydrogen or hydroxide ion concentrations.

A **buffer solution** is one that minimises changes in pH, even when moderate amounts of acid or base are added to it. However, no buffer solution can cope with an excessive addition of acid or alkali.

A solution of sodium ethanoate in ethanoic acid is just such a buffer solution. It operates because the equilibria involved respond to increases in hydrogen or hydroxide ion concentration in such a way as to minimise the increase – another practical application of Le Chatelier's principle.

Note that ethanoic acid and sodium ethanoate must both be present for the buffer solution to be effective. The sodium ethanoate (a salt) dissociates completely to produce ethanoate ions as it dissolves:

$$CH_3COONa(aq) \longrightarrow Na^+(aq) + CH_3COO^-(aq)$$

This complete dissociation influences the dissociation of ethanoic acid, which reaches an equilibrium:

$$CH_3COOH(aq) \rightleftharpoons H^+(aq) + CH_3COO^-(aq)$$

The result is that there are large reservoirs of the acid, CH_3COOH, and its conjugate base, CH_3COO^-.

An increase in hydrogen ion concentration would rapidly lower the pH of water. However, in this buffer solution it shifts the following equilibrium to the left:

$$CH_3COOH(aq) \rightleftharpoons H^+(aq) + CH_3COO^-(aq)$$
$$\text{(mainly from}$$
$$\text{sodium ethanoate)}$$

Hydrogen ions are transferred to the ethanoate ions (of which there are plenty) so that ethanoic acid molecules are formed. A moderate input of hydrogen ions therefore has a marginal effect on the overall pH.

The effect of an alkali, which in water would rapidly increase the pH, is minimised in a similar way. The following equilibrium shifts to the right as hydroxide ions remove protons from ethanoic acid molecules to form ethanoate ions and water:

$$CH_3COOH(aq) + OH^-(aq)$$
$$\rightleftharpoons CH_3COO^-(aq) + H_2O(l)$$

There is an alternative explanation for the way in which this buffer solution copes with an increase of hydroxide ions. The explanation suggests that the hydroxide ions first neutralise any hydrogen ions present, which are then replaced by the dissociation of more ethanoic acid. The fact is that we don't know which mechanism actually operates – so keep it simple. Remember the two components: the weak acid, which counters the addition of hydroxide ions, and the salt of the weak acid, which counters the addition of hydrogen ions.

In general, a buffer solution can be made from an acid and its conjugate base where either the acid or the base is weak. An example of a buffer solution involving a weak base is a solution containing both ammonia and ammonium chloride.

SAQ

16 Ammonia dissociates in water as follows:

$$NH_3(aq) + H_2O(l) \rightleftharpoons NH_4^+(aq) + OH^-(aq)$$

whilst the ammonium chloride is fully ionised:

$$NH_4Cl(aq) \longrightarrow NH_4^+(aq) + Cl^-(aq)$$

a Using the above equations, identify the conjugate acid–base pair in a buffer solution containing ammonia and ammonium chloride.

b Explain how the ammonia/ammonium chloride buffer solution minimises changes in pH on adding dilute aqueous solutions of hydrochloric acid and sodium hydroxide.

c Explain why ammonia solution needs the addition of ammonium chloride to make it a buffer solution.

Answer

'Bicarb' and pH control in blood

Our blood has to maintain a pH of between 7.35 and 7.45. It manages this by utilising buffer solutions, as you can read below.

Oxygen from the air diffuses into your bloodstream in the lungs, and reacts with haemoglobin, Hb. This 'organometallic' compound, the first protein ever to be obtained as a crystalline solid, contains iron – hence its red colour. It reacts with oxygen as shown:

$$Hb + O_2 \rightleftharpoons HbO_2$$

This reaction is easily reversed in tissues all over the body, releasing oxygen for the energy-generating process called aerobic respiration. For example, glucose is oxidised in an exothermic reaction, producing water and carbon dioxide, plus energy. The equation below is a gross over-simplification of the many reactions that it summarises.

$$C_6H_{12}O_6(aq) + 6O_2(g) \longrightarrow 6CO_2(aq) + 6H_2O(aq)$$
$$\Delta H^\ominus = -2802\,kJ\,mol^{-1}$$

Your blood is now left with a waste-disposal problem, which is potentially poisonous. The problem, and part of the solution, lies in the equation below. The rates of both the forward and reverse reactions in the equilibrium are rapid, thanks to the enzyme carbonic anhydrase:

$$H_2O(aq) + CO_2(aq) \underset{}{\overset{\text{carbonic anhydrase}}{\rightleftharpoons}} H^+(aq) + HCO_3^-(aq)$$

The generation of hydrogen ions, if unchecked, would lead to a lowering of blood pH and you would slip into a coma. Your blood needs a buffer.

In fact, it has at least *three*, the most important by far being the buffering action of hydrogencarbonate ion, $HCO_3^-(aq)$. Haemoglobin and plasma, both proteins, also act as buffers, but play much smaller parts.

Hydrogen ions in the blood are mopped up by hydrogencarbonate ions, the equation being the one above, in which the position of equilibrium is well over to the left. The carbon dioxide produced is carried to the lungs and breathed out. Lung infections that inhibit breathing can hinder this extraction process, leading to acidosis – i.e. decrease in blood pH.

The chemistry of pH control in the body is more complex than this section suggests, involving many other ions, particularly when acidosis is severe. The kidneys also play a crucial part. Understanding pH control is vital when treating certain diseases, e.g. coronary thrombosis. Anaesthetists constantly monitor blood pH in long operations that involve heart–lung machines, and may inject controlled amounts of sodium hydrogencarbonate ('bicarb') to cater for a fall in pH (Figure 13.12).

Extension

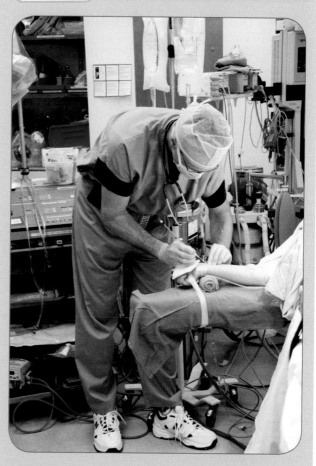

Figure 13.12 Anaesthetists monitor the pH of patients' blood.

Calculating the pH of a buffer solution

We can calculate the pH of a buffer solution given the following data:

- K_a of the weak acid
- the equilibrium concentrations of the conjugate acid–base pair.

The method is demonstrated in Worked example 6.

Worked example 6

A buffer solution was made in which the concentrations were $0.600\,mol\,dm^{-3}$ propanoic acid and $0.800\,mol\,dm^{-3}$ sodium propanoate. The equilibrium constant, K_a, for propanoic acid is $1.35 \times 10^{-5}\,mol\,dm^{-3}$. What is the pH of the buffer solution made?

Step 1 The equation for the equilibrium reaction is:

$$C_2H_5COOH(aq) \rightleftharpoons H^+(aq) + C_2H_5COO^-(aq)$$

from which we can write the equilibrium constant expression:

$$K_a = \frac{[H^+][C_2H_5COO^-]}{[C_2H_5COOH]}$$

Step 2 Rearrange this equation:

$$[H^+] = K_a \times \frac{[C_2H_5COOH]}{[C_2H_5COO^-]}\,mol\,dm^{-3}$$

Step 3 Substitute in the data given:

$$[H^+] = 1.35 \times 10^{-5} \times \frac{0.600}{0.800}\,mol\,dm^{-3}$$

$$= 1.01 \times 10^{-5}\,mol\,dm^{-3}$$

Step 4 Now calculate the pH:

$$pH = -\log_{10}(1.01 \times 10^{-5})$$
$$= -(-4.99) = 4.99$$

SAQ

17 Practise this by calculating the pH of solutions with the following concentrations. Use Table 13.5 for the values of K_a.

   a $0.0500\,mol\,dm^{-3}$ methanoic acid and $0.100\,mol\,dm^{-3}$ sodium methanoate

       Hint

   b $0.0100\,mol\,dm^{-3}$ benzoic acid and $0.0400\,mol\,dm^{-3}$ sodium benzoate.

       Answer

Where buffers can't cope ...

Of course, there is a limit to the efficiency of buffers, as we have indicated previously. Rainwater has a pH of 5.7 in unpolluted regions, because it dissolves carbon dioxide, which in solution forms a dilute solution of the weak acid carbonic acid, $H_2CO_3(aq)$, with a pK_a of 6.4. This buffer solution will accommodate small additions of acid and alkali.

However, in highly polluted industrial regions, or in rural areas that lie downwind of such contamination, the pH of rainwater is around 4, and is known as 'acid rain'. Here the atmospheric pollutant gases are sulfur dioxide and sulfur trioxide, arising from the combustion of fossil fuels containing sulfur. There are also nitrogen monoxide and nitrogen dioxide gases, due mainly to the oxidation of nitrogen in internal combustion engines. These gases dissolve in rainwater and overwhelm the buffering effect (Figure 13.13).

Figure 13.13 Acid rain attacks limestone, which is made mainly of calcium carbonate.

Summary

Glossary

- The Brønsted–Lowry definition of an acid is a proton donor; a base is a proton acceptor.

- Weak acids are only partially ionised in solution; the molecules of strong acids are almost fully dissociated in solution.

- K_w is the ionic product of water: at 298 K, $K_w = [H^+][OH^-] = 1.00 \times 10^{-14}\ mol^2\ dm^{-6}$.

- pH is a measure of $[H^+(aq)]$; it is defined as $pH = -\log_{10}[H^+]$.

- K_a is the dissociation constant for an acid. It is the equilibrium constant for the dissociation of a weak acid, HA:

$$HA(aq) \rightleftharpoons H^+(aq) + A^-(aq)$$

$$K_a = \frac{[H^+][A^-]}{[HA]}$$

- Chemists often use a more convenient scale for comparing acid strengths by using pK_a, defined as:

$$pK_a = -\log_{10}K_a$$

- pH titration curves enable end-points for acid–base titrations to be found. The end-point of a titration is when the quantity of acid is sufficient to exactly neutralise the base present. The curves may also be used to suggest appropriate indicators for a particular acid–base titration.

- A buffer solution minimises pH changes on addition of an acid or a base. A buffer solution consists of an acid and its conjugate base where one of the pair is weak.

- Buffer solutions are important in controlling the pH of many fluids in living organisms, for example in blood.

Questions

1   In sewage plants, biological activity can be reduced by increasing the pH of the water. This is achieved by adding small amounts of solid calcium hydroxide, $Ca(OH)_2$, to the sewage water.
    In all parts of this question, assume that measurements have been made at 25 °C.
    a   The pH of aqueous solutions is determined by K_w.
        K_w has a value of $1.00 \times 10^{-14}\ mol^2\ dm^{-6}$ at 25 °C.
        i   What name is given to K_w? [1]
        ii Write the expression for K_w. [1]
    b   A chemist checked the concentration of aqueous calcium hydroxide, $Ca(OH)_2$,
        in the sewage water by titration with $5.00 \times 10^{-3}\ mol\ dm^{-3}$ hydrochloric acid.

$$Ca(OH)_2(aq) + 2HCl(aq) \longrightarrow CaCl_2(aq) + 2H_2O(l)$$

The chemist titrated $25.00\ cm^3$ of the sewage water with $21.35\ cm^3$ of HCl to
reach the end-point of the titration. Calculate the concentration, in $mol\ dm^{-3}$,
of the calcium hydroxide in the sewage water. [3]

continued

c   The chemist analysed a sample of water from another part of the sewage works and he found that the calcium hydroxide concentration was $2.70 \times 10^{-3}\,\text{mol dm}^{-3}$. Assume that when solid calcium hydroxide dissolves in water, its ions completely dissociate.

$$Ca(OH)_2(s) \longrightarrow Ca^{2+}(aq) + 2OH^-(aq)$$

Calculate the pH of this sample.   [3]

d   After further treatment, the water could be used for drinking. In the drinking water produced, the OH^- concentration was 100 times greater than the H^+ concentration.

What was the pH of this drinking water?   [1]

OCR Chemistry A2 (2816) January 2007   [Total 9]

Answer

2   *In this question, one mark is available for the quality of written communication.*
   a   Describe what is meant by the following terms used in acid–base chemistry.
      ● The Brønsted–Lowry theory of acids and bases.
      ● Conjugate acid–base pairs
      ● Dilute and weak acids.
      Illustrate your answer by choosing suitable examples of acids and bases.
      Write equations where appropriate.   [7]
      Quality of written communication   [1]
   b   The acid dissociation constant K_a of hydrocyanic acid, HCN, is $4.90 \times 10^{-10}\,\text{mol dm}^{-3}$.
      i   Write an expression for the acid dissociation constant of HCN.   [1]
      ii Calculate the pH of a $0.010\,\text{mol dm}^{-3}$ solution of hydrocyanic acid.   [3]

OCR Chemistry A2 (2816) January 2003   [Total 12]

Hint

Answer

3   A student carried out an investigation with aqueous solutions of nitric acid, sodium hydroxide, ethanoic acid and water.
   a   Nitric acid, HNO_3, is a strong Brønsted–Lowry acid.
      i   Explain what is meant by a *strong acid* and a *Brønsted–Lowry acid*.   [2]
      ii What is the conjugate base formed from HNO_3?   [1]
   b   The student diluted $0.015\,\text{mol dm}^{-3}$ nitric acid with an equal volume of water and measured the pH of the diluted acid at 25 °C.
      i   Calculate the pH of $0.015\,\text{mol dm}^{-3}$ nitric acid.   [2]
      ii Calculate the pH of the diluted acid.   [1]
   c   The student measured the pH of a solution of sodium hydroxide as 13.54 at 25 °C.

$$K_w = 1.00 \times 10^{-14}\,\text{mol}^2\,\text{dm}^{-6} \text{ at } 25\,°C.$$

      i   Write down an expression for the ionic product, K_w, for water.   [1]
      ii Calculate the concentration, in mol dm^{-3}, of this solution of sodium hydroxide.   [2]

continued

d The student prepared two solutions.

- Solution **A** was made by mixing together $25\,cm^3$ $0.010\,mol\,dm^{-3}$ aqueous sodium hydroxide with $50\,cm^3$ $0.010\,mol\,dm^{-3}$ ethanoic acid, CH_3COOH. Solution **A** is a buffer solution.
- Solution **B** was made by mixing together $25\,cm^3$ $0.020\,mol\,dm^{-3}$ aqueous sodium hydroxide with $50\,cm^3$ $0.010\,mol\,dm^{-3}$ ethanoic acid, CH_3COOH. Solution **B** is <u>not</u> a buffer solution.

  i What is meant by a *buffer solution*? [1]

  ii Explain why Solution **A** is a buffer solution whereas Solution **B** is not. [4]

e The student measured the pH of water as 7.0 at 25 °C. The student then warmed the water to 40 °C and measured the pH as 6.7.

What do these results tell you about the tendency of water to ionise as it gets warmer? Explain your reasoning in terms of equilibrium. [2]

OCR Chemistry A2 (2816) June 2005   [Total 16]

Answer

4 A student carried out some practical work on acids and alkalis.

a He measured the pH of aqueous solutions of two acids. His results are shown in Table 1 below.

Acid	Concentration/$mol\,dm^{-3}$	pH
HBr	0.0100	2.0
CH_3COOH	0.0100	3.4

Table 1

  i Define pH. [1]

  ii Compare the concentrations and pH values of the two acids in Table 1. Explain what this tells you about the relative strengths of the two acids. [2]

  iii The student mixed together $10\,cm^3$ of $0.0100\,mol\,dm^{-3}$ HBr with $90\,cm^3$ of water. Determine the pH of the diluted acid. Show your working. [2]

b The constant K_w has a value of $1.00 \times 10^{-14}\,mol\,dm^{-6}$.

  i Define K_w. [1]

  ii Calculate the pH of $0.020\,mol\,dm^{-3}$ KOH(aq). Show your working. [2]

c The student pipetted $20.0\,cm^3$ of $0.0100\,mol\,dm^{-3}$ CH_3COOH(aq) into a conical flask.

He then slowly added an <u>excess</u> of $0.0100\,mol\,dm^{-3}$ KOH(aq) from a burette. In total, $50.00\,cm^3$ of the alkali were added.

The pH of the resulting solution was measured throughout the experiment with a pH meter.

The equation for the reaction is shown below.

$$CH_3COOH(aq) + KOH(aq) \longrightarrow CH_3COOK(aq) + H_2O(l)$$

continued

   i Copy the grid below. Sketch the pH curve for this titration on your grid.

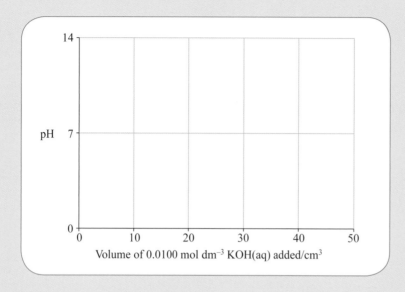

Volume of 0.0100 mol dm⁻³ KOH(aq) added/cm³

[3]

   ii This titration could be carried out using an indicator. The pH ranges for the colour changes of four indicators are shown in Table 2.

Indicator	pH range
clayton yellow	12.2–13.2
thymol blue	8.0–9.6
brilliant yellow	6.6–7.8
resazurin	3.8–6.4

Table 2

Explain which of the four indicators is most suitable for this titration.   [2]

OCR Chemistry A2 (2816) June 2004   [Total 13]

Hint

Answer

5 Methanoic acid, HCOOH, is a weak organic acid which occurs naturally in ants and stinging nettles.

  a Use an equation for the dissociation of methanoic acid to show what is meant by a *weak acid*.   [1]

  b A 1.50×10^{-2} mol dm⁻³ solution of HCOOH has $[H^+] = 1.55 \times 10^{-3}$ mol dm⁻³.

    i Calculate the pH of this solution and give one reason why the pH scale is a more convenient measurement for measuring acid concentration than $[H^+]$.   [2]

    ii Write the expression for K_a for methanoic acid.   [1]

    iii Calculate the values of K_a and pK_a for methanoic acid.   [3]

    iv Estimate the percentage of HCOOH molecules that have dissociated in this aqueous solution of methanoic acid.   [1]

continued

c A student titrated the 1.50×10^{-2} mol dm^{-3} methanoic acid with aqueous sodium hydroxide.

A 25.00 cm^3 sample of the HCOOH(aq) was placed in a conical flask and the NaOH(aq) was added from a burette until the pH no longer changed.

i Write a balanced equation for the reaction between HCOOH(aq) and NaOH(aq). [1]

ii Part of the pH curve for this titration is shown below.

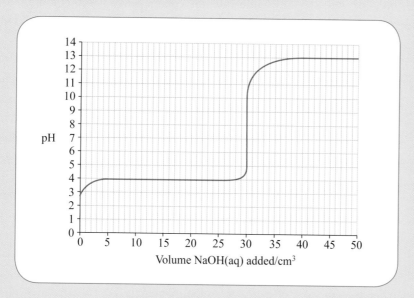

Calculate the concentration, in mol dm^{-3}, of the aqueous sodium hydroxide. [3]

iii Calculate the pH of the aqueous sodium hydroxide.

$$K_w = 1.00 \times 10^{-14} \text{ mol}^2 \text{ dm}^{-6}.$$ [2]

iv The pH ranges in which colour changes for three acid–base indicators are shown in the table.

Indicator	pH range
metacresol purple	7.4–9.0
2,4,6-trinitrotoluene	11.5–13.0
ethyl orange	3.4–4.8

Explain which of the three indicators is suitable for this titration. [2]

OCR Chemistry A2 (2816) January 2006

[Total 16]

Answer

Chapter 14

Lattice enthalpy

e-Learning

Objectives

You have already studied the ionic bonding and lattice structure of sodium chloride (see *Chemistry 1*, Chapter 6). It is important to realise that solid ionic compounds do not form as a result of the transfer of electrons only – overall, forming the ions actually *requires* energy, as you can see if you look at the energy changes involved:

$$Na(g) \longrightarrow Na^+(g) + e^- \qquad \Delta H^\ominus = +496 \, \text{kJ mol}^{-1}$$
$$Cl(g) + e^- \longrightarrow Cl^-(g) \qquad \Delta H^\ominus = -349 \, \text{kJ mol}^{-1}$$
$$Na(g) + Cl(g) \longrightarrow Na^+(g) + Cl^-(g) \quad \Delta H^\ominus = +147 \, \text{kJ mol}^{-1}$$

Yet most ionic solids form easily from their elements. So if transferring electrons is not the reason why ionic compounds form, what is the reason? It is the *huge release in energy* that occurs when the ions of opposite charge combine to form a solid. This is the *lattice enthalpy*, $\Delta H^\ominus_{latt}$.

> The lattice enthalpy, $\Delta H^\ominus_{latt}$ is the enthalpy change when 1 mole of an ionic compound is formed from its gaseous ions under standard conditions (298 K, 101 kPa).

The *gaseous* ions are important here – the equation representing the lattice enthalpy of sodium chloride is:

$$Na^+(g) + Cl^-(g) \longrightarrow NaCl(s)$$
$$\Delta H^\ominus_{latt} = -787 \, \text{kJ mol}^{-1}$$

You can see that the process of bringing together the separate ions in the gaseous state and putting them together into a regular lattice structure releases a large amount of energy. This large exothermic value indicates that the sodium chloride lattice is very stable with respect to the gaseous ions, and cannot easily be pulled apart again. The more exothermic the lattice enthalpy, the stronger the ionic bonds between ions in the solid lattice. Of course, to actually do this process *experimentally* is impossible. So how can we calculate

the enthalpy change when gaseous sodium ions and chloride ions come together to form a solid lattice?

The way in which we calculate the lattice enthalpy is by using a Born–Haber cycle, which is a particular type of Hess's law enthalpy cycle (see *Chemistry 1*, Chapter 16). In a Born–Haber cycle every step from the elements to the ionic compound can be measured, except the lattice enthalpy. The lattice enthalpy can therefore be calculated in the usual way in a Hess's law cycle.

The lattice enthalpy is an exothermic change and always has a negative value.

SAQ

1 Explain what is meant by the terms:
   a enthalpy change
   b exothermic reaction
   c endothermic reaction.

   Answer

2 State Hess's law.

   Answer

The Born–Haber cycle

Let's go through the Born–Haber cycle for lithium fluoride step by step, as shown in Figure 14.1.

We begin with the elements in their standard states, metallic lithium, Li(s), and gaseous diatomic fluorine, $F_2(g)$. From these we can follow two routes to obtain lithium fluoride, LiF(s).

● Route 1 is the direct combination of the elements to give LiF(s); this is the standard enthalpy change of formation, $\Delta H^\ominus_f$. You have used this enthalpy change earlier (*Chemistry 1*, Chapter 16).

● Route 2 is the multi-step route which includes the lattice enthalpy and also gives LiF(s).

From Hess's law, we know that both paths have the same overall enthalpy change, so in route 1 $\Delta H^\ominus_f =$ sum of $\Delta H^\ominus$ for the steps in route 2.

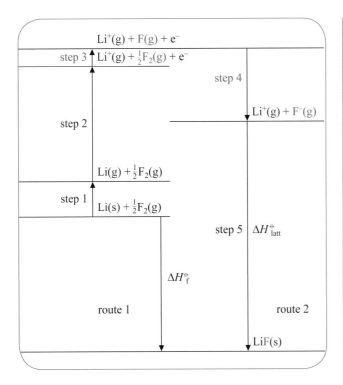

Figure 14.1 Born–Haber cycle for lithium fluoride.

Route 1 involves only one step, so is easily dealt with. This step is the standard enthalpy change of formation of lithium fluoride. The enthalpy change of formation is defined as the enthalpy change when 1 mole of a compound is formed from its elements in their standard states under standard conditions.

$$Li(s) + \tfrac{1}{2}F_2(g) \longrightarrow LiF(s) \qquad \Delta H_f^\ominus = -617\,kJ\,mol^{-1}$$

The overall changes that take place in route 2 can be summarised as follows (see Figure 14.1):
- the elements are converted to individual gaseous atoms (steps 1 and 3)
- these atoms are converted to gaseous ions (steps 2 and 4)
- the ions form the solid (step 5).

Step 1 Converting solid lithium into separate gaseous lithium atoms is called the standard enthalpy change of atomisation, $\Delta H_{at}^\ominus$. This requires energy, so it is an endothermic change.

$$Li(s) \longrightarrow Li(g) \qquad \Delta H_{at}^\ominus = +161\,kJ\,mol^{-1}$$

The **standard enthalpy change of atomisation** of an element is the enthalpy change when one mole of gaseous atoms are formed from the element in its standard state.

Step 2 This step involves removing 1 mole of electrons from 1 mole of gaseous Li atoms to form 1 mole of Li^+ ions. Once again, this is an endothermic change. It is called the first **ionisation energy**, $\Delta H_{i1}^\ominus$. (You met ionisation energies in *Chemistry 1*, Chapter 5.)

$$Li(g) \longrightarrow Li^+(g) + e^- \qquad \Delta H_{i1}^\ominus = +520\,kJ\,mol^{-1}$$

Step 3 This is another enthalpy change of atomisation, but this time half a mole of fluorine *molecules*, $F_2(g)$, are being converted into 1 mole of fluorine *atoms*, $F(g)$. This again is an endothermic change (and also equals half the bond enthalpy of F_2 – you met bond enthalpies in *Chemistry 1*, Chapter 16.)

$$\tfrac{1}{2}F_2(g) \longrightarrow F(g) \qquad \Delta H_{at}^\ominus = \tfrac{1}{2}(+159) = +79.5\,kJ\,mol^{-1}$$

Step 4 Adding an electron to F to form F^- is the first **electron affinity**, $\Delta H_{ea1}^\ominus$. This is an exothermic change – the only exothermic change (besides the lattice enthalpy) in this path of the Born–Haber cycle.

$$F(g) + e^- \longrightarrow F^-(g) \qquad \Delta H_{ea1}^\ominus = -328\,kJ\,mol^{-1}$$

The first electron affinity, $\Delta H_{ea1}^\ominus$, is the enthalpy change when one electron is added to each of one mole of gaseous atoms, to form one mole of gaseous 1– ions:

$$X(g) + e^- \longrightarrow X^-(g)$$

The second electron affinity, $\Delta H_{ea2}^\ominus$, is the enthalpy change when one electron is added to each of one mole of gaseous 1– ions, to form one mole of gaseous 2– ions:

$$X^-(g) + e^- \longrightarrow X^{2-}(g)$$

Step 5 This step represents the **lattice enthalpy**. The two gaseous ions come together to form one mole of the ionic solid, and this is an exothermic change.

$$Li^+(g) + F^-(g) \longrightarrow LiF(s)$$

The enthalpy change for this step is usually unknown and has to be calculated.

How to calculate the lattice enthalpy from a Born–Haber cycle

According to Hess's law,

$$\Delta H_f^\ominus = \Delta H_{at}^\ominus (Li) + \Delta H_{i1}^\ominus + \Delta H_{at}^\ominus (F)$$
$$+ \Delta H_{ea1}^\ominus + \Delta H_{latt}^\ominus$$

This can be rearranged;

$$\text{lattice enthalpy} = \Delta H_f^\ominus - \Delta H_{at}^\ominus (Li)$$
$$- \Delta H_{at}^\ominus (F) - \Delta H_{i1}^\ominus - \Delta H_{ea1}^\ominus$$

In words, the formula is:

lattice enthalpy
= heat of formation – heats of atomisation
– ionisation energy – electron affinity

Putting in the figures:

lattice enthalpy
$$= (-617) - (+161) - (+79.5) - (+520) - (-328)$$
$$= -1049.5 \, kJ \, mol^{-1}$$

SAQ ─────────────

3 Write equations to represent the following standard enthalpy changes:　[Hint]

　a the atomisation of oxygen gas
　b the first ionisation energy of caesium
　c the enthalpy change of formation of potassium chloride
　d the first electron affinity of iodine
　e the atomisation of barium.　[Answer]

4 a Draw a Born–Haber cycle for sodium chloride, naming each step.　[Hint]

---

b Calculate the lattice enthalpy for sodium chloride, given that:

$$\Delta H_f^\ominus (NaCl) = -411 \, kJ \, mol^{-1}$$
$$\Delta H_{at}^\ominus (Na) = +107 \, kJ \, mol^{-1}$$
$$\Delta H_{at}^\ominus (Cl) = +121 \, kJ \, mol^{-1}$$
$$\Delta H_{i1}^\ominus (Na) = +496 \, kJ \, mol^{-1}$$
$$\Delta H_{ea1}^\ominus (Cl) = -348 \, kJ \, mol^{-1}$$

[Answer]

The Born–Haber cycle for magnesium chloride

It is important that you know the Born–Haber cycle for sodium chloride, so make sure you have done SAQ 4 and checked the answer.

Another Born–Haber cycle you must know is the one shown for magnesium chloride (Figure 14.2). It is essentially the same as before, with the same type of steps in each path. However, the magnesium ion is Mg^{2+}, so the gaseous magnesium atom is ionised in *two stages*:

$$Mg(g) \longrightarrow Mg^+(g) + e^-$$

the first ionisation energy, $\Delta H_{i1}^\ominus$

$$Mg^+(g) \longrightarrow Mg^{2+}(g) + e^-$$

the second ionisation energy, $\Delta H_{i2}^\ominus$

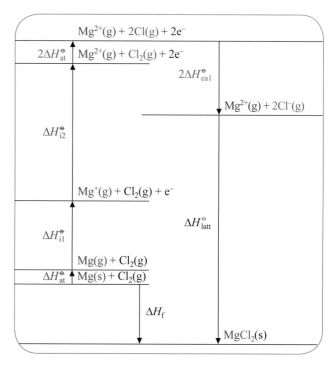

Figure 14.2 Born–Haber cycle for magnesium chloride.

Whenever an ion is formed, it is done in stages, losing or gaining one electron at a time. So, to get to Al^{3+}, you will use three ionisation energies:

$$Al(g) \xrightarrow{\Delta H^{\ominus}_{i1}} Al^{+}(g) + e^{-} \xrightarrow{\Delta H^{\ominus}_{i2}}$$
$$Al^{2+}(g) + 2e^{-} \xrightarrow{\Delta H^{\ominus}_{i3}} Al^{3+}(g) + 3e^{-}$$

The same principle applies to anions. To form O^{2-}, you will use two electron affinities:

$$O(g) + e^{-} \xrightarrow{\Delta H^{\ominus}_{ea1}} O^{-}(g);$$
$$O^{-}(g) + e^{-} \xrightarrow{\Delta H^{\ominus}_{ea2}} O^{2-}(g)$$

One other difference to remember is that two Cl^{-} ions are present in $MgCl_2$, hence $2\Delta H^{\ominus}_{at}$ and $2\Delta H^{\ominus}_{ea1}$ are required in the Born–Haber cycle for $MgCl_2$.

SAQ

5 Draw Born–Haber cycles for:

    a MgO

    b Na_2O.

Hint

Answer

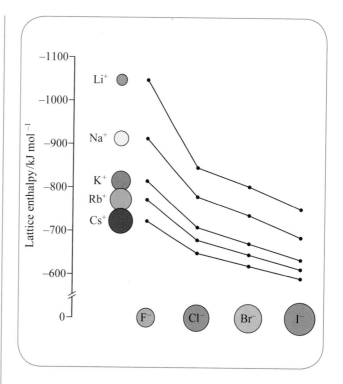

Figure 14.3 Lattice enthalpies of the Group 1 halides.

Trends in the lattice enthalpy

The lattice enthalpy results from the electrostatic forces of attraction between the oppositely charged ions in the solid ionic lattice. The size and charge of the ions can therefore affect the value of the lattice enthalpy.

Size of the ions

The lattice enthalpy becomes *less exothermic* as the size of the ion *increases*.

This applies to both cations and anions. The reason is that as the radius of the ion increases, the attraction between the ions decreases, so the lattice energy is less exothermic. You can see this in Figure 14.3.

The trends in the size of both the cations and the anions are shown, and you can see that the trend in the magnitude of the lattice enthalpy is in the opposite direction (i.e. it gets less exothermic as the size of the ions increases). We say that ions with the same charge have a higher 'charge density' the smaller they are, resulting in stronger electrostatic forces of attraction in the ionic lattice.

Charge of the ions

The lattice enthalpy becomes *more exothermic* as the charge on the ion *increases*.

The effect of the charge of the ion on lattice enthalpy can be seen by comparing LiF with MgO. Both solids have the same giant lattice structure, the Li^{+} ion is about the same size as the Mg^{2+} ion, and the F^{-} ion is about the same size as the O^{2-} ion.

The only difference between the two solids is the *charge* on the ions. Look at the lattice enthalpies for these two compounds:

LiF $\Delta H^{\ominus}_{latt} = -1050 \, kJ \, mol^{-1}$

MgO $\Delta H^{\ominus}_{latt} = -3923 \, kJ \, mol^{-1}$

They are very different. The lattice enthalpy for magnesium oxide is much more negative (more exothermic), which shows that doubly charged ions attract each other more strongly than singly charged ions of the same size. The more highly charged ions will have a higher charge density, resulting in stronger ionic bonds.

Uses of magnesium oxide

The exceptionally high exothermic value for the lattice enthalpy of magnesium oxide means it is a very useful compound in certain situations. The lattice is so strong that it takes a great deal of heat to separate the ions in order to melt the solid (the melting point is 2853 °C). This results in the use of magnesium oxide to line furnaces – we say it is a **refractory lining** (Figure 14.4).

Figure 14.4 Magnesium oxide is used as a lining in furnaces.

Magnesium oxide is also used in high-temperature windows in furnaces, ceramics, wire coatings and flame-retardant particle boards. The strong lattice also means that magnesium oxide is used in anti-corrosion coatings in tankers which carry chemicals.

SAQ

6 For each pair of compounds, suggest which will have the most exothermic lattice enthalpy.
   a CaO and $CaCl_2$
   b KCl and K_2O
   c BaI_2 and SrI_2

Hint

Answer

7 Place the following compounds in order of increasingly exothermic lattice enthalpy:

Li_2O LiF   MgO

Explain why you have placed them in this order.

Answer

Enthalpy change of solution

The energy absorbed or released when one mole of an ionic solid dissolves in sufficient water to form a very dilute solution is called the **enthalpy change of solution** of the compound.

This can be described with an equation like this, using magnesium chloride as an example:

$$MgCl_2(s) + (aq) \longrightarrow MgCl_2(aq)$$

The (aq) on the left of the arrow represents the very large amount of water used.

If the enthalpy change of solution of a compound is negative, or has a small positive value, the compound is likely to be soluble in water. The symbol for the standard enthalpy change of solution is $\Delta H^{\ominus}_{sol}$.

SAQ

8 Look at the enthalpies of solution listed below. What properties of Group 7 compounds do they help to explain?

Hint

sodium chloride	$\Delta H^{\ominus}_{sol} = +3.9\,kJ\,mol^{-1}$
silver chloride	$\Delta H^{\ominus}_{sol} = +65.7\,kJ\,mol^{-1}$
sodium bromide	$\Delta H^{\ominus}_{sol} = -0.6\,kJ\,mol^{-1}$
silver bromide	$\Delta H^{\ominus}_{sol} = +84.5\,kJ\,mol^{-1}$

Answer

Enthalpy change of hydration

When one mole of gaseous ions dissolve in sufficient water to form a very dilute solution the energy released is called the **enthalpy change of hydration** of the ion.

Note that an enthalpy change of hydration is always exothermic due to the attractive forces between the water molecules and the ions. This equation describes the enthalpy change of hydration of calcium ions:

$$Ca^{2+}(g) + (aq) \longrightarrow Ca^{2+}(aq)$$

The symbol for the standard enthalpy change of hydration is $\Delta H^{\ominus}_{hyd}$. The magnitude of $\Delta H^{\ominus}_{hyd}$ is larger (it is more exothermic) for ions that have smaller ionic radii and larger charges. Both these factors increase the charge density of the ions, resulting in stronger forces of attraction between these ions and the polar water molecules.

SAQ

9 a Write an equation to describe the enthalpy of hydration of sodium ions.

  b Write an equation to describe the enthalpy of hydration of chloride ions.

  c Write an equation to describe the enthalpy of solution of sodium chloride.

  Answer

10 a The enthalpies of hydration of Li$^+$ ions and K$^+$ ions are −519 and −322 kJ mol^{-1}, respectively. Predict a value for the enthalpy of hydration of Na$^+$ ions, explaining your decision.

  Hint

  b The enthalpy of hydration of Mg^{2+} ions is −1920 kJ mol^{-1}. Explain why Mg^{2+} ions have a much more exothermic enthalpy of hydration than K$^+$ ions.

  Answer

Using enthalpies of solution and hydration

For an ionic compound the lattice enthalpy, the enthalpy of solution, and the enthalpy of hydration of its ions, are related by this expression:

$$\Delta H^{\ominus}_{latt} + \Delta H^{\ominus}_{sol} = \Delta H^{\ominus}_{hyd}$$

This can be seen clearly in the energy cycle in Figure 14.5, which refers to lithium chloride.

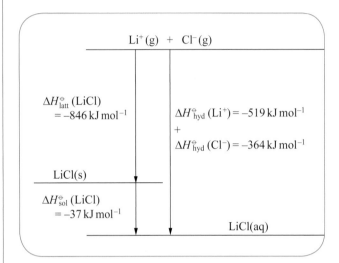

Figure 14.5

Energy cycles like Figure 14.5 can be used to calculate enthalpies of hydration and solution, given suitable data (Worked example 1).

Worked example 1

The lattice enthalpy of sodium fluoride is $-902\,kJ\,mol^{-1}$. The enthalpy of hydration of sodium ions is $-406\,kJ\,mol^{-1}$. The enthalpy of hydration of fluoride ions is $-506\,kJ\,mol^{-1}$.

Draw an energy cycle that includes the lattice enthalpy and enthalpy of solution of sodium fluoride and the enthalpies of hydration of the ions involved, and calculate the enthalpy of solution of sodium fluoride.

Step 1 The energy cycle looks like Figure 14.6.

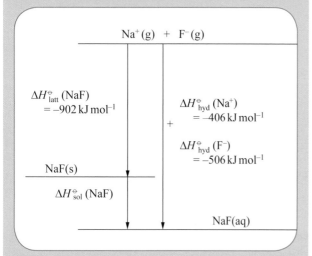

Figure 14.6

Step 2 The enthalpy of solution of sodium fluoride can be calculated using

$$\Delta H^{\ominus}_{latt} + \Delta H^{\ominus}_{sol} = \Delta H^{\ominus}_{hyd}$$

$$-902\,kJ\,mol^{-1} + \Delta H^{\ominus}_{sol}(NaF)$$
$$= -406\,kJ\,mol^{-1} + -506\,kJ\,mol^{-1}$$

$$\Delta H^{\ominus}_{sol}(NaF) = -406\,kJ\,mol^{-1} + -506\,kJ\,mol^{-1}$$
$$+ 902\,kJ\,mol^{-1}$$

$$\Delta H^{\ominus}_{sol}(NaF) = -10\,kJ\,mol^{-1}$$

SAQ

11 The lattice enthalpy of magnesium chloride is $-2592\,kJ\,mol^{-1}$. Its enthalpy of solution is $-55\,kJ\,mol^{-1}$. The enthalpy of hydration of Mg^{2+} ions is $-1920\,kJ\,mol^{-1}$. Calculate the enthalpy of hydration of chloride ions.

Hint

Answer

Summary

- The lattice enthalpy of an ionic solid is the energy change when gaseous ions come together to form one mole of a solid lattice (under standard conditions).

- Lattice enthalpies are exothermic. A strong lattice has a more exothermic lattice enthalpy than a weak lattice. Therefore the lattice enthalpy indicates the strength of the ionic bonding holding a lattice together. The more exothermic the value, the stronger the ionic bonds.

- Lattice enthalpies can be calculated from a Born–Haber cycle, which is a type of Hess's law cycle.

- Each step of the Born–Haber cycle is a separate enthalpy change.

- The standard enthalpy change of atomisation of an element is the enthalpy change when one mole of gaseous atoms are formed from the element in its standard state.

- The value of the lattice enthalpy is affected by the size of the ions making up the lattice, and also by their charge.
  - The smaller an ion, the more exothermic the lattice enthalpy.
  - The higher the charge on an ion, the more exothermic the lattice enthalpy.

- Magnesium oxide is an example of an ionic solid with a large exothermic lattice enthalpy, and therefore it has many uses that require great heat resistance.

- The energy absorbed or released when one mole of an ionic solid dissolves in sufficient water to form a very dilute solution is called the enthalpy change of solution of the compound.

- When one mole of gaseous ions dissolve in sufficient water to form a very dilute solution, the energy released is called the enthalpy change of hydration of the ion.
  - The smaller an ion, the more exothermic the enthalpy change of hydration.
  - The higher the charge on an ion, the more exothermic the enthalpy change of hydration.

- We can use energy cycles to calculate enthalpy changes of solution or hydration, given the necessary data.

Questions

1 The lattice enthalpy of caesium chloride, CsCl, can be calculated using a Born–Haber cycle. The table below shows the enthalpy changes and corresponding data for this cycle.

Enthalpy change		Energy/kJ mol^{-1}
lattice enthalpy of CsCl	A	?
atomisation of caesium	B	+76
atomisation of chlorine	C	+122
1st ionisation energy of caesium	D	+376
1st electron affinity of chlorine	E	−349
formation of CsCl	F	−443

a Match the letter for each enthalpy change to the numbers in the boxes shown below.

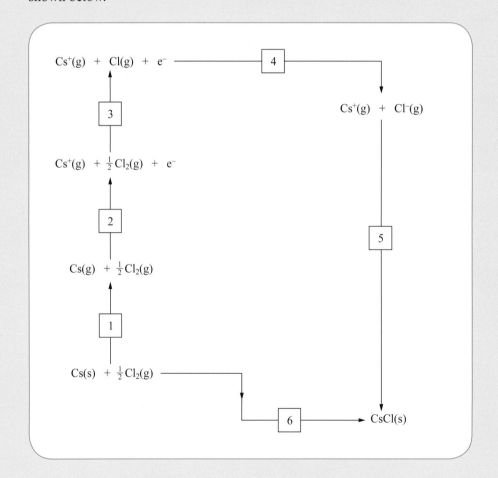

[3]

continued

b Calculate the lattice enthalpy of caesium chloride; give your answer in kJ mol⁻¹. [2]

c The lattice enthalpy of sodium chloride is <u>more exothermic</u> than the lattice enthalpy of caesium chloride.

State and explain the relative strengths of the ionic bonding in sodium chloride and caesium chloride. [3]

d What would you expect to observe when solid caesium chloride is added to water? [2]

e Describe how you would distinguish between aqueous caesium chloride and aqueous caesium iodide using a simple laboratory test. State the observations you would make. [3]

OCR Chemistry A2 (2815/01) June 2002 [Total 13]

Hint

Hint

Answer

2 The table below shows the enthalpy changes needed to calculate the lattice enthalpy of calcium chloride, CaCl₂.

Process	Enthalpy change/kJ mol⁻¹
first ionisation energy of calcium	+590
second ionisation energy of calcium	+1150
electron affinity of chlorine	−348
enthalpy change of formation for calcium chloride	−796
enthalpy change of atomisation for calcium	+178
enthalpy change of atomisation for chlorine	+122

a The Born–Haber cycle below can be used to calculate the lattice enthalpy for calcium chloride.

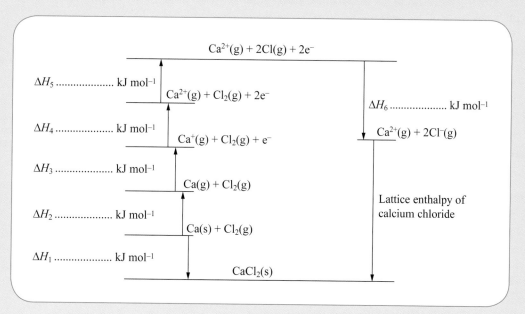

continued

163

    i Use the table of enthalpy changes to complete the Born–Haber cycle by listing the correct numerical values of ΔH_1 to ΔH_6. [3]

    ii Use the Born–Haber cycle to calculate the lattice enthalpy of calcium chloride; give your answer in $kJ\,mol^{-1}$. [2]

    iii Describe how, and explain why, the lattice enthalpy of magnesium fluoride differs from that of calcium chloride. [3]

  b Explain why the first ionisation energy of calcium is less positive than the second ionisation energy. [2]

OCR Chemistry A2 (2815/01) January 2005 [Total 10]

Hint

Hint

Answer

3 *In this question, one mark is available for the quality of spelling, punctuation and grammar.*
The lattice enthalpy of magnesium chloride, $MgCl_2$, can be determined using a Born–Haber cycle and the following enthalpy changes.

Name of process	Enthalpy change/$kJ\,mol^{-1}$
enthalpy change of formation of $MgCl_2(s)$	−641
enthalpy change of atomisation of magnesium	+148
first ionisation energy of magnesium	+738
second ionisation energy of magnesium	+1451
enthalpy change of atomisation of chlorine	+123
electron affinity of chlorine	−349

- Define, using an equation with $MgCl_2$ as an example, what is meant by the term *lattice enthalpy*.
- Construct a Born–Haber cycle for $MgCl_2$, including state symbols, and calculate the lattice enthalpy of $MgCl_2$.
- Explain why the lattice enthalpy of NaBr is much less exothermic than that of $MgCl_2$. [11]

Quality of written communication [1]

OCR Chemistry A2 (2815/01) January 2007 [Total 12]

Hint

Answer

Chapter 15

Entropy

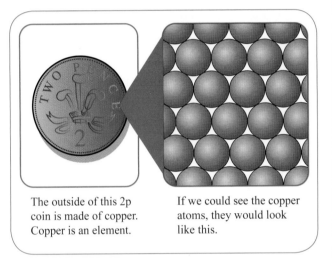

Objectives

Everything is made of atoms. In some substances the atoms are very organised and regularly arranged. Copper is an example of this. The atoms in a piece of copper are regularly arranged; they form a predictable, repeating, pattern (Figure 15.1). A structure like this is said to have a high degree of order – it is an *ordered* structure, in other words.

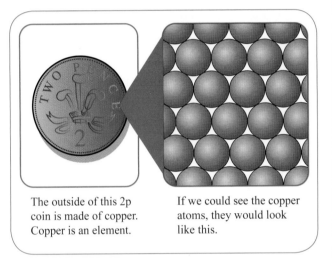

The outside of this 2p coin is made of copper. Copper is an element.

If we could see the copper atoms, they would look like this.

Figure 15.1 The orderly arrangement of copper atoms in a coin.

In other substances, the atoms are very *disorganised* and *irregularly* arranged. A sample of carbon dioxide is an example of this (Figure 15.2). The carbon dioxide molecules are in a much more random and unpredictable arrangement than the atoms in copper. A 'structure' like that of carbon dioxide is said to have a low degree of order – it is a *disordered* arrangement, in other words.

The degree of disorder in a substance is known as the **entropy** of that substance. Different substances have different entropies – different degrees of

disorder. The entropy of a substance can be expressed as a number, with units $JK^{-1}mol^{-1}$ (joules per kelvin per mole). Copper has an entropy of $33.3\,JK^{-1}mol^{-1}$; carbon dioxide has an entropy of $214\,JK^{-1}mol^{-1}$. This is because carbon dioxide has a greater degree of disorder than copper.

When chemical reactions take place, the reacting substances change into the product substances. The total substances before and after the reaction are known as the 'system'. Since the reactant substances are likely to have a different total entropy than the product substances, the chemical reaction causes the entropy of the system to change. A chemical reaction in which the entropy of the system increases makes the system energetically more stable. An understanding of entropy is therefore an important part of explaining why some reactions take place, while others don't.

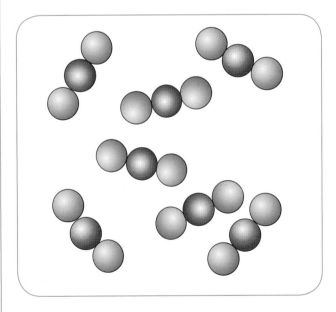

Figure 15.2 Molecules in carbon dioxide.

SAQ

1 What do we mean by the 'entropy of a substance'?

Answer

2 The entropy values of four substances are listed below. All values refer to the substance at 25 °C (298 K), all units are $JK^{-1}mol^{-1}$. Use the data to arrange them from most disordered to most ordered:

copper 33.3
oxygen 205
carbon monoxide 197
water 69.9

Answer

Entropy changes

As a 'rule of thumb', solids have the lowest entropy, and gases have the highest entropy, with liquids and solutions in the middle. Therefore:

- when a solid melts or sublimes there is an increase in entropy
- when a liquid boils there is an increase in entropy
- when a reaction causes an increase in the number of gas molecules there is an increase in entropy
- when a solid dissolves in a solvent there is an increase in entropy.

In all of these cases, the final state is more disordered than the initial state, so entropy increases. The difference in entropy between the reactants and the products in any chemical reaction is called the entropy change of that reaction. It can be calculated as a numerical value and is given the symbol ΔS.

Entropy changes in reactions

The entropy change of a reaction can be calculated if we know the entropy of each reactant and product involved. We calculate it using this equation:

$$\Delta S = \text{(entropy of products)} - \text{(entropy of reactants)}$$

The method is demonstrated in Worked example 1.

Worked example 1

What is the entropy change of the decomposition reaction:

$$NaCl(s) \longrightarrow Na(s) + \tfrac{1}{2}Cl_2(g)?$$

The entropy change is:

(entropy of products) – (entropy of reactants).

Entropy values (from tables of data):

Na 51.0, Cl_2 223, NaCl 72.4, all in $JK^{-1}mol^{-1}$

The entropy change ΔS is $(51.0 + 111.5) - 72.4$

Answer $= +90.1\ JK^{-1}mol^{-1}$

You should note that the entropy data is in joules per kelvin per mole, so the entropy of chlorine has been halved as half a mole of chlorine gas is formed.

SAQ

3 Calculate the entropy changes of the following reactions, and state whether there is an increase or decrease in the disorder of the system as the forward reaction proceeds.

a $N_2(g) + 3H_2(g) \longrightarrow 2NH_3(g)$ (find the entropy change per mole of nitrogen reacted)

b $H_2(g) + Br_2(l) \longrightarrow 2HBr(g)$ (find the entropy change per mole of hydrogen reacted)

(Entropy values: N_2 192, H_2 131, NH_3 193, Br_2 152, HBr 198, all in $JK^{-1}mol^{-1}$)

Answer

4 Explain the entropy changes of the reactions in SAQ 3 by reference to the number of gas molecules involved.

Answer

Free energy

Chemical reactions can release energy as heat, but they can also be used to do useful work. Here are two examples of a chemical reaction doing useful work.

- Burning petrol in a car engine. Work is done by the reaction as the car is propelled forward.
- The chemicals in an electrochemical cell (battery) producing an electric current in a circuit. Work is done by the reaction as the current moves through the components of the circuit.

The maximum useful work that can be done by a chemical reaction is called the *free energy change* of the reaction and is given the symbol ΔG. The units for free energy are joules or kilojoules. ΔG is related to the enthalpy change of the reaction, ΔH, and the entropy change of the reaction, ΔS, by this important equation:

$$\Delta G = \Delta H - T\Delta S$$

This equation is called the Gibbs equation. Free energy is sometimes known as 'Gibbs free energy'. In the Gibbs equation, T is the temperature at which the reaction is taking place. T must be measured in kelvin, not in degrees Celsius. To convert a temperature in degrees Celsius into a temperature in kelvin we have to add 273 to the Celsius temperature. 25 °C is therefore 298 K.

SAQ

5   **a**   Convert 72 °C into kelvin.
    b   Convert 246 K into degrees Celsius.
    c   What is 0 K (absolute zero) in degrees Celsius?
    d   What are the freezing and boiling temperatures of pure water in kelvin?

      (Answer)

The Gibbs equation enables us to calculate the amount of useful work that can be done by the system. This calculation involves the values of ΔH and T, which are measurable experimentally, and ΔS, which is calculated.

Knowing the amount of useful work that can be done by the system is potentially very valuable.

However, even more importantly, if we know the free energy change for a reaction it enables us to predict whether or not it occurs spontaneously.

- If ΔG is negative, the reaction occurs spontaneously.
- If ΔG is positive, the reaction is not spontaneous.
- If ΔG is zero or close to it, i.e. between $+20\,\text{kJ mol}^{-1}$ and $-20\,\text{kJ mol}^{-1}$ (these figures are approximate), the reaction will reach equilibrium, with both reactants and products present.
- If ΔG is more negative than approximately $-20\,\text{kJ mol}^{-1}$, the reaction will be spontaneous and will go to completion.

Why are some reactions spontaneous?

A chemical reaction takes place spontaneously if its free energy change, ΔG, is negative. ΔG is affected by three factors.

- ΔH. This is often the dominant factor. If ΔH is a negative number of large magnitude then ΔG is almost always negative too. Exothermic reactions with a large negative ΔH are nearly always spontaneous. If ΔH is a positive number of large magnitude then ΔG is almost always positive too. Endothermic reactions with a large positive ΔH are very rarely spontaneous.
- ΔS. If ΔS is positive, i.e. if there is an increase in disorder, then $-T\Delta S$ is negative. This can contribute to ΔG being negative, which means the reaction occurs spontaneously. If ΔS is negative, i.e. if there is an decrease in disorder, then $-T\Delta S$ is positive. This can contribute to ΔG being positive, which means the reaction does not occur spontaneously.
- T. This is the only term in $\Delta G = \Delta H - T\Delta S$ that we have any control over. We can choose the temperature of the system. If ΔS is positive then $-T\Delta S$ becomes a larger negative number as T increases, making it more likely that ΔG will be negative and the reaction will occur spontaneously. Changes in which the disorder of the system increases are more likely to be spontaneous at higher temperatures.

There is an important point here. Chemical reactions with a large positive ΔH value (i.e. endothermic reactions) are very rarely spontaneous, because ΔG is positive too. However, a chemical reaction with a small positive ΔH (slightly endothermic) *may* be spontaneous if

- ΔS is positive, *and*
- T is high enough so that $\Delta H - T\Delta S$ is negative.

If we have suitable data we can predict whether or not a reaction will occur spontaneously at a particular temperature (see Worked example 1).

Worked example 2

$$N_2O_4(g) \longrightarrow 2NO_2(g)$$

At 298 K, $\Delta H = +57.2$ kJ per mole of N_2O_4, $\Delta S = +176$ J per kelvin per mole of N_2O_4.

a What is the value of ΔG at 298 K?

Answer: $\Delta G = \Delta H - T\Delta S$,
so $\Delta G = 57\,200 - (298 \times 176)$

Note that ΔH must be converted from kJ to J. This is so that its units are the same as $T\Delta S$.

$\Delta G = 57\,200 - 52\,448$
$= +4752$ J or $+4.75$ kJ per mole of N_2O_4

b What does the answer $\Delta G = +4.75$ kJ mol^{-1} tell us?

Answer: ΔG is positive, so the reaction is not spontaneous. However, ΔG is small, so the reaction is likely to reach an equilibrium with both reactants and products present.

c At what temperature will ΔG be -30 kJ per mole of N_2O_4?

Answer: $\Delta G = \Delta H - T\Delta S$,
so $\quad -30\,000 = 57\,200 - (T \times 176)$

$-87\,200 = -(T \times 176)$

$87\,200 = T \times 176$

$T = \dfrac{87\,200}{176} = 495$ K

continued

d What does this answer mean?

Answer: That the reaction $N_2O_4 \longrightarrow 2NO_2$, will go to completion at a temperature of 495 K (222 °C), since $\Delta G = -30$ kJ per mole of N_2O_4 at this temperature.

Extension

SAQ

6 Chlorine and ethene undergo an addition reaction:

$$Cl_2(g) + C_2H_4(g) \longrightarrow C_2H_4Cl_2(g)$$

At 360 K, $\Delta H = -190$ kJ mol^{-1} and $\Delta S = -121$ J K^{-1} mol^{-1}.
a Write down the Gibbs equation.
b Use the Gibbs equation to calculate ΔG for this reaction at 360 K.
c What do the sign and magnitude of ΔG tell you?
d Why is ΔS for this reaction negative?

Answer

7 The dichloroethane produced in SAQ 6 can undergo an elimination reaction:

$$C_2H_4Cl_2(g) \longrightarrow HCl(g) + C_2H_3Cl(g)$$

At 360 K, $\Delta H = +84.0$ kJ mol^{-1} and $\Delta S = +83.0$ J K^{-1} mol^{-1}.
a Calculate ΔG for this reaction at 360 K.
b What do the sign and magnitude of ΔG tell you?
c How can an endothermic change like this be made to occur spontaneously?
d At what temperature will ΔG for this reaction be -20 kJ per mole? Assume ΔH and ΔS remain constant as temperature varies.
e Why is ΔS for this reaction positive?

Answer

Summary

Glossary

- Entropy is a measure of the 'disorder' of a system.

- A system becomes energetically more stable when it becomes more disordered.

- The entropy is greater in magnitude (becomes more positive in value):
  - when a solid melts, forming a liquid
  - when a liquid boils or evaporates, forming a gas
  - when a solid sublimes, forming a gas
  - when a solute dissolves in a solvent, forming a solution
  - when a reaction produces more gaseous molecules than there are in the reactants.

- The tendency for a process to take place depends on temperature, T, the entropy change in the system, ΔS, and the enthalpy change, ΔH, with the surroundings.

- The feasibility of a reaction is a balance between entropy change and enthalpy change. It is called the free energy change, ΔG, shown by the equation:

  $\Delta G = \Delta H - T\Delta S$.

- We can use $\Delta G = \Delta H - T\Delta S$ to explain how endothermic reactions can produce a negative value for ΔG so are able to take place spontaneously.

Questions

1 Most metals can be extracted by reduction from compounds obtained from their naturally occurring ores. Metals such as calcium and magnesium are normally extracted by electrolysis but it is feasible that calcium oxide could be reduced by carbon, as shown in equation 1.

$$CaO(s) + C(s) \longrightarrow Ca(s) + CO(g) \qquad \text{equation 1}$$

Use the data in the table below to help you answer parts **a–c** below.

	CaO(s)	C(s)	Ca(s)	CO(g)
$\Delta H_f^{\ominus}/\text{kJ}\,\text{mol}^{-1}$	−635	0	0	−110
$S^{\ominus}/\text{J}\,\text{K}^{-1}\,\text{mol}^{-1}$	39.7	5.7	41.4	197.6

a Calculate the standard enthalpy change for the CaO reduction in equation 1.
Give your answer in $\text{kJ}\,\text{mol}^{-1}$. [1]

b Calculate the standard entropy change for the CaO reduction in equation 1.
Give your answer in $\text{J}\,\text{K}^{-1}\,\text{mol}^{-1}$. [1]

c Calculate the minimum temperature at which the carbon reduction in equation 1
is feasible. [5]

OCR Chemistry A2 (sample paper, F325) 2007 [Total 7]

Answer

continued

2 Iron can be extracted from an ore containing Fe_2O_3 by heating it with carbon in a blast furnace. It has been suggested that the chemical reaction could proceed in a number of ways, including the two that follow.

It might take place by a single-step mechanism:
Reaction 1
$Fe_2O_3 + 3C \longrightarrow 2Fe + 3CO$ $\quad \Delta S = +541\,J\,K^{-1}\,mol^{-1}, \Delta H = +489\,kJ$ per mole of Fe_2O_3

Alternatively it might take place by a three-step mechanism:
Reaction 2
$C + O_2 \longrightarrow CO_2$ $\qquad\qquad\qquad \Delta S = +7\,J\,K^{-1}\,mol^{-1}, \Delta H = -394\,kJ\,mol^{-1}$
Reaction 3
$CO_2 + C \longrightarrow 2CO$ $\qquad\qquad\qquad \Delta S = +180\,J\,K^{-1}\,mol^{-1}, \Delta H = +172\,kJ\,mol^{-1}$
Reaction 4
$Fe_2O_3 + 3CO \longrightarrow 2Fe + 3CO_2$ $\qquad \Delta S = +12\,J\,K^{-1}\,mol^{-1}, \Delta H = -27\,kJ\,mol^{-1}$

a **i** Calculate ΔG for reaction 1 at 500 K. [1]
  ii Calculate the temperature at which ΔG for reaction 1 is 0 kJ per mole of Fe_2O_3. [1]
  iii Comment on your answer. [1]
b **i** Calculate ΔG for each of reactions 2, 3 and 4 at 500 K. [3]
  ii Which of these reactions is not spontaneous at 500 K? [1]
  iii Consider your answer to part **b ii**. Calculate the temperature at which ΔG for this reaction is 0 kJ mol^{-1}.
c Estimate a minimum temperature for a blast furnace to operate successfully. [1]
d You should have calculated that the two mechanisms both become feasible at around the same temperature; however, it is believed that the three-step mechanism is the main one occurring in the furnace. Give a possible reason why this is so. [2]

Answer

Chapter 16

Electrode potentials and fuel cells

e-Learning

Objectives

Oxidation and reduction

You will recall from *Chemistry 1*, Chapter 4, that the number of electrons gained or lost by each atom of an element in forming a compound is called its **oxidation state** in that compound. Electrons gained are shown by a negative oxidation state; electrons lost are shown by a positive oxidation state.

Working out oxidation states

Here is a reminder of the rules for determining the values of oxidation states.

1. The oxidation state of uncombined elements (that is, atoms which are not in compounds) is always zero. For example, each atom in $H_2(g)$, $Ne(g)$, $Br_2(l)$, $Co(s)$, $Fe(s)$ or $Cu(s)$ has an oxidation state of zero.

2. For a monatomic ion, the oxidation state of the element is simply the same as the charge on the ion. For example:

ion	Fe^{2+}	Fe^{3+}	Cl^-	O^{2-}
oxidation state	+2	+3	−1	−2

3. The oxidation state of oxygen in compounds is −2, except in peroxides (e.g. H_2O_2), when it is −1, or in OF_2, when it is +2. Hydrogen in compounds is +1, except in metal hydrides (e.g. NaH), when it is −1.

4. The sum of all the oxidation states in a neutral compound is zero. For example, the sum of all the oxidation states in $FeCl_3$ is zero; $[+3 + (3 \times -1) = 0]$.

5. The sum of all the oxidation states in an ion equals the overall charge. For example, the sum of all the oxidation states in VO^{2+} is +2; $[+4 + -2 = +2]$.
    (See also *Chemistry 1*, Chapter 4.)

For example, when titanium burns in oxygen to form an oxide, the titanium atoms each lose four electrons, so titanium has an oxidation state of +4 in this compound. The oxygen atoms each gain two electrons, so oxygen has an oxidation state of −2. The oxide formed is TiO_2 and is called titanium(IV) oxide.

Electrons may also be gained and lost in the reactions of compounds themselves.

*   If a species (i.e. an atom or an ion in a compound) loses electrons in a reaction it is being oxidised.
*   If a species gains electrons in a reaction it is being reduced.

Reduction rarely happens to the ions of s-block elements; any reactions of a compound containing Na^+ ions will almost always give a product containing Na^+ ions – the oxidation state of sodium is +1 before and after the reaction.

Iron, however, forms compounds in the +2 state, containing the Fe^{2+} ion, and in the +3 state, containing the Fe^{3+} ion. During a reaction of a compound containing Fe^{2+} ions each Fe^{2+} ion may lose one electron, giving a product containing Fe^{3+} ions, and vice versa (Figure 16.1).

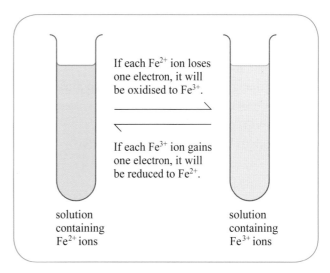

If each Fe^{2+} ion loses one electron, it will be oxidised to Fe^{3+}.

If each Fe^{3+} ion gains one electron, it will be reduced to Fe^{2+}.

solution containing Fe^{2+} ions

solution containing Fe^{3+} ions

Figure 16.1 Iron in the +2 and +3 oxidation states.

Further examples are given in Worked example 1 and Worked example 2.

Worked example 1

What are the oxidation states of copper and chlorine in CuCl and $CuCl_2$?

Rules 2 and 4 above must be used here.

- The oxidation state of chlorine in each compound is –1 as it exists as negative ions with a single negative charge (Rule 2).
- In CuCl the oxidation state of copper is +1 to balance the single negative charge from the chloride ion in a neutral compound (Rule 4).
- In $CuCl_2$ the oxidation state of copper is +2 to balance the two lots of single negative charges from two chloride ions in a neutral compound (Rule 4).

Worked example 2

What is the oxidation state of vanadium in the vanadate ion VO_2^+?

Rules 3 and 5 above must be used here, since VO_2^+ is a compound ion.

- The vanadate ion VO_2^+ has a single positive charge, so the sum of the oxidation states of vanadium and the two oxygens must be +1 (Rule 5).
- The two oxygens in this ion each have an oxidation state of –2 (Rule 3).
- The oxidation state of the vanadium must be +5, since $+5 + (2 \times -2) = +1$.
- The VO_2^+ ion is therefore known as vanadate(V), spoken as 'vanadate five'.

All transition elements may be found in a variety of oxidation states in their compounds. An understanding of oxidation and reduction is therefore central to an understanding of the chemistry of the transition elements (see Chapter 17).

Oxidation and reduction
Remember – OIL RIG.
- **Oxidation Is Loss** of electrons (OIL).
- **Reduction Is Gain** of electrons (RIG).

A species that has been oxidised will have a higher oxidation state after the reaction than before. A species has been reduced if its oxidation state after the reaction is lower than before.

A reactant that causes another reactant to be oxidised in a reaction is called an **oxidising agent**. For example, a substance that reacts with an Fe^{2+} compound giving an Fe^{3+} compound as a product is an oxidising agent. The oxidising agent itself is reduced in the reaction.

A reactant that causes another reactant to be reduced in a reaction is likewise called a **reducing agent**. For example, a substance that reacts with an Fe^{3+} compound giving an Fe^{2+} compound as a product is a reducing agent. The reducing agent itself is oxidised in the reaction.

SAQ

1   In the chemical reaction:

$$Cu^{2+}Cl^-_2 + Fe \longrightarrow Fe^{2+}Cl^-_2 + Cu$$

a   which species gains electrons and is therefore reduced?
b   which species loses electrons and is therefore oxidised?
c   which species is neither oxidised nor reduced?
d   which species is the oxidising agent?
e   which species is the reducing agent?

Answer

2   What is the oxidation state of chromium in compounds that contain the following ions?
a CrO_4^{2-}
b Cr^{2+}
c Cr^{3+}
d $Cr_2O_7^{2-}$

Hint

Answer

3 What is the oxidation state of manganese in the following compounds?

Hint

a MnO_2

b K_2MnO_4

c Mn

d $KMnO_4$

e $MnCl_3$

Answer

f $MnCl_2$

Which oxidation state forms in a reaction?

When an s-block element such as magnesium reacts with an oxidising agent such as dilute acid, the outcome is always the same – a compound containing Mg^{2+} ions. For example:

$$Mg + 2HCl \longrightarrow MgCl_2 + H_2$$

Magnesium is *not* a transition element; it only forms compounds in the +2 oxidation state, so the outcome is quite easy to predict.

However, when a transition element reacts with an oxidising agent there will, on occasions, seem to be more than one possible outcome. For example, when iron metal reacts with dilute hydrochloric acid there are two possible outcomes:

$$Fe + 2HCl \longrightarrow FeCl_2 + H_2$$

or

$$2Fe + 6HCl \longrightarrow 2FeCl_3 + 3H_2$$

Which is the correct equation?

Only one of these two reactions actually takes place, but due to the fact that iron forms stable compounds in the +2 oxidation state *and* the +3 oxidation state, either *might* be correct.

Examining the oxidation states of all the species in these equations shows that the oxidising agent in each case is H^+ ions. H^+ ions are reduced to hydrogen gas so the H^+ ions must be oxidising another species.

We can therefore restate the question as: Is H^+ a strong enough oxidising agent to oxidise iron to Fe^{3+} ions (the second equation) or only as far as Fe^{2+} ions (the first equation)? The answer to this question can be found experimentally, but it can also be predicted using an understanding of standard electrode potentials, which we will look at next.

SAQ

4 For both of the equations for Fe reacting with HCl, give the oxidation number of each species before and after the reaction and identify the reducing agent.

Hint

Answer

Electrode potentials

Reduction reactions involve a substance gaining electrons. For example, metal ions can gain electrons in reactions and be reduced to metals, e.g.

$$Cu^{2+} + 2e^- \rightleftharpoons Cu$$

$$V^{2+} + 2e^- \rightleftharpoons V$$

Equations of this sort are called **half-equations**.

Some metals ions, such as Cu^{2+} ions, are very easy to reduce like this, while other metal ions, such as V^{2+} ions, are much more difficult. Fortunately for us, we can measure the ease with which the reduction takes place – we are not restricted to simple comparative words like 'easier' and 'more difficult'. The measured value is called the **electrode potential** for this reduction. It is measured in volts (V) and is a numerical indication of how favourable (or 'easy') the reduction is. Note that it is a convention that electrode potentials refer to the reduction reaction, i.e. the electrons appear on the left-hand side of the half-equation.

● If the electrode potential is a more positive voltage, the ion on the left is comparatively easy to reduce. For

$$Cu^{2+} + 2e^- \rightleftharpoons Cu$$

the voltage is +0.34 V.

● If the electrode potential is a more negative voltage, the ion on the left is comparatively difficult to reduce. For

$$V^{2+} + 2e^- \rightleftharpoons V$$

the voltage is –1.20 V.

Therefore, it is easier to reduce Cu^{2+} ions to Cu atoms than it is to reduce V^{2+} ions to V atoms.

Remember the convention that electrode potentials refer to reduction reactions. In the reaction above, $-1.20\,V$ refers to

$$V^{2+} + 2e^- \rightleftharpoons V$$

the reduction reaction, and *not* to

$$V \rightleftharpoons V^{2+} + 2e^-$$

which would be an oxidation.

How is the voltage for '$Cu^{2+} + 2e^- \rightleftharpoons Cu$' measured?

In order to measure the electrode potential in volts for this reduction, a rod of pure copper must be placed in a $1.00\,mol\,dm^{-3}$ solution of Cu^{2+} ions (e.g. copper(II) sulfate solution) at a temperature of $25\,°C$ ($298\,K$) (Figure 16.2).

Unfortunately, the electrode potential cannot be measured using this set-up alone. The Cu^{2+}/Cu system described here cannot gain or lose electrons

Figure 16.2 The Cu^{2+}/Cu half-cell.

unless it is connected electrically to a similar system that will either provide or take up these electrons. The Cu^{2+}/Cu system is called a **half-cell**.

In order to work as required and give us a measure of how easy it is to reduce Cu^{2+} ions to Cu atoms, this half-cell *must* be connected to another half-cell. Connecting two half-cells together makes an **electrochemical cell**. An electrochemical cell has a voltage that can be measured and can be used to produce electrical energy, for example, to light a bulb. The sort of batteries that go in torches are simply cleverly packaged electrochemical cells. For convenience their wet ingredients are included in paste form, so they are called 'dry cells'.

Standard electrode potentials

If the Cu^{2+}/Cu half-cell described above is connected electrically to another half-cell then a complete electrochemical cell has been created and we can measure the cell voltage. If the other half-cell consists of a $1.00\,mol\,dm^{-3}$ solution of H^+ ions in contact with hydrogen gas at 1 atmosphere pressure, all at a temperature of $298\,K$, then the voltage measured is called the **standard electrode potential** for the reaction:

$$Cu^{2+} + 2e^- \rightleftharpoons Cu$$

The H^+/H_2 half-cell is called a **standard hydrogen electrode**.

We need a second half-cell of some kind because it is impossible to measure the voltage of the Cu^{2+}/Cu half-cell on its own. Chemists have agreed to use the standard hydrogen electrode as the second half-cell when measuring standard electrode potentials. There is nothing particularly special about the H^+/H_2 half-cell, although the fact that it was chosen in this way makes it significant in electrochemistry.

This seems like quite a fiddly way to collect data, but the data collected is *very* useful.

Look again at your answers to SAQ 3. Manganese can form stable compounds in *five* different oxidation states (Figure 16.3). Using standard electrode potential data it is possible to predict accurately which oxidation state of manganese forms in any particular reaction.

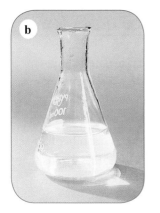

Figure 16.3 The various oxidation states of manganese. **a** Manganese(0), the metal as an element. **b** Manganese(II), as an Mn^{2+} solution. **c** Manganese(III), as an Mn^{3+} solution. **d** Manganese(IV), as solid MnO_2. **e** Manganese(VI), as the MnO_4^{2-} ion. **f** Manganese(VII), as the MnO_4^- ion.

The standard hydrogen electrode

A standard hydrogen electrode is shown in Figure 16.4. Hydrogen gas is introduced into the standard hydrogen electrode near the top and bubbles out slowly from a hole in the glass bell. The platinum electrode allows electrical contact to be made. Platinum ensures good contact between H^+ ions in solution and H_2 molecules so that electrode reactions occur quickly, but being an inert metal it does not take part in any reactions itself. The platinum electrode needs to be coated with finely divided platinum (known as platinum black).

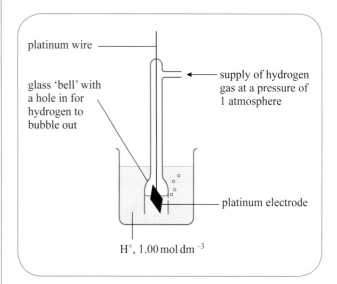

platinum wire

glass 'bell' with a hole in for hydrogen to bubble out

supply of hydrogen gas at a pressure of 1 atmosphere

platinum electrode

H^+, $1.00\,mol\,dm^{-3}$

Figure 16.4 The standard hydrogen electrode.

There are two possible electrode reactions.
- If the other half-cell gives electrons to the standard hydrogen electrode:

$$H^+ + e^- \longrightarrow \tfrac{1}{2}H_2$$

- If the standard hydrogen electrode gives electrons to the other half-cell:

$$\tfrac{1}{2}H_2 \longrightarrow H^+ + e^-$$

The standard hydrogen electrode is used as a *standard reference electrode*. If it is connected to another half-cell then we can measure the electrode potential of the other half-cell *relative* to the voltage of the standard hydrogen electrode. It is a lot like measuring the height of a mountain – the height is always given relative to sea level.

Measuring a standard electrode potential

If all concentrations are $1.00\,mol\,dm^{-3}$, if the temperature is 298 K and if the pressures of any gases used are 1 atmosphere (101 kPa), then these conditions are called **standard conditions**. If an electrochemical cell is made up under standard conditions, using a standard hydrogen electrode as one half-cell and the half-cell under investigation as the second half-cell, then the voltage measured is the standard electrode potential of the half-cell under investigation (Figure 16.5).

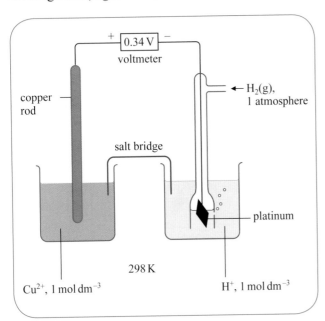

Figure 16.5 Measuring the standard electrode potential of a Cu^{2+}/Cu half-cell.

The **salt bridge** in Figure 16.5 is there to complete the electric circuit. A simple salt bridge can be made by soaking a piece of filter paper in potassium nitrate solution. The salt bridge completes the electric circuit by allowing movement of ions between the two half-cells. It does not allow the movement of electrons – which flow via the wires in the external circuit only.

The voltage of this electrochemical cell is 0.34 V, with the copper half-cell as the positive terminal and the hydrogen half-cell as the negative terminal.

Since conditions are standard and the other half-cell is a standard hydrogen electrode, this means that +0.34 V is the standard electrode potential for the half-cell reaction:

$$Cu^{2+} + 2e^- \rightleftharpoons Cu$$

This value of +0.34 V gives a numerical indication of the tendency of Cu^{2+} ions to receive electrons, and of Cu atoms to lose electrons. It can be used to predict with accuracy which reactions Cu^{2+} ions and Cu atoms will take part in.

The voltage of the electrochemical cell shown in Figure 16.6 is 0.76 V, with the zinc half-cell as the negative terminal and the hydrogen half-cell as the positive terminal.

Since conditions are standard and the other half-cell is a standard hydrogen electrode, this means that −0.76 V is the standard electrode potential for the half-cell reaction:

$$Zn^{2+} + 2e^- \rightleftharpoons Zn$$

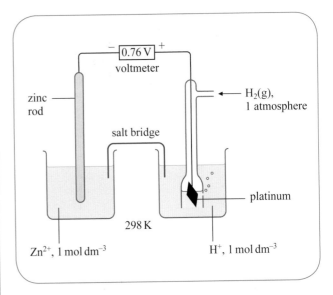

Figure 16.6 Measuring the standard electrode potential of a Zn^{2+}/Zn half-cell.

(Remember the convention that half-equations are written so that the forward reaction is a reduction, with the electrons shown on the left-hand side.) This value of −0.76 V gives a numerical value for the tendency of Zn^{2+} ions to receive electrons, and of Zn atoms to lose electrons. Since it is a more negative value than the value for Cu^{2+}/Cu it means that Zn^{2+} has a *lower* tendency to gain electrons than Cu^{2+} has, and zinc atoms have a *greater* tendency to lose electrons than copper atoms have. This will be explained further in the section 'The meaning of $E^{\ominus}$ values' (page 179). The way in which we can use standard electrode potential values is explained further in the section 'Using $E^{\ominus}$ values to predict whether or not a reaction will occur' (page 181).

The standard electrode potential for a half-cell reaction can therefore be defined as the voltage measured under standard conditions when the half-cell is incorporated into an electrochemical cell with the other half-cell being a standard hydrogen electrode. All conditions must be standard. The polarity of the half-cell within this electrochemical cell gives the sign of the standard electrode potential.

The symbol for a standard electrode potential is $E^{\ominus}$, usually spoken of as 'E standard', with the $^{\ominus}$ sign representing standard conditions. We can therefore write:

$$Cu^{2+} + 2e^- \rightleftharpoons Cu \qquad E^{\ominus} = +0.34\,V$$

$$Zn^{2+} + 2e^- \rightleftharpoons Zn \qquad E^{\ominus} = -0.76\,V$$

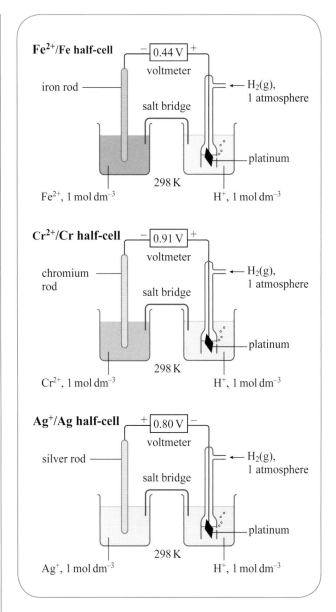

Figure 16.7 Measuring standard electrode potentials.

SAQ

5   Look at the electrochemical cells shown in Figure 16.7.

   a   Write equations for the half-cell reactions in the half-cells on the left of each diagram (i.e. *not* the standard hydrogen electrode). Write each equation as a reduction (gain of electrons), e.g.

   $$Zn^{2+} + 2e^- \rightleftharpoons Zn$$

   b   What are the standard electrode potentials for these half-cell reactions?

   c   List all necessary conditions in each cell.

   Answer

Measuring standard electrode potentials involving two ions

We have considered how the standard electrode potential of a metal in contact with one of its ions can be measured. Standard electrode potentials can also be measured for reductions in which both the species involved are ions. For example:

$$Fe^{3+} + e^- \rightleftharpoons Fe^{2+}$$

The half-cell that is used here must contain *both* Fe^{2+} ions and Fe^{3+} ions, both at a concentration of $1.00\,mol\,dm^{-3}$. A platinum wire or platinum foil electrode is used to make electrical contact with the solution. The Fe^{3+}/Fe^{2+} half-cell is then made into an electrochemical cell with a standard hydrogen electrode as the other half-cell. The measured voltage, the $E^\ominus$ value, is $+0.77\,V$ (Figure 16.8).

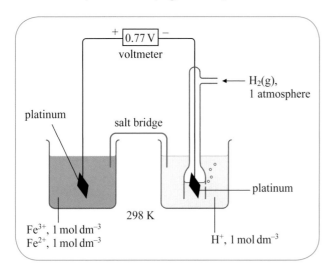

Fe^{3+}, 1 mol dm^{-3}
Fe^{2+}, 1 mol dm^{-3}

Figure 16.8 Measuring the standard electrode potential of an Fe^{3+}/Fe^{2+} half-cell.

Some reductions involve several ionic species. For example:

$$MnO_4^- + 8H^+ + 5e^- \rightleftharpoons Mn^{2+} + 4H_2O$$

The inclusion of H^+ ions here means that acid conditions are necessary for the reduction of MnO_4^- ions (manganate(VII) ions) to Mn^{2+} ions. In order to measure the $E^\ominus$ value for this half-cell, the concentrations of MnO_4^- ions, H^+ ions and Mn^{2+} ions must all be $1.00\,mol\,dm^{-3}$. Once again, electrical

contact is made with a platinum wire or platinum foil electrode. If the voltage to be measured is to be the standard electrode potential for the MnO_4^-/Mn^{2+} half-cell, then the other half-cell must be a standard hydrogen electrode and all conditions must be standard (Figure 16.9).

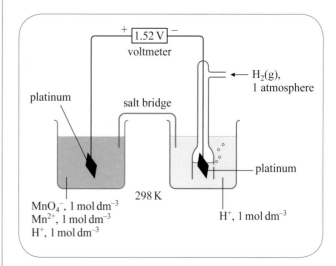

MnO$_4^-$, 1 mol dm^{-3}
Mn^{2+}, 1 mol dm^{-3}
H$^+$, 1 mol dm^{-3}

Figure 16.9 Measuring the standard electrode potential of an MnO_4^-/Mn^{2+} half-cell.

SAQ

6 What is the $E^\ominus$ value for the half-cell shown by the following equation?

$$MnO_4^- + 8H^+ + 5e^- \rightleftharpoons Mn^{2+} + 4H_2O$$

Hint

Answer

7 What are standard conditions?

Hint

Answer

8 Why is platinum used in preference to other metals in half-cells where the reaction itself does not involve a metal element?

Hint

Answer

9 Show, with the aid of a diagram, how you would measure the $E^\ominus$ value for the half-cell shown by this equation:

$$VO^{2+} + 2H^+ + e^- \rightleftharpoons V^{3+} + H_2O$$

Answer

Measuring standard electrode potentials involving non-metals

We can also measure the standard electrode potential for a non-metallic element in contact with a solution of its aqueous ions. As with measuring the standard electrode potential of two ions of the same element in different oxidation states, one difficulty here is how to make electrical contact. The answer again is to use a platinum wire as an electrode.

The platinum wire must be in contact with both the element and the aqueous ions. The standard electrode potential is measured by connecting the half-cell to a standard hydrogen electrode and measuring the voltage produced under standard conditions.

The half-cell on the left of Figure 16.10 involves chlorine gas and chloride ions. The half-equation is therefore:

$$\tfrac{1}{2}Cl_2 + e^- \rightleftharpoons Cl^-$$

The $E^\ominus$ value for this half-cell is +1.36 V.

You should note that the half-equation could also have been written as:

$$Cl_2 + 2e^- \rightleftharpoons 2Cl^-$$

The $E^\ominus$ value for this half-cell is still +1.36 V. The way in which you choose to balance the half-equation makes no difference to the tendency for the element chlorine to gain electrons!

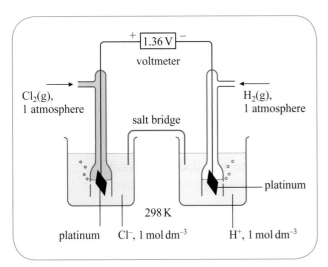

Figure 16.10 Measuring the standard electrode potential of a Cl_2/Cl^- half-cell.

10 a Look at the diagram in Figure 16.11 and write a half-equation for the half-cell on the left.

b What is the $E^\ominus$ value for this half-cell?

Answer

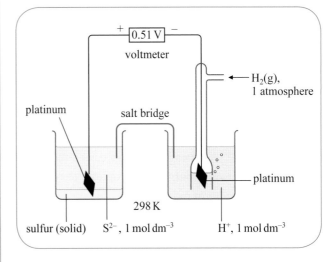

Figure 16.11 Measuring the standard electrode potential of an S/S^{2-} half-cell.

11 Draw a diagram to show how you would measure the standard electrode potential for the half-cell:

Hint

$$\tfrac{1}{2}I_2 + e^- \rightleftharpoons I^-$$

Include the actual $E^\ominus$ value of +0.54 V on your diagram.

Answer

If a cell is made using two identical half-cells, the voltage measured is always zero volts. This means that measuring the $E^\ominus$ for the half-cell:

$$H^+ + e^- \rightleftharpoons \tfrac{1}{2}H_2$$

gives a value of 0.00 V. This value arises because of our choice of a standard hydrogen electrode as reference electrode, but it is still a relevant and useful piece of data.

The meaning of $E^\ominus$ values

You saw in the previous section on measuring $E^\ominus$ values how standard electrode potentials are measured using a half-cell, a standard hydrogen electrode, a salt bridge and a voltmeter. This section begins to explain how useful this data is to us.

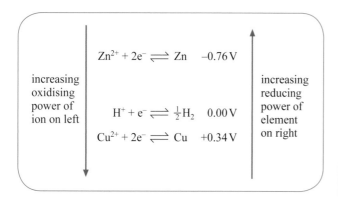

Figure 16.12 Comparing the oxidising power of ions and the reducing power of elements.

$E^\ominus$ values give us a measure of how easy a reduction or oxidation is to carry out. (In this context 'easy' refers to the strength of oxidising or reducing agent required to make a change happen. If a species is 'easy' to oxidise, it can be oxidised by a weak oxidising agent.) This can be summarised in three ways.

- The more positive a value of $E^\ominus$ is, the greater the tendency for this half-equation to proceed in a forward direction.
- The more positive the value of $E^\ominus$, the easier it is to reduce the species on the left of the half-equation.
- The less positive the value of $E^\ominus$, the easier it is to oxidise the species on the right of the half-equation.

Consider the following two half-equations as examples:

$$Cu^{2+} + 2e^- \rightleftharpoons Cu \qquad E^\ominus = +0.34\,V$$

$$Zn^{2+} + 2e^- \rightleftharpoons Zn \qquad E^\ominus = -0.76\,V$$

- Comparing the two half-equations, Cu^{2+}/Cu has a greater tendency to proceed in the forward direction, as its $E^\ominus$ value is more positive. Zn^{2+}/Zn has a greater tendency to proceed in the backward direction, as its $E^\ominus$ value is more negative (Figure 16.12).
- The Cu^{2+}/Cu half-equation has the more positive $E^\ominus$ value, so Cu^{2+} is easier to reduce to Cu than Zn^{2+} is to Zn. Zn^{2+} ions *can* be reduced to Zn atoms, but this requires a stronger reducing agent, with a more negative $E^\ominus$ value than the $E^\ominus$ value for Zn^{2+}/Zn.

- The Zn^{2+}/Zn half-equation has the less positive $E^\ominus$ value, so Zn is easier to oxidise to Zn^{2+} than Cu is to Cu^{2+}. Cu atoms *can* be oxidised to Cu^{2+} ions, but it requires a stronger oxidising agent, with a more positive $E^\ominus$ value than the $E^\ominus$ value for Cu^{2+}/Cu.

SAQ

12 Use the $E^\ominus$ data in Appendix B to answer this question.

   a Of the ions Ag^+, Cr^{2+} and Fe^{2+}, which one needs the strongest reducing agent to reduce it to uncharged metal atoms?   [Hint]

   b Of the atoms Ag, Cr and Fe, which one needs the strongest oxidising agent to oxidise it to an ion?   [Answer]

Using $E^\ominus$ values to predict cell voltages

You have learned how the $E^\ominus$ value of a half-cell can be measured and what the $E^\ominus$ value can tell us about how easy it is to oxidise or reduce a particular species. We can also use $E^\ominus$ values to calculate the voltage of an electrochemical cell made of two half-cells, and to predict whether or not a particular reaction occurs. This section deals with cell voltages.

To recap, if an electrochemical cell is made using two half-cells and a salt bridge, under standard conditions, and if one of the half-cells is a standard hydrogen electrode then the voltage measured is the standard electrode potential of the other half-cell. However, if two half-cells are used, neither of which is a standard hydrogen electrode, then the voltage measured will be the *difference* in the $E^\ominus$ values of the two half-cells.

For the electrochemical cell shown in Figure 16.13, the standard electrode potentials are:

$$Ag^+ + e^- \rightleftharpoons Ag \qquad\qquad E^\ominus = +0.80\,V$$

$$Zn^{2+} + 2e^- \rightleftharpoons Zn \qquad\qquad E^\ominus = -0.76\,V$$

The difference between $+0.80\,V$ and $-0.76\,V$ is $+1.56\,V$ ($+0.80 - (-0.76) = +1.56$) (Figure 16.14). The voltage of this cell is therefore $+1.56\,V$. Since the standard electrode potential of the Ag^+/Ag half-cell

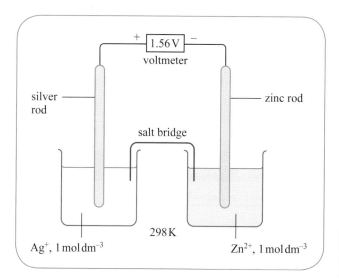

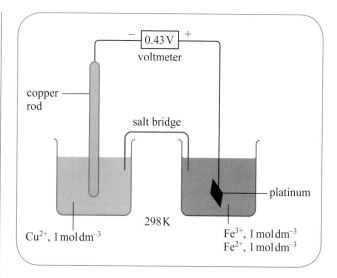

Figure 16.13 An Ag^+/Ag, Zn^{2+}/Zn electrochemical cell.

Figure 16.15 A Cu^{2+}/Cu, Fe^{3+}/Fe^{2+} electrochemical cell.

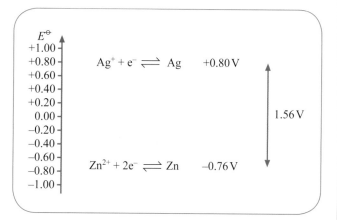

Figure 16.14 The difference between +0.80 V and −0.76 V is +1.56 V.

is more positive, the Ag^+/Ag half-cell will be the positive pole and the Zn^{2+}/Zn half-cell will be the negative pole of the cell.

For the electrochemical cell shown in Figure 16.15, the standard electrode potentials are:

$$Fe^{3+} + e^- \rightleftharpoons Fe^{2+} \qquad E^\ominus = +0.77\,V$$

$$Cu^{2+} + 2e^- \rightleftharpoons Cu \qquad E^\ominus = +0.34\,V$$

The difference between +0.77 V and +0.34 V is +0.43 V (+0.77 − (+0.34) = +0.43). The voltage of this cell is therefore +0.43 V. Since the standard electrode potential of the Fe^{3+}/Fe^{2+} half-cell is more positive, the Fe^{3+}/Fe^{2+} half-cell will be the positive pole, and the Cu^{2+}/Cu half-cell will be the negative pole of the cell.

SAQ

13 a Draw a diagram of an electrochemical cell consisting of a Cr^{3+}/Cr half-cell and a Cl_2/Cl^- half-cell.

b What will be the cell voltage?

c Which half-cell will be the positive pole? All necessary $E^\ominus$ values can be found in Appendix B.

Answer

14 a Draw a diagram of an electrochemical cell consisting of an Mn^{2+}/Mn half-cell and a Pb^{2+}/Pb half-cell.

b What will be the cell voltage?

c Which half-cell will be the positive pole? All necessary $E^\ominus$ values can be found in Appendix B.

Answer

Using $E^\ominus$ values to predict whether or not a reaction will occur

An understanding of standard electrode potentials makes it possible to predict whether or not a particular oxidising agent can or cannot oxidise another named substance under standard conditions. It is also possible to predict whether or not a particular reducing agent can reduce another substance.

To find out whether or not a solution of Cu^{2+} ions can oxidise zinc metal to Zn^{2+} ions, first of all write down the half-equations with their standard electrode potential values:

$$Zn^{2+} + 2e^- \rightleftharpoons Zn \qquad E^\ominus = -0.76\,V$$

$$Cu^{2+} + 2e^- \rightleftharpoons Cu \qquad E^\ominus = +0.34\,V$$

The bottom half-equation has a more positive standard electrode potential value than the top one. This means that the bottom reaction can proceed in a forward direction (meaning Cu^{2+} is reduced to copper) while the top reaction proceeds in a backward direction (meaning zinc is oxidised to Zn^{2+}). Therefore, Cu^{2+} ions *can* oxidise zinc atoms.

To write an equation for this reaction rewrite the two half-equations in the directions in which they will proceed:

$$Zn \longrightarrow Zn^{2+} + 2e^-$$

(the zinc half-equation has been reversed)

$$Cu^{2+} + 2e^- \longrightarrow Cu$$

(this half-equation has been left unchanged).

Adding the two half-equations gives:

$$Zn + Cu^{2+} + 2e^- \longrightarrow Cu + Zn^{2+} + 2e^-$$

Cancelling the two electrons on each side gives:

$$Zn + Cu^{2+} \longrightarrow Cu + Zn^{2+}$$

So, it is this reaction that takes place (Figure 16.16) and *not* its opposite ($Zn^{2+} + Cu \longrightarrow Cu^{2+} + Zn$).

This may seem like a trivial example, involving a reaction you have been familiar with for some years, but it illustrates the predictive power of $E^\ominus$ values. Using $E^\ominus$ values enables you to predict whether or not a reaction can take place (see Worked example 3 and Worked example 4).

Worked example 3

Can chlorine oxidise Fe^{2+} ions to Fe^{3+} ions?

First of all write down the half-equations with their standard electrode potential values:

$$Fe^{3+} + e^- \rightleftharpoons Fe^{2+} \qquad E^\ominus = +0.77\,V$$

$$\tfrac{1}{2}Cl_2 + e^- \rightleftharpoons Cl^- \qquad E^\ominus = +1.36\,V$$

The bottom half-equation, with its more positive standard electrode potential value, will proceed in a forward direction (Cl_2 is reduced to Cl^- ions) while the top reaction proceeds in a backward direction (Fe^{2+} is oxidised to Fe^{3+}). Therefore, chlorine *can* oxidise Fe^{2+} ions. To write an equation for this reaction rewrite the two half-equations in the directions in which they will proceed:

$$\tfrac{1}{2}Cl_2 + e^- \longrightarrow Cl^-$$

$$Fe^{2+} \longrightarrow Fe^{3+} + e^-$$

Adding the two half-equations together and cancelling the electron on each side gives:

$$\tfrac{1}{2}Cl_2 + Fe^{2+} \longrightarrow Cl^- + Fe^{3+}$$

Figure 16.16 As predicted by the $E^\ominus$ values, zinc reacts with Cu^{2+} ions but copper does not react with Zn^{2+} ions.

Worked example 4

Can iodine oxidise Fe^{2+} to Fe^{3+}?

The half-equations and $E^\ominus$ values are:

$$I_2 + e^- \rightleftharpoons I^- \qquad\qquad E^\ominus = +0.54\,V$$

$$Fe^{3+} + e^- \rightleftharpoons Fe^{2+} \qquad E^\ominus = +0.77\,V$$

With a less positive $E^\ominus$ value the top reaction cannot proceed forwards while the bottom reaction proceeds backwards. Iodine *cannot* oxidise Fe^{2+} to Fe^{3+} under standard conditions.

The half-cell that gains electrons is always the one with the more positive $E^\ominus$ value. The half-cell that supplies electrons is always the one with the more negative $E^\ominus$ value.

Remember – positive attracts electrons; negative repels electrons.

SAQ

15 Although iodine cannot oxidise Fe^{2+} to Fe^{3+}, the half-equations in Worked example 4 predict that another reaction involving iodide ions and iron in a particular oxidation state *is* possible. Write an equation for this reaction.

Hint

Answer

The half-equations in Worked example 3 and Worked example 4 both involve one electron only. This will not always be the case.

When using this method to find out whether or not a solution of Ag^+ can oxidise chromium metal to Cr^{3+}, the silver half-equation involves one electron but the chromium half-equation involves three electrons. Writing a balanced ionic equation for the reaction, if it occurs, will involve balancing the number of electrons involved.

Starting as before with the half-equations:

$$Cr^{3+} + 3e^- \rightleftharpoons Cr \qquad E^\ominus = -0.74\,V$$

$$Ag^+ + e^- \rightleftharpoons Ag \qquad E^\ominus = +0.80\,V$$

The bottom half-equation, with its more positive standard electrode potential value, will proceed in a forward direction while the top reaction proceeds in a backward direction. Ag^+ *can* oxidise chromium metal to Cr^{3+} ions. Rewriting the half-equations in the directions in which they will proceed gives:

$$Cr \longrightarrow Cr^{3+} + 3e^-$$

$$Ag^+ + e^- \longrightarrow Ag$$

Before adding these together, the same number of electrons must be involved in each half-equation. In this case that means three electrons, so the bottom equation must be multiplied by three:

$$Cr \longrightarrow Cr^{3+} + 3e^-$$

$$3Ag^+ + 3e^- \longrightarrow 3Ag$$

Adding now gives:

$$Cr + 3Ag^+ + 3e^- \longrightarrow Cr^{3+} + 3e^- + 3Ag$$

Cancelling the electrons gives:

$$Cr + 3Ag^+ \longrightarrow Cr^{3+} + 3Ag$$

The final equation, therefore, says that one chromium atom can be oxidised to a Cr^{3+} ion by three Ag^+ ions, which in turn are reduced to three silver atoms.

SAQ

16 Use the $E^\ominus$ data in Appendix B to predict whether or not the following reactions occur. If a reaction does occur, write a balanced chemical equation for it.

  a Can MnO_4^- ions oxidise Cl^- ions to chlorine in acid conditions (Figure 16.17)?

  b Can MnO_4^- ions oxidise F^- ions to fluorine in acid conditions?

  c Can H^+ ions oxidise V^{2+} ions to V^{3+} ions?

  d Can H^+ ions oxidise Fe^{2+} ions to Fe^{3+} ions?

Answer

Figure 16.17 If the KMnO$_4$(aq) is acidified, would it be safe to do this in an open lab or would chlorine gas be produced?

From SAQ 16d, you now have the answer to the question on page 173: Is H$^+$ a strong enough oxidising agent to oxidise iron to Fe^{3+} ions or only as far as Fe^{2+} ions? It took some time to get here, because some detailed and subtle concepts have been involved. However, if you have mastered the meaning and application of $E^{\ominus}$ values, you now have a powerful tool for assessing whether or not a reaction can occur, and if it does occur which of several possible outcomes arises.

An alternative approach to making predictions is given below. *It is recommended that you choose only one of these two approaches in predicting whether or not a reaction occurs.*

Using cell voltage to predict whether or not a reaction will occur

Alternative approach

The possibility of a reaction occurring has been assessed by looking at the $E^{\ominus}$ values of the two half-equations involved. The half-equation with the more positive $E^{\ominus}$ value will proceed forwards, gaining electrons. The half-equation with the less positive $E^{\ominus}$ value proceeds backwards, supplying electrons. An alternative approach involves manipulation of the two half-equations, followed by examination of the sign of the cell voltage. *It is recommended that you choose only one of these two approaches in predicting whether or not a reaction occurs.*

We shall explain the cell voltage approach using Worked example 5, Worked example 6 and Worked example 7.

Worked example 5

Can bromine oxidise silver metal to Ag$^+$ ions?

The cell voltage approach begins with an equation for the reaction under question. For this example the equation is:

$$\tfrac{1}{2}Br_2 + Ag \longrightarrow Br^- + Ag^+$$

This equation must then be broken down into two half-equations:

$$\tfrac{1}{2}Br_2 + e^- \rightleftharpoons Br^-$$

$$Ag \rightleftharpoons Ag^+ + e^-$$

The $E^{\ominus}$ value for each half-equation is now included. The value is always the data book value and is never a multiple of it. However, for the half-equation that has been written as an oxidation, the sign of the $E^{\ominus}$ must be reversed. For the bromine half-equation the value is simply the data book value of $E^{\ominus}$, +1.07 V, as the half-equation is written in the conventional way, as a reduction. For the silver half-equation the data book value of $E^{\ominus}$ for the reduction

$$Ag^+ + e^- \rightleftharpoons Ag$$

is +0.80 V. The sign of this $E^{\ominus}$ value must be reversed as the process is written as an oxidation, giving −0.80 V.

$$\tfrac{1}{2}Br_2 + e^- \rightleftharpoons Br^- \qquad +1.07\,V$$

$$Ag \rightleftharpoons Ag^+ + e^- \qquad -0.80\,V$$

continued

The two half-equations are now added, and so are the voltages:

$$\tfrac{1}{2}Br_2 + Ag \longrightarrow Br^- + Ag^+ \qquad +0.27\,V$$

Since $+0.27\,V$ is the difference between the two $E^\ominus$ values it will be the measured cell voltage if an electrochemical cell is set up with a Br_2/Br^- half-cell and a Ag^+/Ag half-cell. Here the *sign* of the cell voltage is of great importance. If this process produces a *positive* cell voltage, the reaction as written will occur. This reaction therefore *does* occur, i.e. bromine and silver react to give silver bromide. Bromine will oxidise silver. If the process had produced a *negative* voltage the reaction as written would not occur.

Worked example 6

Can iodine oxidise silver metal to Ag^+ ions?

The equation is:

$$\tfrac{1}{2}I_2 + Ag \longrightarrow I^- + Ag^+$$

The half-equations and voltages are:

$$\tfrac{1}{2}I_2 + e^- \rightleftharpoons I^- \qquad +0.54\,V$$

$$Ag \rightleftharpoons Ag^+ + e^- \qquad -0.80\,V$$

The two half-equations are now added, and so are the voltages:

$$\tfrac{1}{2}I_2 + Ag \longrightarrow I^- + Ag^+ \qquad -0.26\,V$$

The sign of the cell voltage is negative. The reaction does not occur; iodine and silver do not react to give silver iodide. Iodine cannot oxidise silver.

Worked example 7

Can bromine oxidise copper metal to Cu^{2+} ions?

The equation is:

$$Br_2 + Cu \longrightarrow 2Br^- + Cu^{2+}$$

The half-equations and voltages are:

$$Br_2 + 2e^- \rightleftharpoons 2Br^- \qquad +1.07\,V$$

$$Cu \rightleftharpoons Cu^{2+} + 2e^- \qquad -0.34\,V$$

In order to balance the number of electrons, the normal bromine half-equation has been multiplied by two but the $E^\ominus$ value has *not* been multiplied. $E^\ominus$ values are *never* multiplied in this or any other method. The normal copper half-equation has been reversed, so the sign of the $E^\ominus$ value for Cu^{2+}/Cu has been reversed.

The two half-equations are now added, and so are the voltages:

$$Br_2 + Cu \longrightarrow 2Br^- + Cu^{2+} \qquad +0.73\,V$$

The sign of the cell voltage is positive. The reaction occurs; bromine and copper react to give copper(II) bromide. Bromine can oxidise copper atoms to copper ions.

SAQ

17 Use the cell voltage method described in Worked examples 5–7 to answer SAQ 16. Remember that if one half-equation needs multiplying up in order to balance the overall equation for electrons, the $E^\ominus$ value should not be multiplied up.

(Answer)

(Extension)

Limitations of the standard electrode potential approach

As we have seen, standard electrode potentials are measured under standard conditions:

- a temperature of 298 K
- a pressure of one atmosphere (101 kPa)
- all concentrations at $1.00\,mol\,dm^{-3}$.

The actual conditions for a reaction, either in a lab or in industry, are unlikely to be standard. Under such conditions the $E^{\ominus}$ values for the relevant half-equations are still a useful guide to what will or will not occur. If the $E^{\ominus}$ values of the two half-equations involved differ by more than 0.30 V then the reaction predicted by the $E^{\ominus}$ values will nearly always be the one that occurs, even under non-standard conditions of temperature, pressure or concentration.

Where the $E^{\ominus}$ values of the two half-equations are closer than 0.30 V, the actual conditions must be taken into account.

If a half-cell is constructed with non-standard concentrations, its electrode potential can be measured using a standard hydrogen electrode as the other half-cell. The voltage measured is now an E value, not an $E^{\ominus}$ value. Increasing the concentration of a substance on the left of the half-equation will make the E value more positive (or less negative) than $E^{\ominus}$. Increasing the concentration of a substance on the right of the half-equation will make the E value less positive (or more negative) than $E^{\ominus}$. For example, under standard conditions:

$$Fe^{3+} + e^- \rightleftharpoons Fe^{2+} \qquad E^{\ominus} = +0.77\,V$$

- if $[Fe^{3+}]$ is more than $1.00\,mol\,dm^{-3}$, E might be +0.85 V (i.e. greater than $E^{\ominus}$)
- if $[Fe^{3+}]$ is less than $1.00\,mol\,dm^{-3}$, E might be +0.70 V
- if $[Fe^{2+}]$ is more than $1.00\,mol\,dm^{-3}$, E might be +0.70 V
- if $[Fe^{2+}]$ is less than $1.00\,mol\,dm^{-3}$, E might be +0.85 V.

This is an application of Le Chatelier's principle.

0.30 V is given here as a *rough guide* figure only. If $E^{\ominus}$ values differ by over 0.30 V then the reaction predicted by the $E^{\ominus}$ values is *nearly always* the one that occurs. If $E^{\ominus}$ values differ by less than 0.30 V, non-standard conditions *may well* result in an unexpected outcome. If this leaves you desiring a bit more precision, you will have to find out about the Nernst equation!

SAQ

18 The half-cell

$$Cr_2O_7^{2-} + 14H^+ + 6e^- \rightleftharpoons 2Cr^{3+} + 7H_2O$$

has an $E^{\ominus}$ value of +1.33 V. All concentrations in the solutions used to measure this value are, of course, $1.00\,mol\,dm^{-3}$.

a Suggest an E value if:
  i $[Cr_2O_7^{2-}]$ were to be increased
  ii $[H^+]$ were to be decreased
  iii $[Cr^{3+}]$ were to be increased.
b What effect would each of these concentration changes have on the strength of the $Cr_2O_7^{2-}$ solution as an oxidising agent?
c What conditions would you use to make a solution of $Cr_2O_7^{2-}$ as strong an oxidising agent as possible?
d Use Le Chatelier's principle to explain your answer to part c.

Answer

A well-known example of the effect of non-standard conditions is the reaction of MnO_2 with concentrated HCl to make chlorine. This reaction involves MnO_2 being reduced to Mn^{2+} under acid conditions while Cl^- ions are oxidised to Cl_2.

The relevant half-equations are:

$$MnO_2 + 4H^+ + 2e^- \rightleftharpoons Mn^{2+} + 2H_2O$$
$$E^{\ominus} = +1.23\,V$$

$$\tfrac{1}{2}Cl_2 + e^- \rightleftharpoons Cl^-$$
$$E^{\ominus} = +1.36\,V$$

The $E^{\ominus}$ values predict that MnO_2 *cannot* oxidise Cl^- ions to Cl_2 under standard conditions (in fact, chlorine should be able to oxidise Mn^{2+} to MnO_2). However, the $E^{\ominus}$ values are close enough for non-standard concentrations to make a difference. If concentrated HCl is used, the concentrations of H^+ and Cl^- will be well over $1.00\,mol\,dm^{-3}$. Under these conditions the E values might be:

$$\tfrac{1}{2}Cl_2 + e^- \rightleftharpoons Cl^- \qquad\qquad E = +1.30\,V$$

$$MnO_2 + 4H^+ + 2e^- \rightleftharpoons Mn^{2+} + 2H_2O \quad E = +1.40\,V$$

This predicts that under such conditions MnO_2 will oxidise Cl^- ions to chlorine, which is what we observe in practice.

Reaction rate has a role to play too

The rate of a particular reaction may also lead to a prediction based on $E^{\ominus}$ values proving unsatisfactory. Standard electrode potentials can tell you whether or not a particular redox reaction can take place but *not* whether or not it takes place at a useful rate. If predicted to happen, the reaction may happen at an unacceptably slow rate. The $E^{\ominus}$ values can tell us nothing about the rate of the reaction.

One example of this is the lack of a reaction between zinc metal and water. Water contains H^+ ions. The relevant half-equations are:

$$Zn^{2+} + 2e^- \rightleftharpoons Zn \qquad\qquad E^{\ominus} = -0.76\,V$$

$$H^+ + e^- \rightleftharpoons \tfrac{1}{2}H_2 \qquad\qquad E^{\ominus} = 0.00\,V$$

The concentration of H^+ ions in water is well below $1.00\,mol\,dm^{-3}$, but even when this is taken into account, the E values predict that the reaction:

$$Zn + 2H^+ \longrightarrow Zn^{2+} + H_2$$

should occur. Any reaction that does take place, however, is too slow to be observed. Although E values predict that zinc should react with water at $298\,K$ to give Zn^{2+} ions and hydrogen gas, E values cannot predict whether or not this reaction occurs at a reasonable rate. It doesn't! The reaction between zinc and water is very slow indeed.

SAQ

19 Summarise briefly the two limitations to using $E^{\ominus}$ values to predict the feasibility of a reaction.

Hint

Answer

20 If an industrial process relied on a reaction that was impractically slow under normal conditions, how might the chemical engineers in charge try to solve the problem? You should use your knowledge of reaction rates to suggest several different approaches.

Answer

Storage cells

The cells you have studied so far in this chapter are primary cells. A primary cell uses the redox reactions between chemicals to produce electrical energy. When all of the reactants have been converted to products the cell is of no further use and is discarded.

Some cells can be recharged, however. If they are connected to a suitable source of electrical energy the products can be converted back to reactants and the cell can be used again. Such cells are known as 'rechargeable batteries', but better names for them are secondary cells and storage cells.

Car batteries

A car battery consists of several individual cells. In each cell one lead plate and one lead(IV) oxide plate are immersed in sulfuric acid (Figure 16.18).

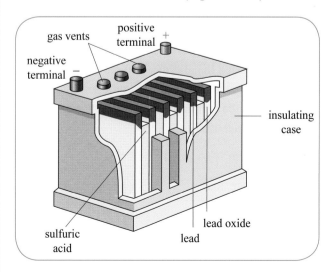

Figure 16.18 The storage cell used in a car.

The relevant half-equations for the electrode reactions are:

$$Pb^{2+}(aq) + 2e^- \rightleftharpoons Pb(s) \qquad E^{\ominus} = -0.13\,V$$

$$PbO_2(s) + 4H^+(aq) + 2e^- \rightleftharpoons Pb^{2+}(aq) + 2H_2O(l)$$
$$E^{\ominus} = +1.47\,V$$

The battery can supply electrical energy, for example to operate the car's starter motor which is electric. When this happens the reaction in the second equation, having the more positive $E^{\ominus}$, proceeds forwards. PbO_2 is reduced to Pb^{2+}.

The first equation, having the more negative $E^{\ominus}$, proceeds backwards. Pb is oxidised to Pb^{2+}. These reactions happen:

$$Pb(s) \longrightarrow Pb^{2+}(aq) + 2e^-$$

at the lead plate, and

$$PbO_2(s) + 4H^+(aq) + 2e^- \longrightarrow Pb^{2+}(aq) + 2H_2O(l)$$

at the lead oxide plate.

This gives an overall cell reaction of:

$$Pb(s) + PbO_2(s) + 4H^+(aq)$$
$$\longrightarrow 2Pb^{2+}(aq) + 2H_2O(l)$$

The $E^{\ominus}$ values can be used to predict the cell voltage:

$$+1.47\,V - (-0.13\,V) = +1.60\,V$$

However, due to non-standard conditions the voltage of each cell is approximately 2 V. A car battery consists of six cells, giving a total of 12 V.

When electrical energy from the battery is not needed, the battery is recharged. Kinetic energy from the car's engine is converted to electrical energy by a device called the alternator, and the electrical energy recharges the battery. This process involves the reverse of the reactions that occur when energy is being taken *from* each cell, i.e.

$$Pb^{2+}(aq) + 2e^- \longrightarrow Pb(s)$$

at the lead plate, and

$$Pb^{2+}(aq) + 2H_2O(l) \longrightarrow PbO_2(s) + 4H^+(aq) + 2e^-$$

at the lead oxide plate.

The overall cell reaction during charging is:

$$2Pb^{2+}(aq) + 2H_2O(l)$$
$$\longrightarrow Pb(s) + PbO_2(s) + 4H^+(aq)$$

You should note that this equation is the reverse of the cell reaction that takes place when the cell is supplying electrical energy.

SAQ

21 a When a car battery is supplying electrical energy, what is the change in oxidation number of lead at:
  i the lead plate?
  ii the lead(IV) oxide plate?
b What is happening to lead at each plate? Justify your answers in two ways.

Answer

22 A common type of rechargeable cell is the nickel–cadmium cell. The relevant half-equations for the electrode reactions are:

$$Cd(OH)_2 + 2e^- \longrightarrow Cd + 2OH^-$$
$$E^{\ominus} = -0.81\,V$$

$$NiO_2 + 2H_2O + 2e^- \longrightarrow Ni(OH)_2 + 2OH^-$$
$$E^{\ominus} = +0.49\,V$$

a Which of these two reactions proceeds in a forward direction, and which proceeds in a backward direction, when electrical energy is being taken from the cell?
b Predict the cell voltage, assuming all conditions are standard.
c Write an equation for the cell reaction that occurs when electrical energy is being taken from the cell.
d Write an equation for the cell reaction that occurs when the cell is being recharged.

Answer

Fuel cells

In the early 21st century most road transport in the developed world is powered by burning hydrocarbon fuels obtained from the fractional distillation of crude oil. These fuels, for example petrol and diesel, will soon be in short supply. They also produce air pollutants, such as soot, carbon monoxide and carbon dioxide, when they burn.

One long-term answer to these problems could be the **fuel cell**. A fuel cell is an electrochemical cell in which a fuel substance gives up electrons at one electrode, while oxygen gains the electrons at the other electrode. The fuel is stored in tanks in the vehicle, and the oxygen comes from the air. When a fuel burns it reacts directly with oxygen, and energy is released as heat. In a fuel cell the energy released produces a voltage difference between the two electrodes. The fuel cell converts the chemical energy stored in the fuel into electrical energy, which can power a vehicle via an electric motor (see Figure 16.19).

Figure 16.19 Fuel cells can be used to power supercars or family run-abouts. They are currently known as Fuel Cell Vehicles, or FCVs. In future they will just be called cars.

Hydrogen–oxygen fuel cells

Fuel cell research has investigated many possible fuels. Hydrogen is one of the most promising. In a hydrogen–oxygen fuel cell the hydrogen is fed in to the cell anode where it reacts on a platinum electrode, forming H^+ ions and releasing electrons (Figure 16.20):

$$H_2 \longrightarrow 2H^+ + 2e^-$$

The electrons travel through an external circuit to the cathode. As they do so their energy is used to drive an electric motor or other device. The H^+ ions also go to the cathode, but they do so by diffusing through

a membrane. At the cathode the H^+ ions and the electrons combine with oxygen to form water:

$$4H^+ + 4e^- + O_2 \longrightarrow 2H_2O$$

The overall reaction in a hydrogen–oxygen fuel cell is therefore:

$$2H_2 + O_2 \longrightarrow 2H_2O$$

This reaction is the source of the electrical energy supplied by the cell. In a fuel cell the anode supplies electrons, and the cathode receives them. This is the opposite of what happens at the electrodes when electrolysis occurs. A fuel cell supplies electrical energy, while electrolysis receives it.

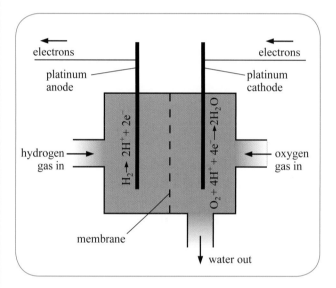

Figure 16.20 A simplified diagram of a hydrogen–oxygen fuel cell.

SAQ

23 What are FCVs?

> Answer

24 In a hydrogen–oxygen fuel cell:
  a what change takes place at the anode?
  b what change takes place at the cathode?
  c how do hydrogen ions reach the cathode?
  d how do electrons reach the cathode?
  e what is the overall chemical reaction?

> Answer

When in use as an energy source, a hydrogen–oxygen fuel cell produces only one waste product – water. This is much better than the soot, carbon monoxide and carbon dioxide produced by burning petrol and diesel. Fuel cells are also more efficient than petrol and diesel engines, so much less energy is wasted as heat.

Research is being carried out into the feasibility of fuel cells that use other fuels – fuels that are 'hydrogen-dense'. A hydrogen-dense, or *hydrogen-rich*, fuel is one which has a high proportion of hydrogen per gram of fuel. Methane is very hydrogen-rich – it is 25% hydrogen by mass. Another possible fuel is methanol. Methanol is only 12.5% hydrogen by mass, but, being a liquid, it is easy to store and it is biodegradable.

SAQ

25 a Justify the statements 'methane is 25.0% hydrogen by mass' and 'methanol is 12.5% hydrogen by mass'. [Hint]

(A_r values: C = 12.0, H = 1.0, O = 16.0)

b Write a balanced chemical equation for the overall reaction that takes place when methanol is used as a fuel in a methanol–oxygen fuel cell.

c Give one advantage that a hydrogen–oxygen fuel cell has over a methanol–oxygen fuel cell. [Answer]

Limitations of hydrogen–oxygen fuel cells

Hydrogen–oxygen fuel cells have great potential, but they have their drawbacks.

- The fuel cells themselves currently have a limited lifetime. Car owners expect the power source of a new car to be good for at least 200 000 km. Fuel cells cannot guarantee this, although it is expected that this problem will be solved.
- Fuel cells are expensive to produce because of the materials that must be used to make the electrodes and the membrane. Their limited lifetime also involves costs incurred in replacing and disposing of used fuel cells.

- Manufacturing fuel cells involves the production of toxic by-products. Making the membrane which allows hydrogen ions to diffuse from the anode to the cathode is one process responsible for the creation of such by-products.
- Hydrogen storage is not straightforward. If stored as a gas it has to be greatly pressurised in order for a fuel tank to store a sufficient amount. This pressure has consequences for the design of the fuel tank, which would have to be extremely strong. Refuelling would also be a problem – a gas-tight seal would have to be created between the vehicle and the hydrogen source.

SAQ

26 A car's fuel tank can hold 40 kg of petrol. 1 kg of petrol releases approximately 5×10^7 J of energy when it burns. The car is 40% efficient. This means only 40% of the energy released when the petrol burns is converted into useful work. 1×10^6 J of work is needed to drive the car 1 km.

a How many joules of energy are released when a full tank of petrol burns?

b How many of these joules of energy are available to move the car forward?

c How far can the car travel on a full tank of petrol? [Answer]

27 An FCV with a similar volume fuel tank can store 400 g of hydrogen at 100 times atmospheric pressure. 2 g of hydrogen release 286 000 J of energy when used in the vehicle's fuel cells. The FCV is 60% efficient. 1×10^6 J of work is needed to drive the car 1 km.

a How many joules of energy are released when a full tank of hydrogen is used in the vehicle's fuel cells?

b How many of these joules of energy are available to move the car forward?

c How far can a car travel on a full tank of hydrogen?

d Comment on your answers to SAQ 26c and SAQ 27c. [Answer]

Hydrogen storage

It is not easy to store sufficient hydrogen in an FCV to give the vehicle an adequate range without refuelling. There are several possible solutions to this problem.

- The hydrogen can be stored in liquid form if it is cooled sufficiently. A $50 \, dm^3$ tank of liquid hydrogen would give an FCV a reasonable range, approaching 200 km ($1 \, dm^3$ is the same as 1 litre). There are many problems with the liquefaction approach, including safety considerations, the weight of the strong, heavily insulated, fuel tanks and the energy costs of liquefying the hydrogen.

- The hydrogen can be adsorbed onto a surface. For this to work the FCV's fuel tank must be packed with an adsorbent material of high surface area. One possible adsorbent surface consists of tightly packed single-walled carbon nanotubes (Figure 16.21).

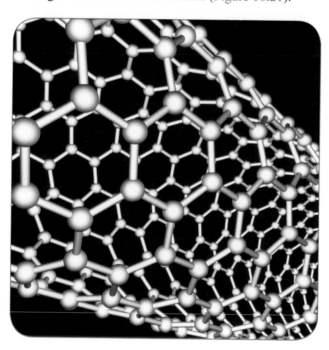

Figure 16.21 Single-walled nanotubes made of rolled-up sheets of carbon atoms.

- The hydrogen can be absorbed by certain metal alloys. This absorption involves the formation of chemical bonds between the metal atoms and the hydrogen, producing substances called hydrides. The hydride formation is reversible so

that the hydrogen is released when required. Some alloys, for example a lanthanum/nickel alloy with formula $LaNi_5$, can store more hydrogen in the same volume tank at normal temperatures than can be stored as a liquid at 20 K ($-253 \, °C$).

At the time of writing this book (2008), the likely solution to the hydrogen storage problem is either adsorption onto carbon nanotubes or absorption by a metal alloy. A combination of these two approaches is also possible. The adsorbers and absorbers currently available do not continue to function efficiently over a sufficiently long time period. The solution that is chosen must use an adsorber or an absorber that will last as long as the rest of the vehicle.

SAQ

28 Find out what the difference is between *adsorption* and *absorption*.

Answer

The hydrogen economy

From the early 20th century to the early 21st century, the need for energy in the developed world has largely been met by burning fossil fuels. It is clear that this 'fossil fuel economy' has a limited future. One possible replacement is an energy economy in which electricity is generated by nuclear fusion or fission and by renewable sources such as wind and wave generators. Since hydrogen can be made by electrolysis of water, our need for a mobile energy source can then be met by hydrogen–oxygen fuel cells. This vision of the future is known as the 'hydrogen economy'. As well as issues which have already been discussed, such as the manufacture and maintenance of fuel-cells, and of hydrogen storage, other obstacles need to be overcome.

- Mechanical engineering that makes and maintains petrol- and diesel-powered vehicles will have to be replaced by mechanical engineering that makes and maintains fuel-cell-powered vehicles.

- Engineering systems will have to be developed to transport hydrogen and to dispense it at filling stations (Figure 16.22).

Figure 16.22 The filling station of the future? How far would you have to go to buy hydrogen today?

- The public will have to be prepared to accept the changes. Human beings are conservative – they like what they know and are used to – and a change of this magnitude is bound to be met with scepticism and reluctance by some people.
- Governments will have to plan for the change to a hydrogen economy. Long-term planning will be essential and will involve legislation to ensure safety, and the development of a hydrogen distribution network.
- Governments will have to be prepared to accept that they may put a lot of work and investment into such long-term planning, but a different political party could reap the rewards of it after a future election victory. Politicians are not good at this sort of thing …

Providing hydrogen

Hydrogen is easy to produce. If a direct electric current (DC) is passed through acidified water the water is electrolysed. It is split into hydrogen and oxygen. This of course requires electrical energy, which in the 20th century was usually provided by power stations burning fossil fuels. Such power stations are highly polluting, and they burn fuels that are going to run out. Unless they are replaced successfully by an alternative, such as nuclear fusion power stations, there will be no hydrogen economy.

FCVs are not a magic answer. A source of electricity is needed to produce the hydrogen. An FCV powered by hydrogen–oxygen fuel cells may emit only water, but if the hydrogen is produced using electricity from a coal-fired power station the FCV will cause more pollution than the petrol engined car it has replaced.

Hydrogen is not a source of energy; it is an energy carrier. Hydrogen can carry energy from a power station to a car in the centre of London. What will provide the energy in the power station? Will it pollute? These questions are still awaiting answers.

SAQ

29 Detail the problems that need to be overcome in order to establish a hydrogen economy.

Answer

Summary

- The oxidation state (oxidation number) of each element in a compound can be calculated by following simple rules.

- An element is oxidised in a chemical reaction if its oxidation state increases; an element is reduced in a chemical reaction if its oxidation state decreases.

- An oxidising agent causes another substance in a reaction to be oxidised. A reducing agent causes another substance in a reaction to be reduced.

- A half-cell can contain either an element electrode in contact with its aqueous ions, or two different aqueous ions of the same element in two different oxidation states using platinum as the electrode.

- The standard electrode potential of a half-cell, $E^{\ominus}$ is defined as the voltage of the half-cell compared with a standard hydrogen electrode.

- The standard electrode potential of a half-cell is a measure in volts of the ease with which one oxidation state in the half-cell can be converted into the other oxidation state.

- Standard conditions are necessary when measuring an $E^{\ominus}$ value.

- Two half-cells put together form an electrochemical cell. The cell voltage of an electrochemical cell can be calculated by finding the difference between the standard electrode potentials of the two half-cells.

- A particular redox reaction will occur if the standard electrode potential of the half-equation involving the species being reduced is more positive than the standard electrode potential of the half-equation involving the species being oxidised.

- A balanced equation can be written for the reaction taking place in an electrochemical cell.

- Under *non-standard* concentrations, a different reaction from the one predicted by standard electrode potentials might take place.

- Although a reaction predicted by standard electrode potentials will occur spontaneously, it may be very slow.

- Storage cells can be recharged by connecting them to a source of electrical energy.

- A fuel cell uses the energy from the reaction of a fuel with oxygen to generate a voltage. For example, a hydrogen fuel cell uses energy from the reaction of hydrogen with oxygen (which produces only water as a by-product) to create a voltage.

- To address the problems associated with oil-based vehicles on our roads, scientists are working on developing FCVs (fuel cell vehicles) which run on hydrogen and hydrogen-rich fuels (such as methane or methanol).

- Hydrogen fuel cells may provide a significant source of energy in the future but there are still issues to overcome first.

Questions

1 Some standard electrode potentials are shown below:

$$E^{\ominus}/V$$

$$Ag^+ + e^- \rightleftharpoons Ag \qquad +0.80$$
$$\tfrac{1}{2}Cl_2 + e^- \rightleftharpoons Cl^- \qquad +1.36$$
$$Cu^{2+} + 2e^- \rightleftharpoons Cu \qquad +0.34$$
$$Fe^{3+} + e^- \rightleftharpoons Fe^{2+} \qquad +0.77$$
$$\tfrac{1}{2}I_2 + e^- \rightleftharpoons I^- \qquad +0.54$$

a Define the term *standard electrode potential*. [3]

b The diagram below shows an incomplete cell consisting of Cu/Cu^{2+} and Ag/Ag^+ half-cells.

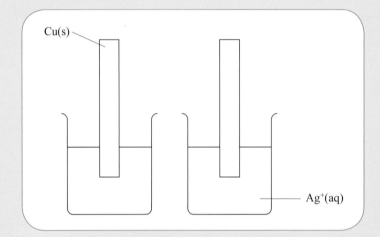

   i Copy, complete and label the diagram to show how the cell potential of this cell could be measured. [2]

   ii On the diagram, show the direction of <u>electron flow</u> in the circuit if a current was allowed. [1]

   iii Calculate the standard cell potential. [1]

   iv Write the overall cell reaction. [1]

c Chlorine will oxidise Fe^{2+} to Fe^{3+} but iodine will not. Explain why, using the electrode potential data. [2]

OCR Chemistry A2 (2815/06) June 2006 [Total 10]

Hint

Answer

2 A cell can be constructed between a Ni^{2+}/Ni half-cell and an I_2/I^- half-cell.

a Draw a labelled diagram of this cell operating under standard conditions. [5]

b The standard electrode potentials for the half-cells in this cell are given below.

   Ni^{2+}/Ni $E^{\ominus} = -0.25\,V$

   I_2/I^- $E^{\ominus} = +0.54\,V$

continued

   i What is the standard cell potential of this cell? [1]
   ii Write equations for the reactions that occur in each half-cell [2]
   iii Write the overall equation for the reaction that occurs in the cell. [1]
   iv State, and explain, the direction of flow of electrons in the external circuit. [1]

OCR Chemistry A2 (2815/06) January 2004 [Total 10]

3 The standard electrode potential of the $\frac{1}{2}Cl_2/Cl^-$ half-cell may be measured using the following apparatus.

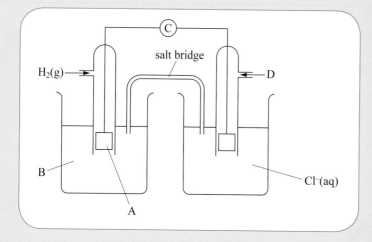

a Suggest suitable labels for **A**, **B**, **C** and **D**. [2]

b The half-cell reactions involved are shown below:

$$\frac{1}{2}Cl_2 + e^- \rightleftharpoons Cl^- \qquad\qquad E^\ominus = +1.36\,V$$

$$H^+ + e^- \rightleftharpoons \frac{1}{2}H_2 \qquad\qquad E^\ominus = 0.00\,V$$

   i What is the direction of flow of electrons through component C? [2]
   ii The values of $E^\ominus$ are measured under standard conditions. What are the standard conditions? [2]

c The half-cell reaction for $ClO_3^-/\frac{1}{2}Cl_2$ is shown below:

$$ClO_3^- + 6H^+ + 5e^- \rightleftharpoons \frac{1}{2}Cl_2 + 3H_2O \qquad E^\ominus = +1.47\,V$$

What does this tell you about the oxidising ability of ClO_3^- compared with Cl_2? Explain your answer. [2]

OCR Chemistry A2 (2815/06) January 2006 [Total 8]

Chapter 17

Transition elements

Objectives

Finding new sources of transition metals

Transition metals are so important to mankind that most reserves will be used up within the next 50 years or so. This means that other sources of transition metals must be found, and one source which may be used is on the ocean floor. Here nodules have been found over large areas, some a few millimetres and some a few metres in diameter (Figure 17.1). These contain mostly manganese and iron oxides but also many other transition metal oxides in smaller quantities.

Figure 17.1 Nodules on the ocean floor could be a future source of transition metals.

Although there are billions of tonnes of these nodules on the ocean floors, there are two problems linked with using them:

● the first problem is the technical expertise required to mine from such an inhospitable place
● the second problem is that, legally, the ocean floors are international property, so ownership of the nodules and the wealth associated with them must be carefully worked out.

This chapter deals with the chemistry of the first row of the transition elements (titanium, Ti, to copper, Cu) which are found in the d block of the Periodic Table, located between Groups 2 and 3. There is a precise definition of a **transition element**:

A transition element is an element that forms at least one ion with a partly filled d subshell.

According to this definition, the transition elements in the first row of the d block are the elements titanium, Ti, to copper, Cu. Scandium forms only one ion (Sc^{3+}), with no electrons in its 3d subshell, whilst zinc forms only one ion (Zn^{2+}), which has a complete 3d subshell. Hence Sc and Zn are not transition elements (see page 197).

The transition elements have certain *physical properties* in common:

● they have high densities
● they are metals with high melting points
● they are hard and rigid, and so are useful as construction materials
● they are good conductors of electricity.

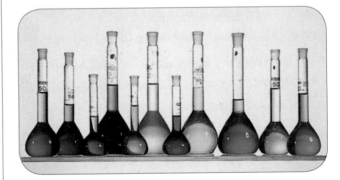

Figure 17.2 From left to right, the strongly coloured solutions of the following transition elements: Ti^{3+}, V^{3+}, VO^{2+}, Cr^{3+}, $Cr_2O_7^{2-}$, Mn^{2+}, MnO_4^-, Fe^{3+}, Co^{2+}, Ni^{2+} and Cu^{2+}.

They also have certain *chemical properties* in common:

- they can show several different oxidation states in their compounds
- they are good catalysts
- they form coloured compounds (Figure 17.2)
- they form complexes with ligands (these terms may be new to you – they are explained later in this chapter).

Electronic structures

Transition metal atoms

The electronic structures of the d-block elements dictate their chemistry, and so are extremely important.

Chemists have a shorthand to show the full subshells in electronic configurations – they use the symbol of the noble gas with the full subshells in square brackets, like this: $[Ar]3d^a \, 4s^b$.

scandium	Sc	$[Ar]3d^1 \, 4s^2$
titanium	Ti	$[Ar]3d^2 \, 4s^2$
vanadium	V	$[Ar]3d^3 \, 4s^2$
chromium	Cr	$[Ar]3d^5 \, 4s^1$
manganese	Mn	$[Ar]3d^5 \, 4s^2$
iron	Fe	$[Ar]3d^6 \, 4s^2$
cobalt	Co	$[Ar]3d^7 \, 4s^2$
nickel	Ni	$[Ar]3d^8 \, 4s^2$
copper	Cu	$[Ar]3d^{10} \, 4s^1$
zinc	Zn	$[Ar]3d^{10} \, 4s^2$

where [Ar] is $1s^2 \, 2s^2 \, 2p^6 \, 3s^2 \, 3p^6$.

If you look at these electronic configurations, you will see that the d subshell is being filled as we move from scandium to zinc, hence the term 'd block' – scandium has one d electron, and zinc has ten, a full d subshell.

The 4s level is filled before the 3d level but the two levels remain very close in energy. We see this closeness illustrated in chromium and copper. Chromium, instead of having a $[Ar]3d^4 \, 4s^2$ structure, has $[Ar]3d^5 \, 4s^1$; it has two half-filled subshells, which gives it greater stability. This exchange is made possible by the closeness of the two subshells. Similarly, copper has a full d subshell and a half-filled 4s shell: $[Ar]3d^{10} \, 4s^1$.

Transition metal ions

As the transition elements are metals they all form *positive* ions, so electrons are *lost* from a transition metal atom when an ion is formed. So the electronic configuration of Fe^{2+} is two electrons less than the electronic configuration of Fe. These electrons are lost from the 4s subshell first, and then the 3d subshell, which means the electronic configuration of Fe^{2+} is:

$$1s^2 \, 2s^2 \, 2p^6 \, 3s^2 \, 3p^6 \, 3d^6$$

As you will see in the next section, transition metals can form several different ions, and iron can form Fe^{3+} as well as Fe^{2+}. The electronic configuration of Fe^{3+} is:

$$1s^2 \, 2s^2 \, 2p^6 \, 3s^2 \, 3p^6 \, 3d^5$$

SAQ

1 Write down the electronic configurations of:
- a Cr
- b Cr^{3+}
- c Cu
- d Cu^{2+}
- e Mn
- f Mn^{2+}

Hint

Answer

Take a look at the electronic configurations of the first element, scandium, and the last d-block element, zinc. For scandium, the only observed oxidation state is +3, so the ion is Sc^{3+}, with the electronic configuration $1s^2 \, 2s^2 \, 2p^6 \, 3s^2 \, 3p^6$. This ion has no d electrons, so does not satisfy the definition of a transition element – scandium is a d-block element but is not a transition element. Now look at zinc. The only observed oxidation state is Zn^{2+}, with the electronic configuration $1s^2 \, 2s^2 \, 2p^6 \, 3s^2 \, 3p^6 \, 3d^{10}$. This ion has a completely filled, not a partially filled, d subshell – so zinc is not a transition element. This is the reason why the compounds of zinc and scandium are white, and not coloured like those of transition elements.

Properties of transition elements and their compounds

Variable oxidation states

Transition elements occur in multiple oxidation states (Figure 17.3).

The most common oxidation state is +2, which occurs when the two 4s electrons are lost (for example Fe^{2+} and Cu^{2+}). But, because the 3d electrons are very close in energy to the 4s electrons, the 3d electrons can quite easily be lost too, so one element can form several different ions by losing different numbers of electrons, and all the ions will be almost equally stable. This closeness in energy between the 3d and 4s electrons also explains why the transition elements have such similar properties to each other.

Table 17.1 shows the main oxidation states of the first row of the d-block elements. The commonly occurring oxidation states are highlighted.

It is worth noting that the highest oxidation state for the first five elements is the same as the total number of 4s and 3d electrons for the element; and for the second five elements, a common oxidation state is +2. It is important that you know the oxidation states of iron and copper in particular, and are able to give the electronic configurations of all their ions.

In transition element chemistry, the changes in oxidation state of the ions are often shown by changes in the colour of the solutions. For example, potassium dichromate(VI) is often used in titrations:

$$Cr_2O_7^{2-}(aq) + 14H^+(aq) + 6e^-$$
orange
$$\longrightarrow 2Cr^{3+}(aq) + 7H_2O(l)$$
green

Element	Oxidation states					
Sc			+3			
Ti		+2	+3	+4		
V		+2	+3	+4	+5	
Cr		+2	+3	+4	+5	+6
Mn		+2	+3	+4	+5	+6	+7
Fe		+2	+3	+4	+5	+6
Co		+2	+3	+4	+5	
Ni		+2	+3	+4		
Cu	+1	+2	+3			
Zn		+2				

Table 17.1 The main oxidation states of the first row d-block elements.

SAQ

2 What is the oxidation state of chromium in:
   a $Cr_2O_7^{2-}$
   b Cr^{3+}?

Answer

Transition elements as catalysts

A catalyst is a substance that speeds up a chemical reaction, without itself being permanently changed in a chemical way (see *Chemistry 1*, Chapter 17). Many transition elements are effective catalysts, and are used in reactions both in the laboratory and in industry.

In the laboratory, you may have seen the decomposition of hydrogen peroxide to water and oxygen:

$$2H_2O_2(aq) \longrightarrow 2H_2O(l) + O_2(g)$$

Figure 17.3 Vanadium and its oxidation states:
a vanadium metal; **b** a solution containing V^{2+} ions; **c** a solution containing V^{3+} ions;
d a solution containing VO^{2+} ions; **e** a solution containing VO_2^+ ions.

At room temperature this reaction is very slow. However, if manganese(IV) oxide is added it acts as a catalyst, and the reaction becomes very rapid.

In industry, one of the best-known reactions that depends on a catalyst is the Haber process, in which nitrogen and hydrogen react to give ammonia (see *Chemistry 1*, Chapter 17):

$$N_2(g) + 3H_2(g) \rightleftharpoons 2NH_3(g)$$

The catalyst used in this reaction is finely divided iron.

Coloured compounds

Transition metal ions in aqueous solution are frequently coloured (see Figure 17.2 and Figure 17.3). Some examples are shown in Table 17.2.

Ti^{3+}	purple
Cr^{3+}	violet (or green)
Mn^{2+}	pink
Fe^{2+}	green
Fe^{3+}	yellow
Co^{2+}	pink
Ni^{2+}	green
Cu^{2+}	blue

Table 17.2 Colours of some aqueous transition metal ions.

Extension

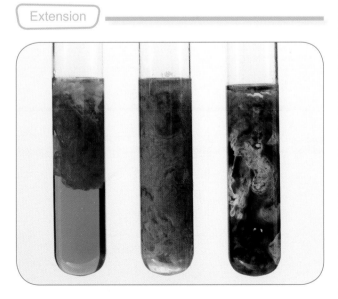

Figure 17.4 Gelatinous precipitates of copper(II) hydroxide, iron(II) hydroxide and cobalt(II) hydroxide.

Precipitating transition metal hydroxides

When we add aqueous sodium hydroxide to a solution of a transition metal ion, a precipitate of the transition metal hydroxide is formed. These precipitates resemble a jelly and so are called '**gelatinous**', and their colour can identify the transition metal ion (Figure 17.4).

$$Cu^{2+}(aq) + 2OH^-(aq) \longrightarrow Cu(OH)_2(s)$$
pale blue

$$Fe^{2+}(aq) + 2OH^-(aq) \longrightarrow Fe(OH)_2(s)$$
green

$$Fe^{3+}(aq) + 3OH^-(aq) \longrightarrow Fe(OH)_3(s)$$
rust

$$Mn^{2+}(aq) + 2OH^-(aq) \longrightarrow Mn(OH)_2(s)$$
cream

$$Cr^{3+}(aq) + 3OH^-(aq) \longrightarrow Cr(OH)_3(s)$$
grey-green

$$Co^{2+}(aq) + 2OH^-(aq) \longrightarrow Co(OH)_2(s)$$
blue-green

Note that gelatinous precipitates can also be formed when ammonia solution is added to the aqueous transition element ion. This is because ammonia is a weak base that exists in equilibrium with ammonium hydroxide in aqueous solution:

$$NH_3(aq) + H_2O(l) \rightleftharpoons NH_4^+(aq) + OH^-(aq)$$

This means that aqueous ammonia is a source of hydroxide ions. For example, aqueous ammonia added to $Mn^{2+}(aq)$ gives a cream precipitate of $Mn(OH)_2$.

SAQ

3 Write equations to predict the reactions between aqueous sodium hydroxide and aqueous solutions of:
   a Ni^{2+}
   b Ti^{3+}

Answer

Complexes

Transition element ions such as Fe^{2+} ions in aqueous solution form a special association with water molecules. Six water molecules can each donate one lone-pair to an Fe^{2+} ion, forming *dative* or *coordinate bonds* to it (Figure 17.5).

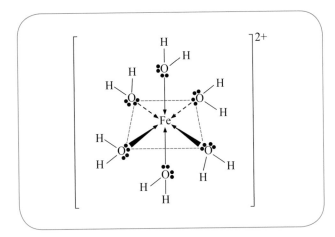

Figure 17.5 $[Fe(H_2O)_6]^{2+}$.

The Fe^{2+} ion and its six bonded water molecules are called a **complex ion**. The ion is written $[Fe(H_2O)_6]^{2+}$. A complex ion consists of a central metal ion with one or more negative ions or neutral molecules coordinately bonded to it. Fe^{2+} and other transition metal ions can form complex ions in solid compounds as well as in solutions.

The transition metals typically form complex ions in this way. The donor of the electron pairs – water in the case of $[Fe(H_2O)_6]^{2+}$ – is called the **ligand**. Each water molecule donates one lone-pair to the Fe^{2+} ion, so water is a **monodentate** ligand. Other ligands can donate two lone-pairs (**bidentate**) (Table 17.3). Ligands donating more than one lone-pair are generally known as **multidentate** (or **polydentate**) ligands.

Type of ligand	Formula	Name
monodentate	H_2O	water
	NH_3	ammonia
	CO	carbon monoxide
	Cl^-	chloride ion
	CN^-	cyanide ion
	NO_2^-	nitrate(III) ion
	SCN^-	thiocyanate ion
bidentate	$NH_2CH_2CH_2NH_2$	ethane-1,2-diamine (en)

Table 17.3 Some of the more common ligands.

4 What is meant by the following terms?
 a complex ion
 b ligand
 c bidentate ligand

Answer

Coordination number

The number of coordinate bonds formed between the ligands and the transition metal ion is called the **coordination number** of the complex ion. Typically the coordination number of a complex ion is four or six.

● Where the ligands are monodentate, this simply means that four or six ligands bond to the central ion, for example $[Ni(CN)_4]^{2-}$ and $[Co(NH_3)_6]^{3+}$ (Figure 17.6).

● With bidentate ligands, such as ethane-1,2-diamine (abbreviated to 'en'), this means that two or three ligands bond to the central ion. $[Ni(en)_3]^{2+}$ is a good example, with a coordination number of six (Figure 17.7).

● Examples of complex ions involving bidentate ligands and a coordination number of four are rare and need not concern us.

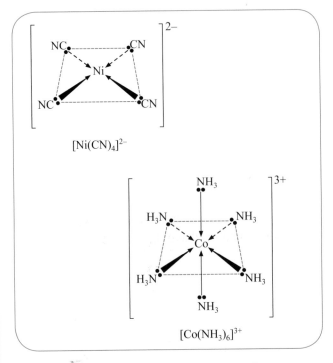

$[Ni(CN)_4]^{2-}$

$[Co(NH_3)_6]^{3+}$

Figure 17.6 $[Ni(CN)_4]^{2-}$ and $[Co(NH_3)_6]^{3+}$ – examples of complex ions containing monodentate ligands.

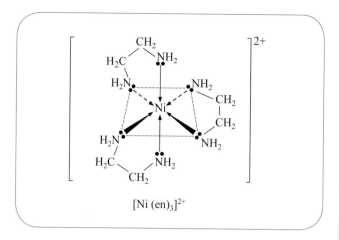

[Ni (en)₃]²⁺

Figure 17.7 $[Ni(en)_3]^{2+}$ – an example of a complex ion containing bidentate ligands.

SAQ

5 a What is meant by the term *coordination number*?

b What is the coordination number of the transition metal ion in the following complexes?

i $[Fe(NH_3)_6]^{3+}$

ii $[CoCl_4]^{2-}$

iii $[Co(en)_3]^{3+}$

iv $[AuCl_4]^-$

c What is the charge on the central transition metal ion in each complex ion in part **b**?

Answer

Shapes of complexes

Where the coordination number is four, the shape of the complex ion will either be square planar or **tetrahedral** (Figure 17.8).

Where the coordination number is six, the shape of the complex ion will be **octahedral** (Figure 17.9). Notice how Figure 17.9 attempts to convey the three-dimensional shape and avoids depicting a planar, hexagonal shape, which would be incorrect.

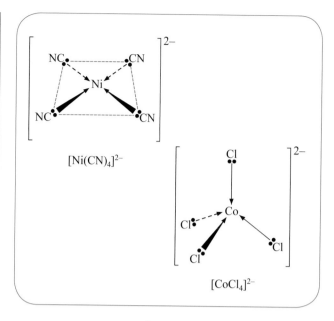

$[Ni(CN)_4]^{2-}$

$[CoCl_4]^{2-}$

Figure 17.8 $[Ni(CN)_4]^{2-}$ is square planar; $[CoCl_4]^{2-}$ is tetrahedral.

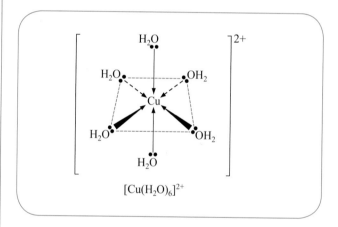

$[Cu(H_2O)_6]^{2+}$

Figure 17.9 $[Cu(H_2O)_6]^{2+}$ is octahedral.

SAQ

6 Draw the 3D shapes of the following complex ions:

a $[Fe(NH_3)_6]^{3+}$

b $[AuCl_4]^-$ (square planar)

c $[FeCl_4]^{2-}$ (tetrahedral).

Hint

Answer

Stereoisomerism in transition metal complexes

Some complex ions exist as **stereoisomers**. Stereoisomers have the same bonds but with different spatial arrangements. Two different types of **stereoisomerism** are observed in transition metal complexes: *cis–trans* isomerism and optical isomerism (Chapter 1 and Chapter 6).

Cis–trans isomerism

In an octahedral complex with four of one monodentate ligand and two of another, the six ligands can be arranged around the central ion in two different ways. Figure 17.10 shows these two ways for the $[CoCl_2(NH_3)_4]^+$ ion. Notice how in the *cis* form the two chloride-to-cobalt bonds form a 90° angle with each other, while in the *trans* form the two chloride-to-cobalt bonds form a 180° angle with each other. In drawing these **isomers** it is again important to draw carefully so that the shape of the molecule is clear.

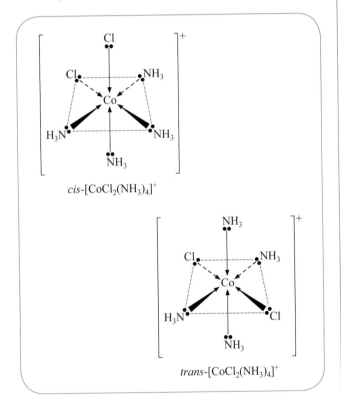

cis-$[CoCl_2(NH_3)_4]^+$

trans-$[CoCl_2(NH_3)_4]^+$

Figure 17.10 *Cis*-$[CoCl_2(NH_3)_4]^+$ and *trans*-$[CoCl_2(NH_3)_4]^+$.

SAQ

7 a Make two more drawings of *cis*-$[CoCl_2(NH_3)_4]^+$ with the two chloride ions in different positions from those shown in Figure 17.10. Remember that the two chloride-to-cobalt bonds must form a 90° angle.

  b Make two more drawings of *trans*-$[CoCl_2(NH_3)_4]^+$, again with the two chloride ions in different positions from those shown in Figure 17.10. Remember that the two chloride-to-cobalt bonds must form a 180° angle.

Answer

You should note that the two new drawings of *cis*-$[CoCl_2(NH_3)_4]^+$ in SAQ 7a simply show the same *cis* isomer from different viewpoints. Similarly, in SAQ 7b you are simply showing the same *trans* isomer from different viewpoints.

Another example, involving a neutral molecule rather than an ion, is $[NiCl_2(NH_3)_2]$. This has a square planar shape and therefore has two stereoisomers (Figure 17.11). Note that *cis–trans* isomerism is not seen in tetrahedral complexes.

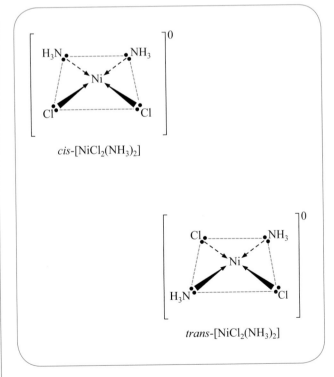

cis-$[NiCl_2(NH_3)_2]$

trans-$[NiCl_2(NH_3)_2]$

Figure 17.11 *Cis*-$[NiCl_2(NH_3)_2]$ and *trans*-$[NiCl_2(NH_3)_2]$.

Cis-platin – fighting cancer

The compound known as platin has the formula $[PtCl_2(NH_3)_2]$. It exists as two stereoisomers. The shape of the platin molecule is therefore square planar. The two stereoisomers are shown in Figure 17.12. The difference between these two stereoisomers is very important.

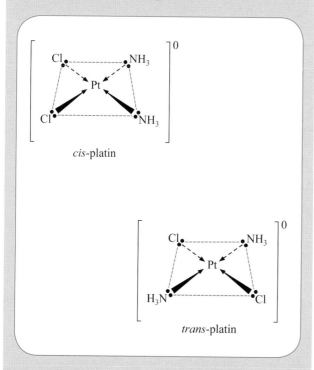

Figure 17.12 *Cis*-platin and *trans*-platin.

Platin binds to the DNA in a fast-growing cell. When such a cell divides, it must first copy its DNA. DNA is a double-stranded molecule. Platin binds the two strands together, making the cell unable to copy its DNA. This makes the cell incapable of division, causing it to die. *Cis*-platin binds much more effectively than *trans*-platin to DNA in the fast-growing cells in cancers. *Cis*-platin is therefore used as an anti-cancer drug; this form of treatment is called chemotherapy. *Cis*-platin has been particularly successful in treating testicular cancer, causing survival rates to increase from 5% to over 95% by 2007.

Optical isomerism

Some octahedral complexes can exist in two forms that are non-superimposable mirror images of each other.

In order to understand this 'non-superimposable mirror image' concept, consider your left and right hands. Your right hand, when viewed in a mirror, looks exactly like your left hand viewed directly, and vice versa, so they are 'mirror images' of each other. However, if you try to put your right hand in exactly the same shape as your left hand, you can't, because the fingernails and knuckles of one hand will face downwards while those of the other hand face upwards. They are 'non-superimposable' (Figure 17.13).

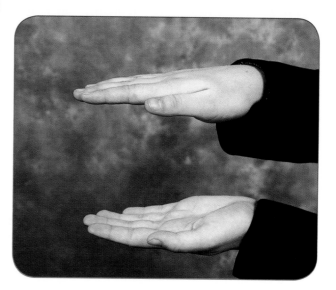

Figure 17.13 Mirror images are non-superimposable.

An example of a compound that shows optical isomerism is $[Ni(en)_3]^{2+}$. The two forms are shown in Figure 17.14.

Normally a sample of $[Ni(en)_3]^{2+}$ contains equal amounts of the two **optical isomers**. If the two forms are separated from each other, then a pure sample of one form is found to rotate the plane of polarised light. This type of stereoisomerism is therefore known as optical isomerism. The two isomers rotate polarised light in opposite directions, one clockwise and the other anticlockwise. In the original mixture these two effects cancel each other out, so no rotation of polarised light is seen.

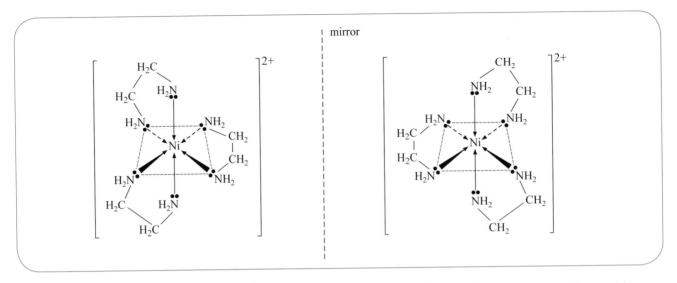

Figure 17.14 The two forms of $[Ni(en)_3]^{2+}$ are mirror images of each other, but they are not superimposable. They are optical isomers.

SAQ

8 The compound $[CoCl_2(en)_2]$, a neutral molecule, exists in three isomeric forms (Figure 17.15). They consist of two *cis* isomers and one *trans* isomer, the two *cis* isomers being non-superimposable mirror images of each other.

a Which diagram shows the *trans* isomer?

b What type of isomerism is shown by the two *cis* isomers?

c Redraw the two *cis* isomers in a way that emphasises that they are in fact non-superimposable mirror images of each other.

d Does $[CoCl_2(en)_2]$ contain Co^{2+} or Co^{3+} ions?

Answer

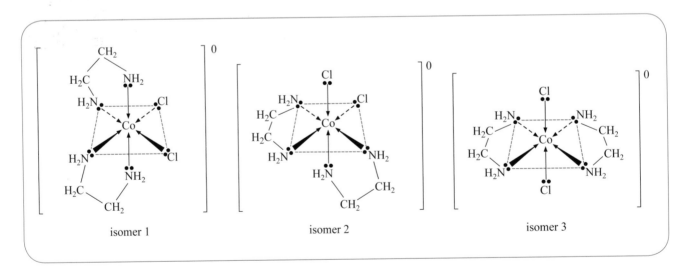

isomer 1   isomer 2   isomer 3

Figure 17.15 $[CoCl_2(en)_2]$ exists in three isomeric forms.

Ligand substitution

In aqueous copper(II) sulfate the Cu^{2+} ion is complexed by six water molecules. The formula of the complex ion is $[Cu(H_2O)_6]^{2+}$. This complex ion gives copper(II) sulfate solution its familiar blue colour.

The water ligands in the copper complex of aqueous copper(II) sulfate can be substituted by other ligands to form a more stable complex. When concentrated hydrochloric acid is added drop by drop, the solution turns yellow as a new complex is formed – the water ligands are substituted by four chloride ion ligands to give $[CuCl_4]^{2-}$:

$$[Cu(H_2O)_6]^{2+}(aq) + 4Cl^-(aq) \rightleftharpoons [CuCl_4]^{2-}(aq) + 6H_2O(l)$$

Sodium chloride can also be used as a source of chloride ions in this reaction.

The water ligands can similarly be replaced by ammonia ligands when concentrated ammonia solution is added, producing a deep blue solution:

$$[Cu(H_2O)_6]^{2+}(aq) + 4NH_3(aq) \rightleftharpoons [Cu(H_2O)_2(NH_3)_4]^{2+}(aq) + 4H_2O(l)$$

Of course, if the ammonia solution is added dropwise and you watch the solution carefully, you will see a pale blue precipitate of $Cu(OH)_2$ appear first and then

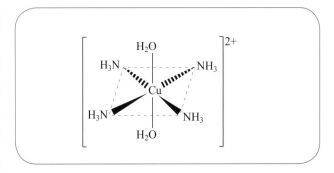

Figure 17.17 The structure of $[Cu(H_2O)_2(NH_3)_4]^{2+}$.

this will dissolve as the deep blue complex between Cu^{2+} and NH_3 is formed (Figure 17.16). Figure 17.17 shows the structure of the octahedral complex.

Aqueous cobalt(II) chloride solution is pink. In this solution the Co^{2+} ion is complexed by six water molecules. The formula of the complex ion is $[Co(H_2O)_6]^{2+}$; this complex gives the solution its pink colour. If a high concentration of Cl^- is added to the solution, ligand substitution takes place:

$$[Co(H_2O)_6]^{2+} + 4Cl^- \rightleftharpoons [CoCl_4]^{2-} + 6H_2O$$

$[CoCl_4]^{2-}$ is blue, so a colour change from pink to blue is seen. As the equation shows, this ligand substitution is reversible; if water is added the colour changes back to pink. This is used as a test to see

$[CuCl_4]^{2-}$	Start here $[Cu(H_2O)_6]^{2+}$	$[Cu(H_2O)_2(NH_3)_4]^{2+}$
This yellow complex forms on adding concentrated HCl.	The well-known blue Cu^{2+} complex with water.	This dark blue complex forms on adding concentrated NH_3.

Figure 17.16 The equations for the changes are:
$$[Cu(H_2O)_6]^{2+} + 4Cl^- \rightleftharpoons [CuCl_4]^{2-} + 6H_2O \quad \text{and} \quad [Cu(H_2O)_6]^{2+} + 4NH_3 \rightleftharpoons [Cu(H_2O)_2(NH_3)_4]^{2+} + 4H_2O.$$

if an unidentified liquid is water. One drop of the liquid is added to cobalt chloride paper. This paper is blue when dry, as $[CoCl_4]^{2-}$ ions are present. If the unidentified liquid is water, $[Co(H_2O)_6]^{2+}$ ions are formed, and the paper turns pink (Figure 17.18).

Figure 17.18 Anhydrous cobalt chloride paper is blue. What liquid is in the pipette? The pink-coloured complex $[Co(H_2O)_6]^{2+}$ shows that the liquid contains water.

SAQ

9 If the cobalt chloride paper on the right of Figure 17.18 is placed on a hot bench mat, the pink circle slowly disappears.

  a Explain what is happening.

  b Name the process occurring.

  c Write a balanced chemical equation for the change.

  Hint

  Answer

Stability constants

The complex ion $[CoCl_4]^{2-}$ is made of one Co^{2+} ion and four chloride ions. Its formation can be represented by the equation:

$$Co^{2+} + 4Cl^- \rightleftharpoons [CoCl_4]^{2-}$$

This process is an equilibrium, and therefore has an equilibrium constant. The equilibrium constant is called the **stability constant** of the complex ion, and has the symbol K_{stab}. For the $[CoCl_4]^{2-}$ complex ion:

$$K_{stab} = \frac{[CoCl_4^{2-}]}{[Co^{2+}][Cl^-]^4}$$

You should note three things.

- The square brackets in this expression are used to mean concentrations, so the charges on ions go *inside* the square brackets.

- The larger the value of K_{stab} the more stable the complex ion is. A more stable complex ion is more likely to form by ligand substitution when the relevant ligand is added to a solution of a less stable complex of the transition metal involved.

- As K_{stab} is an equilibrium constant it will have units, worked out by substituting in the units of concentration into the expression for K_{stab}. For the expression above, the units of K_{stab} are:

$$\frac{(mol\,dm^{-3})}{(mol\,dm^{-3}) \times (mol\,dm^{-3})^4} = mol^{-4}\,dm^{12}$$

Here are some examples of K_{stab} values:

$[Zn(CN)_4]^{2-}$	$K_{stab} = 5 \times 10^{16}\,mol^{-4}\,dm^{12}$
$[Zn(NH_3)_4]^{2+}$	$K_{stab} = 4 \times 10^9\,mol^{-4}\,dm^{12}$
$[Hg(CN)_4]^{2-}$	$K_{stab} = 2 \times 10^{41}\,mol^{-4}\,dm^{12}$
$[FeSCN]^{2+}$	$K_{stab} = 140\,mol^{-1}\,dm^3$

SAQ

10 a Write an expression for the K_{stab} of $[FeSCN]^{2+}$ and of $[Hg(CN)_4]^{2-}$.

  b Which complex is more stable, $[FeSCN]^{2+}$ or $[Hg(CN)_4]^{2-}$?

  Hint

  Answer

11 a Which complex of zinc is more stable, $[Zn(CN)_4]^{2-}$ or $[Zn(NH_3)_4]^{2+}$? Explain your answer.

  b What do you expect will happen if $CN^-(aq)$ is added to a solution containing the $[Zn(NH_3)_4]^{2+}$ complex? Explain your answer, writing an equation for any change that occurs.

  c What do you expect will happen if $NH_3(aq)$ is added to a solution containing the $[Zn(CN)_4]^{2-}$ complex? Explain your answer, writing an equation for any change that occurs.

  Hint

  Answer

Haemoglobin

Haemoglobin is a pigment found in red blood cells. Each haemoglobin molecule includes four Fe^{2+} ions (Figure 17.19). Each Fe^{2+} ion is present as an octahedral complex. Five of its ligands are nitrogen atoms that are part of the haemoglobin molecule; the sixth ligand is a weakly bound water molecule. This water molecule can be replaced by various other molecules, including oxygen and carbon dioxide, so haemoglobin is capable of carrying these substances.

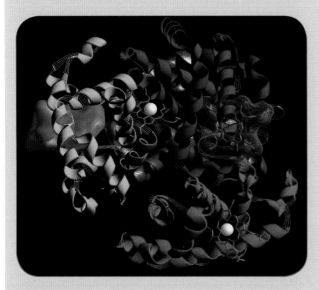

Figure 17.19 A graphic representation of a haemoglobin molecule. The four purple spheres are the Fe^{2+} ions.

When blood reaches the lungs the haemoglobin is exposed to a high oxygen concentration. This causes ligand substitution to take place, and an O_2 molecule then occupies the sixth position around the Fe^{2+} ion. The blood is then pumped to respiring tissues, where there is a high concentration of carbon dioxide and a low concentration of oxygen. Ligand substitution again takes place, and a CO_2 molecule now occupies the sixth position around the Fe^{2+} ion. The oxygen molecule is released to the respiring tissue that needs it, and the carbon dioxide molecule is carried away from the tissue by the red blood cells.

This equilibrium is involved:

$$[Fe(5N)(O_2)]^{2+} + CO_2 \rightleftharpoons [Fe(5N)(CO_2)]^{2+} + O_2$$

'5N' is used here to represent the five nitrogen atoms in the haemoglobin molecule which also act as ligands to each Fe^{2+} ion.

High oxygen concentrations, e.g. in the lungs, cause the equilibrium position to lie to the left, and the haemoglobin carries away the oxygen from the lungs. High carbon dioxide concentrations, e.g. in respiring tissues, cause the equilibrium position to lie to the right, and the haemoglobin carries away the carbon dioxide from the tissues.

Unfortunately, poisonous *carbon monoxide* forms a much more stable complex with haemoglobin than oxygen does. The equilibrium involved is now:

$$[Fe(5N)(O_2)]^{2+} + CO \rightleftharpoons [Fe(5N)(CO)]^{2+} + O_2$$

The position of this equilibrium lies well over to the right, even at low carbon monoxide concentrations. Imagine a person breathes in some carbon monoxide, and $[Fe(5N)(CO)]^{2+}$ forms in their red blood cells. Where oxygen concentrations are high, e.g. in the lungs, the equilibrium position still lies to the right, and the haemoglobin carries carbon monoxide away from the lungs, not oxygen. The blood no longer carries oxygen to the tissues that need it. These tissues stop respiring. Unless the person is removed from the source of carbon monoxide quickly enough, the person will die if sufficient carbon monoxide has been inhaled. This is called carbon monoxide poisoning.

SAQ

12 a How does haemoglobin carry oxygen?

b Why does haemoglobin carry oxygen from the lungs to respiring tissues, and carbon dioxide from respiring tissues to the lungs?

c Why is carbon monoxide gas poisonous?

Answer

Redox behaviour

Transition metals have a variety of different oxidation states and so they can be readily oxidised or reduced. Their redox reactions are an important part of their chemistry, especially as they are used in titrations for many different types of analysis.

Redox reactions

(Note: in this section state symbols have not been put into the equations, to make the species involved stand out more clearly.)

There are many redox reactions involving transition metal ions. One which you must know is the reaction between iron(II) ions (Fe^{2+}) and manganate(VII) ions (MnO_4^-) in acidified aqueous solution. Here is the equation for this reaction:

$$5Fe^{2+} + MnO_4^- + 8H^+ \longrightarrow Mn^{2+} + 5Fe^{3+} + 4H_2O$$
$$\qquad\quad \text{purple} \qquad\qquad\quad \text{pale pink}$$

This type of redox equation can be constructed from two half-equations:

- the half-equation showing oxidation of Fe(II) in Fe^{2+} to Fe(III) in Fe^{3+}:

$$Fe^{2+} \longrightarrow Fe^{3+} + e^-$$

- the half-equation showing reduction of Mn(VII) in MnO_4^- to Mn(II) in Mn^{2+} in the presence of acid:

$$MnO_4^- + 8H^+ + 5e^- \longrightarrow Mn^{2+} + 4H_2O$$

To construct the final equation, write the two half-equations so that the number of electrons in each is the same. This means the first half-equation is multiplied by 5. Then the half-equations can be added together and the electrons on each side of the arrow cancel:

$$5Fe^{2+} \longrightarrow 5Fe^{3+} + 5e^-$$

$$+ \quad MnO_4^- + 8H^+ + 5e^- \longrightarrow Mn^{2+} + 4H_2O$$

$$5Fe^{2+} + MnO_4^- + 8H^+ \longrightarrow 5Fe^{3+} + Mn^{2+} + 4H_2O$$

Any two half-equations can be used in this way to construct a redox equation. Another example is the reaction between aqueous Fe^{2+} ions and hydrogen peroxide, H_2O_2. The Fe^{2+} ions are oxidised to Fe^{3+} ions, and the hydrogen peroxide is reduced to water:

$$Fe^{2+} \longrightarrow Fe^{3+} + e^-$$
$$H_2O_2 + 2H^+ + 2e^- \longrightarrow 2H_2O$$

This time the top half-equation is multiplied throughout by 2. The final redox equation is:

$$2Fe^{2+} + H_2O_2 + 2H^+ \longrightarrow 2Fe^{3+} + 2H_2O$$

Another useful half-equation shows the reduction of orange Cr(VI) in the dichromate ion, $Cr_2O_7^{2-}$, to green Cr(III) in Cr^{3+}. This is another reaction that requires acid:

$$Cr_2O_7^{2-} + 14H^+ + 6e^- \longrightarrow 2Cr^{3+} + 7H_2O$$
$$\text{orange} \qquad\qquad\qquad\quad \text{green}$$

This is the reaction that occurs when primary and secondary alcohols are oxidised to aldehydes and ketones respectively (see *Chemistry 1*, Chapter 13). Acidified potassium dichromate(VI) solution is a common oxidising agent in organic chemistry.

SAQ

13 Construct the redox equation showing the reaction between dichromate(VI) ions and Fe(II) ions in acidic conditions, given

$$Fe^{2+} \longrightarrow Fe^{3+} + e^-$$

and

$$Cr_2O_7^{2-} + 14H^+ + 6e^- \longrightarrow 2Cr^{3+} + 7H_2O$$

Hint

Answer

Redox titrations

The colour changes of redox reactions involving transition metal ions in aqueous solutions can be used to show when a titration has reached the end-point. A good example of this is the redox titration between Fe^{2+} and MnO_4^- in aqueous acid solution:

$$5Fe^{2+} + MnO_4^- + 8H^+ \longrightarrow 5Fe^{3+} + Mn^{2+} + 4H_2O$$

The purple aqueous MnO_4^- is added from the burette into the acidified aqueous Fe^{2+}, and immediately turns pale pink or colourless as it reacts. The end-point of the titration is when all the Fe^{2+} has reacted and a permanent pale purple colour can be seen.

● This redox titration can be used for calculating how much Fe^{2+} is contained in an iron tablet.
● It can also be used for standardising a solution of aqueous $KMnO_4$. It is not possible to weigh out solid $KMnO_4$ to make up into a solution of accurate concentration because the solid $KMnO_4$ is not pure. However, it is possible to find the mass of a piece of pure iron and then to use this reaction to calculate the concentration of the aqueous $KMnO_4$ (see Worked example 1).

Worked example 1

A piece of pure iron wire with a mass of 0.1395 g was converted into Fe^{2+} by reaction with acid, and titrated against aqueous $KMnO_4$ of unknown concentration. The average titre was 26.20 cm^3.

Calculate the concentration of the aqueous $KMnO_4$. The A_r of iron is 55.8.

$$\text{number of moles of Fe} = \frac{m}{A_r} = \frac{0.1395}{55.8}$$
$$= 0.00250 \text{ moles}$$

number of moles of Fe^{2+} = 0.00250 moles

The equation for the reaction in the titration is:

$$5Fe^{2+} + MnO_4^- + 8H^+$$
$$\longrightarrow 5Fe^{3+} + Mn^{2+} + 4H_2O$$

continued

From the equation, 5 moles of Fe^{2+} react with 1 mole of MnO_4^-.

Therefore, the number of moles of $KMnO_4$ in the

$$\text{titre} = \frac{0.00250}{5} = 0.000\,500 \text{ moles}$$

The titre was 26.20 cm^3, which is

$$\frac{26.20}{1000} = 0.0262 \text{ dm}^3.$$

So concentration of $KMnO_4 = \frac{n}{V} = \frac{0.000500}{0.0262}$
$$= 0.0191 \text{ mol dm}^{-3}$$

SAQ

14 0.420 g of iron ore was dissolved in acid, so that all of the iron present in the original ore was then present as Fe^{2+}(aq). The solution obtained was titrated against 0.0400 mol dm^{-3} $KMnO_4$(aq). The titre was 23.50 cm^3.

a Calculate the number of moles of MnO_4^- in the titre.   [Hint]

b Calculate the number of moles of Fe^{2+} in the solution.

c Calculate the mass of iron in the solution (A_r of iron is 55.8).

d Calculate the percentage mass of iron in the 0.420 g of iron ore.   [Answer]

Analysing the amount of copper in an alloy

Many alloys contain copper – for example brass is an alloy of copper and zinc.

If a piece of brass is dissolved in nitric acid (Figure 17.20a), the solution obtained is a mixture of copper(II) nitrate and zinc nitrate (Figure 17.20b). Analysing this mixture can tell us how much copper it contains. If the mass of the original piece of brass is also known, then the composition of the original alloy can be calculated.

The analysis is done by adding an excess of KI(aq) to the mixture containing Cu^{2+} (Figure 17.20c). This causes the precipitation of all the copper as copper(I) iodide:

$$2Cu^{2+} + 4I^- \longrightarrow 2CuI + I_2$$

The amount of iodine produced can then be found by titrating the resulting mixture with a sodium thiosulfate ($Na_2S_2O_3$) solution of known concentration. The thiosulfate ions reduce the iodine back to iodide ions:

$$2S_2O_3^{2-} + I_2 \longrightarrow S_4O_6^{2-} + 2I^-$$

As the end-point of this titration is neared, the brown colour due to the iodine becomes faint (Figure 17.20d). Adding a little starch solution produces a dark blue colour (Figure 17.20e), which in turn disappears when enough sodium thiosulfate solution has been added to react with all the iodine (Figure 17.20f). The disappearance of a dark blue colour is much easier to judge accurately than the disappearance of a pale brown colour.

The two equations above show us that two Cu^{2+} ions produce one iodine molecule, which then reacts in the titration with two thiosulfate ions. The number of moles of thiosulfate added in the titration is therefore the same as the number of moles of copper originally present. From this, the original mass of copper in the alloy can be calculated. The photos in Figure 17.20 show the sequence of events in this process.

Figure 17.20 The sequence of events in the analysis of brass. **a** The brass about to be placed in the nitric acid. **b** The solution containing a mixture of Zn^{2+} and Cu^{2+} ions. **c** The precipitate formed by adding KI, containing Cu^+ ions and iodine. **d** Near the end-point of the titration against $Na_2S_2O_3$. **e** Near the end-point, following the addition of starch. **f** At the end-point – the dark blue colour has disappeared.

15 A 1.00 g piece of brass is dissolved in nitric acid to produce a mixture of copper(II) nitrate and zinc nitrate solutions. An excess of potassium iodide solution is added, causing copper(I) iodide and iodine to form. The iodine formed reacts with 47.80 cm^3 of 0.200 mol dm^{-3} sodium thiosulfate solution.

a How many moles of sodium thiosulfate were needed to react with all the iodine?

b How many moles of Cu^{2+} were present before the potassium iodide solution was added?

c What mass of copper is this? (A_r of copper is 63.5)

d What was the percentage by mass of copper in the original piece of brass?

Answer

Summary

Glossary

- The transition elements are metals with similar physical and chemical properties.

- The electronic configurations of the elements include electrons in the 3d subshell.

- A transition element is defined as having a partly filled 3d subshell in at least one of its ions.

- When a transition element is oxidised, it loses electrons from the 4s subshell first and then the 3d subshell.

- Transition elements can exist in several oxidation states.

- Transition elements are good catalysts because they can transfer electrons easily and provide a site for the reaction to take place.

- Transition metal compounds are often coloured.

- Transition elements react with aqueous hydroxide ions to give precipitates. The colour of the precipitate can be used to identify the transition metal ion.

- Transition elements form complexes by combining with ligands.

- A ligand has an atom with one or more lone-pairs. Ligands bond to transition metal ions by one or more coordinate bonds.

- A ligand that bonds to the transition metal ion by one coordinate bond using one lone-pair is said to be monodentate. A ligand that bonds to the transition metal ion by two coordinate bonds using two lone-pairs is said to be bidentate.

- If the ligands make a total of four coordinate bonds to the transition metal ion, that ion is said to have a coordination number of four.

- If the ligands make a total of six coordinate bonds to the transition metal ion, that ion is said to have a coordination number of six.

- The shape of a four-coordinate complex may be square planar or tetrahedral. The shape of a six-coordinate complex will be octahedral.

- A strong ligand can displace a weak ligand in a complex. This can result in a change of colour.

- Many reactions involving transition elements are redox reactions. Some redox reactions are used in titrations to determine concentrations.

Questions

1 Copper is a typical transition element.
   - It forms coloured compounds.
   - It forms complex ions.
   - It has more than one oxidation state in its compounds.

   a State <u>one</u> other typical property of a transition element.   [1]

   b Dilute aqueous copper(II) sulfate is a blue solution containing $[Cu(H_2O)_6]^{2+}$ ions. A ligand substitution involving $[Cu(H_2O)_6]^{2+}$ is shown below.

$$[Cu(H_2O)_6]^{2+} \xrightarrow{\text{reagent } \mathbf{X}} [CuCl_4]^{2-}$$

   blue solution   yellow solution

   i Suggest a shape for the $[CuCl_4]^{2-}$ ion. Include the bond angles in your diagram.   [2]

   ii State the <u>formula</u> of the ligand in $[CuCl_4]^{2-}$.   [1]

   iii State the name or formula of reagent **X**.   [1]

   iv Explain, with the aid of a balanced equation, what is meant by the term *ligand substitution*.   [2]

   OCR Chemistry A2 (2815) January 2004   [Total 7]

   <u>Hint</u>

   <u>Answer</u>

2 *In this question, one mark is available for the quality of spelling, punctuation and grammar.*

   Iron and its compounds take part in several different types of reaction including ligand substitution, precipitation and redox.

   For each type of reaction:
   - give an example, taken from the chemistry of iron or its compounds
   - state what you would see
   - write a balanced equation for your example.   [9]

   Quality of written communication   [1]

   OCR Chemistry A2 (2815) June 2006   [Total 10]

   <u>Hint</u>

   <u>Answer</u>

   continued

3 Copper and zinc are both d-block elements but only copper is a transition element. Copper forms compounds containing Cu^{2+} or Cu^+ ions but zinc only forms compounds containing Zn^{2+} ions.

a Use the electronic configurations of Cu^{2+} and Zn^{2+} to explain why copper is a transition element and zinc is not. [2]

b Suggest <u>two</u> differences between compounds containing Zn^{2+} and Cu^{2+} ions. [2]

c Brass is an alloy of copper and zinc.

The percentage of copper and zinc in a sample of brass can be determined by reaction with hydrochloric acid. Only zinc reacts, as shown in the equation below:

$$Zn(s) + 2H^+(aq) \longrightarrow Zn^{2+}(aq) + H_2(g)$$

- A sample of brass powder of known mass is added to an excess of $1.00\,mol\,dm^{-3}$ hydrochloric acid.
- The mixture is heated gently and the hydrogen collected is measured once the reaction has finished.

A student analyses a $1.23\,g$ sample of brass, using the method described above. The student collects $76.0\,cm^3$ of hydrogen at room temperature and pressure. 1 mol of gas molecules occupies $24.0\,dm^3$ at room temperature and pressure. Calculate the percentage by mass of copper in the sample of brass. Give your answer to an appropriate number of significant figures. [3]

OCR Chemistry A2 (2815) June 2006

[Total 7]

Hint

Hint

Answer

213

Appendix A

The Periodic Table of the Elements

Key

| relative atomic mass |
| **atomic symbol** |
| name |
| atomic (proton) number |

1	2	3	4	5	6	7	0
							4.0 **He** helium 2
6.9 **Li** lithium 3	9.0 **Be** beryllium 4	10.8 **B** boron 5	12.0 **C** carbon 6	14.0 **N** nitrogen 7	16.0 **O** oxygen 8	19.0 **F** fluorine 9	20.2 **Ne** neon 10
23.0 **Na** sodium 11	24.3 **Mg** magnesium 12	27.0 **Al** aluminium 13	28.1 **Si** silicon 14	31.0 **P** phosphorus 15	32.1 **S** sulfur 16	35.5 **Cl** chlorine 17	39.9 **Ar** argon 18

1.0 **H** hydrogen 1

Transition elements:

45.0 **Sc** scandium 21	47.9 **Ti** titanium 22	50.9 **V** vanadium 23	52.0 **Cr** chromium 24	54.9 **Mn** manganese 25	55.8 **Fe** iron 26	58.9 **Co** cobalt 27	58.7 **Ni** nickel 28	63.5 **Cu** copper 29	65.4 **Zn** zinc 30

Period 4: 39.1 **K** potassium 19 | 40.1 **Ca** calcium 20 | ... | 69.7 **Ga** gallium 31 | 72.6 **Ge** germanium 32 | 74.9 **As** arsenic 33 | 79.0 **Se** selenium 34 | 79.9 **Br** bromine 35 | 83.8 **Kr** krypton 36

88.9 **Y** yttrium 39	91.2 **Zr** zirconium 40	92.9 **Nb** niobium 41	95.9 **Mo** molybdenum 42	[98] **Tc** technetium 43	101.1 **Ru** ruthenium 44	102.9 **Rh** rhodium 45	106.4 **Pd** palladium 46	107.9 **Ag** silver 47	112.4 **Cd** cadmium 48

Period 5: 85.5 **Rb** rubidium 37 | 87.6 **Sr** strontium 38 | ... | 114.8 **In** indium 49 | 118.7 **Sn** tin 50 | 121.8 **Sb** antimony 51 | 127.6 **Te** tellurium 52 | 126.9 **I** iodine 53 | 131.3 **Xe** xenon 54

138.9 **La** lanthanum 57 •	178.5 **Hf** hafnium 72	180.9 **Ta** tantalum 73	183.8 **W** tungsten 74	186.2 **Re** rhenium 75	190.2 **Os** osmium 76	192.2 **Ir** iridium 77	195.1 **Pt** platinum 78	197.0 **Au** gold 79	200.6 **Hg** mercury 80

Period 6: 132.9 **Cs** caesium 55 | 137.3 **Ba** barium 56 | ... | 204.4 **Tl** thallium 81 | 207.2 **Pb** lead 82 | 209.0 **Bi** bismuth 83 | [209] **Po** polonium 84 | [210] **At** astatine 85 | [222] **Rn** radon 86

[227] **Ac** actinium 89 ••	[261] **Rf** rutherfordium 104	[262] **Db** dubnium 105	[266] **Sg** seaborgium 106	[264] **Bh** bohrium 107	[277] **Hs** hassium 108	[268] **Mt** meitnerium 109	[271] **Ds** darmstadtium 110	[272] **Rg** roentgenium 111

Period 7: [223] **Fr** francium 87 | [226] **Ra** radium 88

Elements with atomic numbers 112–116 have been reported but not fully authenticated.

Lanthanides (•)

140.1 **Ce** cerium 58	140.9 **Pr** praseodymium 59	144.2 **Nd** neodymium 60	144.9 **Pm** promethium 61	150.4 **Sm** samarium 62	152.0 **Eu** europium 63	157.2 **Gd** gadolinium 64	158.9 **Tb** terbium 65	162.5 **Dy** dysprosium 66	164.9 **Ho** holmium 67	167.3 **Er** erbium 68	168.9 **Tm** thulium 69	173.0 **Yb** ytterbium 70	175.0 **Lu** lutetium 71

Actinides (••)

232.0 **Th** thorium 90	[231] **Pa** protactinium 91	238.1 **U** uranium 92	[237] **Np** neptunium 93	[242] **Pu** plutonium 94	[243] **Am** americium 95	[247] **Cm** curium 96	[245] **Bk** berkelium 97	[251] **Cf** californium 98	[254] **Es** einsteinium 99	[253] **Fm** fermium 100	[256] **Md** mendelevium 101	[254] **No** nobelium 102	[257] **Lr** lawrencium 103

Appendix B

Standard electrode potentials

Electrode reaction	$E^{\ominus}/V$
$Ag^+ + e^- \rightleftharpoons Ag$	+0.80
$Br_2 + 2e^- \rightleftharpoons 2Br^-$	+1.07
$Cl_2 + 2e^- \rightleftharpoons 2Cl^-$	+1.36
$Cr^{2+} + 2e^- \rightleftharpoons Cr$	−0.91
$Cr^{3+} + 3e^- \rightleftharpoons Cr$	−0.74
$Cr_2O_7^{2-} + 14H^+ + 6e^- \rightleftharpoons 2Cr^{3+} + 7H_2O$	+1.33
$Cu^+ + e^- \rightleftharpoons Cu$	+0.52
$Cu^{2+} + 2e^- \rightleftharpoons Cu$	+0.34
$Cu^{2+} + e^- \rightleftharpoons Cu^+$	+0.15
$F_2 + 2e^- \rightleftharpoons 2F^-$	+2.87
$Fe^{2+} + 2e^- \rightleftharpoons Fe$	−0.44
$Fe^{3+} + e^- \rightleftharpoons Fe^{2+}$	+0.77
$Fe^{3+} + 3e^- \rightleftharpoons Fe$	−0.04
$2H^+ + 2e^- \rightleftharpoons H_2$	0.00
$I_2 + 2e^- \rightleftharpoons 2I^-$	+0.54
$Mn^{2+} + 2e^- \rightleftharpoons Mn$	−1.18
$MnO_4^- + 8H^+ + 5e^- \rightleftharpoons Mn^{2+} + 4H_2O$	+1.52
$Ni^{2+} + 2e^- \rightleftharpoons Ni$	−0.25
$O_2 + 4H^+ + 4e^- \rightleftharpoons 2H_2O$	+1.23
$O_2 + 2H_2O + 4e^- \rightleftharpoons 4OH^-$	+0.40
$Pb^{2+} + 2e^- \rightleftharpoons Pb$	−0.13
$SO_4^{2-} + 4H^+ + 2e^- \rightleftharpoons SO_2 + 2H_2O$	+0.17
$Sn^{4+} + 2e^- \rightleftharpoons Sn^{2+}$	+0.15
$V^{2+} + 2e^- \rightleftharpoons V$	−1.20
$V^{3+} + e^- \rightleftharpoons V^{2+}$	−0.26
$VO^{2+} + 2H^+ + e^- \rightleftharpoons V^{3+} + H_2O$	+0.34
$VO_2^+ + 2H^+ + e^- \rightleftharpoons VO^{2+} + H_2O$	+1.00
$VO_3^- + 4H^+ + e^- \rightleftharpoons VO^{2+} + 2H_2O$	+1.00
$Zn^{2+} + 2e^- \rightleftharpoons Zn$	−0.76

Answers to SAQs

Chapter 1

1 a

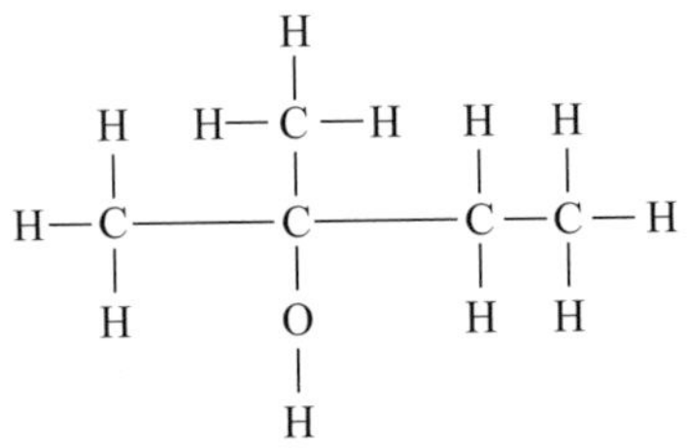

b

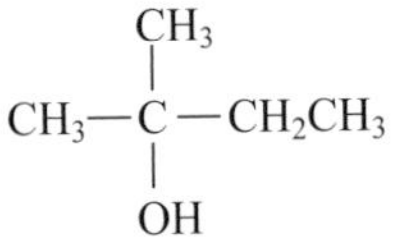

CH₃—C(CH₃)—CH₂CH₃ with OH

Alternatively: CH₃C(CH₃)(OH)CH₂CH₃

c

2 C_4H_9Br

3 a 3-chloro-4,5-dimethylheptane.
b 1-methyl-3-nitrobenzene.
c Bromoethanoic acid.

4 a $NH_2CH_2CO_2H$
b

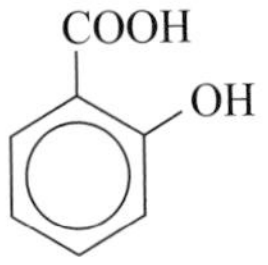

c

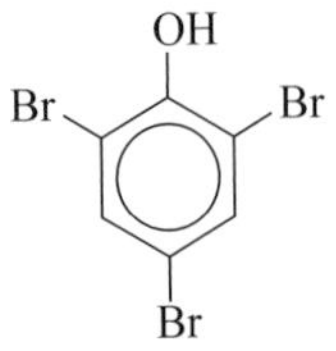

5

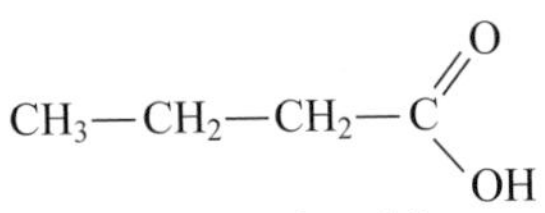

(butanoic acid)

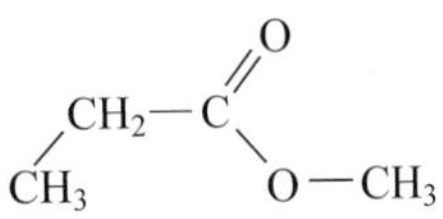

(methyl propanoate)

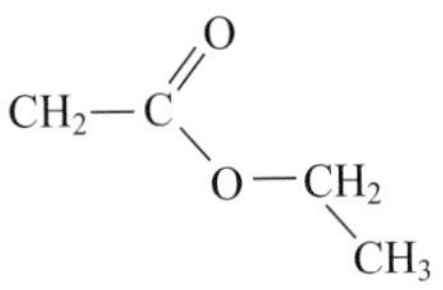

(ethyl ethanoate)

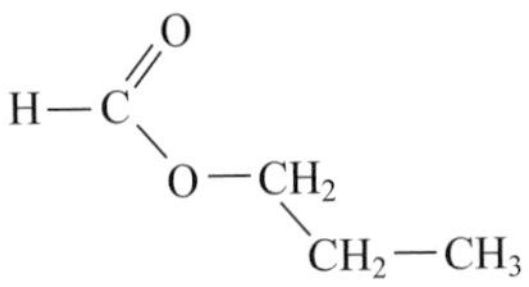

(propyl methanoate)

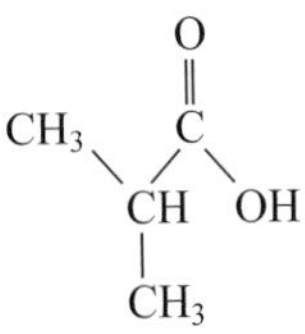

(2-methylpropanoic acid)

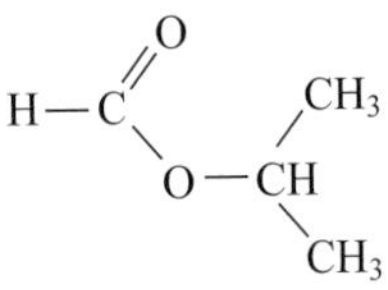

(1-methylethyl methanoate)

6

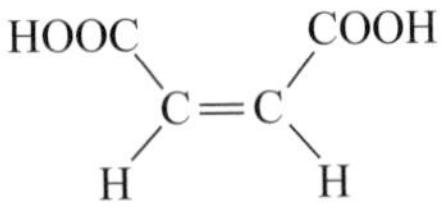

cis-butenedioic acid
(Z)-butenedioic acid

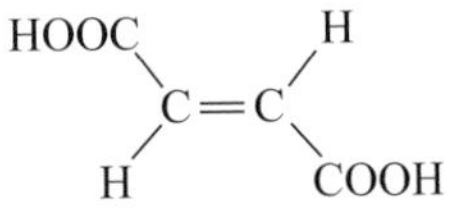

trans-butenedioic acid
(E)-butenedioic acid

7 a Homolytic fission is when a covalent bond is broken to form two (free) radicals.
b The two propagation steps constitute a chain reaction. In these steps chlorine radicals, Cl•(g), are consumed *and* regenerated. As long as there is a sufficient supply of chlorine, Cl_2, and ethane, the reaction will continue.

8 Two moles of bromine, Br_2.

9 a An electrophile is a reagent which accepts an electron-pair as it attacks an electron-rich centre, leading to the formation of a new covalent bond.
b The $CH_2BrCH_2^+$ carbocation, formed in the initial attack by Br_2, reacts with a water molecule (or an OH^- ion from water) to form 2-bromoethanol.

10 A nucleophile is a reagent which donates a lone-pair of electrons as it attacks a centre (such as a carbon atom) which has a partial positive charge, δ+. The attack results in the formation of a new covalent bond.

Chapter 2

1 a 6 electrons (one from each carbon atom in the benzene ring).
b 2p orbitals (one from each of the six carbon atoms).
c Once involved in π bonding, these electrons are no longer associated with any one particular carbon atom.

2 All the bonds are the same length.
Benzene does not behave like an alkene with C=C double bonds. For example, it does not easily undergo addition reactions.
The enthalpy of hydrogenation is not as exothermic as predicted from the theoretical value calculated using Kekulé's model.

3 a

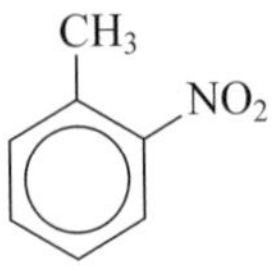

1-methyl-2-nitrobenzene

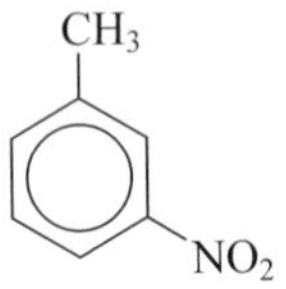

1-methyl-3-nitrobenzene

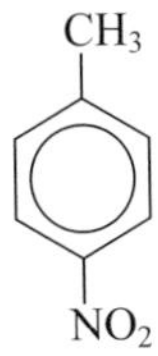

1-methyl-4-nitrobenzene

b

O$_2$N — CH$_3$ — NO$_2$ (2,4,6-trinitromethylbenzene structure with NO$_2$ at bottom)

4

$\overset{\delta+}{}$ $\overset{\delta-}{}$
Cl---Cl→AlCl$_3$ $\longrightarrow$ (+ ring) + [AlCl$_4$]$^-$

$\downarrow$

(chlorobenzene ring) + HCl + AlCl$_3$

5 a The attacking species involved in the addition to benzene is a (free) radical.

b The attacking species involved in the addition of chlorine to an alkene is an electrophile.

6 a, b

phenolic –OH group
ether
aldehyde

7 a Potassium phenoxide and water.

b

(ring)—OH + KOH $\longrightarrow$ (ring)—O$^-$K$^+$ + H$_2$O

8 The bromine molecule is polarised by the delocalised π electrons on phenol. (The enhanced reactivity of the benzene ring, caused by the –OH group, is also required. Note that aqueous bromine will not react with benzene – a halogen carrier, such as FeBr$_3$ is needed.)

Chapter 3

1 The hydrocarbon parts of the molecules are only attracted to other molecules by weak, instantaneous dipole–induced dipole forces (van der Waals' forces). The carbonyl group has a permanent dipole and will hydrogen bond to water molecules via a lone-pair on the C=O group. Aldehydes and ketones with less than four carbon atoms are miscible (they mix freely) with water because the intermolecular forces in the mixture are similar in strength to those in the separate liquids. As the length of the carbon chain is increased, the van der Waals' forces increase and start to dominate the physical properties of the aldehydes and ketones. If the larger molecules were to dissolve, they would disrupt the hydrogen bonding between water molecules, so these compounds remain immiscible with water.

2 a Butan-1-ol should be heated gently with acidified dichromate(VI); the butanal should be distilled off immediately.

b CH$_3$CH$_2$CH$_2$CH$_2$OH + [O]
$\longrightarrow$ CH$_3$CH$_2$CH$_2$CHO + H$_2$O

c Butan-1-ol should be refluxed with acidified dichromate(VI); the butanoic acid should be distilled off after at least 15 minutes' refluxing.

d CH$_3$CH$_2$CH$_2$CH$_2$OH + 2[O]
$\longrightarrow$ CH$_3$CH$_2$CH$_2$COOH + H$_2$O
Alternatively:
CH$_3$CH$_2$CH$_2$CH$_2$OH + [O]
$\longrightarrow$ CH$_3$CH$_2$CH$_2$CHO + H$_2$O
followed by
CH$_3$CH$_2$CH$_2$CHO + [O] $\longrightarrow$ CH$_3$CH$_2$CH$_2$COOH

3 a

OH
H$_3$C — CH$_2$ — CH — CH$_3$

b H$_3$C — CH$_2$ — CH$_2$ — CH$_2$OH

4 a Nucleophilic addition.

b Hydride ion, H$^-$.

c

propan-1-ol

5 With pentanal a silver mirror is observed forming on the inside surface of the test tube but no change is seen with pentan-3-one. With pentanal, the aldehyde is oxidised to the carboxylic acid (pentanoic acid) by Ag$^+$ ions in the Tollens' reagent, which are reduced themselves to Ag metal in the redox reaction. On the other hand, ketones, such as pentan-3-one, cannot be oxidised to carboxylic acids by mild oxidising agents so no change is seen with Tollens' reagent.

Chapter 4

1 a Ester.

b Carboxylic acid.

c Ester.

2 a Zn + 2CH$_3$CH$_2$COOH $\longrightarrow$ (CH$_3$CH$_2$COO)$_2$Zn + H$_2$

b Na$_2$CO$_3$ + 2HCOOH $\longrightarrow$ 2HCOONa + CO$_2$ + H$_2$O

c MgO + 2CH$_3$COOH $\longrightarrow$ (CH$_3$COO)$_2$Mg + H$_2$O

d

(ring)—COOH + NaOH

$\longrightarrow$ (ring)—COONa + H$_2$O

3 a

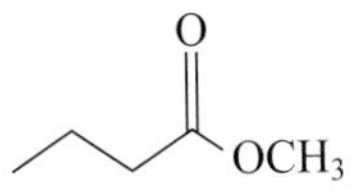

methyl butanoate 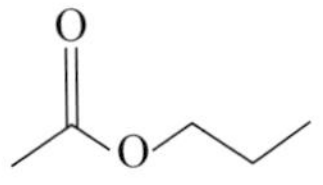   propyl ethanoate

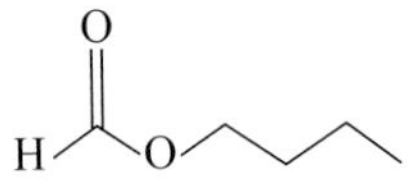

butyl methanoate

b

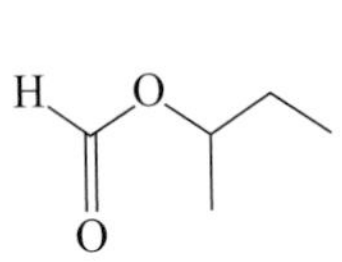

1-methylpropyl   2-methylpropyl   1,1-dimethylethyl
methanoate   methanoate   methanoate

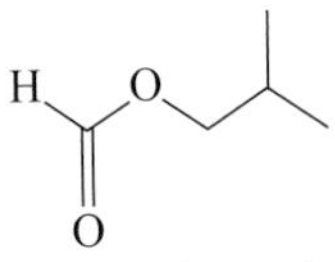

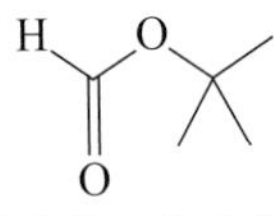

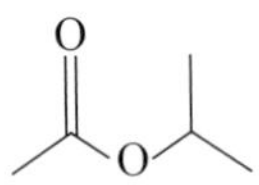

1-methylethyl   methyl 2-methylpropanoate
ethanoate

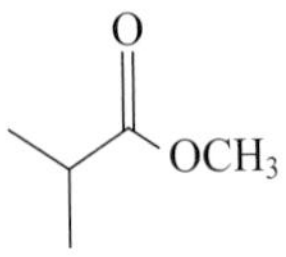

Pentanoic acid, $CH_3CH_2CH_2CH_2COOH$, and other isomeric carboxylic acids.
Methoxybutan-2-one, $CH_3OCH_2COCH_2CH_3$, and other isomers with an ether plus a ketone or an aldehyde group.
Cyclic isomers are also possible.
For example:

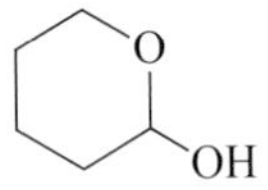

4 a

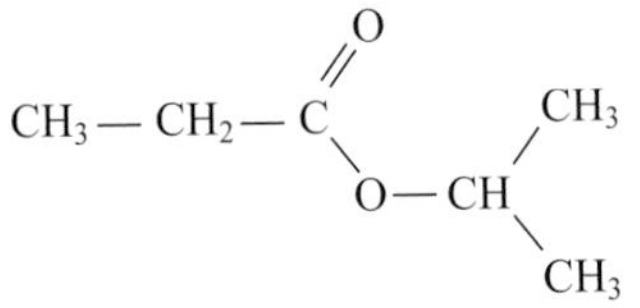

b Propanoic acid and propan-2-ol.

c

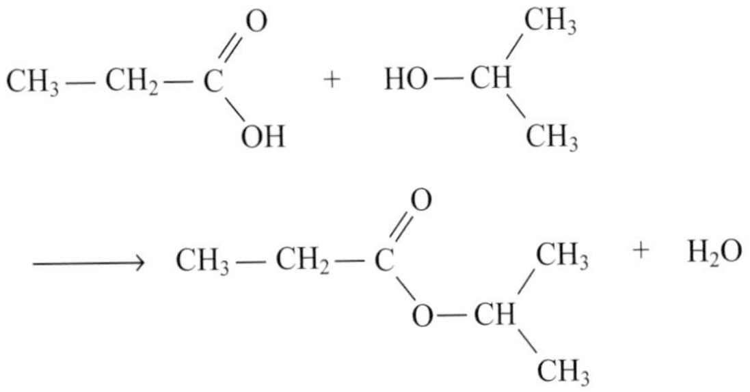

5 a Butyl methanoate.

b

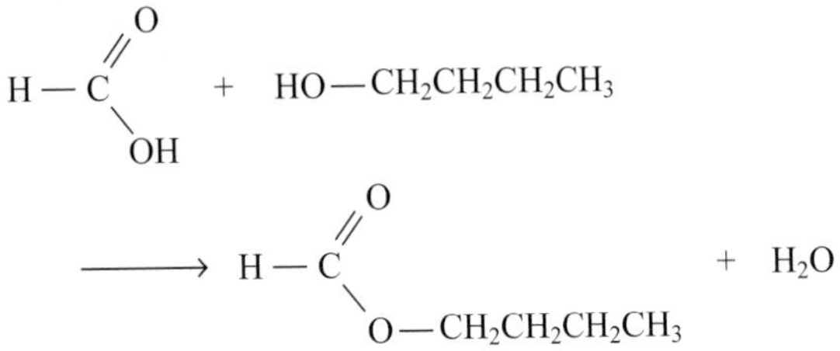

6

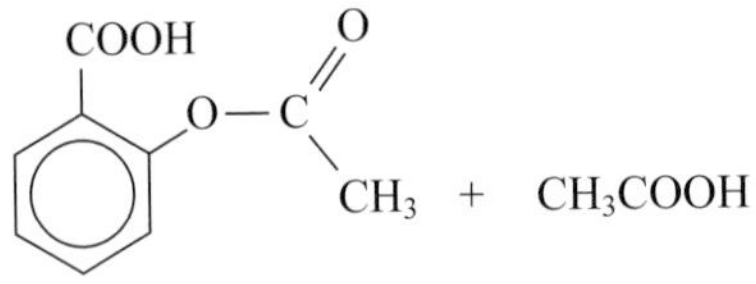

$+ CH_3COOH$

7 a

$COOCH_3(l) + NaOH(aq)$

$COONa(aq) + CH_3OH(aq)$

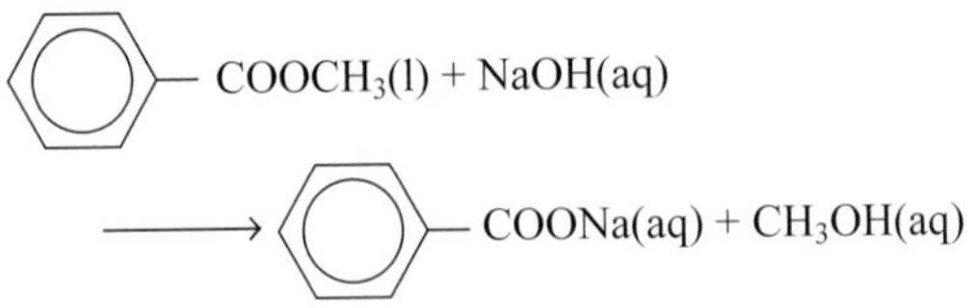

sodium benzoate   methanol

b $CH_3CH_2COOCH_3(l) + H_2O(l)$

$\xrightleftharpoons{H^+(aq)} CH_3CH_2COOH(aq) + CH_3OH(aq)$

propanoic acid   methanol

8 a Water.
b Esterification.
c 3
d

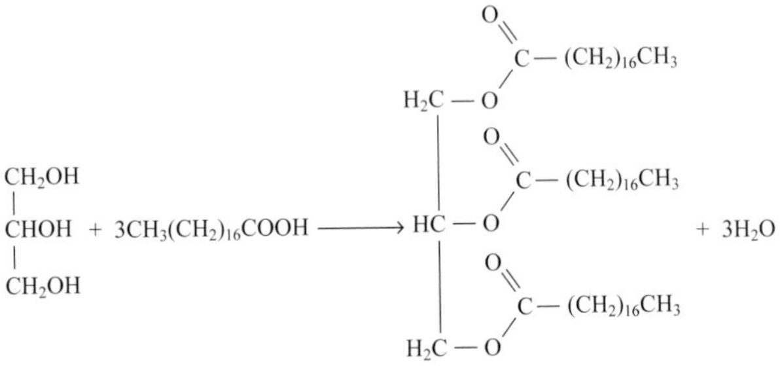

$+ 3H_2O$

9 a

b

c (9Z,12Z)-octadec-9,12-dienoic acid.

10 a 9%
b 86%
c 69%
d 17%
e There are no C=C bonds so you don't need to indicate their positions.

11

12 C18,3(9,12,15)

13 *Advantages of biofuels:*
- conserve our diminishing supplies of fossil fuels
- plants absorb CO_2 as they grow, reducing the greenhouse effect
- biodegradable if spilled.

Disadvantages of biofuels:
- not 'carbon-neutral' as yet
- deforestation to gain more land to grow the crops, destroying habitats and reducing rainforest
- crops used for fuel instead of food, affecting prices and causing hardship in developing countries.

Need a balanced argument with a well-reasoned conclusion.

Chapter 5

1 a Butylamine.
   b Amine **C**: $C_2H_5NHCH_3$.

2 a Propylamine, $CH_3CH_2CH_2NH_2$
   b 4-aminophenol,

   H_2N—⬡—OH

3 a $CH_3CH_2CH_2CH_2NH_2 + HNO_3$
      $\longrightarrow CH_3CH_2CH_2CH_2NH_3{}^+NO_3{}^-$
   b H_2N—⬡—OH + HCl
      $\longrightarrow$ $^-ClH_3N^+$—⬡—OH
   c H_2N—⬡—OH + NaOH
      $\longrightarrow H_2N$—⬡—$O^-Na^+ + H_2O$

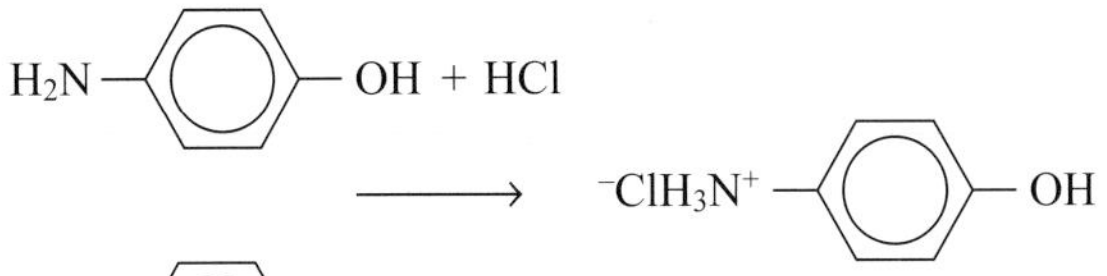

4 a H—O—⬡—N═N—⬡—O—H

   b HO—⬡—NH_2 + HNO_2 + HCl
      $\longrightarrow$ HO—⬡—$N_2{}^+Cl^-$ + $2H_2O$

   c HO—⬡—$N_2{}^+Cl^-$ + ⬡—OH
      $\longrightarrow$ HO—⬡—N═N—⬡—OH + HCl

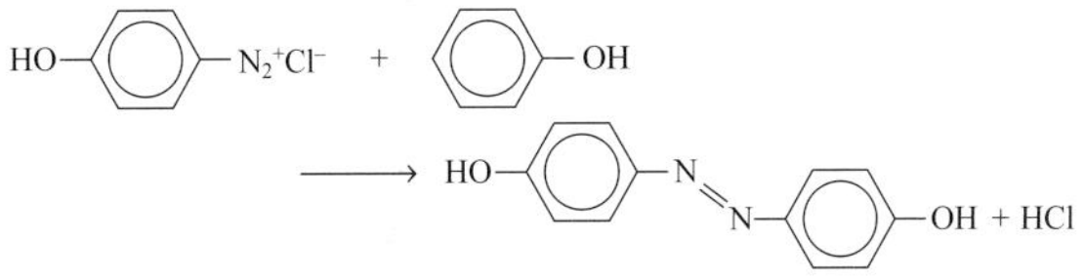

Chapter 6

1 a $HOOCCH_2NH_3{}^+Cl^-$(aq)
   b $NH_2CH_2COO^-Na^+$(aq)

2 a $HOOCCH_2NH_2$(aq) + HCl(aq)
      $\longrightarrow HOOCCH_2NH_3{}^+Cl^-$(aq)
   b NH_2CH_2COOH(aq) + NaOH(aq)
      $\longrightarrow NH_2CH_2COO^-Na^+$(aq) + H_2O(l)

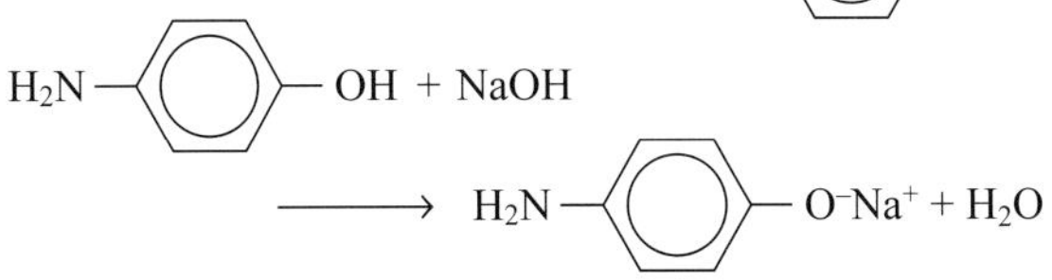

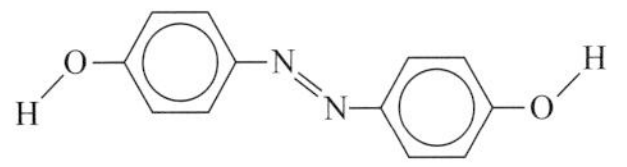

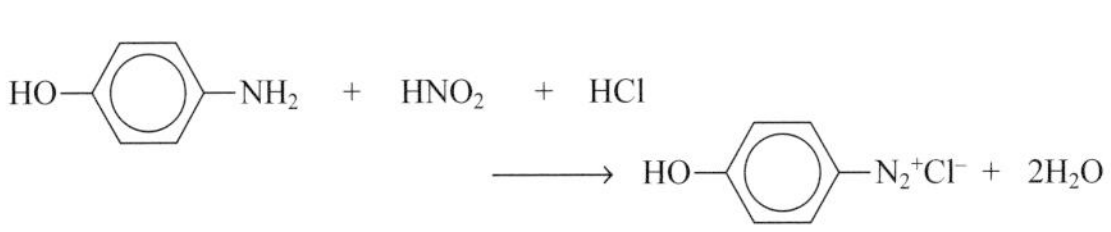

3 The concentration of the lysine zwitterion is at a maximum at about pH 9.5. The side group (R) on the α-amino acid is basic in its nature.

4 a (structure) or (structure)

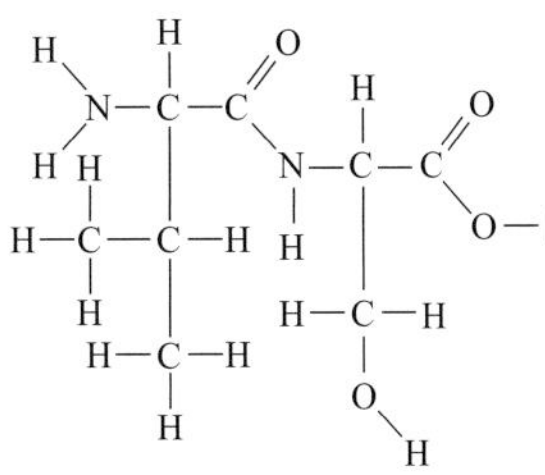

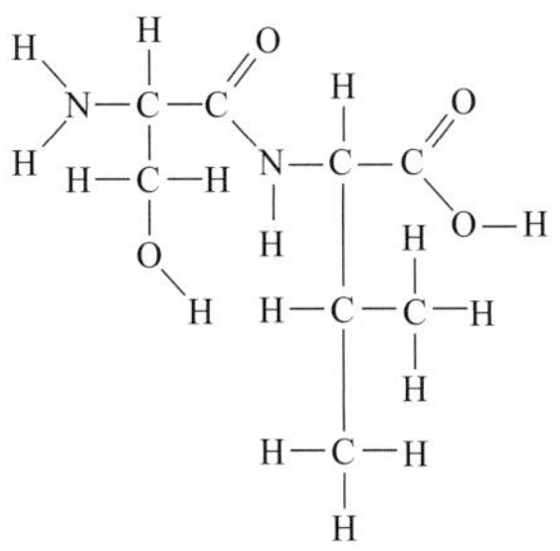

   b Water.
   c Condensation reaction.

5 a (structure with labels: amide; bonds that may be broken by hydrolysis; ester)

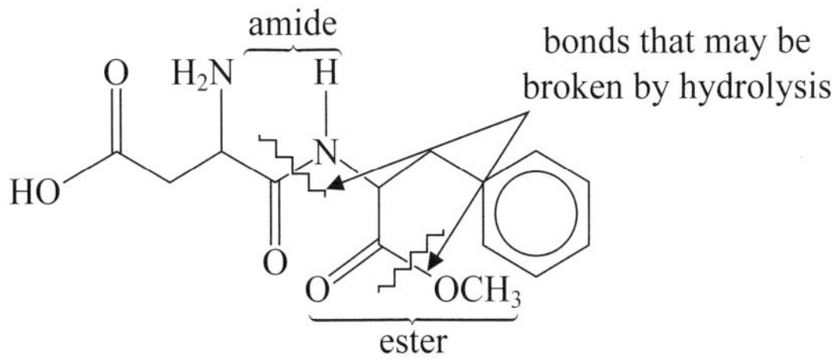

   b (structure) + $2H_2O$

      $\longrightarrow$ (structure) + CH_3OH + (structure)

      2-aminobutanedioic acid (aspartic acid)   methanol   2-amino-3-phenylpropanoic acid (phenylalanine)

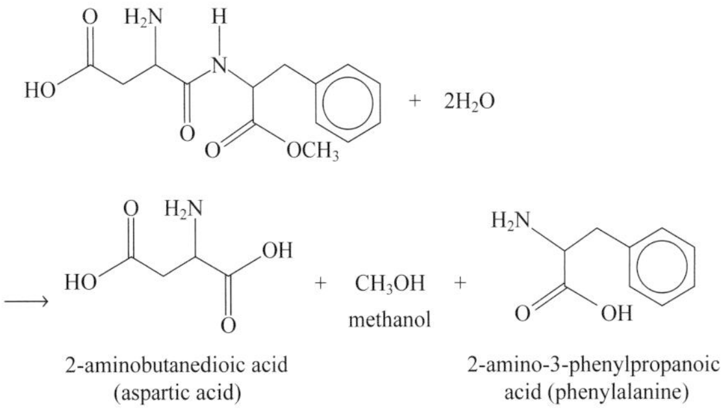

6 Only compound A has *cis–trans* isomers. The isomers are:

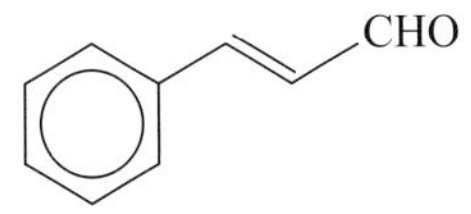

   (structure) CHO   (structure) CHO
   trans (E) 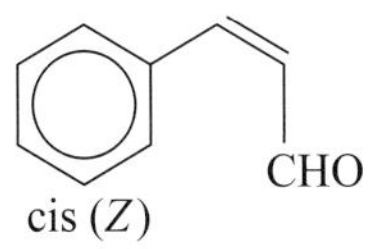   cis (Z)

7 a $CH_3CH_2\overset{*}{C}HBrCH_3$

   b (structure with NH_2 and * label)

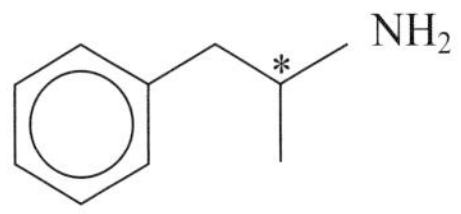

   c (structure with OH, N, *, HO groups)

8 (two structures with CH3, H, H2N, COOH, HOOC, NH2 and mirror plane)

9 a (two structures with $CH(CH_3)_2$, CH_2, C, H_2N, COOH, HOOC, NH_2, H and mirror plane)

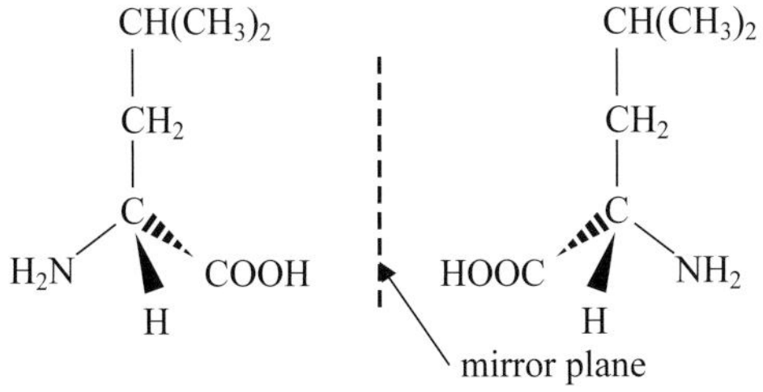

   b H_2N—$\overset{*}{C}$—COOH with $\overset{*}{C}HCH_2CH_3$ and CH_3

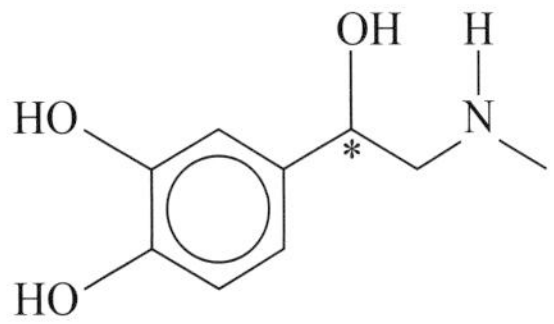

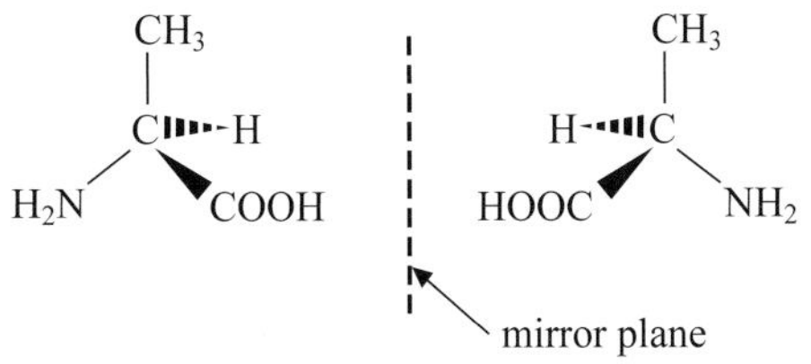

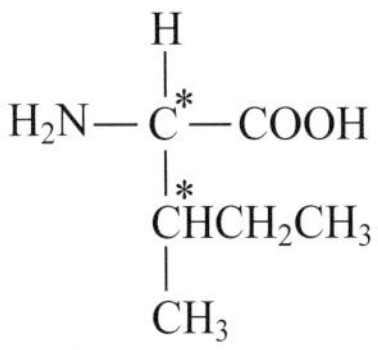

Chapter 7

1 a

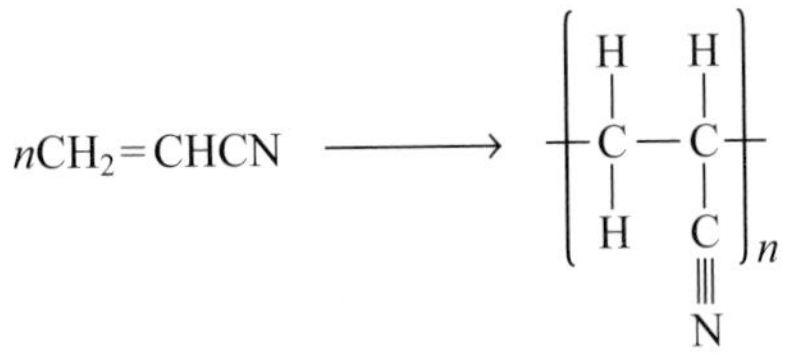

$$nCH_2 = CHCN \longrightarrow$$

b Repeat unit:

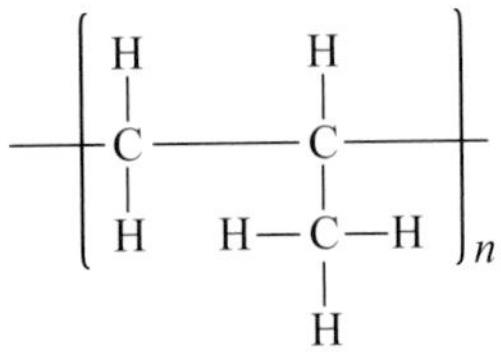

poly(propene)

Monomer:

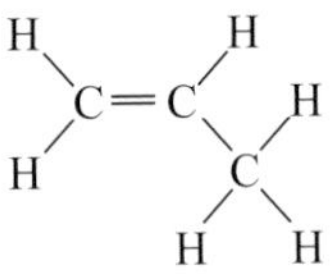

propene

2 a

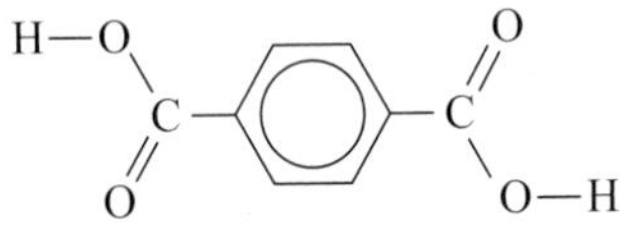

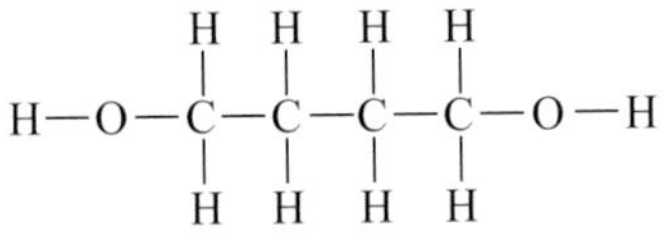

b

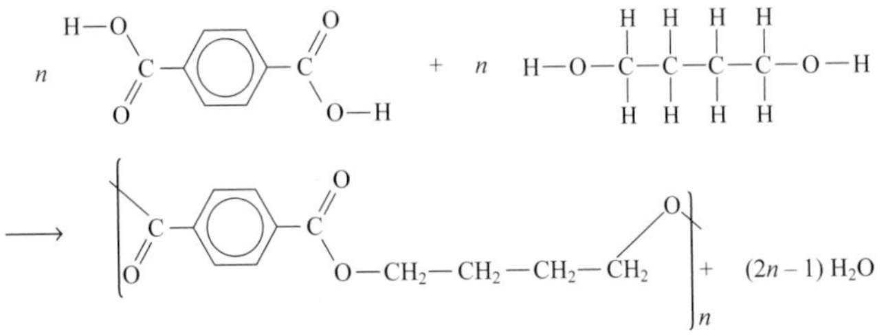

$+ (2n - 1) H_2O$

3 a

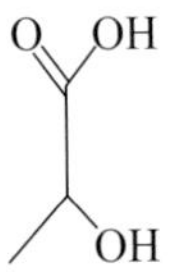

or

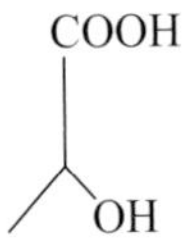

b

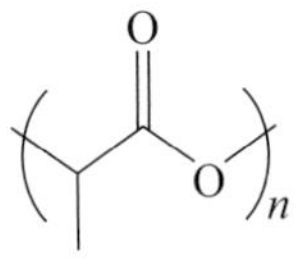

or

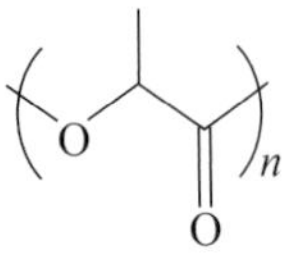

4 a

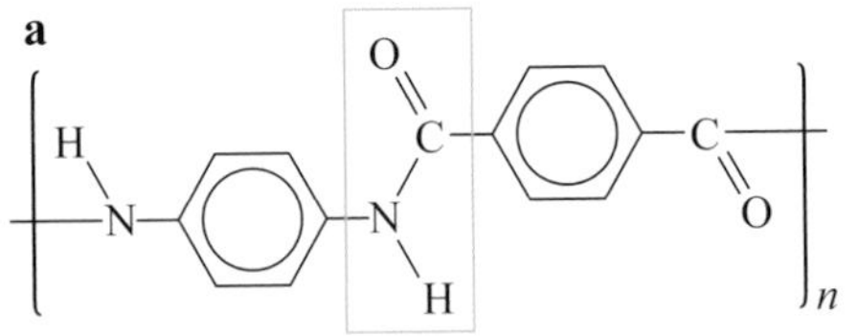

amide link

b

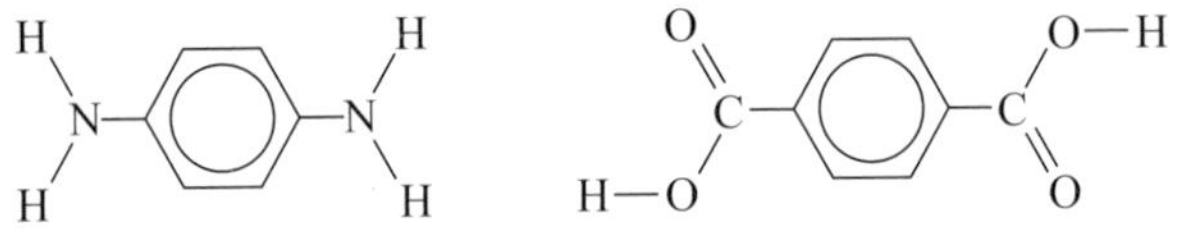

c

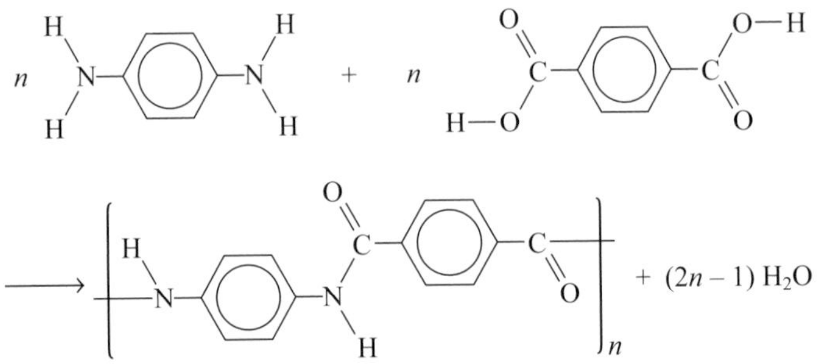

$+ (2n - 1) H_2O$

d Only one type of monomer is used to make poly(ethene), whereas there are two different monomers used to make Kevlar.
Poly(ethene) is made in an addition polymerisation reaction in which the polymer is the only product. However, Kevlar is made in a condensation polymerisation reaction in which water is produced as well as the polymer.
Kevlar and poly(ethene) are both polymers consisting of long-chain molecules involving many repetitions of a relatively simple repeat unit.

5 Some points to look for:
Advantages: biodegradable; made from renewable resources; grease/oil resistant; does not contaminate food; transparent; machinable.
Disadvantages: PLA contaminates other plastics collected for recycling; slightly more expensive than plastics such as poly(chloroethene) – although traditional plastics will become more expensive as crude oil runs out; can develop a 'haze' over time; shrinks if heat-sealed too near its melting temperature; fields used for crops used as raw material for PLA could be used for growing food.

Chapter 8

1

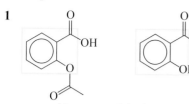

aspirin   2-hydroxybenzoic acid
(salicylic acid)

salicin

2 Compound **C**, as it has the same structure as the parts marked with a blue box in the answer to SAQ 1. However, compound **A** has the same number of electrons in the same orbitals as aspirin and therefore has a similar shape too.

3 Compound **B**.

4 a $H_2C = CH_2$

$\downarrow$ HCl(aq)

CH_3CH_2Cl

$\downarrow$ heat with alcoholic ammonia under pressure

$CH_3CH_2NH_2$

b ⬡—CHO

$\downarrow$ heat with H_2SO_4(aq) and $K_2Cr_2O_7$(aq)

⬡—CO_2H

$\downarrow$ heat with ethanol and acid catalyst

⬡—$CO_2CH_2CH_3$

c $CH_3CH_2CH_2CH_2Br$

$\downarrow$ reflux with NaOH(aq)

$CH_3CH_2CH_2CH_2OH$

$\downarrow$ reflux with H_2SO_4(aq) and excess K_2Cr_2O7(aq)

$CH_3CH_2CH_2COOH$

d $CH_3CH_2COCH_3$

$\downarrow$ warm with $NaBH_4$ in water

$CH_3CH_2CHOHCH_3$

$\downarrow$ distil from mixture with conc. H_2SO_4 and KBr(s)

$CH_3CH_2CHBrCH_3$

$\downarrow$ heat with alcoholic NH_3

$CH_3CH_2CHNH_2CH_3$

5 a Less dosage required; reduces risk of side-effects as the unwanted enantiomer might present a health hazard.

b Reduces the chances of litigation against the drug company as a result of side-effects caused by the unwanted enantiomer.

6 Thalidomide was prescribed to pregnant women as a sedative during the early 1960s. For a time it was the preferred sedative during pregnancy as the alternatives, such as valium, were addictive. Unfortunately, one of the stereoisomers of thalidomide proved to have disastrous side-effects, causing babies to be born with congenital deformities (teratogenicity). Not surprisingly, thalidomide was quickly withdrawn from use and law suits were filed against the manufacturers to compensate those affected and to help finance their care. (Note, however, that thalidomide racemises in the body, so even giving the drug as a pure enantiomer would not have prevented the problems.)

7 Points to include:
- Racemic mixture produced in traditional synthetic routes. This results in the need to separate the mixture of enantiomers. This can use large volumes of organic solvents which have to be disposed of, along with the unwanted enantiomer. The process will also use more chemicals, which require natural resources.
- Enzymes are stereo-specific.
- Whole organisms can be used (avoiding the need to isolate enzymes).
- Fewer steps in process, resulting in more efficiency.

Chapter 9

1 a Calcium carbonate.
b Ethanol.

2 Any *two* of the following:
- Thin-layer chromatography is faster than paper chromatography.
- The thin layer may be made from different solids. So a wide variety of mixtures can be separated by careful choice of the mobile and stationary phases.

- Thin-layer chromatography can be used for quickly selecting the best conditions for larger-scale separations.
- Thin-layer chromatography works with very small samples.

3 Compound 1: $R_f = \dfrac{1.5}{12.5} = 0.12$

Compound 2: $R_f = \dfrac{9.1}{12.5} = 0.73$

Compound 1 has a greater affinity for the thin layer than does compound 2. As the thin layer is silica gel, compound 1 is more polar than compound 2.

4 a By measuring the difference in time between the injection of the sample and the centre of the peak for a component.

  b The relative areas under the peaks represent the relative amounts of the components in the mixture.

5 The relative height of its peak compared to the sum of the heights of all the peaks.

6 a **A** methanol, CH_3OH
  B ethanol, C_2H_5OH
  C butan-1-ol, $CH_3CH_2CH_2CH_2OH$
  D 2-methylbutan-1-ol

$$CH_2-CH_2-\overset{\overset{\displaystyle CH_3}{|}}{C}-CH_2OH$$

  b Using peak heights:

Peaks	A	B	C	D
% of total	6.7	66.7	13.3	13.3

7 a 9 minutes.
  b About 180–190.
  c By comparing its mass spectrum to a database of known spectra.

Chapter 10

1 Ethanol contains H atoms so it produces (3) peaks of its own on the proton NMR spectrum, making it more complicated to interpret.

2 a 3 peaks, corresponding to the 3 different types of ^1H atom in propanal: CH_3CH_2CHO
  b The CH_3 peak will be split into a triplet (as the adjacent C atom is bonded to two ^1H atoms, so $n = 2$ and $n + 1 = 3$).

3 a

Chemical shift, δ/ppm	Relative number of protons	Splitting pattern
1.2	3	triplet
2.0	3	singlet
4.1	2	quartet

b From the splitting patterns given, the following can be deduced.
- To produce a triplet, the three protons at chemical shift 1.2 must be adjacent to a $-CH_2-$ group.
- To produce a quartet, the two protons at chemical shift 4.1 must be adjacent to a $-CH_3$ group.
- To produce a singlet, the three protons at chemical shift 2.0 must have no protons on the adjacent carbon atom.

c The types of protons are as follows:

Chemical shift, δ/ppm	Type of proton
1.2	CH_3-R
2.0	$\overset{\overset{\displaystyle O}{\|}}{-C}-CH_3$
4.1	$-O-CH_2-R$

The presence of the C=O group is supported by the infrared data, as $1750\,cm^{-1}$ is the absorption frequency for this bond.

d The structure of the compound is

$$CH_3-C\overset{\displaystyle O}{\underset{\displaystyle O-CH_2-CH_3}{<}}$$

4 Methyl propanoate has the following structure:

$$CH_3-CH_2-C\overset{\displaystyle O}{\underset{\displaystyle O-CH_3}{<}}$$

The chemical shifts and splitting patterns are as follows:

Type of proton	Chemical shift, δ/ppm	Relative number of protons	Splitting pattern
CH_3-O	3.3–4.3	3	singlet
CH_3-R	0.7–1.6	3	triplet
$\overset{\overset{\displaystyle O}{\|}}{-C}-CH_2-R$	2.0–2.9	2	quartet

5 The peak at 5.4 ppm would disappear.

6 The carbon atom in the benzene ring that is bonded directly to the ethyl group.

7 A single peak, somewhere between 110 and 165 ppm.

8 a 3 peaks, one for the C atom in $-CH_3$, one for $-CH_2-$ and one for $-CH_2OH$.
  b 2 peaks, one for the C atoms in the two $-CH_3$ groups and one for $-CHOH$.

9 a ● Mass spectrometry to find M_r from the molecular ion peak and a possible structure for the molecule.

● IR to identify the functional groups C=O and O–H in the acid. Or use NMR.

b ● Mass spectrometry to find M_r and a possible structure.

● IR to identify the C=O group in the ester. Or use NMR.

c ● Mass spectrometry to find Mr and a possible structure.

● NMR to identify the chemical groups containing protons and find their arrangement in the molecule.

● IR to identify the functional groups –OH and C=O.

Chapter 11

1 a Infrared.

b 2.00×10^{-13} s

2 Experimental evidence shows that the rate of reaction is directly proportional to the concentration of cyclopropane. If the concentration of cyclopropane is halved, the rate of reaction is halved.

3 Table 11.2 has more accurate data as the tangents drawn were longer, giving larger triangles.

4 The reaction is first order with respect to cyclopropane and first order overall.

5 By titrating small samples of the reaction mixture with standardised base, for example $1.00\,\mathrm{mol\,dm^{-3}}$ aqueous sodium hydroxide, at set times during the chemical reaction you could find the concentration of hydrochloric acid as the reaction progressed. You could also monitor this concentration using either a pH meter or a conductivity meter. Both devices respond to changes in hydrogen ion concentration, which is itself an indication of the concentration of hydrochloric acid over time.

6 Remember that the temperature of the reaction mixture must be constant throughout.

a We cannot tell. This data can be explained if the reaction is first order with respect to both reactants, in which case both reactants affect the rate. Alternatively the data can be explained if the reaction is second order with respect to one reactant and zero order with respect to the other, in which case only one reactant affects the rate.

b Several approaches are possible. To provide a fair test, the experiment should be designed to study the effect of changing the concentration of only one

reagent. One approach is to ensure a large excess of methanol. Relative to the concentration of HCl, the methanol concentration could then be assumed to be constant. This would allow the concentration of the acid to be monitored. The data obtained would enable the order with respect to HCl to be deduced.

7 Separate experiments need to be conducted. In each experiment, the concentration of just one reactant is allowed to change, with other reactants present in excess. The effect of changing the concentration of $H^+(aq)$ can be investigated by the addition of a strong acid (such as sulfuric acid). Similarly, the effect of changing the concentration of $Cl^-(aq)$ can be investigated by the addition of sodium chloride.

8 a The reaction rate = $k\,[N_2O_5]$, so the order of the reaction is 1.

b $k = 1.05 \times 10^{-5}\,\mathrm{s^{-1}}$

9 a reaction rate = $k\,[H^+]\,[CH_3COCH_3]\,[I_2(aq)]^0$ (in effect, reaction rate = $k\,[H^+]\,[CH_3COCH_3]$ as $[I_2(aq)]^0 = 1$)

b Substituting data from experiment 1 in the rate equation:

$10.9 \times 10^{-6}\,\mathrm{mol\,dm^{-3}\,s^{-1}}$
$= k \times 1.25\,\mathrm{mol\,dm^{-3}} \times 0.5 \times 10^{-3}\,\mathrm{mol\,dm^{-3}}$

$$k = \frac{10.9 \times 10^{-6}\,\mathrm{mol\,dm^{-3}\,s^{-1}}}{1.25\,\mathrm{mol\,dm^{-3}} \times 0.5 \times 10^{-3}\,\mathrm{mol^{-1}\,dm^3\,s^{-1}}}$$

$= 1.74 \times 10^{-2}\,\mathrm{mol^{-1}\,dm^3\,s^{-1}}$

10

Chapter 12

1 Experiment 1, $K_c = 0.276$; experiment 4, $K_c = 0.272$.

2 a $CH_3COOH + CH_3CH_2OH \rightleftharpoons CH_3COOCH_2CH_3 + H_2O$

b 0.1728 mol

c $0.5000 - 0.1728 = 0.3272$ mol

d $K_c = \dfrac{[CH_3COOCH_2CH_3][H_2O]}{[CH_3COOH][CH_3CH_2OH]}$

e $K_c = \dfrac{(0.3272) \times (0.3272)}{(0.1728) \times (0.1728)}$

$= 3.59$

3 If we call the number of moles of products at equilibrium M1 and M2, and the number of moles of reactants at equilibrium M3 and M4, and the total volume is V, then the concentrations of the substances at equilibrium are $\dfrac{M1}{V}, \dfrac{M2}{V}, \dfrac{M3}{V}$ and $\dfrac{M4}{V}$.

The expression for K_c is

$$\frac{\dfrac{M1}{V} \times \dfrac{M2}{V}}{\dfrac{M3}{V} \times \dfrac{M4}{V}}$$

The 'Vs' all cancel, so $K_c = \dfrac{[M1] \times [M2]}{[M3] \times [M4]}$

and so the total volume is irrelevant.

4 The 10 moles of hydrogen iodide begin to dissociate, forming hydrogen and iodine:

$$2HI(g) \rightleftharpoons H_2(g) + I_2(g)$$

For every molecule of iodine formed, two molecules of hydrogen iodide have to split up. To form 0.68 moles of iodine molecules, 2×0.68 moles of hydrogen iodide must dissociate. This means a total loss of 1.36 moles of hydrogen iodide, from 10 down to 8.64 moles.

5 **a** $K_c = \dfrac{[N_2O_4(g)]}{[NO_2(g)]^2}$ units are $dm^3\,mol^{-1}$

b $K_c = \dfrac{[NO_2(g)]^2}{[NO(g)]^2[O_2(g)]}$ units are $dm^3\,mol^{-1}$

c $K_c = \dfrac{[NH_3(g)]^2}{[N_2(g)][H_2(g)]^3}$ units are $dm^6\,mol^{-2}$

6

	$H_2(g)$	$CO_2(g)$	$CO(g)$	$H_2O(g)$
Initial concentration/ mol dm^{-3}	10.0	90.0	0	0
Equilibrium concentration/ mol dm^{-3}	10.0 − 9.47 = 0.53	90.0 − 9.47 = 80.53	9.47	9.47

$$K_c = \frac{[CO]\,[H_2O]}{[H_2][CO_2]}$$

$$= \frac{9.47 \times 9.47}{0.53 \times 80.53}$$

$$= 2.10$$

(No units as in this homogeneous reaction, i.e. all reactants and products are in the same state, the total moles of reactants = total moles of products, so the units cancel out.)

7 The forward reaction is exothermic, so an increase in temperature causes the equilibrium to shift to the left. There are less products and more reactants at equilibrium. K_c decreases.

8 **a** The equilibrium position shifts to the left. This is because the forward reaction is exothermic and higher temperature favours the endothermic backward reaction, thereby lowering the temperature according to Le Chatelier's principle. K_c decreases. (The higher temperature will, however, cause an increased rate of reaction.)

b The equilibrium position shifts to the right. This is because the forward reaction causes a decrease in the number of gas molecules so higher pressure favours the forward reaction, thereby decreasing the pressure according to Le Chatelier's principle. K_c is unchanged. (The higher pressure will also cause an increased rate of reaction.)

c The equilibrium position is unchanged. K_c is unchanged. (The catalyst will, however, cause an increased rate of reaction.)

Chapter 13

1 **a** $H_2SO_4(l) + H_2O(l) \rightleftharpoons H_3O^+(aq) + HSO_4^-(aq)$
  B–L acid   B–L base   B–L acid   B–L base

b $CH_3COOH(aq) + H_2O(l) \rightleftharpoons CH_3COO^-(aq) + H_3O^+(aq)$
  B–L acid   B–L base   B–L base   B–L acid

c $CH_3NH_2(aq) + H_2O(l) \longrightarrow CH_3NH_3^+(aq) + OH^-(aq)$
  B–L base   B–L acid   B–L acid   B–L base

d $NH_3(g) + HCl(g) \longrightarrow NH_4^+(s) + Cl^-(s)$
  B–L base   B–L acid   B–L acid   B–L base

2 Pure water is a poor conductor of electricity, which shows that it contains very few ions that can carry a direct current.

3 $K_c = \dfrac{[H^+][OH^-]}{[H_2O]}$

K_c is very small, so the concentrations of the products must be very much smaller than the concentration of water itself. This indicates that only a tiny proportion of pure water exists at any one time as protons and hydroxide ions, a deduction backed by the evidence that water is a poor conductor of electricity.

4 **a** $H_2SO_4 + CuO \longrightarrow CuSO_4 + H_2O$
   and $2H^+ + O^{2-} \longrightarrow H_2O$

b $H_2SO_4 + Na_2CO_3 \longrightarrow Na_2SO_4 + H_2O + CO_2$
   and $2H^+ + CO_3^{2-} \longrightarrow H_2O + CO_2$

c $H_2SO_4 + Mg \longrightarrow MgSO_4 + H_2$
   and $2H^+ + Mg \longrightarrow Mg^{2+} + H_2$

d $H_2SO_4 + 2KOH \longrightarrow K_2SO_4 + 2H_2O$
   and $H^+ + OH^- \longrightarrow H_2O$

5 **a** Energy $= 200\,g \times 4.2\,J\,g^{-1}\,°C^{-1} \times 13.5\,°C = 11\,340\,J$

b $100\,cm^3$ of $2.00\,mol\,dm^{-3}$ acid contain 0.200 moles of H^+ ions. $100\,cm^3$ of $2.00\,mol\,dm^{-3}$ alkali contain 0.200 moles of OH^- ions. This will produce 0.200 moles of water.

c Enthalpy change of neutralisation $= \dfrac{-11340}{0.200}$
   $= -56\,700\,J\,mol^{-1}$ or $-56.7\,kJ\,mol^{-1}$

6 **a** 3.5
  b 2.0
  c 7.4

7 a pH = 0.0

b pH = 0.3

c The aqueous solution contains 3.00 g of hydrogen chloride, HCl, per dm^3. To find the pH we need the hydrogen ion concentration in $mol\,dm^{-3}$.

The relative molecular mass of HCl = (1.0 + 35.5) = 36.5.

Thus the concentration of hydrogen chloride

$= \dfrac{3.00}{36.5}\,mol\,dm^{-3} = 0.0822\,mol\,dm^{-3}$.

Because the hydrogen chloride dissociates completely to form hydrogen ions and chloride ions, the concentration of hydrogen ions is $0.0822\,mol\,dm^{-3}$.

The pH of this acid $= -\log_{10}[H^+] = -\log_{10}[0.0822] = 1.09$.

d Potassium hydroxide dissociates completely in solution:

$$KOH(s) \xrightarrow{\text{water}} K^+(aq) + OH^-(aq)$$
$$\text{0.001 mol} \qquad \text{0.001 mol} \quad \text{0.001 mol}$$

The concentration of hydroxide ions is the same as the concentration of the potassium hydroxide.

$K_w = [H^+][OH^-] = 1.00 \times 10^{-14}\,mol^2\,dm^{-6}$

so

$[H^+] = \dfrac{1.00 \times 10^{-14}\,mol^2\,dm^{-6}}{[OH^-]}$

$= \dfrac{1.00 \times 10^{-14}\,mol^2\,dm^{-6}}{0.001\,mol\,dm^{-3}}$

$= 1.00 \times 10^{-11}\,mol\,dm^{-3}$

The pH of this acid $= -\log_{10}[H^+] = -\log_{10}[10^{-11}] = 11.0$

e Sodium hydroxide ionises completely in aqueous solution:

$$NaOH(s) \xrightarrow{\text{water}} Na^+(aq) + OH^-(aq)$$

The relative molecular mass of NaOH
= (23.0 + 16.0 + 1.0) = 40.0

An aqueous solution containing 0.200 g of NaOH

per dm^3 contains $\dfrac{0.200}{40.0}$ mol NaOH, i.e.

$5 \times 10^{-3}\,mol\,dm^{-3}$. The concentration of hydroxide ions is therefore $5.00 \times 10^{-3}\,mol\,dm^{-3}$.

$K_w = [H^+][OH^-] = 1.00 \times 10^{-14}\,mol^2\,dm^{-6}$

Therefore $[H^+] \times 5.00 \times 10^{-3} = 1.00 \times 10^{-14}$

$[H^+] = \dfrac{1 \times 10^{-14}}{5 \times 10^{-3}} = 2.00 \times 10^{-12}\,mol\,dm^{-3}$

Therefore pH $= -\log_{10}[H^+] = -\log_{10}(2.00 \times 10^{-12})$
$= 11.7$

8

Acid	Base
HNO_3	NO_3^-
H_2SO_3	HSO_3^-
$[Fe(H_2O)_6]^{3+}$	$[Fe(H_2O)_5(OH)]^{2+}$
HF	F^-
HNO_2	NO_2^-
HCOOH	$HCOO^-$
C_6H_5COOH	$C_6H_5COO^-$
CH_3COOH	CH_3COO^-
CH_3CH_2COOH	$CH_3CH_2COO^-$
$[Al(H_2O)_6]^{3+}$	$[Al(H_2O)_5(OH)]^{2+}$
$CO_2 + H_2O$	HCO_3^-
$SiO_2 + H_2O$	$HSiO_3^-$
HCO_3^-	CO_3^{2-}
$HSiO_3^-$	SiO_3^{2-}
H_2O	OH^-

9 a $K_a = \dfrac{[H^+]^2}{[\text{benzoic acid}]}$

Therefore $[H^+] = \sqrt{6.3 \times 10^{-5} \times 0.020}$
pH $= -\log_{10}[H^+] = 2.95$

b pH = 3.5. Aqueous solutions of aluminium salts are surprisingly acidic. An accidental tipping of aluminium salts into a reservoir in Cornwall created tap water acidic enough to dissolve copper from pipes and to worry large numbers of people about the possibility of being poisoned.

c pH = 2.4

10 a $1.26 \times 10^{-3}\,mol\,dm^{-3}$

b $2.00 \times 10^{-4}\,mol\,dm^{-3}$

c $6.31 \times 10^{-12}\,mol\,dm^{-3}$

11 a $[H^+]$ is $5.01 \times 10^{-5}\,mol\,dm^{-3}$.
K_a is $1.26 \times 10^{-7}\,mol\,dm^{-3}$.

b $0.0500\,mol\,dm^{-3}$ propanoic acid has a pH of 3.1. $[H^+]$ is $7.94 \times 10^{-4}\,mol\,dm^{-3}$. K_a is 1.26×10^{-5}.

c $0.0100\,mol\,dm^{-3}$ methanoic acid has a pH of 2.9. $[H^+]$ is $1.26 \times 10^{-3}\,mol\,dm^{-3}$. K_a is 1.58×10^{-4}.

12 Strong acid–strong base: the slope of the graph is steep over the range pH 3.5 to pH 10. Any indicator with a colour change range within these limits is suitable: bromocresol green, methyl red, bromothymol blue or phenolphthalein. The others in the table are not suitable.

13 Strong acid–weak base: the slope is steep over the range 7.0–2.0. The indicators we could use are methyl yellow, methyl orange, bromophenol blue, bromocresol green or methyl red. We might get away with using bromothymol blue, but all the others in the table are unsuitable.

14 Weak acid–strong base: methyl orange starts changing colour when the pH is 3.2 and stops at pH 4.4, so you would see no colour change with this indicator.

15 a Strong acid–weak base: methyl orange or bromophenol blue.

b Strong acid–strong base: bromocresol green, methyl red, bromothymol blue or phenolphthalein.

c The equilibrium constant for aspirin is similar to that of methanoic acid, so aspirin is a weak acid. Potassium hydroxide is a strong base, so the sensitive region for the indicator would be in the range pH 7–11. Phenolphthalein would be the best choice of indicator.

16 a The conjugate acid is NH_4^+ and the conjugate base is NH_3.

b When dilute hydrochloric acid is added, the additional hydrogen ions are accepted by the ammonia molecules. You can think of the additional H^+ ions reacting with the OH^- ions in the equilibrium mixture shown below (forming H_2O):

$$NH_3(aq) + H_2O(l) \rightleftharpoons NH_4^+(aq) + OH^-(aq)$$

The position of equilibrium then shifts to the right to replace OH^- ions removed from the mixture. When dilute sodium hydroxide is added, the position of equilibrium shifts to the left, to remove the additional $OH^-(aq)$ ions.

c Because NH_3 is a weak base there will not be enough NH_4^+ ions in the equilibrium mixture of an ammonia solution (as the equilibrium lies well over to the left) to remove additional OH^- ions (alkali) added.

17 a The equation for the equilibrium reaction is

$$HCOOH(aq) \rightleftharpoons H^+(aq) + HCOO^-(aq)$$

from which we can write the equilibrium constant expression:

$$K_a = \frac{[H^+][HCOO^-]}{[HCOOH]}$$

Rearranging this equation:

$$[H^+] = K_a \times \frac{[HCOOH]}{[HCOO^-]} \text{ mol dm}^{-3}$$

Substituting the data given produces:

$$[H^+] = 1.6 \times 10^{-4} \times \frac{0.0500}{0.100} \text{ mol dm}^{-3}$$

$$= 8.00 \times 10^{-5} \text{ mol dm}^{-3}$$

so pH $= -\log_{10}(8.00 \times 10^{-5})$
$= -(-4.096) = 4.10$

b Using the method in part **a**, pH = 4.8

Chapter 14

1 a The energy change associated with a chemical reaction.

b A chemical change in which energy is released to the surroundings; $\Delta H^\ominus$ is negative.

c A chemical change in which energy is taken in from the surroundings; $\Delta H^\ominus$ is positive.

2 The total enthalpy change for a chemical reaction is independent of the route by which the reaction takes place, provided initial and final conditions are the same.

3 a $\frac{1}{2}O_2(g) \longrightarrow O(g)$

b $Cs(g) \longrightarrow Cs^+(g) + e^-$

c $K(s) + \frac{1}{2}Cl_2(g) \longrightarrow KCl(s)$

d $I(g) + e^- \longrightarrow I^-(g)$

e $Ba(s) \longrightarrow Ba(g)$

4 a

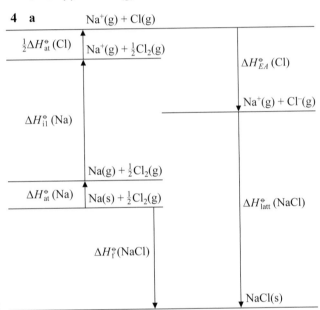

b -787 kJ mol^{-1}

5 a

b

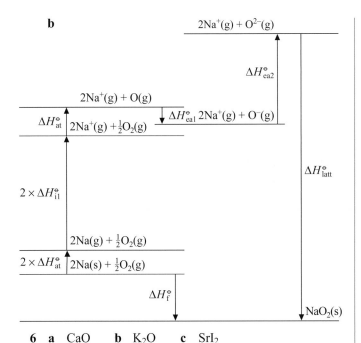

6 a CaO **b** K_2O **c** SrI_2

7 LiF, Li_2O, MgO.
LiF is composed of singly charged ions so has the least attraction between ions, Li_2O has one doubly charged ion, and MgO has two doubly charged ions so has the most attraction between ions.

8 Sodium bromide has a negative enthalpy change of solution. It is soluble in water. Sodium chloride has a small positive enthalpy change of solution. It is soluble in water. Silver chloride and silver bromide have larger positive enthalpy changes of solution. They are insoluble in water.

9 a $Na^+(g) + (aq) \longrightarrow Na^+(aq)$
b $Cl^-(g) + (aq) \longrightarrow Cl^-(aq)$
c $NaCl(s) + (aq) \longrightarrow NaCl(aq)$

10 a A sensible prediction for the $\Delta H_{hyd}^{\ominus}$ of Na^+ would be around $-420\,kJ\,mol^{-1}$ (the actual value is $-406\,kJ\,mol^{-1}$). This is larger in magnitude (or *more exothermic*) than the value for K^+ as Na^+ has a smaller ionic radius than K^+ and therefore a higher charge density. It is smaller than the value for Li^+ as Na^+ has a larger ionic radius than Li^+ and therefore a lower charge density.
b Mg^{2+} is more highly charged *and* has a smaller ionic radius (due to one less occupied shell of electrons) than K^+ so has a much higher charge density, therefore the $\Delta H_{hyd}^{\ominus}$ of Mg^{2+} is much more exothermic than the $\Delta H_{hyd}^{\ominus}$ of K^+.

11 $\Delta H_{latt}^{\ominus} + \Delta H_{sol}^{\ominus} = \Delta H_{hyd}^{\ominus}$
$-2592\,kJ + -55\,kJ = \Delta H_{hyd}^{\ominus}(Mg^{2+}) + 2 \times \Delta H_{hyd}^{\ominus}(Cl^-)$
$-2647\,kJ = -1920\,kJ + 2 \times \Delta H_{hyd}^{\ominus}(Cl^-)$
$-2647\,kJ + 1920\,kJ = 2 \times \Delta H_{hyd}^{\ominus}(Cl^-)$
Therefore $\Delta H_{hyd}^{\ominus}(Cl^-)$ is $-363.5\,kJ\,mol^{-1}$.

Chapter 15

1 The entropy of a substance is the degree of disorder of that substance.

2 Starting with most disordered, therefore the one with the highest entropy: oxygen, carbon monoxide, water, copper.

3 a $386 - (393 + 192) = -199\,J\,K^{-1}\,mol^{-1}$. The entropy change is negative. There is a decrease in the disorder of the system.
b $396 - (131 + 152) = +113\,J\,K^{-1}\,mol^{-1}$. The entropy change is positive. There is an increase in the disorder of the system.

4 a The entropy change is negative and there is a decrease in the disorder of the system because there is a decrease in the number of gas molecules involved.
b The entropy change is positive and there is an increase in the disorder of the system because there is an increase in the number of gas molecules involved.

5 a $72\,°C + 273 = 345\,K$
b $246\,K - 273 = -27\,°C$
c $0\,K - 273 = -273\,°C$
d $273\,K$ and $373\,K$

6 a $\Delta G = \Delta H - T\Delta S$
b $\Delta G = -190\,000 - (360 \times -121) = -146\,440\,J\,mol^{-1}$ or $-146\,kJ\,mol^{-1}$
c ΔG has a large negative value. The reaction is spontaneous and goes to completion.
d The reaction causes a reduction in the number of gas molecules, so there is a decrease in the disorder of the system.

7 a $\Delta G = \Delta H - T\Delta S$
$\Delta G = +84\,000 - (360 \times 83.0) = +54\,120\,J\,mol^{-1}$ or $+54.1\,kJ\,mol^{-1}$
b ΔG has a positive sign and its magnitude is well over $+20\,kJ\,mol^{-1}$. This reaction will not occur spontaneously at $360\,K$.
c If the reaction takes place at a sufficiently high temperature so that $\Delta H - T\Delta S$ becomes negative it will occur spontaneously.
d $\Delta G = \Delta H - T\Delta S$
$-20\,000 = +84\,000 - (T \times 83.0)$
$T = \dfrac{104\,000}{83} = 1253\,K$
e The reaction causes an increase in the number of gas molecules, so there is an increase in the disorder of the system.

Chapter 16

1 **a** Cu^{2+}
   b Fe
   c Cl^-
   d Cu^{2+}
   e Fe

2 **a** +6
   b +2
   c +3
   d +6

3 **a** +4
   b +6
   c 0
   d +7
   e +3
   f +2

4 *First reaction:*
Fe: $0 \longrightarrow +2$; reducing agent
H: $+1 \longrightarrow 0$; oxidising agent
Cl: -1 and -1
Second reaction:
Fe: $0 \longrightarrow +3$; reducing agent
H: $+1 \longrightarrow 0$; oxidising agent
Cl: -1 and -1

5 *For the Fe^{2+}/Fe half-cell:*
   a $Fe^{2+} + 2e^- \longrightarrow Fe$
   b $-0.44\,V$
   c Fe^{2+}: $1.00\,mol\,dm^{-3}$
For the Cr^{2+}/Cr half-cell:
   a $Cr^{2+} + 2e^- \longrightarrow Cr$
   b $-0.91\,V$
   c Cr^{2+}: $1.00\,mol\,dm^{-3}$
For the Ag^+/Ag half-cell:
   a $Ag^+ + e^- \longrightarrow Ag$
   b $+0.80\,V$
   c Ag^+: $1.00\,mol\,dm^{-3}$
In all three cells the temperature must be 298 K
and in the standard hydrogen electrodes the $H^+(aq)$
concentration must be $1.00\,mol\,dm^{-3}$, the H_2 pressure
must be 1 atmosphere (101 kPa) and electrical contact
must be made by platinum.

6 $+1.52\,V$

7 298 K, all gases at a pressure of 1 atmosphere (101 kPa),
all relevant concentrations at $1.00\,mol\,dm^{-3}$.

8 Platinum does not take part in reactions. It is an
inert electrode.

9
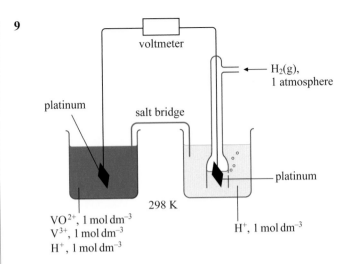

10 a $S + 2e^- \rightleftharpoons S^{2-}$
   b $E^\ominus = -0.51\,V$

11
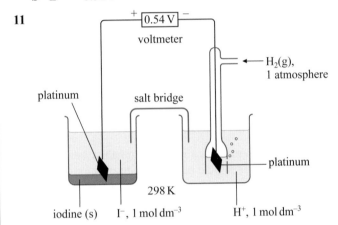

12 a Cr^{2+}
   b Ag

13 a
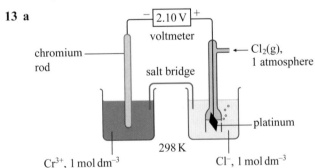

   b $1.36 - (-0.74) = 2.10\,V$
   c Chlorine half-cell.

14 a

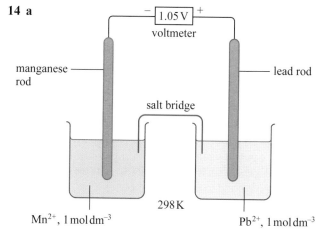

b $(-0.13) - (-1.18) = 1.05\,V$
c Lead half-cell.

15 $Fe^{3+} + I^- \longrightarrow Fe^{2+} + I_2$

16 a Yes.
$MnO_4^- + 5Cl^- + 8H^+ \longrightarrow Mn^{2+} + \frac{5}{2}Cl_2 + 4H_2O$

$MnO_4^- + 8H^+ + 5e^- \rightleftharpoons Mn^{2+} + 4H_2O$, with its *more* positive $E^\ominus$ value, will proceed in a forward direction while $Cl_2 + 2e^- \rightleftharpoons 2Cl^-$ proceeds in a backward direction.

b No.
$MnO_4^- + 8H^+ + 5e^- \rightleftharpoons Mn^{2+} + 4H_2O$, with its *less* positive $E^\ominus$ value, cannot proceed in a forward direction while $F_2 + 2e^- \rightleftharpoons 2F^-$ proceeds in a backward direction.

c Yes.
$V^{2+} + H^+ \longrightarrow \frac{1}{2}H_2 + V^{3+}$

$2H^+ + 2e^- \rightleftharpoons H_2$, with its *more* positive $E^\ominus$ value, will proceed in a forward direction while $V^{3+} + e^- \rightleftharpoons V^{2+}$ proceeds in a backward direction.

d No.
$2H^+ + 2e^- \rightleftharpoons H_2$, with its *less* positive $E^\ominus$ value, cannot proceed in a forward direction while $Fe^{3+} + e^- \rightleftharpoons Fe^{2+}$ proceeds in a backward direction.

17 a Cell voltage $= 1.52 - 1.36 = +0.16\,V$, therefore yes.
b Cell voltage $= 1.52 - 2.87 = -1.35\,V$, therefore no.
c Cell voltage $= 0.00 - (-0.26) = +0.26\,V$, therefore yes.
d Cell voltage $= 0.00 - 0.77 = -0.77\,V$, therefore no.

18 a i $E =$ more than $1.33\,V$
  ii $E =$ less than $1.33\,V$
  iii $E =$ less than $1.33\,V$
 b i Stronger oxidising agent.
  ii Weaker oxidising agent.
  iii Weaker oxidising agent.
 c High concentration $Cr_2O_7^{2-}$, high concentration H^+, low concentration Cr^{3+}.

d Increasing the concentrations of reactants forces equilibrium to shift to the right in order to reduce these concentrations. Therefore, E goes up and the $Cr_2O_7^{2-}/H^+$ solution becomes a stronger oxidising agent.

19 $E^\ominus$-based predictions refer to standard conditions, but lab conditions are not usually standard. (However, if the $E^\ominus$ values for the two half-equations differ by more than $0.30\,$volts, $E^\ominus$-based predictions are usually correct.)
$E^\ominus$ values may predict that a reaction will occur, even though in reality the reaction may have such a slow rate that it is not observed.

20 Add a catalyst; increase temperature; increase concentration of dissolved reactants; increase pressure of gaseous reactants; increase surface area of solid reactants.

21 a i 0 to +2
  ii +4 to +2
 b Lead is oxidised at the lead plate. Its oxidation number is increasing; it is losing electrons. Lead is reduced at the lead oxide plate. Its oxidation number is decreasing; it is gaining electrons.

22 a $NiO_2 + 2H_2O + 2e^- \longrightarrow Ni(OH)_2 + 2OH^-$ has a more positive $E^\ominus$ so it proceeds forwards.
$Cd(OH)_2 + 2e^- \rightarrow Cd + 2OH^-$ has a less positive $E^\ominus$ so it proceeds backwards.
 b $1.30\,V$
 c $Cd + NiO_2 + 2H_2O \longrightarrow Cd(OH)_2 + Ni(OH)_2$
 d $Cd(OH)_2 + Ni(OH)_2 \longrightarrow Cd + NiO_2 + 2H_2O$

23 Fuel cell vehicles.

24 a Hydrogen loses electrons forming H^+ ions (oxidation).
 b Oxygen gains electrons and combines with H^+ ions forming water (reduction).
 c By diffusing through a membrane.
 d Via the external circuit.
 e $2H_2 + O_2 \longrightarrow 2H_2O$

25 a Methane is CH_4.
One mole of methane has a mass of $16.0\,g$, out of which $4.0\,g$ is hydrogen.
$$\frac{4.0}{16.0} \times 100\% = 25.0\%$$
Methanol is CH_3OH.
One mole of methanol has a mass of $32.0\,g$, out of which $4.0\,g$ is hydrogen.
$$\frac{4.0}{32.0} \times 100\% = 12.5\%$$
 b $CH_3OH + 1\frac{1}{2}O_2 \longrightarrow CO_2 + 2H_2O$
(or $2CH_3OH + 3O_2 \longrightarrow 2CO_2 + 4H_2O$)

c A hydrogen–oxygen fuel cell produces water as its only product. A methanol–oxygen fuel cell also produces carbon dioxide, which may be responsible for global warming.

26 a $40 \times 5 \times 10^7 = 2 \times 10^9\,J$

b $2 \times 10^9\,J \times 0.4 = 8 \times 10^8\,J$

c $\dfrac{8 \times 10^8}{1 \times 10^6} = 800\,km$

27 a $400 \times 143\,000 = 5.72 \times 10^7\,J$

b $5.72 \times 10^7\,J \times 0.6 = 3.43 \times 10^7\,J$

c $\dfrac{3.43 \times 10^7}{1 \times 10^6} = 34.3\,km$

d The range of the FCV between refuelling is far too small when compared with the petrol-engined car in SAQ 26.

28 If a material adsorbs hydrogen then the hydrogen is stored on the surface of the material.
If a material absorbs hydrogen then the hydrogen is stored in the bulk of the material.

29 The problems include:
- high production costs of hydrogen–oxygen fuel cells
- toxic chemicals used in the production of hydrogen–oxygen fuel cells
- limited lifetime of hydrogen–oxygen fuel cells
- the cost of replacing and disposing of spent hydrogen–oxygen fuel cells
- the development of new engineering skills associated with the maintenance of hydrogen–oxygen fuel cells
- the development of new engineering skills associated with the supply of hydrogen
- problems associated with storing and transporting hydrogen, including difficulty in storing a large amount of a gas, energy costs of liquefaction, safety issues, adsorption or absorption methods are still in development, adsorbers and absorbers have a limited working lifetime
- public reluctance to accept hydrogen as a new fuel
- political reluctance to commit to expensive long-term planning
- the need for a large-scale source of electrical energy to supply the hydrogen.

Chapter 17

1 a $[Ar]3d^5 4s^1$

b $[Ar]3d^3$

c $[Ar]3d^{10}4s^1$

d $[Ar]3d^9$

e $[Ar]3d^5 4s^2$

f $[Ar]3d^5$

2 a +6

b +3

3 a $Ni^{2+}(aq) + 2OH^-(aq) \longrightarrow Ni(OH)_2(s)$

b $Ti^{3+}(aq) + 3OH^-(aq) \longrightarrow Ti(OH)_3(s)$

4 a A central positive ion with one or more ligand species datively bonded to it.

b An atom, neutral molecule or negative ion which is able to use one or more lone-pairs to bond datively to a positive ion.

c A ligand with two lone-pairs which can each form a dative bond to a positive ion.

5 a The number of dative bonds formed between the ligands and the central positive ion in a complex ion.

b i 6

ii 4

iii 6

iv 4

c i 3+

ii 2+

iii 3+

iv 3+

6 a

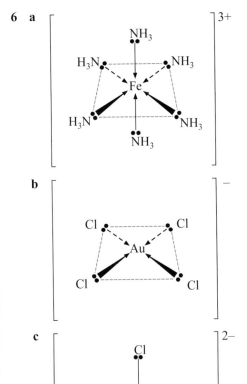

7 a

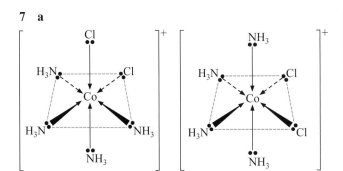

b

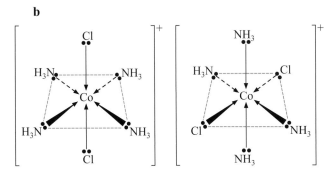

8 a The *trans* isomer is isomer 3.

b Optical isomerism.

c

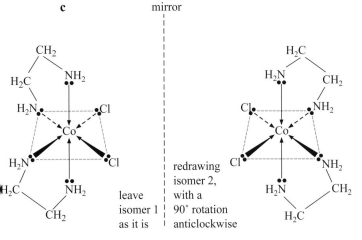

redrawing
isomer 2,
with a
90° rotation
anticlockwise

leave
isomer 1
as it is

d Co^{2+}

9 a The heat of the bench mat makes the water evaporate. $[CoCl_4]^{2-}$ ions are formed and the pink circle turns blue like the rest of the paper.

b Ligand substitution.

c $[Co(H_2O)_6]^{2+} + 4Cl^- \longrightarrow [CoCl_4]^{2-} + 6H_2O$
or $[Co(H_2O)_6]^{2+} + 4Cl^- \rightleftharpoons [CoCl_4]^{2-} + 6H_2O$

10 a $\dfrac{[FeSCN^{2+}]}{[Fe^{3+}][SCN^-]}$

$\dfrac{[Hg(CN)_4{}^{2-}]}{[Hg^{2+}][CN^-]^4}$

b $[Hg(CN)_4]^{2-}$ as its K_{stab} is (much) larger.

11 a $[Zn(CN)_4]^{2-}$ since its K_{stab} is larger.

b CN– ligands will substitute for NH_3 ligands in $[Zn(NH_3)_4]^{2+}$, forming $[Zn(CN)_4]^{2-}$. This happens because $[Zn(CN)_4]^{2-}$ is more stable than $[Zn(NH_3)_4]^{2+}$.
equation:

$$4CN^- + [Zn(NH_3)_4]^{2+} \longrightarrow 4NH_3 + [Zn(CN)_4]^{2-}$$

c Nothing happens (except at very high concentrations of ammonia). Nothing happens because $[Zn(CN)_4]^{2-}$ is more stable than $[Zn(NH_3)_4]^{2+}$.

12 a As a ligand to an Fe^{2+} ion in a haemoglobin molecule.

b Haemoglobin carries oxygen from the lungs because oxygen concentration in the lungs is high, so ligand substitution occurs at the Fe^{2+} ions. Haemoglobin carries carbon dioxide from respiring tissues because carbon dioxide concentration in the respiring tissues is high, so ligand substitution occurs at the Fe^{2+} ions.

c Carbon monoxide gas forms a more stable complex with Fe^{2+} ions than oxygen does. The carbon monoxide molecules remain bound to the Fe^{2+} ions even in situations where the oxygen concentrations are high. The haemoglobin therefore fails to transport oxygen to the respiring tissues that need it.

13 $6Fe^{2+} + Cr_2O_7{}^{2-} + 14H^+ \longrightarrow 6Fe^{3+} + 2Cr^{3+} + 7H_2O$

14 a $23.50\,cm^3 = 0.02350\,dm^3$
$n = V \times c$
so $n = 0.02350 \times 0.0400 = 0.000\,940$ moles

b The equation for the reaction in the titration is:

$$5Fe^{2+} + MnO_4^- + 8H^+ \longrightarrow 5Fe^{3+} + Mn^{2+} + 4H_2O$$

Therefore the number of moles of Fe^{2+}
$= 5 \times 0.000\,940 = 0.00470$ moles

c moles of Fe = moles of Fe^{2+} = 0.00470 moles
mass of Fe = $n \times A_r = 0.00470 \times 55.8 = 0.262$ g

d percentage mass of iron = $\dfrac{0.262}{0.420} \times 100\% = 62.4\%$

15 a $\dfrac{47.8}{1000} \times 0.200 = 0.00956$ mol

b 0.00956 mol

c $0.00956 \times 63.5 = 0.60706$ g

d $\dfrac{0.60706\,g}{1\,g} \times 100\% = 60.7\%$

The final answer has been rounded to 3 significant figures as that is the accuracy of the data.

Glossary

acid dissociation constant K_a is the equilibrium constant for a weak acid HA:

$$K_a = \frac{[H^+][A^-]}{[HA]}$$

Unit: $mol\,dm^{-3}$.

addition polymerisation A polymerisation reaction in which a polymer is formed by a repeated addition reaction.

adsorption chromatography A method of chromatography where separation of polar solute molecules is achieved by their being held on the surface of a polar solid stationary phase.

aliphatic compound An organic compound that does not contain any arene rings.

alkanes Hydrocarbons containing C–C single bonds only.

alkenes Hydrocarbons containing a C=C bond.

amino acids Naturally occurring building blocks of protein molecules. The structure of an amino acid consists of a carboxylic acid group and an amino group attached to the same carbon chain.

amphoteric Amphoteric substances can behave as an acid or a base, depending on the conditions.

arenes Hydrocarbons containing one or more benzene rings.

aromatic compound An organic compound which contains one or more arene rings.

bidentate A bidentate ligand has two lone-pairs of electrons which can form two separate dative covalent bonds to a transition metal ion.

bifunctional Describes an organic compound containing two functional groups, for example amino acids, which contain the amino group and a carboxylic acid functional group.

biodiesel A fuel made by processing vegetable oils extracted from crops such as oilseed rape.

buffer solution A solution that minimises changes in pH, even when moderate amounts of acid or base are added to it. It consists of an acid and its conjugate base, where one of the pair is weak.

chiral centre (or chiral carbon) A (carbon) atom in a molecule attached to four different groups.

chromatography The separation of dissolved substances by their different speeds of movement through or over a separating material.

complex ion A transition metal ion bonded to one or more electron-donating species (ligands) by dative covalent bonds from the ligands to the metal.

condensation polymerisation A polymerisation reaction in which the monomers are joined together by condensation reactions.

conjugate pair In an acid–base equilibrium there are two conjugate acid–base pairs:
- the acid in the forward reaction and the base in the reverse reaction
- the base in the forward reaction and the acid in the reverse reaction.

coordination number The number of dative bonds formed between the ligands and a central transition metal ion in a complex.

coupling reaction The reaction in which a diazonium dye is formed.

delocalised When electron pairs are shared between three or more atoms as, for example, in benzene.

diazonium ion An organic cation whose formula is $R–N_2^+$, where R is an aryl or alkyl group.

diazotisation The reaction of phenylamine and nitrous acid (nitric(III) acid), at below 10 °C, in which a diazonium salt is formed as an intermediate in the production of diazonium dyes.

diglyceride A compound formed when any *two* of the alcohol groups in propane-1,2,3-triol have been esterified.

displayed formula A formula which shows all the covalent bonds and all the atoms present.

dynamic equilibrium An equilibrium is dynamic at the molecular level; both forward and reverse processes occur at the same rate; a closed system is required and macroscopic properties remain constant.

E/Z (*cis–trans*) isomerism Isomerism in alkenes that have two different groups on each of the carbon atoms involved in the double bond. A *cis* (or *Z*) isomer has identical groups on the same side of the double bond. A *trans* (or *E*) isomer has identical groups on opposite sides of the double bond. E/Z (*cis–trans*) isomerism occurs because a C=C bond cannot rotate.

electrochemical cell An exothermic chemical reaction set up as two half-cells in two separate containers so that the energy released can produce an electric current between them.

electrode potential The voltage measured for a half-cell. Another half-cell is essential for this measurement to be made.

electron affinity (first) The enthalpy change when one electron is added to each of one mole of gaseous atoms, to form one mole of gaseous ions.

electrophilic addition The type of reaction in which an electrophile, which accepts a pair of electrons from a C=C double bond, reacts with an alkene resulting in addition across the double bond. No other product is formed in the reaction.

electrophilic substitution The type of reaction in which one or more hydrogen atoms are replaced in a benzene ring following attack by an electrophile. The benzene ring retains its system of delocalised electrons at the end of the reaction.

empirical formula The simplest whole-number ratio of the elements present in a compound.

enantiomers Optical isomers.

enthalpy change of hydration The energy released when one mole of gaseous ions dissolves in sufficient water to form a solution of infinite dilution.

enthalpy change of solution The energy released when one mole of an ionic solid dissolves in sufficient water to form a solution of infinite dilution.

entropy The degree of disorder of a system, measured in $J K^{-1} mol^{-1}$.

ester An organic compound (represented as R^1COOR^2, in which R^1 and R^2 are alkyl or aryl groups) formed by the reaction of an alcohol with a carboxylic acid, using a strong acid catalyst.

esterification The acid-catalysed formation of an ester from a carboxylic acid and an alcohol.

fatty acids Long-chain carboxylic acids obtained from oils or fats. Monounsaturated fatty acids contain one carbon–carbon double bond. Polyunsaturated fatty acids contain more than one carbon–carbon double bond.

fuel cell A source of electrical energy which comes directly from energy stored in chemicals in the cell, one of which is oxygen, which may come from the air.

functional group An atom or group of atoms that gives specific chemical properties to a molecule.

gelatinous Jelly-like.

general formula A formula which may be written for each homologous series (for example, C_nH_{2n+2} for alkanes).

half-cell Half of an electrochemical cell. One half-cell supplies electrons, the other half-cell receives electrons.

half-equation An equation that describes what is happening in one half-cell. Alternatively, in a redox reaction a half-equation can be used to describe only the reduction reaction or only the oxidation reaction.

homologous series A series of organic molecules with the same functional group. Compounds in the same homologous series show similar chemical properties.

indicators These can change colour at a particular pH value.

initiation The first step in a radical substitution in which the radicals are generated by heat or ultraviolet light.

integration trace A stepped line on an NMR spectrum which helps us identify the relative numbers of each type of proton (^1H) present in a compound. The area under a peak on the spectrum is proportional to the height of the step superimposed on it.

ionic product of water $K_w = [H^+][OH^-]$ $= 1.00 \times 10^{-14} mol^2 dm^{-6}$ at 25 °C.

ionisation energy The first ionisation energy is the energy needed to remove one electron from each atom in one mole of gaseous atoms of an element. Successive ionisation energies are the sequence of first, second, third, fourth, etc., ionisation energies needed to remove the first, second, third, fourth, etc., electrons from each atom in one mole of gaseous atoms of an element. (Note: From the second ionisation energy onwards, successive electrons are removed from positively charged gaseous ions.)

isoelectric point The pH of a solution in which an amino acid will be at its maximum concentration of zwitterion.

isomers Compounds with the same molecular formula but with different arrangements of atoms.

lattice enthalpy The enthalpy change when one mole of an ionic compound is formed from its gaseous ions under standard conditions (298 K, 101 kPa).

Le Chatelier's principle When any of the conditions affecting the position of a dynamic equilibrium are changed, then the position of that equilibrium will shift to minimise that change.

ligand A species that can use one or more lone-pairs to form dative covalent bonds to a transition metal ion, forming a complex ion.

mobile phase The solvent in the chromatography process which moves through the column or over the paper. It is either a liquid or a gas.

molecular formula A formula which shows the total numbers of atoms of different elements present in a molecule of the compound.

molecular ion (M^+) The ion formed by the loss of one electron from a complete molecule during mass spectrometry.

monodentate A monodentate ligand can use one lone-pair of electrons to form one dative covalent bond to a transition metal ion.

monoglyceride A compound formed when only *one* of the alcohol groups in propane-1,2,3-triol has been esterified.

monomer The small molecule used to build a polymer molecule.

monounsaturated Describes a fatty acid containing one carbon–carbon double bond.

multidentate A multidentate ligand has more than one lone-pair of electrons and can form more than one dative covalent bond to a transition metal ion.

nitrating mixture A mixture of concentrated nitric and sulfuric acids used to produce NO_2^+ – an electrophile that can nitrate benzene rings.

nomenclature The international system of naming compounds such as organic compounds.

nucleophilic addition The type of reaction in which a carbonyl compound reacts with a nucleophile (a species that can donate a pair of electrons).

nucleophilic substitution The type of reaction in which a nucleophile displaces another group from around a carbon atom that has a partial positive charge.

octahedral The shape that six atoms, ions or molecules take up around a central atom; the bond angles will be 90°.

optical isomers Molecules that are non-superimposable mirror images of each other. The two isomers (known as enantiomers) rotate the plane of polarised light in opposite directions.

optical resolution The separation of a mixture of optically active isomers (enantiomers).

order of reaction The power to which the concentration of a reactant is raised in the rate equation. *Zero-order* indicates that the reactant concentration does not affect the rate, rate $\propto$ [A]^0. *First-order* indicates that the reactant concentration is directly proportional to the rate, rate $\propto$ [A]^1. *Second-order* indicates that the square of the reactant concentration is directly proportional to the rate, rate $\propto$ [A]^2.

oxidation state (or oxidation number) A number (with a positive or negative sign) assigned to the atoms of each element in an ion or compound. Oxidation states are determined using a set of rules devised by chemists.

oxidising agent A species that takes one or more electrons away from another species in a reaction.

partition The division of solutes between two phases. For example, in chromatography the movement of a solute in a solution is determined by its relative solubilities in the mobile phase and in the stationary phase.

peptide link The amide link (–NHCO–) in polypeptides and proteins.

pharmacological activity The effectiveness of a drug.

photodegradable Describes a plastic that is broken down by light.

plastic Capable of being moulded into a new shape. The word is commonly used as a general term for 'polymer'.

polyamide A polymer with repeating amide links made by condensation polymerisation, e.g. nylon, Kevlar.

polydentate A polydentate ligand has more than one lone-pair of electrons and can form more than one dative covalent bond to a transition metal ion.

polyunsaturated Describes a fatty acid containing two or more carbon–carbon double bonds.

primary amine An amine in which the nitrogen atom is bonded to *one* alkyl group and two hydrogen atoms.

primary structure The sequence of amino acids in a protein.

propagation The stage in a radical substitution which constitutes the two reaction steps of the chain reaction.

rate constant The proportionality constant k in a rate equation (rate = k[A]^m[B]^n).

rate-determining step The slowest step in a reaction mechanism.

receptor molecule A molecule that medicines or other agents bind to in the body.

reducing agent A species that donates one or more electrons to another species in a reaction.

refractory lining The material used to form the inner surface of a furnace.

repeat unit The smallest section of a polymer which, when repeated, gives the polymer.

retardation factor (R_f value) Measured from chromatograms:

$$R_f = \frac{\text{distance moved by centre of solute spot}}{\text{distance moved by front of mobile phase}}$$

retention time The time taken for a component of a mixture to pass through a gas chromatography column.

salt bridge A piece of filter paper soaked in potassium nitrate solution used to make electrical contact between the half-cells in an electrochemical cell.

secondary amine An amine in which the nitrogen atom is bonded to *two* alkyl groups and one hydrogen atom.

skeletal formula A formula which shows the carbon skeleton only – hydrogen atoms are omitted and other atoms are shown as in a structural formula. For example, the skeletal formula of propylcyclohexane is:

solute A substance dissolved in a solvent.

solvent A liquid or gas used to dissolve substances.

stability constant An equilibrium constant, known as K_{stab}, that gives information on the stability of a complex ion. More stable complex ions have larger values of K_{stab}. (The units of K_{stab} can vary.)

standard conditions A temperature of 298 K, all solutions at a concentration of 1.00 mol dm^{-3}, all gases at a pressure of 1 atmosphere (101 kPa).

standard electrode potential The electrode potential of a half-cell when measured with a standard hydrogen electrode as the other half-cell. All conditions must be standard. If this value is negative the half-cell donates electrons to the standard hydrogen electrode. If this value is positive the half-cell receives electrons from the standard hydrogen electrode.

standard enthalpy change of atomisation The enthalpy change when one mole of gaseous atoms are formed from an element in its standard state.

standard hydrogen electrode A half-cell in which hydrogen gas at a pressure of one atmosphere (101 kPa) bubbles into a solution of 1.00 mol dm^{-3} H$^+$ ions. Electrical contact is made with platinum wire. This half-cell is given a standard electrode potential of 0.00 V; all other standard electrode potentials are measured relative to it.

stationary phase The separating material in chromatography, such as solid particles packed into a column, water held in the fibres of paper, or a viscous liquid coated onto a solid surface.

stereoisomerism Isomerism in which molecules have the same structural formula but the atoms are in a different spatial arrangement.

stereoisomers Molecules containing the same atoms with the same order of bonds but with different spatial arrangements of atoms.

structural formula A formula which shows how the atoms are joined together in a molecule.

structural isomers Isomers which have the same molecular formula but different structural formulae.

support An inert material such as paper that carries the stationary phase in chromatography.

systematic The systematic name is the name of an organic compound, following internationally agreed rules.

termination The step at the end of a radical substitution reaction in which two radicals combine.

tertiary amine An amine in which the nitrogen atom is bonded to *three* alkyl groups.

tetrahedral The shape that four atoms, ions or molecules take up around a central atom; the bond angles will be 109.5°.

thermoplastic Describes a plastic which softens when heated, enabling it to be remoulded.

thermosetting Describes a plastic that cannot be softened by heating once it is formed.

three-dimensional formulae The structural formula of an organic compound using wedged lines and dotted lines for bonds (wedged line = bond pointing forwards, dotted line = bond pointing backwards). An ordinary line indicates a bond in the plane of the paper. For example, the three-dimensional formula of methane is:

transition element A metal element that forms at least one ion with a partially filled d subshell. Not zinc or scandium.

triglyceride A compound formed when all *three* of the alcohol groups in propane-1,2,3-triol have been esterified.

zwitterion An 'internal' salt of an amino acid, in which the –COOH group donates a proton to the –NH$_2$ group: $^{-}$OOC–CHR–NH$_3$$^{+}$.

Index

236